THE *Art* OF
ART THERAPY

THE *Art* OF
ART THERAPY

What Every Art Therapist Needs to Know

JUDITH A. RUBIN

Routledge
Taylor & Francis Group
New York   London

Routledge
Taylor & Francis Group
270 Madison Avenue
New York, NY 10016

Routledge
Taylor & Francis Group
27 Church Road
Hove, East Sussex BN3 2FA

Printed in the United States of America on acid-free paper
10 9 8 7 6 5 4 3 2 1

International Standard Book Number: 978-0-415-96094-6 (Hardback)

Library of Congress Cataloging-in-Publication Data

Rubin, Judith Aron.
 The art of art therapy : what every art therapist needs to know / by Judith Aron Rubin. -- 2nd ed.
   p. ; cm.
 Includes bibliographical references and index.
 ISBN 978-0-415-96094-6 (hardback : alk. paper)
 1. Art therapy. I. Title.
 [DNLM: 1. Art Therapy. WM 450.5.A8]

RC489.A7R83 2011
616.89'1656--dc22   2010035022

Visit the Taylor & Francis Web site at
http://www.taylorandfrancis.com

and the Routledge Web site at
http://www.routledgementalhealth.com

Contents

Acknowledgments

There is no way I could have written and produced either the first or the revised edition by myself. I want to express my gratitude to the individuals listed next.

First Edition (1984)

Elinor Ulman, publisher of the *American Journal of Art Therapy*, for permission to reprint portions of Chapter 6, which first appeared as part of a panel discussion, "Transference and Counter-transference in Art Therapy" (1982, Vol. 21, pp. 10–12).

Linda Gantt (art therapist) and *Eleanor Irwin* (drama therapist), for wading through the entire manuscript and giving freely of their advice and suggestions for improvement.

Frann Salley and *Elaine Wade*, graduate student interns in the Creative and Expressive Arts Therapy Program at Western Psychiatric Institute and Clinic (WPIC), for reading, proofing, and photocopying.

Gladys Agell (president of the American Art Therapy Association) and *Irene Jakab* (president of the American Society of Psychopathology of Expression) for agreeing to read and comment on the text prior to publication.

Ann Alhadeff, my editor at Brunner/Mazel, with whom it was a pleasure to work.

Jacob Malezi, Norman Rabinovitz, Sheila Ramsey, Norman Snyder, photographers.

Nona Rubin, for typing the first draft.

Herb, Jenny, and *Jonathan*, for being my understanding family while I wrote it.

Second Edition (2011)

Elizabeth Stone Matho, art therapy educator and colleague, for going through every chapter and making detailed and thoughtful suggestions for improvement within the text that were extremely helpful. Because she had not read it before, her fresh eyes added a new viewpoint.

Randy M. Vick, former director of the art therapy training program at the School of the Art Institute of Chicago, for reading through the text and making general suggestions for improving the book as well as specific ones for each chapter. Because he had used this book in teaching, he was able to incorporate feedback over the years from his students.

Herb Rubin, patient husband, for tolerating me writing on a laptop computer not only at home but also everywhere we went for the better part of a year.

Shaun McNiff, Joy Schaverien, Lynn Kapitan, and *Catherine Moon,* respected colleagues who agreed to read and comment on the text prior to publication.

Contributors to the DVD. All of the art therapists whose work is included in the DVD, who are listed separately in Appendix B.

John Mittner, art therapist and filmmaker, for formatting the final version of the DVD much better than I was able to do myself.

Jon Cobert, musician and composer, for giving permission for the use of the music he composed and recorded for the EMI DVD, "Creative Healing in Mental Health: Art & Drama in Assessment & Therapy."

Foreword to the Revised Edition

In 2009, I completed a revision of an introductory textbook in art therapy, *Introduction to Art Therapy: Sources and Resources* (Rubin, 2009). At the time, I reviewed the literature in the field since the first edition of that volume a decade earlier and discovered that there had been 200 new books on art therapy published during that period of time. When the first edition of this book saw print in 1984, there were a total of 31 books on the topic, and there are now well over 300. In other words, the literature of the profession has increased 10-fold. The field is indeed growing, and that growth is increasingly rapid; more people have written about what they do, and many more specific topic areas have been addressed.

So, the first question I asked myself when my publisher suggested revising this book was whether it was really likely to make a contribution today to either the training or the professional development of art therapists. Did it make sense to spend time revising it? After discussing the issue with colleagues and taking another look at what else has become available, I finally concluded that, despite the proliferation of other writings in the field, this one remains different, so I decided to go ahead.

It has been reassuring to realize that, although there have been many developments in art therapy itself and many changes in the delivery of human services, the general principles that are the core of this book still seem valid to me. Indeed, at the risk of sounding grandiose, the "basics" of art therapy as I understand them are virtually timeless. That is, the majority of the recommendations seem for the most part to be as appropriate now as they did over 25 years ago when I first wrote them.

Some of the language describing the various conditions, settings, and ways of thinking about therapy has of course changed during this period of time. Although I have made every effort to be "politically correct," I know that I may still have offended some and apologize in advance if I have. However, in my view of art therapy, the words are not as important as the music; that is, what you *call* someone is not as important as whether you really *respect* them.

To secure objective feedback from others, I asked a number of colleagues to comment on the book prior to the revision and was given excellent guidance by those who had used *The Art of Art Therapy* in teaching over the years. I thank the many whose ideas have helped me, including Joan Bloomgarden, Randy Vick, and Elizabeth Stone Matho, all of whom have been involved for decades in training art therapists. Matho's and Vick's extensive and detailed suggestions for changes were especially invaluable.

While the essential message of the original book remains the core of the revised edition, there are also a great many modifications. At the suggestion of my consultants, I have tried to make the tone somewhat less formal and more direct. I have also rearranged the order of the last two sections. Since the field of art therapy as well as the delivery of services in mental health, education, and the community have expanded greatly in the interim, I have tried to include those changes that seem most relevant.

In addition, I have also tried to make the language more reader friendly by addressing the reader as "you" wherever possible rather than talking about "one" or "the art therapist." I tried to be gender neutral, but it ended up being much less awkward to keep the feminine pronoun for the art therapist (most of whom are still women, although that fortunately is changing) and the masculine for the patient or client (although of course those we serve are not limited to males). It was an arbitrary decision in 1984 and it still is, but it makes the text flow better so I ended up retaining it.

Finally, because the art therapy literature has grown so extensively since the first edition of this book was published, it no longer seems necessary or appropriate to list the kinds of recommended readings by those in other disciplines that seemed essential in 1984 when the available books in art therapy were so few and there were few training programs and no certification examination.

At the end of many chapters, there are references to the literature cited in the text, as well as recommended readings in that domain if they are not included in the chapter references and if they are germane to the topic of the chapter. On the other hand, many chapters did not require specific references, and for some topic areas, there is no relevant recommended readings list. Either or both are included only if they seemed appropriate. In addition, there is also an alphabetical list, "Books on Art Therapy and Related Areas," at the end of this volume. Many books broadly cover a multitude of topics. Others are more specific, which is generally evident from their titles.

One major addition is a DVD to illustrate the topics in the text. It is a series of segments corresponding to the five sections of the book and the chapters in each. There is a description of the DVD in Appendix B, detailing its contents and acknowledging the source materials and the art therapists who contributed them.

Preface

Although it may be presumptuous of me to think that I could describe "the art of art therapy," I want to be sure from the start that you know my own reservations about the title. This book is not intended to be *the* definitive, unalterable statement about *how to do art therapy*. Actually, I cannot imagine how such a book could ever be written. That is because one of my firmest beliefs is that all therapists—art therapists included—need to find a style that is synchronous with their personalities and that cannot be the same for all practitioners. Nevertheless, given inevitable and appropriate differences among clinicians, it seems to me that there are in fact some general understandings necessary for effective art therapy with *any* kind of person and in *any* sort of setting. Added to these "generic" foundations is the specific knowledge essential for different sorts of work with specific kinds of people in diverse contexts. These I have tried to sketch out in this volume.

My motivation for writing this book in 1984 and revising it in 2010 was and remains an uncomfortable feeling of distress when hearing or reading about some work in art therapy. Too often, the art therapist, while clearly gifted and knowledgeable in certain areas, seems to be sadly lacking in others.

It has often been my impression—I think valid—that the individual is not even *aware* of such deficits. Perhaps, I reasoned, the necessary understandings for doing good art therapy had never been spelled out clearly. This book is an attempt to do just that and to do it in a simple and straightforward way.

There is one potential pitfall due to those characteristics of effective art therapists that have little to do with *knowing* any kind of information and more to do with *being* a certain kind of person. For this reason, I have added to my descriptions what you should *know*, some statements on how you should *be*—with the awareness that the particular form such being takes will vary among individuals.

While I am skeptical about the *teachability* of such traits, it is clear to me that they often become available to people after profound learning experiences—like good supervision or effective psychotherapy. At the very least, I believe that any art therapist can *strive* to be more open, flexible, creative, and caring. And, since these attributes seem essential to good work in art therapy, it would be wrong to omit them.

In a way, the whole book is an attempt to describe what goes into making a good art therapist and no doubt is modeled on individuals I have known and admired in this and other fields. Among them are psychoanalysts, psychologists, psychiatrists, other kinds of therapists, teachers, and artists. Among them, too, are my earliest models of loving and caring—my father, my mother, and my grandmother—to whose memory this book is warmly dedicated,

Judith Aron Rubin

Introduction

In thinking about what constitutes the art of art therapy, it seemed to me that—to put it simply—there is an *art* part and a *therapy* part, both of which are essential. In elaborating these, it seemed that there was also an area I have called *the interface,* in which the therapeutic evocation of and responding to the patient's art are central. The book therefore begins with these three main sections.

In the first, "The Art Part," there are chapters on knowing the basic elements of art—materials, processes, and products—in regard to form, content, and symbolic language. The second portion, "The Therapy Part," includes the knowledge that any therapist needs to have about development, dynamics and deviations, and the conditions of therapeutic change. In addition to knowing therapy in general, you also need to know art therapy in particular and to know your identity as a person and a professional, the fourth chapter in Part 2.

In the third portion, "The Interface," there are chapters on knowing how to stimulate and then to deal with the art made and shared in therapy, including setting the stage, evoking expression, enabling creation, and facilitating reflection. There is also a chapter on working artistically, helping people through art in an aesthetically and humanly sensitive way.

Although the aspects of art therapy in this book seem applicable to all possible contexts, there are particular "knowings" and perhaps "beings" necessary for the best kind of practice in specific situations. These are detailed in the fourth section of the book, "Applications," with chapters on different populations, settings, and modes of art therapy, including thoughts about the kinds of skills and understandings that are needed to work with particular people in particular places in specific ways.

In addition to the "basics" of art therapy discussed in the first three sections and the specifics elaborated in the fourth, there are also some "extras," of concern primarily to those who guide others in providing direct service. Chapters on each area comprise the fifth portion of the book, "Related Service," and include teaching, supervision, consultation, research, and theory.

Despite the need for knowledge specific to each situation, I believe the essentials outlined in this book have virtually universal applicability. The basics, and even the extras, seem to me to be valid generalizations that can be translated in a variety of ways. In regard to population, they are true for work with children, adolescents, adults, the elderly, as well as those with a wide variety of conditions.

In regard to setting, they are true for work in outpatient clinics, inpatient hospitals, schools, rehabilitation centers, community studios, and any other place where an art therapist might practice. In regard to mode, they are true for work with individuals, families, and groups. And in regard to theoretical orientation, they are true no matter where you might be on the continuum of art *as* therapy to art *in* therapy and seem valid whether your favored frame of reference is humanistic, cognitive, behavioral, psychodynamic, multicultural, spiritual, intermodal, or systemic.

I am convinced, therefore, that this book is relevant and helpful for all who use art diagnostically or therapeutically. I hope that it can say something useful to beginners as well as to advanced practitioners. While it is directed primarily to art therapists, it could be used by any mental health professional who incorporates art into clinical work, whether social worker, psychologist, psychiatrist, occupational therapist, or recreational specialist.

This is not so much a book on "how to *do* it" as it is a book on "how to *think* about what you do." I suspect there is no one among us who cannot profit from thoughtful reflection on their clinical work. For myself, writing this book has provided just such an opportunity, both in 1984 and again, after 48 years in the field, in 2011. It is my hope that it will provide you with a similar kind of stimulation, to think and act with increasing clarity about "the art of art therapy."

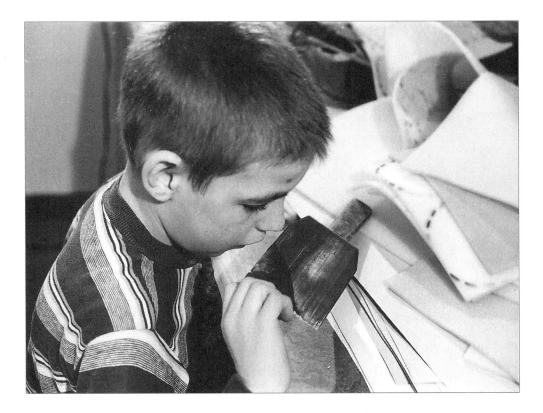

A boy examines a variety of art materials before deciding what he wants to use in his creative work.

PART 1

The Art Part

The visual arts are a rich and complex realm, encompassing history, aesthetics, criticism, and the work of the artist in the studio. While it would be nice to know all aspects in detail, it is not really necessary to be an accomplished historian, aesthetician, or critic. Neither is it essential to be an accomplished worker in all possible art media. Proficiency in any of these can take a lifetime. There are, however, certain kinds of understanding and knowledge that matter more than others for a practicing art therapist. It is these that I emphasize, with the awareness that it is always an asset to know more rather than less about any facet of the visual arts.

There are three chapters in this section, each touching on a different aspect of the art part of art therapy, dealing with the basics: materials, processes, and products. In each chapter, I focus on those elements most critical for the practicing art therapist, although I am aware that I may well have omitted aspects that others would consider essential, like the vast new horizons opened up by the digital age.

In fact, I considered adding a section on the additional options for expression made possible through the use of technology (cf. Malchiodi, 2000). Long ago, I explored the use of film, photography, and stop-motion animation with patients of all ages and am energized by the exciting new options for both art therapists and their clients in the growing varieties of digital media. I am especially hopeful about the potential for computer-based programs to expand the range of artistic expression that is possible for those with serious physical disabilities, as well as for those who might live too far away to enter your studio.

These new developments offer thrilling possibilities and are likely to become more important in art therapy over time as the next generation, who can master and offer them, comes of age. There is an active discussion group on digital art therapy on the Internet, itself a reflection of the rapid growth of these new forms of communication. (http://www.linkedin.com/groups?home=&gid=2172516&trk=anet_ug_hm&goback=%2Eanh_87161_1264520522160_1%2Eanh_2172516).

Perhaps it is a reflection of my age, but I am still convinced that materials that can be touched and shaped by the hands offer a kind of direct sensory experience that is perhaps—even more than before—badly needed by people in this era of virtual reality and technology. For that reason, as well as the fact that most work in art therapy has been with paint, chalk, and clay, the focus of the art part remains traditional art media.

Art is, after all, the core of art therapy. It is my belief that it can and should remain central, no matter how much training or experience you may have had in verbal psychotherapy. Some individual art therapists who have gone on for further study in another mode of treatment have moved more and more into words, with less and less use of art in their work with patients.

I had some concerns when I began studies in psychoanalysis in the 1970s that I, too, might find verbal psychotherapy more attractive. Sitting next to Edith Kramer on a panel in 1979, I was startled when she told me she was sure that I would end up becoming a child analyst rather than an art therapist. I suppose that I might have gone in that direction.

Much to my surprise and delight, however, I discovered that the training in other ways of eliciting and viewing clinical material resulted not only in enhanced expertise, but also in a deeper appreciation of the value of expressive media and of the visual modality in work with other people. Even when the communication is only in words, it is remarkable how often the question, "Is there an *image* that goes with that thought?" elicits a response that can lead to greater awareness and understanding.

I begin this book with the art part, because that is the element that makes art therapy different from other forms of treatment. It makes art therapy more attractive to some and more unattractive to others. It may enhance a person's self-esteem or ability for self-expression, but it can also be threatening for many.

Whatever the assets and liabilities of using art in work with people, however, it is the unique and central modality of the art therapist, no matter what the therapist's level of expertise. The three chapters in this section are not only basic but also interdependent, because there can be no *products* unless raw *materials* are transformed via a creative *process* into art.

References

Malchiodi, C. A. (2000). *Art therapy and computer technology*. London: Kingsley.

A girl has selected her art materials from a supply table and is taking them to her working space so she can create with them.

A blind boy explores the finger paint medium in all its richness.

CHAPTER 1

Knowing Materials

Introduction

When you think of making art, you naturally think of using some sort of medium with which to create. It might be a brush with tempera paint, a chunk of water-based clay, or a set of brightly colored markers. Such materials are the core of what we do. To put it simply, without media and tools, there can be no art. While there is indeed such a thing as mental imagery, and people of all ages *do* think in pictures, for such images to become art they must be concretized in some way.

What Kind of Materials?

In the visual arts, this is done through the use of materials. Art therapists tend to prefer simple media and processes to more complex ones for several reasons. First, the more unstructured the medium, the more an individual will be able to project on it. Since art therapists hope to evoke personally meaningful creations, it makes sense that you would not wish to impose in any way on the client's natural imagery. So it follows that unstructured art materials like paint, clay, or pastels allow for an infinite range of visual constructions, offering each client the opportunity to find their own style.

Conversely, to paint by numbers or pour clay into molds is *not* an art activity, although art materials are indeed used. Similarly, making a potholder with cotton loops, a pleasant activity resulting in a useful product, greatly restricts the kind of design that is possible, despite the fact that people are free to choose the colors and how they want to use them within a square metal loom. Such circumscribed tasks require following directions—a laudable capacity, but not one that involves the essence of art therapy, which is helping people to find their own imagery and in so doing to find their authentic selves. While all art materials impose their own intrinsic limits, there is in each the possibility of highly personal work by every individual.

Another reason why art therapists prefer simple media is a practical one. Most art therapy sessions, especially in clinical settings, are limited in time. While it is possible in ongoing art therapy to work on an individual or group project that extends over days, weeks, or even months, there are many contexts in which such work is out of the question—as in a brief assessment or with a group whose membership does not remain consistent, such as open studio groups in hospitals.

There is much to be said for media that permit the creation of satisfying products within the space of an art therapy session. This allows for consideration of the product as well as the process within a single time frame, when the impulses involved in the making are still very much alive. Since we assume that any creation reflects ideas and feelings inside the maker at the time of its creation, being able to reflect on art at the moment it comes into being offers a powerful opportunity for learning about the self.

There is yet another reason why simple, direct media appeal to art therapists, which is the fact that they can be used by individuals of all ages with little or no instruction. As people often tell us, we offer materials that could be "used by a child." And indeed, beginners of all ages can quickly learn to successfully manipulate chalk, paint, or clay. However, because art therapists are often called upon to give technical help, you also need to know how to use materials effectively and how to convey that knowledge to others. Teaching, a vital component of the work, is done in the service of helping the artists to successfully make their own statements—to say, with pencil or paint or clay, what it is they want to say (cf. Chapter 10, this volume).

In addition to preferring materials that are *simple* and *unstructured,* art therapists have sufficient respect for media to use only those that are *sturdy* and *effective.* This does not, as some people imagine, mean that you need to offer the most expensive art supplies. Indeed, a reasonably strong grade of white drawing paper (60–80 lb.) is adequate for most media, and the highest quality would be unnecessarily extravagant. Newsprint, on the other hand, while the cheapest, is also the most likely to tear.

Indeed, it is vital to avoid inexpensive materials that lead to frustration. It is better to have boxes with 8 colors of decent-quality markers than to have sets of 16 colors that dry up too rapidly. Sometimes, less-expensive materials are even easier to manipulate than more costly ones, which is true, for example, of different brands of oil-based clay or some colored chalks vs. some pastels. What does matter is that the material be strong enough to withstand the pressures of normal usage, and that it does what it is supposed to do.

Respect for materials is reflected not only in choosing those that are of reasonably good quality and will work predictably, but also in caring for all media and tools with genuine concern. Brushes should therefore be washed right away with soap, paper should be stored neatly, clay and tempera paint should be maintained at a usable consistency, and so on. Not only does such good care extend the value of limited resources, but also it makes a statement to the client about the value of the materials. This is analogous to the even more important message conveyed to the client through your handling and storage of the individual's art products. Is it possible to be respectful of a person and to be at the same time careless about his creations? I think not.

Knowing Media Well Enough to Help Others

Given these general requirements—for media that are simple, sturdy, and well maintained— what other things should concern an art therapist about materials? First, you should be aware of the unique capabilities of different media, surfaces, and tools in order to be able to offer adaptive solutions to people's problems in the actualization of their creative intentions. Most central, I believe, is sufficient experience with the use of those offered so that you can assist in technical matters.

For example, if you do not know about the use of armatures to support three-dimensional modeled work, you cannot help someone whose clay figure keeps collapsing with anything but their feelings of frustration. Similarly, if a person wants to build up the texture of acrylic paint, it is important to know not only that it is possible, but also which available materials would work. Or, when someone wants to represent overlapping with transparency, it may be up to you to suggest cellophane or tissue paper as workable ways to concretize such an idea.

The essential types of material are actually few in number, but you need to know each in depth. There are the *surfaces* on which people may work, which include papers of various weights, colors, and sizes, as well as cardboards of different kinds, canvases, Masonite, wood, and more. You need to be familiar with all of the commonly available kinds of paper, and to know the limitations and capacities of different types, in order to help someone select the most facilitating size and kind of surface for a drawing, painting, or collage. Knowing the range of possible papers and other surfaces helps you to provide the client with appropriate choices, without which there may be considerable unnecessary frustration.

As for *drawing materials,* you need to be familiar with all kinds of pencils—soft, hard, colored, charcoal, and those designed for normally resistant surfaces, such as transparency pencils or china markers. You also need to know about different kinds of pens—those with a variety of nibs for use with ink, ballpoints, roller ball, felt tipped, and so on. There are many kinds of ink and watercolor markers now available, each with different possibilities, in various sizes and ranges of hues (and even odors). Then there is charcoal, both natural and pressed, and in pencil form.

As for crayons, there is not only the traditional wax variety in a range of sizes and shapes but also others made of solid paint (like oil crayons and PaintStiks) and those more closely related to chalk (like Conté crayons). Finally, there are chalks and pastels, which come in many different shapes and sizes, with varying degrees of softness. What is essential is that you be aware of the many potential drawing tools and of the most appropriate surfaces for each kind and variation.

There is a similar range of possibilities in *painting media,* with many varieties of each type available. Watercolors come soft in tubes or hard in pans; tempera comes in blocks, liquid, and powder form; and there are other water-based media as well, like gouache and casein.

Finger paint can be created in different textures, using a variety of available bases (such as soap flakes or liquid detergent or the many "cooked" types, for which recipes are available); there is also the commercially prepared variety in moist or powder form. Finally, there are the more costly painting media, such as oils (which now come in a water-soluble form as well) and acrylics, available in tubes or as a liquid.

Manufacturers continue to create new types of paint and new ways of delivering it, like "tempera markers," liquid tempera paint in plastic bottles that can be squeezed and applied in dots, lines, or masses. As with drawing tools, it is essential to know about the many types of paints available so you can help people find what they need.

Another central creative mode in art therapy is three-dimensional work with *modeling materials.* Here, you need to know about clay—all kinds—from those that are fired in a kiln, to those that are designed to be baked in a kitchen oven or air-dried. In addition to natural or man-made clay with a water base that hardens, you need to know about oil-based clay, which does not get hard and comes in a variety of colors and degrees of pliability. Then, there are the modeling doughs, some that are commercially prepared, and many that can be created using a variety of available recipes.

Finally, there are commercial modeling preparations in plastic or powder form with a wide range of qualities, such as Sculpey, a polymer clay available in a variety of weights and colors, to be baked and painted, or Model Magic, an exceptionally soft dough that can be baked and kneaded by weak hands, whether young, old, or disabled. You need to be familiar not only with the many types of modeling materials available, but also with the particular characteristics of each one and with appropriate tools and surfaces for work with each.

There are also a number of other materials that can be used for *three-dimensional construction,* from papier-mâché to Pariscraft to stiff paper to wire, fabric, yarn, wood, plastic, and others. Again, it is important to be familiar with the possibilities as well as with the particular tools and processes appropriate to each. Tools include such basics as scissors, brushes, and modeling tools, as well as different kinds of knives, staplers, string, and adhesive materials, such as tapes and glues. There is a wide variety available, each with its particular capabilities and appropriate uses. If working with wood, metal, or stone, it is important to know about the special tools used with these materials and how they work.

To keep up with *new developments* in creative materials, it is extremely helpful to regularly receive catalogs from commercial distributors. Most useful are those that cover a broad range, from professional to school art supplies, so that you can find what is needed and available within your budget. Criteria for selection should include not only cost but also the kind of simplicity of use referred to in this chapter.

When selecting or suggesting materials for anyone, you need to consider the relevance of the medium to any creative intention in addition to its ability to be used successfully by a particular person or group. In this regard, it is essential to be aware of the degree of difficulty of the medium as well as the perceptual-motor capacities of those who will be using it.

Also relevant to supply decisions are management aspects, like the complexity of distribution or cleanup. Certainly, the amount of time and the space available have to be taken into account, as well as the accessibility of water, soap, and other resources. Just as all art therapists do not have unlimited budgets for materials, so all do not work in optimal settings for creating art. It is often necessary to find a workable compromise between the ideal materials and those that are feasible within realistic constraints.

In a severely limited work situation, especially where you need to be highly selective about what materials are made available, a wide-ranging awareness of possibilities is an essential condition for the best-informed choices. Such broad-based knowledge about materials cannot be acquired merely from looking at catalogs or reading books about what to do with different media.

It is only available, I believe, through direct personal experience with the widest possible variety of media, tools, and processes. You need not be an *expert* with clay or paint or pastel, but you must have used the different varieties of each sufficiently to know their capacities and to help someone else work successfully with them.

Knowing the capacities of materials is fortunately quite fascinating, for media and tools each have particular things that they can and cannot do, and there are indeed more and less successful ways of using them. In addition, they have many qualities to which we respond emotionally as well as cognitively. Finger paint is not only smooth, moist, thick, and colorful, but also, because of its abundance and texture, it can be experienced as plentiful or messy, whether or not the hands contact it directly.

Clay can stimulate feelings of disgust as well as feelings of pleasure; it can seem cold and unyielding as well as soft and manipulable. While these possible responses are partly a function of what the client brings to the experience, they are also dependent on the particular qualities of the material.

Such projections occur in response to tools and processes as well as media, so that a thick, long-handled brush can seem powerful to one person and unwieldy to another.

Pounding a nail into wood can be felt as an exciting release of aggressive energy or as an anxiety-provoking forbidden act. Sanding wood can be experienced as a loving kind of caress or as a hostile kind of attack.

"If You Were an Art Material, Tool, or Process, What Would You Be?"

An exercise I have found useful with trainees never fails to demonstrate the capacity of materials and processes to elicit meaningful personal responses. In this experience, each person is asked to think about which medium, tool, or process he or she might be. Some wish to be paint because they want to feel fluid and colorful, while others identify with paint because they often feel out of control. It is important to be as aware of the symbolic qualities of materials as of their pragmatic aspects. Only then is it possible to appreciate the full impact on the people you serve of their encounter with different media and tools.

While it is tempting to go into further detail about the practical and symbolic aspects of each of the basic kinds of materials and tools used by art therapists, such information already exists in books that concentrate in depth on different media and processes. What is essential is to have not only a cognitive awareness of what is available but also an appreciation of the "personality" of each medium, tool, and process—what it can and cannot do, and how it relates to developmental levels in terms of difficulty and symbolic meaning.

Such an awareness can only be gained through substantial personal experience with the medium, tool, or process. Ideally, this experience should be under the supervision of an expert in the area, who can teach the essential skills needed to make the material do its work for the artist. In my opinion, only an art therapist who can assist a patient in the use of a medium is legitimately entitled to offer it.

The challenge of how much to "teach" and how much to allow the person to find his or her own way is one of many that call for clinical as well as educational judgment, a subject to be covered in other chapters. Meanwhile, no judgments will be well made if you do not have the "basics" under your professional belt, and all, I am sure, would agree that the materials with which we work are central. Equally important are the processes, both therapeutic and artistic, by which we transform media into products, the subject of the next chapter.

Recommended Readings

Hinz, L. D. (2009). *Expressive therapies continuum.* New York: Routledge.
Moon, C. H. (Ed.). (2010). *Materials and media in art therapy.* New York: Routledge.
Sherwood, P. (2004). *The healing art of clay therapy.* Melbourne, Australia: ACER.

A teenager is absorbed in carving a sculpture from a block of hard foam.

Active involvement in a creative process often means "letting go."

CHAPTER 2

Knowing Processes

What Do We Mean by Process in Art Therapy?

Without some kind of creative working process, media and tools do not become art. A jar of paint and a brush do not become a painting until an individual uses one to place the other on a surface. Although the processes of working with different media are closely related to the physical characteristics of each, there is a wide range of possibilities.

As with materials, it is essential that you be aware of these so that you can help clients to have the fullest and most satisfying experience with whatever is offered. The challenge here, as elsewhere, is to know when to intervene (which can take a wide variety of forms) and when to leave the person to his own devices. Some general thoughts about the creative process may help to guide this challenging decision-making act.

Exploring

I believe that, whatever the age of the client, the natural and organic way to begin with any material is to explore. Just as you experiment with a new toy or get to know a new person, the initial step with a new medium is exploration. This is contrary to the common educational way of beginning by instructing the person in how to properly use a material or tool. My own conviction is that therapy itself is an exploratory process, one in which it is hoped that people discover and understand their own ideas and feelings, which eventually help them to be more in charge of their lives. One of the positive aspects of art therapy is that we can offer experiences of exploration and discovery through media as well as words.

I hope, therefore, that all art therapists would become comfortable with inviting people to explore materials they are encountering for the first time. In order for this to be possible, you need to be comfortable with the idea that there may be no finished product, that some technical elements may be less than optimal, and that the client is likely to experience some confusion with the ambiguity of not having a well-defined, goal-oriented task. Indeed, most individuals do find it necessary to create "something" at some point during their explorations with materials since there seems to be a universal need to organize experience in a coherent way.

Some art therapists may object that an invitation to "explore," especially if it includes a playful component such as "fooling around" to see what will happen with the medium, is antithetical to the nature of art, which is to make a formed, finished product. Yet a quick glance at the literature on the creative process, whether by artists or psychologists, quickly assures us that this kind of playful experimentation is an essential element in genuine creative work of any sort.

Perhaps more significant, it is also seen as a necessary condition for gaining access to unconscious ideas and feelings, as in the "free association" of psychoanalysis. Like free verbal association, exploring freely with materials is far from easy, eliciting many defenses and organizing phenomena in response to ambiguity and confusion. A number of art therapy techniques have been specifically developed as a way of attempting to help patients to bypass these normal resistances, to get more rapidly in touch with less-conscious kinds of imagery. These include such approaches as modeling with a blindfold on or using a scribble as projective stimulus for a picture.

For many years, I asked workshop participants, after doing a scribble drawing, whether they thought they would have come up with an image like the one they developed had they been given a blank sheet of paper and asked to draw anything they wished. Almost universally, the answer was in the negative. When asked what they might have done if a free drawing had been requested, most thought of either abstract designs or well-practiced schemata, often stereo-typed and impersonal. The opportunity to "find" an image in a scribble is also a welcome excuse for most to feel less sense of responsibility (and therefore shame) for what emerges.

There are many such ways to help people to enter a more relaxed, free process of creation. The possibilities are limited only by the imagination of the art therapist. My own preference is to utilize such stimuli only when necessary, such as in short-term workshops or some assessment interviews, and in therapy only when an individual or group seems "stuck" in some way.

What seems most natural to me, in order to help clients to experience a genuine creative process, is to create a physical and psychological environment in which such freedom becomes truly possible. Then, encouraging the kind of exploration and nonjudgmental playing with the possibilities of what materials can do can enable the most meaningful and most personal experience. Having done art therapy since 1963 with people of all ages, I am convinced that this kind of beginning is possible for everyone.

The essential conditions for such a "framework for freedom" include sufficient, organized, and predictable space and time—as well as a trusting, interested, accepting, and supportive attitude on the part of the clinician. Only if you are honestly convinced of each individual's potential creativity in art is it possible to convey such confidence. Moreover, such an open approach to the creative process can evoke a good deal of anxiety in some, so that you also need to be able to help people to deal with the stresses and frustrations of relative freedom.

What is critical, however, is a clear understanding that the creative process for anyone must grow out of such a free exploration of possibilities. While this is most important at the outset, it is also true for many moments later in time—when someone may have mastered the use of a medium, for example, but has not yet permitted himself to freely explore its full expressive potential.

Incubating and Organizing

In every creative process of any worth, there is also a time for "incubation," for allowing the mind to work quietly, without conscious deliberation, on the creative problem at hand.

You need to respect this phenomenon, to permit putting work aside for a period of time, or simply looking at it without making any changes, in order for this kind of subterranean problem solving to occur. Not only can you allow such periods of reflection, but you can also promote them in a variety of ways, especially when someone's anxiety creates pressures for premature closure.

And, equally familiar, there is the need in any creative process for organizing, putting together, arranging, and elaborating the finished work. Materials vary in their ability to be reworked, so there may be greater value for art therapy in those that permit change over time (such as clay kept moist), as opposed to those that do not (such as wood, once carved). Parenthetically, digital media permit virtually unlimited possibilities for control, for doing and undoing, which makes them an exciting option for those who have never had much control over their lives, such as at-risk adolescents. The work of art therapist Brian David Austin with such young people using computer-generated animation is a fine example (http://www.theanimationproject.org).

In any case, while there is often value for a client in having to make irrevocable decisions (such as where to saw or carve the wood), it is always the art therapist's job to monitor the technical progress of the work so that its development will permit maximal modification by the artist until it has reached a satisfying finished state. This might involve such a simple intervention as suggesting that someone arrange the parts of a collage or construction before gluing them down in order to be able to rearrange them if they want to before the final decisions are made.

Here, you might ask if your own aesthetic judgment ought to be part of what is offered to the client. I believe that your job is to facilitate the expression and aesthetic judgment of that individual, not to impose your own. There are situations for which it might be helpful to suggest that someone look only at a portion of a larger work (covering the rest visually) or perceive the product from a distance or a different perspective (such as upside down). I would conceptualize such acts on your part as facilitating the client's ability to make aesthetic decisions about what is "best" or "right."

This is analogous to my feeling about technical assistance—that it be offered only when needed to help the client to make a personally meaningful and practically durable product. Thus, it is unfair to let someone use a material on a surface to which you know it will not adhere permanently or to model a form that you know will crack in the drying process. Similarly, it seems somewhat inhumane to silently allow a client to struggle to cover a huge surface with a tiny brush or marker when you know that a larger brush or marker is available for such a task. With respect for the patient as artist, however, your role is the sharing of such information, not the mandating or prohibiting of any specific act, regardless of practicality.

Reinforcing Creative Behavior

So far, this chapter has emphasized the creative process using art media in the most general sense. There are also some specific aspects of creative thinking and behaving that are highly relevant for art therapists. These are the capacities found by psychologists to be characteristic of creative people, whether studied anecdotally or experimentally. These traits usually include *fluency, flexibility, elaboration,* and *originality.* Each of these can be promoted and encouraged in a client's experience with art in therapy, and each relates significantly to the larger task of creative problem solving in life.

Fluency refers to the capacity to generate many ideas in response to a problem, such as how to combine particular shapes, colors, or figurative concepts in a work of art. While having a large number of ideas is not essential for an artist, being able to play with multiple possibilities for dealing with life problems is helpful to everyone and is often a dilemma for our clients, who tend not to see the many alternatives open to them. I believe that the very experimentation with art, with no dangers or consequences in reality, can actually be a preparation for a more courageous exploration of possibilities in real life. Certainly, the more ideas generated for solving the artistic problem itself, the more solutions from which to choose. The people we see typically have various kinds of blinders on, largely for self-protection but which narrow their view of their options.

Flexibility refers to the ability to perceive the same thing in different ways, to shift gears from one frame of reference to another, and to deal with unforeseen events with minimal frustration. It is intimately related to most notions of mental health, for which the extremes of both rigidity and fluidity are signs of disorder. Flexibility in the use of materials and tools in art-making processes is more likely if it is valued by the art therapist, who can actively reinforce instances of such behavior by the client.

While *elaboration* may be the least intimately related to mental health—the primary goal in art therapy—it is still relevant and worthy of both encouragement and reward. Like fluency, the ability to elaborate—to extend, decorate, and refine—can result not only in more beautiful art creations but also in a more adaptive response to life challenges. To be able to stick with a problem or piece of art once the initial inspiration has passed enables the momentary "high" to be translated into something lasting. And, in most situations, it allows the individual to achieve greater success and fulfillment than are found with the most "inspired"—but undeveloped—ideas and products.

As for *originality,* this is the aspect of creativity most often thought of by the average person. Yet, as Ecclesiastes pointed out in the Bible, there is rarely anything really new under the sun. Every artist, great or amateur, has been inspired by the work of others. This is true even of the so-called primitive, naïve, or folk painters who have had no formal training. What seems most critical in art therapy is that each person be enabled to find their own "true self" by discovering and developing preferred media, style, or thematic modes. Even though the artwork may remind a historian of one or another well-known artist, what matters is that the work feel right and authentic to the client, whatever the mix of outside inspiration and inside generation that went into its creation. As D. W. Winnicott, who invented the term, once wrote: *"Only the true self can be creative and only the true self can feel real."*

This is an area fraught with hazards for the practicing art therapist for you cannot help but have media, style, and content preferences of your own. What is essential is to be aware of your tastes so as to avoid influencing clients either overtly or subtly. There is a striking similarity among the artwork of different individuals in some publications on art therapy as well as quite a few in art education. One cannot help but assume that the worker, probably unwittingly, has influenced the art of the client or student by responding even nonverbally in either a positive (reinforcing) or negative (punishing) fashion to what has been made, both during and after the working process.

In order to help each individual to really discover and develop his or her own genuine style, you need to behave in as neutral a fashion as possible about the aesthetic elements therein, with the highest value placed on the authenticity of the art for the person involved. I believe this is the only position consonant with respect for the individual, his worth, and his art as an extension of himself.

This is as true for work that appears to be "copied" as for that which seems totally original. Copying after all is a tried-and-true technique for learning to be an artist. Why should it not be permissible for a patient to do so? The fact that something has been copied from whatever source (art, photograph, work of another person in the group) does not mean that it is not authentic for the individual who made it. Being nonjudgmental about all the work that is created is much harder than you might realize. As artists, we are especially vulnerable to liking some creations more than others (which is inevitable), but our investment in the aesthetic appeal of art makes it especially hard to "keep a straight face" and neither disclose our own preferences nor subtly reinforce them.

Being Open-Minded and Flexible

As for processes of work with art media per se, there are two aspects that I feel are critical for art therapists. The first concerns the possibilities inherent in any material, which are never limited to those known as most common or usual. Such flexibility in thinking about art processes becomes especially vital in work with those who have disabilities—for whom modifications of media, tools, and surfaces may be absolutely essential conditions for creative work.

Even with those who are not challenged in any sensory or physical domain, an openness to unexpected possibilities is an asset in art therapy. Such a stance is helpful, whether responding to a child's spontaneous impulse to use oil paints with his fingers or trying to figure out a way to make it possible for a person to draw with paint when he cannot control a thin brush but could manage a long-handled cotton swab.

Observing the Process

The other area that seems vital for art therapists is a sensitivity to the temporal and spatial aspects of the art process engaged in by another. While some attempts have been made to classify such aspects of creative work, such as deliberate versus spontaneous types of artists (Burkhart, 1962), close observation by educators and clinicians indicates a rich and variegated range of possibilities in the rhythms of any individual's work during the course of a single session and over a period of time (cf. Rubin, Schachter, & Ragins, 1983). There seems to be more awareness in art therapy of whether an individual uses a medium "appropriately" than of more subtle qualitative aspects of the art process—differences in cognitive and creative styles.

While some such aspects of the working process are reflected in the finished product, most can only be seen through close observation of the doing itself. This includes what precedes and follows the work in regard to materials as well as associated behaviors during the use of the media chosen. It involves words, facial expressions, body movement, and tone and the interaction of all of these in the totality of the individual's behavior, all of which are fascinating to observe.

It includes such aspects of being as activity vs. passivity, tension vs. relaxation, awkwardness vs. coordination, impulsivity vs. deliberation, or distractibility vs. involvement, all in relation to the art process itself. Even dimensions such as rigidity vs. flexibility, compulsivity vs. freedom, or constriction vs. openness can be thought of not only in relation to products but also in regard to the working process.

Similarly, attitudes toward the process can be reflected in the way the person engages with the materials. Reactions of disgust vs. pleasure or reluctance vs. eagerness can be inferred through facial expressions, body movements, and all kinds of associated verbalization, including that which appears unrelated to the ongoing artmaking. The point, which is difficult to articulate since it involves largely nonverbal phenomena, is that you need to be attentive to all aspects of the client's working process. The reason is simple. Everything is diagnostic "data" that is available and should therefore be noted throughout treatment, not only at the time of assessment or evaluation.

Even some of the objectively specifiable aspects of process, such as the *sequence* in which items are made, are not necessarily noticed automatically. You need to learn to record and to retrieve such information through practice, until recalling the order of creative events becomes as automatic as the coordination required to type, to ride a bicycle, or to drive a car once you have mastered these skills.

It is not too difficult to learn to note a product's place in a series, and it is possible, especially in individual art therapy, to note the sequence of actions within a single work of art. If you believe as I do that all behavior is lawful and unfolds in a *psychologically* meaningful way—what Freud called "psychic determinism"—such close observation becomes extremely valuable for understanding both the person and his creative product.

Since detailed notation of all behaviors associated with a creative process is indeed demanding, it is no wonder that you might shrink from such a difficult task. The main compensation for the high level of attentiveness necessary, however, is that the payoff in ultimate understanding is considerable. Being an active observer can also be a great deal of fun. If you are to make use of an individual's working process as part of your database about that person, then you need to learn how to observe accurately and sensitively and on many dimensions simultaneously.

Turning your energies toward active observation also lessens the likelihood of one of the greatest abuses in the field of art therapy—the therapist's intrusiveness during the creative process. It takes a good deal of experience and trial and error with each client to find the optimal level of intervention over time as well as during any particular creative act. What is essential is that you have sufficient respect for the person's creative process not to interfere with its organic evolution.

Ironically, this is more likely to happen in groups because of the impossibility of intervening with everyone at once, although the difficulty of observing the kinds of subtle aspects of process noted is also greater. You will have to make choices—with a family, for example—whether to observe an individual's working process or to focus on the interactions between family members.

In either case, however, I am convinced that time spent observing carefully is time well spent for learning and understanding, which is your responsibility. Observation also allows the client to engage without interruption in a more natural kind of creative process than if you are active in any other way.

Am I suggesting that you never intervene when someone is working quietly? Not at all. There are times when such an intervention is called for, as when a neurotic client is using his absorption in the art process primarily as an escape from difficult issues in the therapeutic situation, or when an isolated member of a group is unable to initiate contact with others, yet needs some affirmation from the therapist.

I am simply suggesting that, in my experience, art therapists err more often on the side of intrusiveness, perhaps because they mistakenly think they are not doing their proper therapeutic jobs if they remain silent. I once saw a book, however, with the lovely title *Art Is a Quiet Place*. And so it is, or at least it should be.

In summary, the creative process itself is an essential element of art therapy, regardless of your particular theoretical orientation. To make such an experience available to clients, you must not only know the specific processes of work with particular materials but also know and respect the conditions essential to genuine creative activity. If you do, then you will provide a "framework" for artistic freedom as well as for growth.

References

Burkhart, R. C. (1962). *Spontaneous and deliberate ways of learning.* Scranton, PA: International Textbook.

Rubin, J. A., Schachter, J., & Ragins, N. (1983). Intra-individual variability in human figure drawings: A developmental study. *American Journal of Orthopsychiatry, 53,* 654–667.

Recommended Readings

Berensohn, P. (1972). *Finding one's way with clay.* New York: Simon & Schuster.

McNiff, S. (1998a). *Art-based research.* London: Kingsley.

McNiff, S. (1998b). *Trust the process.* Boston: Shambhala.

Nicolaides, K. (1941). *The natural way to draw.* New York: Houghton Mifflin.

Richards, M. C. (1962). *Centering.* Middletown, CT: Wesleyan University Press.

Sometimes, the process of working with materials requires close attention and careful control.

A girl with anorexia nervosa drew this self-portrait during a family art therapy session, enabling her parents to grasp how distorted her body image really was. It was a powerful communication that allowed them for the first time to empathize with her struggle.

CHAPTER 3

Knowing Products

Understanding the Art Product

Knowing art products is simple, according to some. You just learn the meanings of different elements, and you can then translate the messages in patients' art, saying with conviction, "*This* [shape, color, or subject matter] means *that.*" Of course, there are meanings in products, in formal qualities, and in content, but they are not to be found in neat formulas or simple recipes. Those generalizations in current usage are useful as an indication of possibilities, sometimes probabilities, but never certainties. Human beings, after all, are complex creatures, as is their expressive behavior and the products that arise therefrom.

There is a strong emphasis in art therapy, however, on products that are the visible, concrete outcome of any creative process. While I do not subscribe to the notion implied by some that there can be "art therapy" without art materials (with the patient as medium and the clinician as artist?), I do feel that an overemphasis on the product can deflect your attention from the *person* and the process by which he or she creates it. At times, this concern with the product may not only create observational blind spots but also lead to nontherapeutic interventions, like working on a patient's creation to "improve" it, thereby implicitly devaluing the person.

Despite the tendency to sometimes put too much emphasis on art products with both clients and other professionals, learning to read the language of art is essential to good art therapy. Indeed, without an aesthetically and psychologically trained eye, you do not really deserve to be thought of as a clinician. There is no question that psychologically sophisticated vision is needed to be able to decipher issues related to development, deviance, and dynamics and to use all components of the language of art—form, content, and the relationships between the two.

Ironically, an underemphasis on the art product is also a hazard. The "anything goes" approach practiced by some, because of a misunderstanding of the meaning of ideas like catharsis and creative freedom, is actually a devaluation of the "Art" part of art therapy. As Elinor Ulman once wrote, "Anything that is to be called art therapy must genuinely partake of both art and therapy" (1961, pp. 10–20). This concept was well stated by one of my advisors on this revision:

> The erroneous notion that simply spilling out feelings will be therapeutic has generated misunderstanding and has been advocated where it can actually be unhelpful for some patients and even dangerous for others. Those who advocate this form of practice do not understand the unconscious (although they believe they are working with it), and often devalue the concept of craftsmanship in the making of an art product. They don't understand that while a patient comes to understand that art therapy is less about making "beautiful art," than about accurately expressing something meaningful about himself through visual means, most who are invested in the process of creation do care about the art product. Caring about the product can occur on a variety of levels, from the purely symbolic to a truly aesthetic investment. It is of course most authentic for the therapist to care about the art product on any level where the patient invests himself. (E. Stone, personal communication, January 2010)

Having found an optimal place, where there is neither an over- nor an underemphasis on the product, in order to be able to "read" anything at all from patient art, you must be able to perceive and to decipher the language of art itself.

How to Look at the Product

There are two essential ways to regard any art product, whether you are thinking developmentally, existentially, or psychodynamically: in terms of *form* and in terms of *content*. There is also, as with art and therapy, an *interface* between the two, where form itself becomes the content of the work of art, as in the work of Janie Rhyne (1979) in her doctoral dissertation, where she requested line drawings to represent feeling states.

Some art therapists have an unfortunate bias in this regard, focusing primarily on either element to the exclusion of the other. While emphasizing one item at a time can be useful as a learning exercise, it cannot do justice to the richness of any art creation, which necessarily includes both, each with vital messages for the clinician.

Knowing Form

The formal elements in art are many and include not only general ones (such as organization) but also those specific to particular media (such as color or shading). There are some elements that apply to work in all materials. These include the degree of organization, clarity, completeness, originality, age appropriateness, expansiveness, simplicity, activity, and balance of the work. The first five items are related primarily to quality, while the last four relate more to style. Yet, even such dimensions as these, while applicable to all two- and three-dimensional products, are manifest in distinct ways as a function of the medium involved.

Specific to different media are additional formal qualities, all of which should be part of the mental checklist of any competent art therapist. Pencil drawings, for example, can be considered in terms of line quality, which itself includes such distinct variables as darkness, thickness, sharpness, smoothness, and the relationship of the line to other formal elements (such as mass or space). With the addition of color in a drawing medium (whether pencil, crayon, or chalk), you can also assess such aspects as hue and intensity, and with a fluid medium (such as marker or paint), the quality of the strokes becomes relevant, with categories somewhat different from those appropriate to pencil or crayon.

The interaction between these formal elements must also be considered. Are some colors linear and others in masses? How do they relate in space? Do they touch or are they separated, and, if separated, is it by space or by line? What are the relative sizes of different elements and their sequence in the making of a product? Close observation of the latter is a major source of information, as when the artistic statements are revised in some way, such as erasing parts of a pencil drawing, undoing what has been made with clay, or covering over what has been done in paint.

While the artist considers all such formal elements in relation to aesthetic criteria, the art therapist is also concerned with their significance in terms of development, personality style, coping strategies, and symbolic meaning. Thus, each aspect of a work of art is rich in multiple messages.

A mass of yellow paint can be seen not only in terms of its intensity or solidity but also in regard to its placement on the page, its relationship to other elements in the painting, its relative size, its particular shape, and its symbolic meaning for the individual. Does it imply flatness or three-dimensionality, lightness or heaviness? Is it meant to be something, or does it resemble something when ideas are projected onto it by the artist?

When in the context of the entire sequence of events does it get placed in the picture space? Is it modified in any way by the artist in the course of completing the work? What developmental level is suggested by its form in the context of the whole? From what developmental level are the thematic issues it represents? Does it seem to be primarily expressive or primarily defensive? And so on.

These are complex questions, and there is no recipe book that is really valid for understanding art. But, *the more you look, the more you will be able to see*, and sophisticated looking with what might be called "the third eye" is analogous to listening with "the third ear" as recommended by psychoanalyst Theodor Reik (1948).

Knowing Content

The content of a work of art would seem at first glance to be a fairly simple matter, but upon reflection it, too, becomes complicated. For content in any communication, whether verbal, visual, or gestural, can be considered in at least two ways: manifest (what is visible) and latent (the symbolic meaning that is behind it). And, if you embrace the psychoanalytic theory of mental topography, content can be thought of as emanating from conscious, preconscious, or unconscious levels of the mind.

While these two ways of categorizing content are connected, that relationship, too, is not as simple as it seems. For manifest content, while presumably conscious, is not always something of which the maker is aware. In fact, what is "visible" can even come as a surprise ("Oh! I didn't realize I had drawn a bird here!"), suggesting that it emanates from a preconscious rather than a fully conscious level of mental awareness.

It is also useful to think of content in terms of the *themes* therein, which can be classified in regard to *developmentally* relevant issues (attachment, separation, individuation, etc.) and can also be thought of *dynamically* (e.g., aggression toward others, toward the self, etc.). In order to make such determinations about the meanings inherent in the represented or projected content of a work of art, it is best to have observed the sequence involved in its creation and the many associations, both verbal and nonverbal, expressed by the artist.

The art alone is never enough, yet in its associative context (like the dream) it is a rich source of understanding. This context includes behaviors directly related to the particular product, as well as those that precede and follow it. The repetition of either form or content is a signal that something is significant to the artist. Repeated images within a product or in different products will alert you to the intensity of the client's message, although a single subtle "slip" of form or content can be equally important, albeit less comfortable for the person to perceive or express.

Content can be quite logical, making conceptual as well as perceptual sense. It can also be quite illogical, either perceptually (as in the work of Escher) or conceptually (as in art created during psychosis). While both form and content may be parallel on the logic continuum, they can also be diametrically opposed—as with an orderly, clearly depicted drawing, painting, or sculpture of creatures that are pure fantasy. It is sometimes said that images are the main language of "primary process" thought, while words provide a tongue for what Freud called the "secondary process." Yet, either words or images can express primary or secondary process thought, as in neologisms (primary process words) or surrealistic art (secondary process imagery).

So content is not simply a matter of identifying the "what" of a deliberately depicted image or a projected visual idea and then classifying it developmentally or symbolically. This is just the first stage of understanding, and even at that level, you also need to consider the spatial and temporal relationship of one aspect of subject matter to another. A wild animal baring its teeth alone on a picture space is a far different statement from the same animal shown inside a cage. Even an animal plus a cage is a different equation, depending on whether the cage or the animal is created first.

And in this complex area of form/content relationships, we need to consider what is usually called "style," whereby the manner itself, in which formal elements are expressed, carries a kind of symbolic meaning. Style is often thought of in human and dramatic ways, such as "voluptuous," "passionate," "cold," "detached," "loose," or "fussy."

While all of these elements of art are visible in the finished product, anyone who has observed the process from start to finish knows that much of the drama therein is hidden in the final outcome. To be able to derive the richest and most therapeutically useful understanding from art products, it is optimal to observe the entire process of their creation. Such aspects as sequence, tempo, rhythm, and all verbal and nonverbal behaviors are indeed associations to the elements in an artistic product. Unlike a dream, revealed in consciousness but produced in sleep, art is created while awake, its very evolution visible to both artist and therapist. Associations to art (nonverbal as well as verbal) are assumed to reflect something about the art maker.

This holds true for all art therapists, even if you do not consider yourself to be operating from a deep psychological point of view. As my very humanistic colleague Randy Vick wrote as part of his critique of this book, "I contend however that if you don't buy into the notion of *projection*, the rest of the concepts underlying Art Therapy collapse like a house of cards" (Personal communication, February 21, 2007; italics in the original). In other words, most art therapists believe, as pioneer art therapist Bernie Levy used to say, that "the picture is the person."

Projection was initially defined as a defense mechanism by analysts Sigmund and Anna Freud, and it can indeed serve the function of protecting a person from knowing about, for example, his hostile impulses by ascribing them to someone else or expressing or seeing them in a picture. It can also be thought of as a way of making sense of the world, especially of other people (where it takes the form of "transference") and of ambiguous stimuli. It is especially useful in group art therapy, in which each group member can project ideas that concern him onto the artwork of every other member. Thus, everyone can learn not only from their own creations but also from those of the others.

Because projection is ubiquitous, it presents a huge challenge to the art therapist, who needs to know herself very well—her inner psychic reality, not just her artistic tastes—in order *not* to project her own meanings onto anyone else's creative product. Subtracting yourself from the equation when regarding, responding to, and understanding client art is a discipline that requires constant attention. As you get to know clients well, you begin to "know" what they are saying in their artwork, but you always need to be cautious about unwittingly adding your own projections to the mix.

Because I believe that the deepest understanding for anyone comes from within, it does not make sense to impose either form or content on the patient. Only when what has been created comes as completely as possible from the individual can its meaning be fully valid for understanding that person. Of course, there are exceptions, which will be discussed in the Interface section of the book. But for the purpose of knowing people by their products, our comprehension is most valid when based on something emanating as fully as possible from the person himself.

One of the most confused and confusing areas in art therapy, as pointed out by my colleague Randy Vick in his consultation on this revised edition, concerns "interpretation." For most people, this means knowing and often telling the client what his or her artwork "means." Because there is an intense desire to be understood on the part of the client and a strong wish to help on the part of the therapist, the temptation to gratify that wish is there from the start. On the other hand, it is also true that many people fear what they will learn from what the therapist "sees" in their artwork, what unpleasant truth they will find out about themselves that they do not already know.

In fact, there were many in the early days of art therapy who actually thought they could "read" patients from their art. The truth is that art therapists are not omniscient interpreters, but it is also true that because of our training and experience we can indeed "see" more in patient art than many other professionals. Generalizations about meanings, whether of colors, symbols, or placement, are a useful source of hypotheses that bubble up in your mind when observing the creation of and engaging in reflection on a client's artwork. For most of us, however, the most valid "meaning" is one co-constructed with the client, in a respectful partnership in which the patient, rather than the art therapist, is the "expert" on his or her own creation.

In addition to advising that I confront the issue of interpretation, Randy also suggested that this chapter include a consideration of other uses of patient artwork, not just those in the interpersonal context of therapy. One of course is the archiving and preservation of case material, certainly a responsibility of the art therapist. This can be complicated by the occasional destruction of artwork by clients, as well as the wish to take something home or keep it in their hospital rooms. Since I believe strongly that the art belongs to its creator, the best way I have found to meet such needs is to use a camera to record the artwork when the person does not want it to be kept on a shelf or in a folder.

At one time, many art therapists worried that exhibiting or reproducing a client's artwork was a form of exploitation. However, in my experience, most individuals are absolutely delighted to have their work valued sufficiently for someone to want to exhibit it in a show or reproduce it in a book or on a calendar. If you or anyone in the institution wants to reproduce or exhibit a patient's artwork, it is essential that written permission be obtained. Indeed, such a requirement is built into the ethical codes that govern the work of art therapists. It is simply respectful to do so.

And, speaking of respect, just as respect for materials is shown by how they are stored, displayed, and handled, so respect for people's art is demonstrated in how the art therapist regards, takes care of, and stores it. There are many possible ways of doing so, from portfolios to shelves to folders to containers, but the goal should always be to handle, store, and display client art with the utmost concern and respect.

The art, after all, is an extension of the person, and so how it is dealt with conveys a loud message about how you regard the individual who created it. If there is one thing all therapists want clients to get out of their treatment, it is increased self-esteem, which, in my opinion, is another way of saying more self-respect. In addition to helping people to feel better about themselves because they have mastered an art process, feeling good about what they have created is hugely valuable.

Recommended Readings

Arnheim, R. (1969). *Visual thinking*. Berkeley: University of California Press.

Cohen, B. M. (Ed.). (1986/1994). *The diagnostic drawing series rating guide*.

Cohen, B. M., & Cox, C. T. (1995). *Telling without talking*. New York: Norton.

Gantt, L., & Tabone, C. (1998). *The formal elements art therapy scale: The rating manual*. Morgantown, WV: Gargoyle Press.

Jakab, I. (1998). *Pictorial expression in psychiatry* (2nd ed.). Budapest: Akademiai Kiado.

Levy, B. I. (1979). Videotape. "Art therapy: An introduction." Craftsbury Commons, VT: Art Therapy Publications.

Malchiodi, C. A. (1998). *Understanding children's drawings*. New York: Guilford Press.

Reik, T. (1948). *Listening with the third ear*. New York: Farrar, Straus.

Rhyne, J. (1979). Drawings as personal constructs: A study in visual dynamics. Unpublished doctoral dissertation, University of California, Santa Cruz.

Silver, R. A. (2007). *The Silver drawing test and draw a story: Assessing depression, aggression, and cognitive skills*. New York: Routledge.

Simon, R. (1992). *The symbolism of style*. New York: Routledge.

Ulman, E. (1961). Art therapy: Problems of definition. *Bulletin of Art Therapy*, *1*, 10–20.

Feelings about the self are involved in the making and showing of most creative products.

The art therapist observes closely as a blind boy creates "A Street" using torn foam rubber shapes.

PART 2

The Therapy Part

This section of the book is rather generic in that the subject matter is potentially relevant for all kinds of therapists or counselors. However, since the term *therapy* is so casually bandied about with so many different meanings, it may be helpful to note those aspects of psychology, psychopathology, and psychotherapy that are most critical for art therapists specifically.

As with the art part, it never hurts to know more, and particular settings or populations may demand further understanding in one or another area. Any art therapist has an ethical, as well as a professional, responsibility to gather that additional knowledge in order to do the job properly. Just as a painter may need to learn more about wood sculpture in order to reach troubled adolescents who are easily "turned on" to that mode of expression, so a therapist who has worked primarily with individuals may need to study family systems and therapy if asked to do family art evaluation or therapy at a child guidance center.

There are, however, some basics, as with art, that every art therapist should know—basics that do not enter your head through intuition or osmosis, but that require some kind of study, formal or informal. These basics are the subject matter of the first three chapters in this section. The initial one deals with development, both normal and abnormal; the second deals with deviations from normal development and psychological functioning, both individual and interpersonal; and the third deals with therapy, focusing on the necessary framework, the relationships therein, and the process of treatment over time. In each, general understandings are briefly noted, along with some specific issues relevant to art therapy in particular.

A final chapter deals with knowing art therapy and being an art therapist. This includes becoming clear about your identity through understanding the relationship of art to other action therapies—such as activity, occupational, and recreation therapy—as well as to other creative therapies—such as music, drama, and dance therapy.

In addition to knowing how art therapy is similar to and different from related disciplines, attention is also given to the beliefs seen as necessary for the effective art therapist. Finally, there is a brief description of some of the personal qualities that seem essential for a good art therapist, including knowledge of the self. With the foundation laid in the first two sections of the book, it then is possible to go on to the art therapy situation itself, which is the subject matter of the third portion, The Interface.

Mother-child art activities help to clarify attachment issues for parent, therapist, and child.

Monsters are one way for children to give artistic form to aggressive impulses and ambivalent feelings.

CHAPTER 4

Knowing Development

The Importance of Knowing Normal Development

Knowing normal human development is vital to the practice of good art therapy. While you might suppose that the most important aspect for an art therapist is what happens over time in using materials, by itself that is far from sufficient. Although a detailed knowledge of development in drawing, painting, and modeling is essential in order to recognize deviations from the norm, art expression cannot be arbitrarily divorced from the totality of human growth. Art therapists, while we work with and through art, are ultimately responsible for understanding and helping the human beings who become our clients as whole people.

You might also imagine that a detailed knowledge of normal development is vital only if an art therapist works primarily with children. Although that sounds reasonable, I believe that no adult can be fully understood without an awareness of the historical roots of his or her problems. Different theories of personality and psychotherapy place varying degrees of emphasis on early origins of behavior, but all agree that symptoms result from something that has happened externally and been processed internally, whether in the distant past or the recent present. A person's history can be viewed through many different and varied developmental lenses, but understanding how someone's problems came to be is always part of the solution.

Whatever the age of the person you are trying to help, it is best for any effort at understanding or helping to know about someone's development over time, as well as their "roots," both biological and psychosocial. The old dichotomy of *nature versus nurture* has slowly been supplanted by a more complex understanding of multiple causation.

Whether thought of narrowly in terms of birth order or broadly in terms of the socioeconomic/cultural matrix, any individual's development reflects a dynamic interaction between genetic givens and environmental influences. Both kinds of information are relevant when you take a historical, developmental perspective, regardless of the patient's age at the time of referral.

However, reading or taking a developmental history is as limited in usefulness as requesting or seeing a drawing if you do not know how to make sense of it. To classify, categorize, and fully comprehend historical information, it is essential to have a frame of reference, a clear conception of normal and abnormal development. At the risk of oversimplifying, I would like to suggest that there are some aspects of development that matter more than others for the practice of good art therapy. In addition to knowing normal artistic progression, you need to be familiar primarily with social and emotional development and secondarily with the specific functions involved in creating and perceiving works of art.

In other words, while it is helpful to know the expectable ages and sequences for the mastery of major developmental tasks, it is especially important to be familiar with what usually happens in the areas of sensory and perceptual functioning as well as in reality testing and synthesizing. This becomes critical if you work with cognitively impaired individuals of any age, who often require some pre-art preparatory or remedial activities of a sensory/perceptual nature in order to be able to eventually use art materials creatively. Similarly, although it is helpful to be familiar with all aspects of normal motor development, it is vital to know in detail about the specific fine motor behaviors involved in working with art materials.

But physical development cannot really be understood independently of psychological growth, any more than cognitive development can be looked at independently of emotional maturation. In fact, a steadily growing body of evidence about the intimate relationship between soma and psyche (body and mind) seems to validate hypotheses about the frequent influence of stress on certain physiological disorders, such as migraine headaches or ulcerative colitis. Although there is no question about the reality of the symptoms, the interdependence of mental and physical functioning is so great that the degree of impairment may be greatly magnified by psychological variables.

For example, I find myself thinking of a number of children with whom I worked who suffered from what psychologists called a "specific learning disability" and who did indeed test as deviant from the norm in such areas as auditory or visual processing. Yet many of these children, after a period of successful art therapy, turned out to be able to learn mathematics or reading at a much higher level and faster rate than was earlier thought possible.

That does not mean, by the way, that whatever neurological impairment presumably involved in the learning disability was magically reversed, or that the children tested any differently on diagnostic instruments. It does mean, however, that the psychological problems that compounded the physiological ones, once removed, no longer inhibited the full use of the child's mental capacities—including the ability to benefit from the remedial teaching of compensatory learning strategies.

I also think of many blind youngsters I have seen, whose sensory handicap could not be undone, but who after therapy were able to learn more easily and to move more freely than before. It was not the blindness, but the inhibitions caused by the maladaptive coping mechanisms used by these children, that had made mastering Braille or benefiting from mobility training so difficult.

In fact, it is not uncommon for apparently appropriate remedial efforts to be made in regard to specific problems, which eventually turn out to be psychological in origin and therefore require a different kind of therapy. I think of an almost-mute girl with a severe articulation disorder, who was referred for art therapy after a painfully long history of evaluations, diagnoses, and treatments by doctors, developmental specialists, and speech therapists. Although she had suffered several convulsions, and there was indeed some mild mental retardation, her dramatic response in expressive therapy revealed that the blocks that had stood in her linguistic and intellectual path were largely psychological.

Within less than a year of weekly individual sessions, she was talking more clearly and with fairly well-organized language, surprising all who knew her—her parents, her teacher, her former speech therapist, and myself as well. While she had also progressed several grade levels in basic skills during the year of treatment, she was still better off in a special class where she could get the greater personal attention that was optimal for her. But she no longer required speech therapy or medication and was able to move along quite normally into adolescence.

There have even been some instances in my experience in which almost all of an apparent disability turned out to have been psychological in origin. A boy of 18, who had been in classes for the retarded throughout his academic life, had scored consistently low on intelligence tests. However, after a little over a year of individual expressive therapy (stimulated by a period of suicidal depression), not only was he feeling happier and more outgoing but he was also moved into the regular high school program, on a normal educational track for the first time in his life. Perhaps the fact that he was also blind and had a seizure disorder affected the ability of diagnosticians to see the latent intelligence in this boy. This case, while tragic and ironic, is also profoundly instructive and serves as a reminder that the arts are often able to elicit the healthy capacities of patients when other modes cannot. Whether it was the working through of his rage, the pleasure in his own creativity, or both, the experience with art therapy for this youngster revealed that what had been seen as a genetic given (his retardation) was a functional developmental delay.

Professionals and parents are used to thinking of some physical symptoms like enuresis as possibly psychological in origin. This seems to be less true, however, for inhibitions in learning or motility, which are often seen as neurologically or physiologically based. Both enuresis and learning disabilities tend to run in families, so there is clearly a genetic component. But both can be exacerbated by and can cause stress because of the embarrassment and frustration of the symptoms.

As we begin to understand more fully the complexity and plasticity of the brain, it is likely that a treatment such as art therapy might turn out to be useful, because the very nature of the modality involves the activation of different parts of the human mind. Given the need for integration and synthesis in organized thought and action, a visual *and* verbal modality, which involves translation from one mode into the other, has tremendous potential for the promotion of higher and healthier mental functioning.

And it is, after all, primarily mental functioning with which any psychotherapist is concerned. It therefore makes sense that the most important aspect of development for an art therapist to be knowledgeable about is mental—both cognitive and affective. I found Erik Erikson's thinking about development (1964) to be especially helpful because he included more of the sociocultural matrix, long before many others realized how important it was.

To consider *both* cognition and affect seems important, especially since both are involved in the creation of art. To my mind, the work of Stanley Greenspan (1980) is still a good model for integrating both domains. Although early developmental study emphasized childhood and adolescence (Freud, 1965), it is also useful to supplement your frame of reference with investigations of infancy (Greenspan & Wieder, 2005) and the years of adulthood (Vaillant, 1977, 2002).

This book is not the place to restate specifics about psychological development that are detailed elsewhere. But, as with media and processes, it might be appropriate to remind ourselves of the importance of *all* stages and phases and of the special significance of certain aspects of normal development that have a bearing not only on the client's inner world but also on the way in which he or she relates to the art therapist.

The therapeutic dyad, for example, comes into being based on a person's early experiences of attachment (Cassidy & Shaver, 2008). Erikson's studies of the gender differences in "inner and outer space" have been confirmed by later studies of feminine development in which the importance of connection and relationships have been found to be paramount (Jordan, 1997; Jordan, Kaplan, Miller, & Stiver, 1991).

So, whenever it is possible to find out about someone's history, it is helpful to inquire. With a child, you might ask about the meaning of the particular pregnancy to both parents, especially the mother. Also critical is the way in which the child, as an infant, adjusted to the stimuli and demands of the physical and social world. What kind of temperament was inborn and how was it perceived and felt by the mother, especially in terms of her own way of being (Chess, Thomas, & Birch, 1965)? Was there a comfortable "fit" between mother and child, or was there tension and dyssynchrony (Lewis & Rosenblum, 1974)?

And, as the child became aware of his separateness, how did both partners in the twosome deal with the tasks and phases of the separation-individuation process (Mahler, Pine, & Bergmann, 1975/2000)? When the world changed for the child from a dyadic to a triadic one, how did he deal with the challenge of incorporating beloved but inherently rivalrous others (father, siblings) into his life space? Was he able to venture and explore as his universe expanded? How did he relate to those beyond the family circle: peers, babysitters, teachers? What were the school years like in regard to learning, social behavior, and all of the developmental tasks of childhood?

What happened in adolescence—that period of massive change, inevitable instability, and potential for both pain and pleasure (Erikson, 1980)? And so on, through the primary psychosexual and psychosocial tasks of young, middle, and late adulthood (Erikson & Erikson, 1997). Regardless of the age of the patient, it is important to ask for childhood recollections in general, and it is remarkably useful to inquire about the person's *earliest memory*. Whatever is recalled is sure to be significant, and often one image of the distant past will stimulate others. Even though we now know even more than in the past that memory is a complex phenomenon, this is a helpful historical question.

You may be wondering why it seems so important to know anything about a client's history in order to understand his problems. Whether the person in distress is a child or an adult, the very fact that there is an inability to cope with the demands of life in the present means that at some point or other, his development did not proceed in a completely adequate fashion (with the possible exception of "reactive" disorders). Even cognitive-behavioral therapists agree that it is important to learn the history of any maladaptive behaviors or thoughts. The assumption is that they have been learned in the past, whether recently or some time ago.

If you think of human development as similar to building with blocks—something like a pyramid, in that so many vital tasks occur in early childhood—then it makes sense that, if there are weaknesses or gaps at any point along the line, they will create a structure with an inherent vulnerability to stress. Even though certain developmental tasks may not have been fully accomplished, the biological maturational thrust of succeeding stages will demand dealing with later tasks, which the individual is poorly equipped to master.

In other words, a person who has not fully resolved a separation-individuation process in early childhood has many difficulties with succeeding phases and may be unable to master later challenges, such as the definition of his sexual or personal identity. Many of the clues about developmental lags, fixation points, or arrests are available in the client as he presents himself in the present.

His behavior and his artwork both give hints and even indications of unresolved issues and the developmental levels to which they belong. Knowing normal development in art is essential for any art therapist who looks at a drawing, painting, or sculpture. It is striking that, even though his ideas were formulated in the 1940s, Viktor Lowenfeld's (1957) description of the stages of graphic development have remained dominant in art therapy education.

A knowledge of normal development in general and in art specifically is, of course, critical for accurate assessment and eventual treatment (Golomb, 1992; Milbraith & Trautner, 2008). Since art therapists work with all expressive visual media, and with many populations deviating in complex ways from the norm, we have much to discover regarding the "mapping" of normal and atypical art development beyond what is already known about such limited expressive activities as human figure drawing (Rubin, 2005).

We probably also have a good deal to add to the growing knowledge base about hemispheric dominance and the functions of different parts of the brain. We can contribute little, however, if we have not fully digested and integrated the many bits and pieces of developmental knowledge about art expression already available. This is a difficult task because the information comes from a variety of disciplines, including child development, art education, developmental psychology, and psychoanalysis.

A well-informed art therapist ought to be aware of what is already known about art development and ought to have integrated such knowledge into his or her clinical vision so that developmental determinations can be easily and securely made in response to the art product.

It is also especially important to be familiar with what is known about the particular mental functions involved in creative work. There is evidence from the investigations of psychologists that intelligence and creativity, as they are currently defined and measured, are independent capacities (Getzels & Jackson, 1962). In this context, Howard Gardner's conceptualization of "multiple intelligences" is also relevant, especially because it is evident that some individuals are high in one domain but low in another (Gardner, 1983, 1999).

So, in addition to understanding what is known about the overall development of the intellect and its ability to solve problems, it is also important to be familiar with what is known about the growth and development of creative thinking abilities. Related, but not identical, are the areas of fantasy, imagination, and play, all of which are necessarily involved in any creative act. The growth over time of the capacity to think and act symbolically, as well as to differentiate fantasy from reality, is particularly critical for art therapists, working as we do in a symbolic mode.

Of equivalent interest, then, is a person's creative history, as far back as the individual (and, if a child, the parents) can remember. What kind of play activities and materials were preferred in infancy, early childhood, latency, and adolescence? If an adult, what is the current place of the arts in the client's life? And, whatever the age, what is the role of fantasy, imagination, and daydreaming for this person? How much of the person's thinking is *visual* rather than *verbal* (cf. Arnheim, 1969)?

A history is useful as a way of validating your clinical "hunches" about *when* things went off a normal track. Making sense out of a history, however, requires more than a coherent sense of normal development. It also requires an ability to relate what you have learned about a person's past to the hypotheses you have developed based on what goes on in art interviews—behavior, images, and associations.

Taking a History Using Art

If you are involved in the diagnostic assessment of an individual, in addition to being able to discover a great deal through both process and products, it is also possible to use art to look more directly at a person's history. Many ways of asking patients to represent themselves over time have been suggested, usually as a pictorial or abstract representation of feelings, events, or people over the life span—perhaps on a long roll of paper. Sometimes this is called a "life line."

The important thing is that you invite the person to show the ups and downs and significant people, places, and events in his life representationally, symbolically, or abstractly. As with a verbal history, what is selected and how it is expressed are both significant. Another approach is to ask for representations (pictorial or abstract) of self or others (such as family) at one or more moments in the past, in the present, and perhaps in the future as well. The powerful, expressive language of form and color adds an ineffable dimension to the usual verbal history-taking exercise.

Whether art is involved in the data-gathering process, when all of the available information on someone's life story is in, then you can begin to organize that information for a fuller understanding of the problems bringing the person to therapy. My own theoretical bias is psychoanalytic, and I find Anna Freud's (1965) Developmental Profile to be an extremely useful way of organizing clinical data, including historical information (Eissler, Kris, & Solnit, 1977). There are, of course, other formal and informal ways of conceptualizing the past and its influence on present functioning. What matters most is not the specific frame of reference used, but that there be some coherent framework in your mind for making psychological sense out of a client's developmental history.

Regardless of your theoretical orientation, a clear image of normal development is essential in order to identify any kind of distortion or deviation. Although definitions of abnormality vary considerably from one frame of reference to another, and there are many who find diagnostic classifications inadequate, you cannot function in a psychiatric setting without some understanding of various kinds of psychopathology and of the terms used to categorize different kinds of psychic disorders. The most commonly used system is the *Diagnostic and Statistical Manual of Mental Disorders* put out by the American Psychiatric Association (APA); the most current is the revision of the fourth edition (*DSM-IV-TR*; APA, 2000; Millon, Krueger, & Simonsen, 2010).

Similarly, you cannot function in an educational setting without a clear comprehension of the current understanding and coding for different types of exceptionality. The Web site of the Council for Exceptional Children, a special education organization, lists the main types of exceptionality, along with descriptions of each (http://www.cec.sped.org/Content/NavigationMenu/NewsIssues/TeachingLearningCenter/ExceptionalityArea/?from=tlcHome). The same considerations apply to social and emotional development, neither of which can be viewed in isolation from the norms of the individual's environmental and cultural matrix.

In any case, when development goes awry at any point in a person's life, whether the disability is inborn or acquired as the result of some physical or psychological stress, then subsequent development is necessarily affected. It is helpful not only to be able to name the problem but also to understand its historical origins. Whether a phobia is being treated by behavior modification or psychoanalytic art therapy, it helps greatly to know the history of the person, if only in regard to the symptom. I also believe that developmental understanding leads to the most meaningful kind of psychological comprehension, including any sort of formulation of deviations (abnormal psychology or psychopathology), the area considered in the next chapter.

References

American Psychiatric Association. (2000). *Diagnostic and statistical manual of mental disorders* (4th ed.). Washington, DC: Author.
Arnheim, R. (1969). *Visual thinking.* Berkeley: University of California Press.
Cassidy, J., & Shaver, P. R. (Eds.). (2008). *Handbook of attachment* (2nd ed.). New York: Guilford Press.
Chess, S., Thomas, A., & Birch, H. G. (1965). *Your child is a person: A psychological approach to childhood without guilt.* New York: Viking Press.
Eissler, R. S., Kris, M., & Solnit, A. J. (Eds.). (1977). *Psychoanalytic assessment: The diagnostic profile.* New Haven, CT: Yale University Press.
Erikson, E. H. (1964). *Childhood and society* (2nd ed.). New York: Norton.
Erikson, E. H. (1980). *Identity and the life cycle.* New York: Norton.
Erikson, E. H., & Erikson, J. M. (1997). *The life cycle completed.* New York: Norton.
Freud, A. (1965). *Normality and pathology in childhood.* New York: International Universities Press.
Gardner, H. (1983). *Frames of mind.* New York: Basic Books.
Gardner, H. (1999). *Intelligence reframed.* New York: Basic Books.
Getzels, J. W., & Jackson, P. W. (1962). *Creativity and intelligence.* New York: Wiley.
Golomb, C. (1992). *The child's creation of a pictorial world.* Berkeley: University of California Press.
Greenspan, S. I. (1980). *Intelligence and adaptation: An integration of psychoanalytic and Piagetian developmental psychology.* New York: International Universities Press.
Greenspan, S. I., & Wieder, S. (2005). *Infant and early childhood mental health: A comprehensive, developmental approach to assessment and intervention.* Arlington, VA: American Psychiatric Publishing.
Jordan, J. V. (Ed.). (1997). *Women's growth in diversity.* New York: Guilford Press.
Jordan, J. V., Kaplan, A. G., Miller, J. B., & Stiver, I. P. (1991). *Women's growth in connection.* New York: Guilford Press.
Lewis, M., & Rosenblum, L. A. (Eds.). (1974). *The effect of the infant on its caregiver.* New York: Wiley.
Lowenfeld, V. (1957). *Creative and mental growth* (3rd ed.). New York: Macmillan.
Mahler, M. S., Pine, F., & Bergmann, A. (2000). *The psychological birth of the human infant.* New York: Basic Books. (Original work published 1975)
Milbraith, C., & Trautner, H. M. (Eds.). (2008). *Children's understanding and production of pictures.* Cambridge, MA: Hogrefe & Huber.
Millon, T., Krueger, R. F., & Simonsen, E. (2010). *Contemporary directions in psychopathology: Scientific foundations of the DSM-V and ICD-11.* New York: Guilford Press.
Rubin, J. A. (2005). *Child art therapy* (3rd ed.). New York: Wiley.
Vaillant, G. E. (1977). *Adaptation to life.* Boston: Little, Brown & Co.
Vaillant, G. E. (2002). *Aging well.* Boston: Little, Brown & Co.

Recommended Readings

Colarusso, C. A. (1992). *Child and adult development: A psychoanalytic introduction for clinicians.* New York: Plenum Press.
Fein, S. (1976). *Heidi's horse.* Pleasant Hill, CA: Exelrod Press.
Viorst, J. (1986). *Necessary losses.* New York: Simon & Schuster.

A girl draws with markers during her individual art therapy at a child guidance center.

Understanding an individual's internal world is critical to helping through art therapy.

CHAPTER 5

Knowing Dynamics and Deviations

Theoretical Underpinnings

Knowing dynamics, as I am using the term, has to do with knowing why people function as they do, that is, understanding the psychological causality of behavior in a broad sense and of symptoms (deviations) in a narrow one. As with development, you ought to be familiar with all of the major theories of personality and psychopathology currently in use, as well as deeply and thoroughly knowledgeable about at least one.

Despite tremendous strides in the last several decades in the investigation and understanding of the neurobiological substrate, which has revolutionized the treatment of serious mental disorders, the experts are still far from being able to quantify all of the influences and outcomes in this complex area. Existing theories represent useful hypotheses about why people act and think as they do and are important to know about, not only in order to communicate with colleagues but also to further your efforts at understanding and helping clients through art.

The decades since the first edition of this book was published have seen the increasing dominance of biological psychiatry (Wender, 1981), including studies indicating more neuronal plasticity than was earlier thought possible. While the use of antidepressant and other psychiatric drugs has increased in the hands of general practitioners as well as psychiatrists, there have been encouraging findings about the ability of the brain to change and for the potential of modifications through psychotherapy (Siegel, 1999, 2007).

Meanwhile, the ideas and theories covered in a book I edited in 1987 and revised in 2001, *Approaches to Art Therapy,* are still being used by most people who try to help others through art and other therapies (Corey, 2008; cf. also Hogan, 1997; Rappaport, 2009). Although there are significant differences between different theoretical approaches, there are also many commonalities. In fact, my own belief is that they are rarely mutually exclusive and are more often complementary.

Each can be conceptualized as one of numerous blind men examining an elephant, focusing on one aspect of human psychology more than another. Or, they can be thought of as propositions that vary because the angles from which they sight their subject are not the same; or, they can be seen as different stains on a microscope slide, which enable different aspects of the phenomenon studied to become clearly visible (Hedges, 1983). The exciting challenge is to integrate these partially perceived truths from the particular perspective of art therapy itself and the creative process that is its core.

Pragmatically, no therapist can function in the mental health world of today without an awareness of the major theoretical approaches to understanding and modifying human behavior: behavioral, cognitive, nondirective, humanistic, existential, postmodern, narrative, Jungian, Freudian, and all of the many formulations based on the last, especially those based on developmental observation as well as those known as intersubjective, relational, or interpersonal.

Similarly, an art therapist in an educational setting must be familiar with different theories and explanations of learning problems and their remediation. As noted in Chapter 4, an art therapist also needs to know and understand the labels for both psychopathology and exceptionality in current usage.

Understanding the Client

Although it is somewhat artificial to separate theories of psychodynamics from questions of nosology, I do so largely because art therapists experience frequent confusion in this area. All too often there is a defensive use of diagnostic terminology, as if by labeling a patient with a word we automatically understand *why* he behaves as he does.

Whether the label is one describing overt behavior (such as "oppositional") or implying causality (such as "passive-aggressive"), having named the problem, the etiology seems to be assumed as simple and known. This confusion seems even greater when the label is one with multiple referents and conjures up a constellation of both etiology and symptomatology, such as "borderline" or "schizophrenic."

While it is true that we have a responsibility to be familiar with and to comprehend current diagnostic terminology, the desire for simple formulations may be as pervasive in this area as in that of understanding patient artwork. Hence, there is the rush to label without understanding or its opposite—to reject labeling as irrelevant and disrespectful. Neither the baby nor the bathwater seem to be well served in either of these two extremes.

The hard work is to try to understand what is wrong and why, and how that came to be the case. Assessment should not be a meaningless activity conducted to be able to get an insurance company to pay for treatment by finding and listing a diagnosis. Understanding what is going on is absolutely critical to helping people, but it is certainly not a simple matter.

Descriptive labeling of psychological problems came into fashion with the *Diagnostic and Statistical Manual of Mental Disorders* (DSM), which is now almost 60 years old (the first was in 1952), and it helped greatly by classifying psychological problems descriptively. It is published by the American Psychiatric Association and, along with the mental disorders section of the international medical coding system, the *International Classification of Diseases* (ICD), has been useful because it is descriptive and allows people to communicate more effectively than before it existed (cf. Millon, Krueger, & Simonsen, 2010).

If a disorder can be best treated by certain medications (as in the use of lithium and related chemicals for bipolar disorder), knowing what is wrong can lead to more effective treatment. However, it can work the other way; finding the proper treatment can help in differential diagnosis as in the following story. One of my young adult patients had a psychotic break and became virtually catatonic while in the hospital following a second suicide attempt. While she had been clearly depressed during her previous hospitalization, she had not been psychotic and the treatment team was stumped. Only after she was given lithium, which led to a dramatic improvement, was the psychiatrist in charge able to determine that she suffered from bipolar disorder.

Although they differ regarding the importance of etiological understanding for the patient himself, all current theories seem to agree that people with psychological problems are unable, for some reason, to deal comfortably and effectively with the tasks and stresses of their lives. Whether the disorder is pervasive and extensive or narrowly confined to some particular area, all approaches try to define as specifically as possible the reasons why the patient is unable to cope in a healthy, adaptive way.

Naturally, the therapeutic approach will depend heavily on a therapist's understanding of the causes of the problem. Some feel that maladaptive behaviors are learned and can therefore be unlearned, as in behavior modification or cognitive and cognitive-behavioral therapy. Others are convinced that overt symptomatology, although possibly modifiable, is but the tip of an internal conflictual iceberg that itself must be resolved (melted through insight) in order for the person to function freely, as in psychoanalytic therapies.

Whether the patient is seen individually, as part of a group, or with his family, you need to have some way of understanding what goes on inside of him and why. As with developmental theory, I have found the psychoanalytic approach to psychodynamics to be the most useful in my own work. The notion that there are different parts of the personality that can be in painful tension seems to "fit" the clinical data of both people and their art products.

That there are drives or strivings in all of us, and that successful living involves finding ways of satisfying our yearnings that are acceptable to ourselves and our environment, makes good common as well as clinical sense. Perhaps it is the comprehensiveness of analytic theory that makes it seem so useful, although I suspect that there are other reasons why I and many other art therapists find it so congenial (McWilliams, 1994, 1999).

For example, any artist knows from direct experience of the process that the source of creativity is rarely clear or articulate at a conscious level. Sensing that the imagery and gestures we employ come from some place within, artists have always been like depth psychologists, exploring and expressing the inner self. It makes sense, then, that art therapists would be attracted to depth psychological theories that postulate a dynamic unconscious, like those of Freud and Jung. I have had the rare personal advantage of undergoing full classical (Freudian) psychoanalytic training with both children and adults—a rich experience involving simultaneous personal analysis, didactic instruction in theory and technique, and closely supervised clinical work with patients.

Since the children I saw in analysis used art media extensively, it was possible to apply the theoretical understanding of psychodynamics to patient art as well as to other forms of expression, like dreams and mental imagery. After graduation from the Psychoanalytic Institute and going into full-time private practice, I was able to use art in adult analyses as well, sometimes extensively.

There is no question that, having invested a great deal of time, energy, and money in the study of psychoanalysis, I am certainly far from unbiased. But it is also relevant that I was drawn to study that particular approach because the supervisors who were most helpful to me in my first decade as an art therapist were all analysts.

Psychodynamic theory and therapy have continued to evolve during the past several decades, with more emphasis on the interpersonal situation between the therapist and the patient from a relational and collaborative point of view (Mitchell & Aron, 1999; Wachtel, 2008), as well as a recent emphasis on what is known as "positive psychology," based on two converging strands of work, by psychologists Mihaly Csikszentmihalyi (1998) and Martin Seligman (2002). The former did his early research in the phenomenon of "flow," in the context of creative behavior. The latter looked at how and why psychotherapy works and has focused on people's strengths and capacities. Since art therapy, more than most clinical approaches, also reveals people's strengths and capacities, it is no surprise that this approach has become popular among art therapists within a short period of time.

Despite my own bias for understanding dynamics in terms of internalized conflict, I do respect other orientations when the art therapist fully understands what she is doing. For that reason, asking respected colleagues to write about their particular approaches for *Approaches to Art Therapy* made a good deal of sense, both in 1987 and for the revision in 2001. Most studies of the effectiveness of psychotherapy have concluded, however, that the most significant variable is *not* the theoretical orientation of the therapist, but rather the ability of that individual to empathize with and to relate to the patient. The perceived "fit" between the therapist and the patient seems to be what matters most.

Although this would imply at the extreme that it is not knowing about art or therapy but simply being the right sort of person that is the only thing that leads to success, that is a rather foolish conclusion. While such findings do validate the importance of personal qualities in effective therapy, they do not thereby nullify the need for understanding and helping in a clearly conceptualized fashion.

As I look back now at my earliest work with schizophrenic youngsters in art therapy in 1963, when I had little formal knowledge or training, I think that any success I may have had was due to the healing power of the modality along with some relevant personal qualities. But I also believe quite firmly that had I known then what I know today, I could have done a much better job of helping those children.

Although I learned much through supervision and other experiences about both theory and technique, it seems to me that the most useful learning for my work in art therapy has been primarily in a richer and clearer understanding of intrapsychic functioning within a developmental frame of reference.

In addition to general issues of psychological functioning and its development under normal and pathological conditions, you need to know in some detail and depth about the particular dynamics of creative behavior, especially in the visual arts. Admittedly theoretical, like all such hypotheses, those notions about why human beings are motivated to create are most relevant to our work as art therapists.

As with other aspects of psychology, it is important to be familiar with all of the most common theoretical formulations. Whether you agree with theories that regard the creative act as primarily compensatory or with those that see it as a striving for self-actualization is not as important as being aware of different ways of perceiving its motivation and meaning.

Moreover, since human beings do not grow and develop in isolation but in relation to others, it is impossible to think about psychodynamics without considering interpersonal relationships as well. Even those who are convinced that psychological problems can become internalized do not deny or disavow the importance of interpersonal dynamics, whether in the family, the peer group, or the therapeutic dyad.

Although some theories give more weight to environmental effects than others, and some approaches intervene directly with the interpersonal matrix (like family art therapy), all ways of understanding psychological functioning and stress include both the individual and his relationships with others.

It is therefore essential to understand interpersonal as well as intrapsychic dynamics. In addition to reading and learning about how and why people relate as they do, it is extremely helpful to have the experience of being a member of an unstructured group that examines its own process. Whether the group is thought of as a learning experience or as psychotherapy, an absence of predefined structure allows group dynamics to emerge naturally, organically, and dramatically.

Anyone who has been involved in such an intensive group experience, like those modeled on the work of Wilfred Bion (1961) known as the "Tavistock method," knows much more about the powerful forces at work in a group than any amount of reading alone can convey. Although individual dynamics and developmental considerations are relevant to understanding group process, there are also many additional ways of conceptualizing families and other systems that take into account the forces among and between multiple individuals.

As with a developmental history, art materials can be used in many different ways to elicit meaningful data about the family, the group of origin. Most approaches to family art evaluation include a request for some open-ended work from each member (free product or one developed from a scribble, initial, or other stimulus), some representation of the family by each member, and some joint art task in which all participate. In addition to the interpersonal dynamics that become evident in the symbolic content of the products, behavioral data are also available for the art therapist, who can observe the many formal and informal reactions to one another among family members.

While comprehending group process and dynamics is vital for group art therapy, and knowing about family systems is essential for family art therapy, these understandings are equally relevant for the art therapist who sees individuals. Even in a one-to-one situation, there is in fact a group in the room.

In reality, it is the therapist and the patient, but in "psychic reality," there may be others "present," particularly from the past, in varied and complex ways. Since the understanding of what is going on in a therapy situation and why has some elements specific to that very unique and special event, the following chapter on therapy itself deals with knowing the framework, the relationship, and the nature of the therapeutic process over time.

References

Bion, W. R. (1961). *Experiences in groups*. New York: Basic Books.

Corey, G. (2008). *Theory and practice of counseling and psychotherapy* (8th ed.). Belmont, CA: Brooks/Cole.

Csikszentmihalyi, M. (1998). *Finding flow*. New York: Basic Books.

Hedges, L. (1983). *Listening perspectives in psychotherapy*. New York: Aronson.

Hogan, S. (Ed.). (1997). *Feminist approaches to art therapy*. New York: Routledge.

McWilliams, N. (1994). *Psychoanalytic diagnosis*. New York: Guilford Press.

McWilliams, N. (1999). *Psychoanalytic case formulation*. New York: Guilford Press.

Millon, T., Krueger, R. F., & Simonsen, E. (2010). *Contemporary directions in psychopathology: Scientific foundations of the* DSM-V *and* ICD-11. New York: Guilford Press.

Mitchell, S. A., & Aron, L. (Eds.). (1999). *Relational psychoanalysis*. New York: Analytic Press.

Rappaport, L. (2009). *Focusing-oriented art therapy*. London: Kingsley.

Rubin, J. A. (Ed.). (1987). *Approaches to art therapy*. New York: Brunner/Mazel.

Rubin, J. A. (Ed.). (2001). *Approaches to art therapy* (2nd ed.). New York: Brunner-Routledge.

Seligman, M. E. P. (2002). *Authentic happiness: Using the new positive psychology to realize your potential for lasting fulfillment*. New York: Free Press.

Siegel, D. J. (1999). *The developing mind: Toward a neurobiology of interpersonal experience*. New York: Guilford Press.

Siegel, D. J. (2007). *The mindful brain: Reflection and attunement in the cultivation of well-being*. New York: Norton.

Wachtel, P. (2008). *Relational theory and the practice of psychotherapy.* New York: Guilford.

Wender, P. H. (1981). *Mind, mood, and medicine: A guide to the new biological psychiatry.* New York: Farrar Straus & Giroux.

Recommended Readings

Engel, L., & Ferguson, T. (1990). *Imaginary crimes.* Lincoln, NE: Authors Choice Press.

Freud, A. (1936). *The ego and the mechanisms of defense. Writings of Anna Freud* (Vol. 2). New York: International Universities Press.

Solomon, M., & Siegel, D. (Eds.). (2003). *Healing trauma: Attachment, mind, body and brain.* New York: Guilford Press.

Art therapy involves helping a person not only to create but also to reflect on the product and the experience. The art therapist is writing down the child's story about his finger painting.

A woman smiles while using her favorite medium, thick poster chalk, and talking to the therapist. Being comfortable with the materials and the clinician are essential to successful art therapy.

CHAPTER **6**

Knowing Therapy

Knowing the Framework

One area often neglected in art and other therapies is what I have called the *framework*—the physical and psychological conditions one establishes within which art therapy becomes possible. Only in a certain kind of clearly bounded and conceptualized "frame" is an individual of any age able to fully and freely let go of his usual inhibitions, whether verbal or artistic. A feeling of safety and continuity is an essential condition for revealing to another the private aspects of the self. A secure and predictable environment is also needed in order for a person to be able to create authentically with art media. Such conditions for creative work have already been alluded to in the chapter on processes.

Physically, you need to create an environment that has a minimum of distraction and a maximum of conditions facilitating creativity. The latter would include adequate lighting, seating, working surfaces, and a clear and attractive arrangement of a variety of art media, with materials for drawing, painting, sculpting, and constructing. All of these should be kept as constant as possible, thereby creating a feeling of security as well as the possibility of independent functioning on the part of the client.

As for space, it is ideal if there is the possibility of both closeness and distance, openness and privacy—if there are sufficient options so that the client can be next to or far from others, including the therapist. Although you might under certain conditions (such as a brief evaluation) want to structure the space so as to maximize the possibility of observing the person while he works, in general it is best to allow the individual some freedom in determining the degree of closeness, especially in the beginning of the therapy.

With a family or a group, similar considerations are valid. Again, it is important to have adequate lighting, working space, and a variety of clearly arranged materials, all of which are consistent from one session to the next. On the other hand, you might also want, for diagnostic or therapeutic reasons, to structure the situation so as to maximize interaction (such as sitting at a round table or restricting materials so that sharing becomes necessary), without specifically mandating it (as in a request for a joint project).

In general, in art therapy over time with both families and groups, I have a personal preference for flexibility within a secure framework. This means providing options in working spaces, as well as media and themes, in order to allow individuals to determine their own distance and degree of interaction with other clients as well as with the therapist.

I suspect that such a preference for an open-ended approach is another reason why I found psychoanalysis so congenial, for one of the assumptions of that technique is that people will, given maximum freedom (of verbalization), express what is needed in order to understand their focal concerns and conflicts. Although the art therapy situation is radically different from that of adult analysis, in which the patient is on the couch and restricted to verbalization, the basic premise that free expression (association) is the optimal route to the pain within (which is causing problems) still holds. This is, in fact, the essential technique in child analysis, in which an open-ended kind of stance invites the youngster to play, draw, or talk as the spirit moves him.

The framework in art therapy need not be as explicit or rigid as in classical psycho-analysis, but it must be as clearly understood and provided in order for the client to feel fully secure. This is more difficult in the psychological arena than in the physical, where the pressures for a variety of responses are inevitably strong, regardless of the person's age. For this reason, it is essential that you be clear about your own boundaries, which necessarily reflect your conceptualization of the nature of art therapy and the consequent role of the clinician.

Although these notions differ from one individual and theory to another, what matters most is that you be consistent. This applies to all behaviors in the presence of and regarding the client and requires being clear about your own set of "rules and regulations." These "rules" refer to considerations such as limits—limits on client behavior (such as prohibiting destruc-tion of property) as well as on therapist behavior (such as not becoming socially involved).

They refer in a broader and more complex manner to the ways in which you continually monitor your verbal interventions, whether running commentary, inquiry, confrontation, or interpretation. Moreover, in art therapy, you also need to be clear in your own mind about guidelines for nonverbal interventions as well, especially in regard to the art process and products.

Some think that the best therapeutic stance is being spontaneous, free, flexible, respond-ing intuitively to the patient and his art. While that may seem on the face of it to be "creative," such behavior is really undisciplined, unthinking, and—more important—not therapeutic. For whatever your theoretical persuasion, an art therapist ought to know in general what personal position you might take in regard to a client at any stage of the therapeutic process.

It seems to me that the artistry of good therapy lies in being flexible, but within certain guidelines, rather than being either rigidly unbending or fluidly unpredictable. Neither of these extremes represents a useful model to a troubled person, who requires an image of freedom with order, energy with control. Neither chaotic freedom nor constricting control represents anyone's notion of mentally healthy functioning. All psychotherapeutic theories and techniques aim, ultimately, at enabling people to be in charge of and able to use the energy and abilities they possess, rather than being dominated by inner forces against their will.

In addition to the romanticized notion of the "spontaneous" art therapist, there is another image that I find equally anti-therapeutic (despite its popularity with some exis-tential clinicians)—that of the "authentic" art therapist who shares her "real self" with the patient. While it may be appropriate and helpful to convey personal information in certain times and places and for certain individuals, this is the exception rather than the rule. The main reason is that the sharing of such information reduces your usefulness as an object of projection (in analytic therapy, the "transference") on the part of the client. And even if you are not analytically inclined, the client's perception of the therapist, like his perception of anything else, reveals more about him the less he knows about your reality.

A secondary reason for thinking it is unwise to disclose personal information is that it can so easily be exhibitionistic and self-indulgent, although a clever clinician can usually rationalize that it is being done in the patient's interest. After all, an art therapist is supposed to use her time and skill in the service of the client, not of herself. This seems so obvious that it should not need to be said, but I feel a grave concern about situations I have observed that suggest that some therapists are meeting their own needs at the expense of those they are supposed to be helping.

Of course, no one would enjoy being an art therapist if the work did not fulfill some genuine personal needs, but you should still be able to remove your selfish strivings from the actual therapeutic arena. This is often difficult because the patient may demand—may even plead for—behaviors on your part that would be gratifying to both, like asking you to work on his painting or to go out for coffee after a session. It is important to remember that therapy is not primarily an arena for gratification of either client or clinician, despite the fact that to sustain the tensions and frustrations of the work there must be some genuine pleasures for both.

Knowing the Relationship

A therapist cannot work with someone over any substantial period of time without establishing some kind of working relationship. Whether formalized in a written or oral contract or informally agreed upon and whether explicit or implicit, therapy must be a collaborative partnership if it is to endure the inevitable stresses and strains of any internal change process. Some have called the establishment of a solid working relationship a therapeutic or working "alliance," a useful concept.

For, despite your striving for neutrality in regard to what the client presents, the work of therapy implies that both partners are allied in an effort to help the client to get well and to live better. With a group or a family, there must be alliances with all members individually as well as a kind of working agreement with the unit.

Although most writers have emphasized the task of involving the *client* in this pact, I believe that it takes time for *both* partners to make a genuine commitment. The client, it is true, needs to overcome any distrust and anxiety he may feel about this new person and strange new venture. But, the *therapist* also undergoes a progressive understanding of the client, his needs, and his potential, which enables you to fully invest in the mutual task.

Both therapist and client are likely to experience anxiety, frustration, discouragement, and even despair over the course of any sustained treatment. The alliance enables both to endure such strains and defines the relationship, even in its darkest hours, as a mutual partnership based on a fairly high level of trust and commitment on both sides.

Art therapists are in a rather favorable position in the establishment of an alliance with patients since what we offer is not only ourselves but also our modality. In a sense, then, the client forms an alliance over time with both the therapist and the creative process. While art materials can be threatening, it is also true that they do not talk back, and that with increasing skill a patient can learn to make them say what he wants them to say. He also learns that they can help him to both express and understand himself and that they are part of what is offered by the art therapist, who also offers her clinical as well as her creative expertise. The patient gradually becomes attached to the art making as well as to the therapist in an unconflicted, goal-directed way as a means to get well.

Parenthetically, art media are probably useful in the establishment of an alliance because they are intrinsically pleasurable in a sensory/manipulative way. They may even minimize the pain involved at many stages of the therapeutic process, from assessment through treatment to termination.

Also, for the person who is able to learn to use materials to make products of which he feels proud, there is yet another aspect. Because creative activity has its own rewards, there are continual reinforcements of the patient as artist, which go beyond sensorimotor pleasure and provide genuine enhancement of both self-esteem and self-confidence or, one could say, healthy narcissism (liking yourself).

All of these rewards, intrinsic to the creative process, add a continual, intermittent reinforcement feature to art therapy. Such a schedule is known to be the most likely to promote continuation of the associated behavior, so it is not surprising that a patient's commitment to the creative process and to art therapy itself tends to grow over time. Not only are you the person providing these opportunities and therefore someone positive, but also the opportunities themselves have sufficient built-in gratification to enable an alliance to form relatively rapidly and to become increasingly firm.

Of course, it is well known that any kind of therapy (even a behavioral or cognitive treatment) stirs up less-rational kinds of feelings and wishes in the patient (transference) and in the clinician (countertransference). I believe that the concept of transference is an especially congenial one for art therapists since it parallels what we already know about symbolism in visual expression.

Just as a color or an image can "stand for" something because of an individual's past experience, so do people project ideas and feelings onto other human beings. Given the need to make sense of experience, people tend to fill in what they do not know about any new person, just as they tend to complete a visual "gestalt." Moved by both the need to organize the outside world and the pressure of inner conflicts, all human beings tend to perceive new people on the basis of past experience with significant others and in relation to still-active strivings.

The conditions that facilitate transference reactions are much like those that foster the emergence of genuine personal material in art. For the latter purpose, unstructured media are presented in a safely bounded but free situation, encouraging individuals to find and express their own imagery (Rubin, 1982).

In a similar fashion, you can present yourself in a relatively neutral way, so that the patient can project feelings and ideas reflecting unresolved conflicts on you, just as he projects his inner world onto the art materials. You can make good use of that tendency to distort what is perceived in terms of what is inside—to see the present through lenses colored by the past. Since there are many kinds of gratifications and non-neutral behaviors inevitable in art therapy, these will of course influence the kind of transference that develops.

In giving someone materials, for example, you are a "feeder," offering supplies that may be experienced as good and plentiful or as bad and insufficient. The expectation that a client will use materials to make a product may be viewed as unreasonably demanding or as affirming the person's potency and creative powers. Encouraging someone to think for himself may be felt as supporting his autonomy or as abandoning him unfairly. When offering potentially messy media in a permissive setting, you may be perceived as a benign parent who allows sensory play or as a seducer who invites the client to engage in forbidden pleasures.

In limiting destructive uses of materials, you may be experienced as a restrictive policeman or as a helpful guardian controlling dangerous impulses. When teaching about a medium or process, you can be felt as generous or as interfering. In looking at the artwork, you may be experienced as encouraging either voyeurism or exhibitionism and in either case can be seen positively (as giving permission for desired acts) or negatively (as inviting forbidden behavior).

When asking questions, you may be perceived as an intruder, worming your unwelcome way into the person's private, creative world. Conversely, such inquiries can be experienced as an affirmation of the artwork, an indication of the importance to you of the patient and his productions. In all of these functions, essential to therapy through art but not through words, you are responded to in both realistic and distorted (transferential) ways, reflecting both your role and the client's reactions to it.

Another unique aspect of transference in art therapy is the likelihood of a distorted response not only to the person of the therapist, but also to the media, the processes, and the products themselves. Materials such as clay or finger paint, for example, can evoke pleasure but can also arouse disgust. A process like the hammering of nails into wood can lead to a feeling of potency or, if aggression is too threatening, can be invaded by anxiety. The products also take on meaning in relation to the state of the transference. A creation offered to an art therapist can as easily be a "bomb" as a "love gift." A patient can feel not only narcissistic pride but also shame in the showing of his self-creation to another.

In addition, art also makes possible a range of concrete, sometimes even creative, ways of expressing the transference to the therapist. As with putting an idea into words, putting an idea into a gesture or a form can also reduce the pressure to act out directly either loving or hostile impulses. Clay, for example, can be caressed with affection or pounded with hostility. It can be formed carefully or impulsively and can be lovingly decorated or angrily stabbed. Anger can be expressed by refusing to use materials or by insisting on hiding the product from the eyes of the therapist.

Transference wishes or fears may be represented in more or less disguised ways, as in beautiful or ugly pictures of the therapist or another authority figure. The treatment itself can also be represented—as a prison when the artist feels trapped or a haven when he feels comfortable. And, instead of acting out his wishes, the client in art therapy can create images of happy marriages or violent battles, with any degree of disguise necessary for him at that stage of treatment.

At times, such representations may provide sufficient indirect gratification and may successfully bind anxiety to such an extent as to be justly termed *sublimation*. A mark of successful sublimation is that it frees further energy for constructive work. Some believe that the promotion of transference via an art therapist's relative neutrality lessens the likelihood that sublimation will be achieved. Sublimation may indeed be interfered with by transference at moments when interpersonal pressures become overwhelming. However, a more insidious hazard lies in the failure to recognize subtly manifested transference reactions, which can themselves create formidable resistance to the treatment process.

An awareness of transference reminds us that behavior with art materials, or the style of the work itself, can defend against unwelcome transference reactions as easily as it can express them. For example, a client might use insufficient paint to deny his strong urge to take it all. Or, he might try to please a defensively idealized therapist through "pretty" or self-consciously "expressive" productions, thereby avoiding awareness of conflicted, anxiety-provoking impulses. What is essential here, as with more direct expressions of transference reactions, is that you be aware of the likelihood of a patient's hidden instinctual/defensive agenda.

Equally important is an awareness of counter-transference, that is, the distorted responses to the client, his art, or both, that emanate from your own internal world. As with transference, in addition to the usual factors, there are elements that are peculiar to the art therapy situation. Since you are also an artist, you must be careful not to let your enthusiasm for the quantity or quality of a patient's products influence you unduly.

We do need to be on the side of the client's creative self, but we should neither exaggerate nor denigrate a person's productions. The challenge is to support and express appreciation of authentic work without explicitly passing judgment on its aesthetic quality. Indeed, as noted earlier, one hazard for an art therapist is letting the subtle promotion of your own favorite media, content, or style interfere with facilitating the client's mode of expression. Similarly, it can be difficult for a creative artist to provide expressive media for others while not always able to use it herself, which can stimulate frustration and even envy.

Knowing yourself well enough to spot your counter-transferential distortions is probably the most difficult area of all, despite your familiarity with the topic. Knowing yourself internally—knowing how you function and why you feel and think and behave as you do—is a lifelong and difficult task. Unless you are as gifted as Freud or Jung, who were able to analyze themselves, you will probably need some help from a more objective clinical other.

Although my own preference for self-knowledge is the detailed journey through the mind provided by psychoanalysis, I would not recommend that route for every art therapist. But, I have come to feel that anyone taking responsibility for modifying the psyches of other people through the powerful modality of art has a responsibility to undergo some personal psychotherapy.

The primary reason, of course, is so that your own conflicts, distortions, and characterological as well as conflictual hang-ups will not interfere with your ability to fully empathize with and help your clients. Just as transference reactions are helpful symbolic routes to the client's inner world, so counter-transference responses, promptly identified and understood, can often provide useful clues to the person's transference or other aspects of his personality.

Unlike a strictly verbal clinician, an art therapist can also use her own artwork as an aid to self-understanding, in addition to helping the patient. Portraits of patients made outside the therapy session can, for example, help you to identify and comprehend counter-transference responses, especially when explored with the help of your own therapist or clinical supervisor.

During a session, you can communicate in a variety of ways by means of your creative imagery, whether working jointly, in turn, or alongside the patient. As with any other intervention, it is essential that the therapist who chooses to converse with a patient through art consider what it means to her to do so as well as the probable impact of her activity and imagery on the person she is trying to help. Most important, any art therapist who uses her own creations must be especially alert to the transference and counter-transference implications of such potent nonverbal interactions.

I personally feel that trying to limit the transference in art therapy is futile, although modifying its expression is often essential to productive work. Distorted reactions to the therapist, both loving (positive) and hostile (negative), are powerful and, when attended to, can be used for understanding and as an agent of change.

The greatest danger for art therapists lies in ignoring or minimizing the presence of transference. Whether or not it is analyzed, unrecognized it can cause intense resistance and can bring about premature termination as easily in art therapy as in psychoanalysis. The wisest course in my opinion is to encourage its expression and to do your best to understand its manifestations. Only then can you make an informed decision regarding whether it would be best to manipulate, to interpret, or even occasionally to gratify a particular transferential wish.

Margaret Naumburg (1953), an analytically oriented art therapy pioneer, believed that the transference in art therapy was lessened in intensity because of the degree of libido invested in the art object itself. In one sense, the product functions as a kind of "transitional object" (Winnicott, 1953) and is, like the toddler's blanket, an object of "transaction" between patient/child and therapist/mother (Schaverien, 1992). I do not believe that the artwork dilutes the transference, however, which inevitably develops more or less rapidly in any kind of therapy.

I do feel, though, that the presence of the product modifies what occurs, and that there are pressures toward certain *forms* of transference in art therapy, as suggested here. Because there is so much gratification, for example, the likelihood of an initial positive transference is great.

In a study comparing same-day art and drama interviews with 24 youngsters, it was found that the art products tended to have more positive content, with a higher frequency of nurturance themes, while the majority of the dramas had more negative content, with a higher frequency in them of injury to the self (Rubin & Irwin, 1975). The "feeder" aspect of the art therapist's role and the admiring "gleam-in-the-eye" mother (Kohut, 1971)—who approves of controlling one's (anal/art) products and applauds one's (phallic/art) display or performance—combine to produce a high frequency of maternal transferences in art therapy, especially in the early stages of treatment.

Knowing Stages of Therapy

In any therapeutic journey, whether relatively long or relatively short, whether fairly intense or rather superficial, there are certain predictable stages or phases. This is true whether you are working with an individual, a family, or a group. Just as it is important to be aware of the framework and the relationship in therapy, so it is useful to know what is likely to happen and the sequence in which it normally unfolds. Most books on counseling and psychotherapy are rather global in this regard, talking about a clearly defined opening or initial phase, a more variable middle phase, and a differentiated termination or ending phase. This is true regardless of the theoretical orientation of the therapist (Corey, 2008).

While these three major segments are always present, I believe that they can be further broken down, and that to do so is helpful to the practitioner. Not only does it sharpen your ability to assess where the client is on the ladder or road of therapeutic progress, but also it is helpful as a guide to what you can expect and potentially promote as the next likely stage of the treatment.

As with normal development, there is always regression as well as progression; there is always overlapping and the potential presence of all stages throughout the entire process. Nevertheless, the steps outlined in a publication on individual work with children (Rubin, 2005) also seem applicable to work with all age levels and combinations of people, although there are additional issues peculiar to groups (Yalom & Leszcz, 2005) and families (Goldenberg & Goldenberg, 2008) at each stage.

In the beginning of treatment, the therapist's goals are primarily the establishment of a good alliance and, secondarily, the gaining of a fuller understanding of the problems clients bring, even if there has been prior diagnostic work. To make the beginning phase as comfortable and appealing as possible, the clinician is generally more supportive and less demanding or confronting than would be appropriate later.

Fortunately, minimal intervention works equally well for the gathering of diagnostic information and the assessment of the particular issues causing problems in the individual, family, or group. The only structure that might be imposed during this first stage is that which the art therapist feels is necessary to enhance the comfort level of the client(s). For the client, the initial stage is primarily one of finding out what is expected of him, getting to know the clinician, the media, and the peculiarities of what happens in art therapy. It is also a period marked by a kind of testing of the waters in order to be clear about the nature and boundaries of this particular situation. In the area of limits, it is best, as noted earlier, to be clear, firm, and open about them. Such a stance is immensely useful to the patient, who needs to develop trust in the framework, as well as in the clinician and the modality.

If things go well, the client gradually feels secure and comfortable and begins to develop a feeling of trust in the therapist, the most significant index of a valid alliance. Trust becomes evident in art therapy, not only in how people behave and what they disclose verbally, but also in what they are able to express visually. As with testing, the development of trust is rapid for some and slow for others.

Only when there is sufficient trust, however, can the client begin to take risks, revealing verbally and nonverbally those wishes and fears that have been hidden, from himself as often as from others. As the communication process unfolds and he is able to risk new ways of creating as well as conversing, there is the possibility of facing the issues that have emerged. To face that which has not been acknowledged before is difficult for anyone. The very anxieties that led to keeping the threatening ideas out of awareness are re-stimulated as they begin to unfold.

These fears, usually out of proportion to the stimulus, cause many natural protective reactions, so that defensiveness and resistance, which may seem to have been reduced since the initial phase, return in full force. It is my conviction that without such self-protective reactions there is probably not any kind of useful therapy occurring. That is, it is only when a person is able to come close to the disabling areas of conflict that he or she is ever likely to overcome them, whether the treatment aims at an educative or an insightful kind of learning.

In any case, periods of resistance in art therapy are marked by all of the defenses characteristic of verbal expression, including an unwillingness to create, the use of impersonal imagery, a turning to (cartoon) humor, a regression to earlier forms of (art) behavior, and a compulsive fussing over details. There may be a willingness to create but an unwillingness to reflect on either process or product. There may also be a superficial compliance with both doing and discussing, which masks a stubborn inner refusal to divulge anything personal or affect laden.

Whether the unwelcome impulse is focused on the therapist (as in transference resistance) or on some other person (like emerging hostility toward a child, spouse, or parent), the ensuing resistance should be understood as a natural defensive reaction. It is the client's way of protecting himself from what appears to be an intolerable outcome (such as annihilation, loss of boundaries or of control, loss of a significant other or of that person's love, violent retaliation from a rival, or an overwhelming sense of guilt) should the impulse be expressed.

It is in the process of risking the communication and the subsequent confrontation of previously denied ideas and feelings that much of the change in psychotherapy occurs. Such change seems to take time for most people, and it is best if the therapeutic contact can continue long enough for a genuine "working through" to take place. This involves looking not just once but many times at difficult issues—learning about not only the feared impulses but also one's habitual ways of coping (defenses), some of which have not worked well in the past.

During this period, there is usually a sharply intensified feeling of cyclicity in the therapy, of an "open" session followed by a "closed" one, or of a series of relatively free meetings succeeded by several marked by inhibition or regression. It is almost as if the psyche has to continually balance disclosure with closure, as if the need to maintain equilibrium operates not only momentarily but also over time. Sometimes resistance can seem like an endless stalemate and can stimulate powerful counter-transference in the therapist, who can feel discouraged and may distance emotionally.

What is most helpful during this period of facing, understanding, and eventually accepting what has been feared is a sustained empathic awareness of the depth of the client's anxiety. Sometimes an aptly timed and well-worded interpretation can help to move things forward; sometimes you must simply wait and deal with your own frustration. Only if you can sustain the tensions of the working-through phase is there much likelihood that the client will be able to tolerate them.

The penultimate stage is in the development and integration of a new image of the self, in both a passive and an active sense. To see yourself as a separate, integrated person (good-and-bad) and as competent (able to work, to play, and to love) is only possible if you are able to actualize those self-perceptions in behavior. From thinking, which Freud called "trial action," to doing usually takes time. And, it often requires support from the therapist, who helps the client's newly developed self to take its "first steps" safely and effectively, like any good parent (McWilliams, 2004; Solomon & Siegel, 2003; Wachtel, 2008).

Needless to say, such a new image and sense of self is only possible if the client has been able to give up maladaptive coping mechanisms and to fully accept what he has discovered in the facing and understanding stages of the therapeutic process. Accepting is very different from knowing about. It is as much an affective event as a cognitive one. Just saying the words is meaningless; behaving and feeling differently are the only valid indices. In the process of accepting previously denied or devalued aspects of yourself, you must also give up old ways of being in the world.

Between the disruption of old structures and the formation of new ones, there is usually a period that can be threatening, when old coping mechanisms are no longer available but new ones are not ready for action. This is a painful, often empty-feeling time, when the threat of loss of self or of control can seem overwhelming. No matter how unhappy the client or family, the renunciation of old ways of perceiving, feeling, and behaving is immensely difficult.

I believe that the inertia that seems to accompany any significant change process is never laziness or even the pull of entropy but rather a self-protective clinging to the known, the familiar, the predictable. For the unknown is always fraught with danger, despite its exciting appeal for the venturesome.

Even the people who attend personal growth art therapy groups, who are highly motivated to improve the quality of their lives, who suffer normal discontent rather than crippling illness—even such relatively healthy and secure individuals inevitably discover a good deal of internal resistance to change during both art expression and reflection. Whatever the source of the anxiety about change, it is ubiquitous and accounts for the time it takes for people not only to practice new ways of being but also to become comfortable with them—to fully integrate them. There is a necessary mourning—of the loss of old fantasies, goals, and images—which also takes time. Giving up impossible or inappropriate strivings is just as difficult as letting go of old defense mechanisms.

The biggest loss, inevitable in any therapy, lies in the loss of the therapist—the termination process, when the separating task becomes preeminent. Art therapy, like any other form of therapy, helps clients to separate fact from fancy, fantasy from reality, and in a deeper sense, to separate from their disorder and any secondary gain it may provide. To help people to accept all such separations, there must be a strong attachment to the therapist, both as a real person and as a transference object (Wallin, 2007).

The separation-individuation process between a client/child and a therapist/parent is a powerful potential learning and reworking experience and a painful and intense one as well. Attention should always be paid to the significance of termination, especially when the client has been seen as part of a group or in a milieu setting. While the transference may not be as intense, it may be just as powerful (and, with needy clients, is often instant). Even if there has been relatively little transferential involvement with the therapist, there is still a need to pay attention to all of the feelings, fantasies, and especially fears involved in saying good-bye, in letting go.

Sometimes the client has little choice. The treatment ends, not because all goals are reached, but because of some extrinsic factor: the insurance money runs out, the therapist is leaving the facility, the program has been discontinued, the parents decide to withdraw the child, and so on. With the more ideal conditions available in some outpatient settings and in private practice, it is possible to involve clients in setting the termination date. I believe this is best, although there is often much ambivalence and indecision around the task. Even when the setting of the date is out of the client's control, the individuals should be encouraged to say something about *how* the ending period should proceed. Deciding what to do on the last day, for example, can provide an opportunity for some active mastery in the otherwise helpless situation of having to end while perhaps not feeling ready.

Art products can play a special role at the time of termination. If they have been stored as part of the treatment, they provide a splendid and vivid basis for re-viewing the therapy, whatever its duration and scope. A client may choose to keep all or some or to give all or some to the art therapist. In either case, the art becomes a transitional object for both partners in the therapeutic adventure. It carries in it a piece of the treatment for the client and a piece of the person for the therapist.

Another unique aspect of termination in art therapy is that the client, ideally, does not just identify with the therapist's clinical perspective, as in all forms of treatment. From direct experience as well as through identification, he may come away from art therapy with a strong sense of his own creative potential as an artist.

He will also have learned, through practice and imitation, to look at his personal "visions"—his dreams and imagery as well as his art—and to use them as a way of further understanding himself. Any tolerance he has learned from his therapist for his own forbidden fantasies or wishes should also be felt for his artistic inadequacies.

Whether he feels talented and desires further training or has simply discovered that he can express, enjoy, and understand himself through art, he may very well want to continue in this modality as well as in the kind of self-therapy that should be the outcome of any successful treatment—the ability to monitor and be comfortably in charge of oneself.

So another way to help a client to terminate art therapy is to facilitate the likelihood that the person will be able to continue his creative growth as well as to continue to reflect and understand himself—a goal of all psychotherapy. Perhaps the means will be a good-bye gift of art supplies for the client who is too poor to buy his own or is exceptionally needy of some concrete evidence of the therapist's concern. Or, perhaps an art therapist will provide information to the client, the family, or the referral source about where to buy appropriate materials or how and where to find further instructional or recreational art experiences. Perhaps it will seem appropriate to make referrals to specific teachers or art centers, just as you might refer a client to another therapist.

Because of the nature of the modality, the client can carry on concretely with the creative work on his own or with the help of a professional who is an artist or teacher, not necessarily a therapist. In this sense, the client can carry over into his real life an activity that, although it was a means of inpatient or outpatient treatment, can continue as a normal, creative way of sustaining balance and finding fulfillment as a healthy, productive human being. In that way, art therapy can sometimes make the separation involved in termination not only easier to handle, but also more likely to be successful.

References

Corey, G. (2008). *Theory and practice of counseling and psychotherapy* (8th ed.). Belmont, CA: Brooks/Cole.

Goldenberg, H., & Goldenberg, I. (2008). *Family therapy: An overview* (7th ed.). Belmont, CA: Thomson.

Kohut, H. (1971). *The analysis of the self.* (The psychoanalytic study of the child, Monograph No. 4). New Haven, CT: Yale University Press.

McWilliams, N. (2004). *Psychoanalytic psychotherapy.* New York: Guilford Press.

Naumburg, M. (1953). *Psychoneurotic art.* New York: Grune & Stratton.

Rubin, J. A. (1982). The role of transference and countertransference in art therapy. *American Journal of Art Therapy, 21,* 10–12.

Rubin, J. A. (2005). *Child art therapy* (3rd ed.). New York: Wiley.

Rubin, J. A., & Irwin, E. C. (1975). Art and drama: Parts of a puzzle. In I. Jakab (Ed.), *Psychiatry and art* (Vol. 4, pp. 193–200). New York: Karger.

Schaverien, J. (1992). *The revealing image: Analytical art psychotherapy in theory and practice.* London: Routledge.

Solomon, M., & Siegel, D. (Eds.). (2003). *Healing trauma: Attachment, mind, body and brain.* New York: Guilford Press.

Wachtel, P. (2008). *Relational theory and the practice of psychotherapy.* New York: Guilford.

Wallin, D. J. (2007). *Attachment in psychotherapy.* New York: Guilford Press.

Winnicott, D. W. (1953). Transitional objects and transitional phenomena: A study of the first not-me possession. *International Journal of Psycho-Analysis, 34,* 89–97.

Yalom, I., & Leszcz, M. (2005). *Theory and practice of group psychotherapy* (5th ed.). New York: Basic Books.

Recommended Readings

Jordan, J. V. (2009). *Relational-cultural therapy.* Washington, DC: American Psychological Association.

Linley, P. A., & Joseph, S. (Eds.). (2004). *Positive psychology in practice.* New York: Wiley.

Knowing what to say, as well as how and when to say it, are both necessary for making effective verbal interventions in art therapy.

Helping a person to reflect on the experience of creating, as well as on the product itself, is essential to doing effective art therapy.

CHAPTER 7

Knowing Art Therapy

What You Need to Know

As suggested, being an artist and a nice human being is not enough to make you a good art therapist. To permit the fullest possible use of art for the purpose of healing, you must *know* certain things, must *believe* in others, and must *be* a certain sort of person. Only if these three conditions are met is it possible to achieve genuine *artistry* as an art therapist.

Before you can function as an art therapist with patients or clients, you need to know a great deal about *art*. Most important are the necessary understandings and information about materials, processes, and products, as detailed in the first three chapters. In the area of *therapy*, you need to know a good deal about development (normal and abnormal), about dynamics (individual and group), and about the therapeutic process (the framework, the relationship, and the stages).

To begin synthesizing what you know about art and about therapy, it is vital to be clear about your identity as an art therapist. This is as necessary for private work with patients as it is for public interchange with colleagues. Since art therapy is a hybrid discipline, it is superficially similar to a wide variety of other fields, from art education to play therapy to occupational, recreational, and activity therapy.

Since all of these may involve the use of art materials by individuals or groups, they can look strikingly alike to the naïve observer. Even the clinician's behavior may be similar, whether helping someone to use materials appropriately or asking questions about process or product. Nevertheless, art therapy is different from all of these fields, despite some over-lapping areas with each.

While there are often superficial similarities between art and the other action therapies (recreation, activity, and occupational therapy), there is a deeper affinity between art and the other creative expressive therapies (music, movement, drama, poetry, and phototherapy). Although the primary modality in each is distinct, it is also true that human beings, espe-cially in a situation that promotes freedom of expression, often move spontaneously from one mode to another.

Children frequently create dramas while they draw or sculpt; adolescents and adults sometimes write poetry on their paintings. Such spontaneous shifts have led me in my own work to a multimodal approach. While it is especially appropriate for the very young, it is also applicable to adolescents, adults, families, and groups. Although I do respect those who are able to facilitate work in more than one art form and who believe in an inter-modal approach (Atkins, 2002; Atkins, Williams, & Suggs, 2007; Knill, Levine, & Levine, 2005; McNiff, 2009; Pearson & Wilson, 2009), I have never thought of myself as doing "expressive therapy" because I have never felt capable of doing it, not because I do not think it is a good idea.

I prefer when possible to collaborate with an expert in another modality since my own skills are limited in creative areas other than art, but I feel comfortable with permitting or even encouraging a shift of mode during the working process when it seems to be appropri-ate. I think of myself throughout as an art therapist, not an expressive arts therapist, a play therapist, or an activities therapist, for the art process is always at the center of my work. For Natalie Rogers (1993), who was trained both as a dancer and as an artist, "the creative connection" is internal and totally authentic.

Issues of identity in a synergistic discipline such as art therapy have naturally been of concern from the first. It is necessary not only to relate the two components (art and therapy) in a way that makes sense but also to differentiate art therapy, as noted earlier, from its activity cousins and its creative arts siblings. There are even times when you may need to clarify, for a colleague or a patient, the distinctions between art therapy and the use of art by other kinds of clinicians as in the diagnostic drawings requested by some psychologists or the paintings used by some psychiatrists.

When a psychologist, psychiatrist, social worker, or counselor uses art extensively in his or her work, is that person then an art therapist? This is a difficult question since it is highly likely that anyone using art a great deal is something of an artist himself, such as counselor Sam Gladding (2005), Gestalt therapist Joseph Zinker (1977), psychiatrist Mardi Horowitz (1983), or psychoanalyst Marion Milner (1957, 1969).

Nevertheless, even for those who have a sincere affinity for art and who employ it clini-cally, if their primary identity is something else, art is then seen as an adjunct—used when perceived as useful or appropriate, but not always, or usually central to the individual's pro-fessional work as a therapist. By contrast, the art therapist's primary modality is art, despite the fact that the talking time may occasionally exceed the doing time, or that there may even be sessions when the pressure to talk is so great or the depression so profound that the person does not create with media.

These instances are the exception, however, and the "rule" is that in most art therapy, all or part of every meeting is spent creating or looking at art. Whether the art is thought of primarily as a vehicle for sublimation (art as therapy—healing through the creative process) or for communication (art in psychotherapy), the art process and product always occupy considerable time and space.

In addition to the ongoing task of defining your use of art in therapy, it is most helpful to become informed in some detail about those related disciplines mentioned above. Only then can distinctions be clearly made, both for yourself and for the society in which you work as a professional. While it is necessary to know what art therapy *is*, it is perhaps even more important to know what it is *not*.

You can only be clear about how you are different from your professional relatives if you also know a great deal about them, so it follows that an art therapist ought to be knowl-edgeable about her closest relations, especially the other arts and activity therapies. Only by knowing how art therapy is similar to and different from occupational, recreational, or play therapy can you discuss intelligently with colleagues or patients what art therapy in particular has to offer.

Art therapy is a unique profession, with the entry level for practitioners only after 2 years of full-time training at the master's level. This is necessary because doing art therapy in the fullest sense requires combining a deep understanding of art and the creative process with an equally sophisticated understanding of psychology and psychotherapy—knowing well all of the areas discussed in this book so far, as well as how to put them together in the best therapeutic way—the subject of the next section.

In the years since the first edition of this book was published, an awareness of "art therapy" as an idea has become part of our culture. This heightened consciousness of the healing power of art has also bred a great deal of confusion. It seems therefore even more imperative in the fast-changing world of the 21st century to clarify the often-blurry distinctions between trained art therapists and others providing therapeutic art activities.

This includes artists in residence (Herbert, Deschner, & Glazer, 2006; Riccio & Rollins, 2001; Rollins & Mahan, 1996), art teachers, and volunteers who provide therapeutic art activities to individuals under stress, from homeless shelters to hospitals (Graham-Pole, 2000). There will probably never be enough trained art therapists to meet the immense human need for the healing power of art. So in my opinion, these developments are to be welcomed. In the best of all possible worlds, volunteers or artists who offer art to those in need would be supervised and trained by art therapists. However, even when this ideal situation is not possible, it is vitally important to educate the public and professionals who have something to say about who offers art and about the difference between a volunteer artist and a trained art therapist.

The main reason for educating others is so that those who are vulnerable are more likely to be treated through art by someone who is trained and, because of that training, is also more likely to help and less likely to do harm. Art is a wonderful medicine, but that is largely because it is so potent. Using art with people who are fragile requires skill, sensitivity, and the kind of knowledge that only comes after many hours of supervised practice. Thus, the need for public education and awareness regarding how art therapists are different from others bearing crayons and paper to those in pain.

Art is a powerful tool—one that, like the surgeon's, must be used with care and skill if it is to penetrate safely beneath the surface. Using media with those who are significantly disabled or disturbed (even without analysis of process or product) requires an understanding not only of art but also of the world of those with whom you are working. The use of art as a symbolic communicative medium is a clinically demanding task that carries with it both a tremendous potential and an equally great responsibility.

A parent, teacher, or artist without clinical training can indeed provide people with genuinely helpful—and in many ways "therapeutic"—art experiences. Caution is required, however, in the use of such experiences for a deeper understanding or remediation of internal psychological problems. There, in both diagnosis and treatment, close clinical supervision in the learning phases and early work stages of art therapy seems to me to be not only desirable but also essential.

Dealing with those who are already vulnerable, or "opening up" others in a way that creates a certain vulnerability, can be either helpful or harmful. One need not be afraid to do many wonderful and meaningful things with people in art, but one must always respect the importance and the uniqueness of an individual's emotional life. One also grows to respect, with some awe and humility, the potency of art, especially in the context of those special human relationships promoted in art therapy.

What You Need to Believe

Belief is not the same as knowledge, despite the fact that most people try hard to justify their convictions on some rational basis. The beliefs that I feel are essential for an art therapist concern the need, the right, and the capacity of every human being to be creative. Only if you are convinced of the need can you motivate those who at first appear apathetic or resistant.

Only if you are convinced of the right can you work effectively with those severely disabled individuals for whom fully formed art may never be possible, but who deserve the opportunity to develop to the utmost whatever sensory and creative potential they possess. And only if you are convinced that every person has the ability to be a creative artist can you sincerely strive to find the song in the soul, the poetry in the person, whatever the medium or modality.

I think that another necessary belief is in art therapy itself, which probably involves a sincere conviction that both art and therapy can help people—and, on a personal level, that you can enable that to happen. Unless someone really believes in art therapy as a treatment modality, she may be tempted to engage in the kind of clever or naïve mislabeling that often serves short-term personal or political goals.

If, however, she knows that she is *not* doing art therapy until and unless she is trained as a therapist, then she is not likely to masquerade as an "art therapist," even though she may be offering art to a deviant population or in a treatment setting. Although this was a more common problem when the first edition of this book was written, the growth of "healing arts" and the popularity of using art in clinical work by other therapists has created a new set of concerns about misrepresentation.

It is actually not a matter of *where* a therapist works or *whom* she serves that makes an activity *art therapy*. What does matter is the *goal* (therapy) and the use of art as the primary modality in the pursuit of that goal of human growth in a more than momentary way. Even when that is the case, however, there is sometimes a temptation to call what one is doing something else because of the pervasive anxiety attendant on the word *therapy*. This is less true now, although the term *counseling*, which used to mean career advising, has become more common and is generally less threatening.

The common fears of patients about being harshly exposed or manipulated in a painful way may be confirmed whenever anyone calls herself an "art therapist" without the requisite training. Although the profession has grown in the past three decades, this is still unfortunately the case in many settings; administrators seem strangely comfortable with calling an art school graduate with no psychology background a *therapist* despite the fact that they would never allow such an individual to give psychological tests or make a psychiatric diagnosis.

While this situation is of concern primarily to trained practitioners and their professional associations, I hope that it will become the concern of all who believe in the healing power of art and the creative right of each human being to safe and ethical treatment. While I was revising this section, a respected colleague noted on an Internet listserv that a play therapist without proper training was advertising a course on the use of "art therapy" with children. Even though the American Art Therapy Association worked hard to obtain "title protection" for the credential ATR (registered art therapist), there is still the possibility of misunderstanding and misrepresentation.

I have also believed that art therapists do not own art any more than we own therapy. In fact, I have always been in favor of helping other trained mental health professionals to use art (which they do anyway) more effectively with their patients. Such usage preceded the development of the specialized profession of art therapy and can certainly coexist.

Certainly those artists who offer healing experiences to people under stress, despite the fact that they are not clinicians, have the right to do so, and many are gifted and passionate in their work. However, it is our job to educate them about the limitations of what they can do and to offer guidelines for safety.

In addition, I believe that most of the time, when "art therapy" is described as such but is not conducted by a trained art therapist, the intent is not malicious. But it is indeed confusing to the public and even to others in mental health. Again, I see it as the responsibility of the art therapy community to educate others so that they understand the difference, which hopefully will facilitate the hiring of qualified art therapists not only for direct service but also as supervisors, consultants, and teachers of others who want to use art in a broadly therapeutic fashion. These roles are discussed in the last section of this book, on related service. But first, I want to return to what is required of a good art therapist by talking not about knowing or believing but about *being*.

Who You Need to Be

Perhaps even more important than believing in yourself or in art therapy is *being* the right sort of person. There is no single best personality for good art therapy, any more than there is only one right way to behave as an art therapist. But some characteristics do seem to be essential and are probably potential in most people, although they are sadly undeveloped or inhibited in many. Nevertheless they are important, perhaps vital, and the challenge is to develop them in yourself. These necessary qualities include some related to creative thinking, such as fluency, flexibility, originality, and an ability to take risks, to tolerate ambiguity, and to regress in the service of the ego. Certainly, you must have experienced the creative process yourself in order to be an effective art therapist.

In contrast to some of my colleagues, however, I do not believe that you need to be an actively practicing, exhibiting artist. Rather, what is essential is that you have known, in some depth and at a personal level, what it means to create with art media—the pain as well as the pleasure, the tension as well as the release. In addition, it is important to be able to use your own creative activity, even if you are not showing in galleries or selling work, for your personal pleasure and the self-care that all psychotherapists need.

Incidentally, I find it really intriguing that art therapists do not always behave *creatively* in their clinical work, despite the fact that most are practicing artists. How is it that people can be comfortable manipulating essentially unpredictable materials, enduring and even enjoying the inevitable tensions of the creative process, yet so often seem unable to adopt the same attitude in regard to their work as therapists?

Perhaps, having identified themselves as artists before they became therapists, they are understandably cautious about tapping what they know to be powerful, but not easily controlled, inner energies in the service of this new identity. Indeed, they are right to be cautious—for while it is necessary to gain access to those potent resources, it is also essential to control their overt expression and to do so within some clearly bounded framework. In art, this framework is provided largely by the medium, shaped by the artist's intent; in therapy, it is provided by the treatment context and the role of the clinician within that frame of reference. It is for that reason that an art therapist needs to be clear about the boundaries of her behavior so that she can have the same kind of secure framework she provides for her patients.

Given that caution, and with sufficient knowledge about both art and therapy in your mental storehouse, I submit that an effective art therapist is a person who enjoys the challenge of using creative thinking in the service of the therapeutic task at hand. I believe this is true whether the clinical questions are about the *what* of symbolic meaning, the *why* of behavior, or the *how* and *when* of intervention.

The persistent search by some art therapists for simple answers to complex questions suggests that they are not yet comfortable with using their own creativity in finding their own solutions. Yet the challenge of understanding and helping each new human being, of solving the mystery of how to help each person to find and enjoy his creative potential—in art and in life—is for me, and for many others, the source of continuing stimulation and pleasure in the work of art therapy.

Although it goes without saying, you cannot be any kind of a therapist if you do not genuinely like other people, and the kind of people who end up in treatment are not always easy to like. So it is necessary to be the kind of person who enjoys relating to those who may be wary or inhibited as human beings as well as in their art. You also need to be genuine, to behave in a real and human way.

I am often surprised by the comments I consistently get from trainees after I conduct a family art evaluation with one of them, that they "never knew it was possible to be so *natural* with patients." You can be authentic and friendly, without being either seductive or effusive, and you can still maintain a good deal of therapeutic distance and neutrality in regard to your private self.

As for your private self, as noted earlier, it is vital to get to know and accept as much of yourself as possible, whether you end up exploring your inner world through art therapy or some other form of treatment. Such self-knowledge is essential, partly because you can never fully empathize with patienthood until you have experienced it, and, more important, because you cannot use yourself well as a therapeutic instrument in the service of another when you are responding unconsciously to your own "unfinished business" (unresolved conflicts).

I do not have strong feelings about *when* in your life such an undertaking is best, but I do think it helps to be in therapy *while* you are practicing art therapy so that the ways in which your own conflicts affect your work can be examined directly. I am increasingly convinced that it is only through a capacity for empathy and for truly following the patient that really artistic work can be done. I suspect that it is not possible to allow yourself to "feel with" another in any depth unless you are genuinely comfortable with all aspects of your own psyche.

I am also convinced that no amount of the right knowledge alone is sufficient to make a person a fine clinician. This knowledge, while an essential condition, must still be applied with conviction in work with other human beings. The artistry involved in outstanding therapy through art may depend, in the final analysis, as much on personality as on technique. No amount of scientific knowledge will make for good art therapy if it is not applied in a sensitive and artistic way by a human being who can relate effectively to others in the special fashion needed for successful treatment.

While all of these concerns about what you *know*, what you *believe*, and what sort of person you *are* may seem peripheral to the topic (the art of art therapy), they are really the bedrock—the foundation on which good art therapy must rest. I do not mean to imply that they are accomplished in any sort of neat chronological sequence: that you learn, believe, and become in some sequential order, according to a prescribed plan of action. Rather, it is necessary for growth to be continuous and ongoing in all of these areas throughout your lifetime.

Learning and knowing about both art and therapy should expand and deepen over time, just as a developing person will naturally expand and deepen his values and himself as a human being. Nevertheless, I am convinced that you cannot be any more artistic as an art therapist than you can be as a painter if you do not *know* the "basics," if you do not truly *believe* in human potential, and if you do not have the *personality* and the ability to sustain all aspects of the role.

These are the necessary conditions for artistry, which does not, despite the mythology, spring full blown from anyone who is not properly prepared. As noted, this is a challenging lifelong task, which is a good thing since none of these can be easily accomplished, and all of them require consistent and persistent effort. The rewards, however, are immense, for the more successful you are as an art therapist, the greater the gratification of such work.

References

Atkins, S. (2002). *Expressive arts therapy: Creative process in art and life.* Boone, NC: Parkway.

Atkins, S., Williams, L. D., & Suggs, M. S. (2007). *Sourcebook in expressive arts therapy.* Boone, NC: Parkway.

Gladding, S. T. (2005). *Counseling as an art* (3rd ed.). Washington, DC: American Counseling Association.

Graham-Pole, J. (2000). *Illness and the art of creative self-expression.* Oakland, CA: New Harbinger.

Herbert, G., Deschner, J. W., & Glazer, R. (2006). *Artists-in-residence.* New York: Creative Center.

Horowitz, M. J. (1983). *Image formation and psychotherapy.* New York: Aronson.

Knill, P. J., Levine, E. G., & Levine, S. K. (2005). *Principles and practice of expressive arts therapy: Toward a therapeutic aesthetics.* Toronto: E*G*S Press.

McNiff, S. (2009). *Integrating the arts in therapy.* Springfield, IL: Thomas.

Milner, M. (1957). *On not being able to paint.* New York: International Universities Press.

Milner, M. (1969). *The hands of the living God.* New York: International Universities Press.

Pearson, M., & Wilson, H. (2009). *Using expressive arts to work with mind, body and emotions.* London: Kingsley.

Riccio, L. L., & Rollins, J. (2001). *ART is the HeART.* Washington, DC: WVSA Arts.

Rogers, N. (1993). *The creative connection: Expressive arts as healing.* Palo Alto, CA: Science and Behavior Books.

Rollins, J., & Mahan, C. (1996). *From artist to artist-in-residence: Preparing artists to work in pediatric healthcare settings.* Washington, DC: Rollins.

Zinker, J. (1977). *Creative process in Gestalt therapy.* New York: Brunner/Mazel.

Recommended Readings

Brooke, S. L. (Ed.). (2006). *Creative arts therapies manual.* Springfield, IL: Thomas.

Case, C., & Dalley T. (2006). *The handbook of art therapy* (2nd ed.). London: Routledge.

Chaiklin, S., & Wengrower, H. (2009). *The art and science of dance/movement therapy: Life is dance.* New York: Routledge.

Davis, W. B., Gfeller, K. B., & Thaut, M. H. (2008). *An introduction to music therapy: Theory and practice.* Washington, DC: American Music Therapy Association.

Johnson, D. R., & Emunah, R. (Eds.). (2009). *Current approaches in drama therapy* (2nd ed.). London: Kingsley.

Malchiodi, C. A. (Ed.). (2003). *Handbook of art therapy.* New York: Guilford Press.

Malchiodi, C. A. (Ed.). (2004). *Expressive arts therapies.* New York: Guilford Press.

Mazza, N. (2003). *Poetry therapy: Theory and practice.* New York: Routledge.

Moon, B. L. (2007). *Introduction to art therapy* (2nd ed.). Springfield, IL: Thomas.

Rubin, J. A. (Ed.). (2001). *Approaches to art therapy* (2nd ed.). New York: Brunner-Routledge.

Wadeson, H. (2010). *Art psychotherapy* (2nd ed.). New York: Wiley.

The art therapist in a Veterans Affairs hospital is focused on both the patient and the painting process in which he is engaged.

A well-set "stage" allows time and space for quiet contemplation and thoughtful decision making.

PART 3

The Interface

The interface is that area where art and therapy meet, the synergistic core of the work of the art therapist. It is best if it takes place within a matrix of knowledge about art and therapy, as outlined in the first two portions of this book. For art therapy to happen, however, the stage must be set: first in the institution, then with the referring individuals, and finally in the art therapy room itself.

The first chapter of this section describes all aspects of setting the stage—moving from the larger to the smaller arena, from the preparation distant in time to that immediately before and at the outset of the art therapy session.

The second step in the work of the art therapist is evoking expression—stimulating the individual or group to use creative media in some way. This involves not only asking people to do something with materials but also deciding in advance as well as on the spot what to request, suggest, or offer. These issues and ways of thinking about them are dealt with in the second chapter in this section.

While people are working, the art therapist's primary job is facilitating creation—helping the individual or group to work most productively with the materials available. This task of enabling clients to create during the working process is examined in the third chapter in this section.

When the working time is over, the therapist's role lies primarily in looking and reflecting—helping the patients to learn about self and others from the products that were created. This aspect is discussed in the fourth chapter of this section, which focuses on the perception and discussion of art for therapeutic goals.

Each of these facets of the art therapy process is treated in a separate chapter, which may imply that they always occur in the sequence in which they are discussed. It is often true, however, that two or more will be happening simultaneously, or in an alternating sequence, for any individual patient.

Within a group, of course, different people will usually be at different stages in the creative process at the same moment in time, and this will shift throughout the session. For any single art therapy product or process, however, it is always true that the stage must be set, the expression evoked, facilitated, looked at, and understood. In all of these activities, the art therapist uses knowledge about art and therapy in a way that helps people to grow.

How an art therapist accomplishes each of these tasks is a measure of her artistry, her ability to synthesize what she knows in the course of each clinical moment. It is easy to talk in generalizations about how to be a good art therapist. The challenge is to be able to integrate your knowledge sufficiently to respond with genuine spontaneity and in a way that is optimally in tune with the client's needs. That, of course, is not so easy. It takes time, practice, close supervision, personal reflection, and, most important, a flexible approach to your work and an awareness of the lifelong need for improvement.

The best clinicians I know tend to be the most modest, about both their technique and their theoretical formulations. They are the least doctrinaire and the most open-minded. They tend to make good supervisors, teachers, and consultants as well as good therapists. I think this is true not only because they know a great deal and are able to communicate it well, but also because they are secure enough to be comfortable with the notion that they can never know it all.

A man is intensely engaged in creating his chalk drawing, oblivious to other artists in the group.

A woman in an art therapy group finds a quiet place where she can become absorbed in her painting and will not be disturbed.

CHAPTER **8**

Setting the Stage

Laying the Groundwork

The first step is setting the stage for the art therapy encounter. But, before art therapy can occur in any sort of institution, there must have been some prior groundwork, which involves getting the agency to a point at which it is willing to support the work of an art therapist. In dealing with institutions, it is necessary to think, as with families or groups, in terms of the entire system.

Entering a system and harnessing its energies in a way that is conducive to the growth and development of an art therapy program requires more than tact and knowledge about art therapy. As in working with a family, it helps immensely if you can look intelligently at personnel and program in a larger context, which means knowing "systems analysis." When you are able to identify the values and the power structure of an institution, you can then develop a plan for moving in the desired direction. As with the assessment of individuals and families, both a historical (developmental) and a dynamic perspective are useful ways to conceptualize any social system, whether it is a hospital, a school, or a community arts center.

During the early 1980s, I moved from direct clinical work with outpatients to the administration and supervision of therapy with inpatients. Although I had begun my own career in the same hospital and had consulted to people who worked with inpatients there for 20 years, this change in my full-time responsibilities made me acutely aware of the many differences between the two kinds of settings. The specific strategies that had worked for program development in a child guidance center were not necessarily best for growth in a psychiatric hospital.

In both places, however, understanding the development, dynamics, power, and values of the system were highly relevant. Although getting past the front door is a long way from working with a client, how you deal with administrators in terms of such issues as space, time, supplies, and relationship to the rest of the institution will determine in large part what will be possible in the face-to-face encounter.

Another principle that makes pragmatic sense in therapy also makes sense in dealing with institutions. It takes time for any substantial transformation to occur, and even more time for it to become integrated. If you have a fairly clear sense of how and why the system currently functions and an equally sure sense of the kind of art therapy program that might eventually serve its needs, you can start where the system is (like starting where the client is) and work toward your goal, dealing with resistances on a collective basis, just as you do with an individual or a group in art therapy.

These considerations, by the way, do not apply only to treatment or educational settings, in which most art therapists still work. They also apply to churches, shelters, and community organizations and art centers. More and more, art therapy has moved from the clinic to the community. If you are setting up a storefront open studio, you need to deal with your neighbors and the community and building in which you will be offering art therapy, just as you need to do in a hospital or clinic. This became apparent to me many years ago when I was involved in running some community-based programs.

After Dr. Martin Luther King's assassination in 1968, a number of concerned people in our neighborhood—which was not yet very integrated and bordered on a then all-black neighborhood—decided to start a "Freedom School." I became the director, knowing that I could recruit volunteers from the arts therapy community, in which there were many who cared about social justice and were disturbed by the riots in Pittsburgh after Dr. King was assassinated.

One of the first questions was where such an effort might be located. We ended up having classes at a church and a community center, both in a Black neighborhood bordering the mostly White neighborhood in which I lived. In addition to finding volunteers to do the teaching, most of whom were in the arts therapies, it was vital to work with those in both of the volunteer settings so as not to disrupt or intrude upon their usual activities.

It was also important that we find ways to meet the needs of these institutions, which had generously offered their space, so some of the activities were added at their request. For example, the community center asked if we planned to offer Black history, and although the original vision was to reach children, we agreed that adults could also benefit. By asking around the community, we were fortunate to find a high school teacher who offered to teach that class at night.

I had a similar experience in the 1970s when I was in charge of running summer creative arts programs funded by Pittsburgh Model Cities—a part of President Lyndon Johnson's War on Poverty. Finding appropriate sites in the two designated "model" (poor) neighborhoods, one racially mixed and the other all African American, was a political as well as a practical task. It required meeting with community leaders in both South Oakland and the Hill District and exploring not only which community centers might have the space to house the programs but also where they would be most welcome. As with the Freedom School, it was necessary to plan with each center to meet their needs as well as to create quality arts programs. It was also important to set the stage in terms of personnel by hiring individuals who could work comfortably and be acceptable in each community.

Although neither of these programs was labeled as "therapy" in the narrow sense of the word, both were "therapeutic" interventions through the arts in a larger sense. The Martin Luther King Freedom School was a community response to the fiery destructive riots in Pittsburgh that had followed King's assassination in April 1968. It became even more urgent after the helplessness and concern felt by all of us after Robert Kennedy was assassinated in early June.

The summer of 1968 was traumatic for the city as well as the nation, especially for the neighborhood where the school took place. It was therapeutic (helpful) for concerned citizens, White and Black, to be able to do something positive and to teach through the arts the values for which both King and Kennedy had stood. I thought of the effort as a kind of community-based collective attempt at self-therapy.

The Model Cities Arts programs were part of a national campaign to wage war on poverty by making various services available, especially to young people, so that they would have an opportunity to thrive like those who were more advantaged. The Head Start early intervention program was also part of Johnson's efforts to undo the wrongs that had concerned both King and Kennedy.

The summer creative arts program was done through the Community Services Department of the Pittsburgh Child Guidance Center, and I was the coordinator. The hope was to help the youngsters in this program—who were more at risk than others because of their impoverished lives—so the thrust was therapeutic, as was the ongoing supervision of the workers in it.

Many of them were arts therapists, and I met for several days in advance of beginning the programs to sensitize them to emotional issues. I also met weekly for half a day with the staff at each of the two centers as well in a kind of group supervision. In addition to being able to refer individual families to community mental health agencies, the close staff supervision allowed the program to truly become one that promoted wellness and prevented disturbance (secondary prevention in mental health).

Beginning Art Therapy Treatment

In any case, once the green light has been given for art therapy to become a reality, the first step is planning for the actual encounter. Whatever the situation, you are probably going to be talking to somebody—the referral source, the treatment team, the client—about the reasons you are being asked to see the person or group and their expectations of what you can offer.

This is a delicate transaction, requiring artistry on your part outside the art room. While the specifics of what you might say will vary from one situation to another, a good general principle is to be careful in listening to what is being requested, covertly as well as overtly, and to ask any clarifying questions you might have in a clear and diplomatic way.

If it is the client or parent who makes the initial contact, as in private practice, then this interaction is really the beginning of the treatment process and needs to be handled with as much care as the first meeting. In general, I attempt to avoid any more telephone interaction than seems necessary, preferring to reserve as much as possible for the initial face-to-face encounter.

Setting the stage with a referring professional is a somewhat different matter, for often that person will be presenting the recommendation to the client or family. Sometimes, a bit of education may be necessary, including ideas about what to say. How people are prepared by you or someone else will certainly affect how they approach art therapy, at least initially.

In some situations, it is necessary to remain silent when you might otherwise prefer to speak since too much information can also confuse or frighten your audience—whether referring clinician, parent, or client. It is important in early stage-setting encounters to be as unthreatening as possible, to listen carefully, especially "between the lines" or with your "third ear," and to form as much of a beginning "alliance" as is feasible with the person who makes the initial contact, whoever that individual may be.

Considerations of Time and Space

Some decisions that might need to be made in advance concern time and space. In both, there may be realistic constraints that limit the options, although usually, if one or another seems essential to the chances of success, you will be able to explore creatively, with the others involved, a "good enough" solution to the problem. Although this may seem minor, I include it because I have often been surprised at how passive and helpless some art therapists seem to feel about issues of time or space. While it is true that you frequently have to make do with less of either than you wish, it is my impression that being clear in your mind about the necessary minimum helps considerably in making workable arrangements.

For example, I have found it simply impossible to conduct a meaningful family art evaluation in less than 1 hour; 1.5- or 2-hour sessions are much more fruitful time spans. I would never, therefore, agree to do a full evaluation in a half hour. In that instance, I would probably suggest that the family work together on a mural and discuss it before and after as a way of getting a glimpse of their interactive style. But, I would also make it clear to the referring clinician that the longer period would be much richer since the hypotheses generated by any single task might then be confirmed or refuted by behavior in others (checks and balances).

The issue of time is an important one, although it is sometimes seen by art therapists as either insignificant or inflexible. Naturally, the optimal length of an individual or group session will depend on many relevant variables, including the attention span of the patient, the number of people involved, and the goals of the art therapy activity.

It is best to be open minded and flexible in your thinking about time, although it is also necessary to be firm about whatever boundaries are established. Nevertheless, while exploring how to work best with groups on the unit for those patients with schizophrenia, I had an experience that reminded me that one should withhold expectations about any group, regardless of the diagnostic label.

Indeed, much to my surprise, these hospitalized schizophrenics were able to become deeply involved in a creative art process and subsequent discussion lasting as long as 3 hours. Length of art therapy sessions should of course be planned as realistically as possible, but with an openness to modifications as indicated, such as the gradual lengthening of the group time that occurred with the patients on this unit.

Frequency of meetings is also significant and should be approached with flexibility and imagination. In establishing an inpatient program with a wide variety of populations, we had the luxury of being able to experiment with group and individual work at varying intervals, from daily to weekly. We were also able to explore some of the benefits—especially in short-term work due to the pressures of "managed care"—of seeing patients more often.

The amount, location, and kind of space available are clearly relevant issues when setting the stage for art therapy. Sometimes, you are offered only one option, sometimes many.

When I consulted to a school for the deaf, for example, the room they had picked out for the pilot art therapy program seemed to the administrators to be best. After seeing it, however, I was uneasy about its size and location, so I asked if I might look for alternatives, to which they agreed. After exploring the building, I was able to find another room that seemed to me more appropriate for the activity—ample daylight, a "cozier" space for individual work, proximity to a water source, and so on.

On many of the inpatient units of the psychiatric hospital in which I worked, the art therapists ended up running groups in a space that at first seemed to me to be ridiculous—the kitchen. But on most of the floors (all locked), the kitchen was a spacious room with a large round table and several smaller ones, good lighting, ample storage space for supplies and patient artwork, and easy access to water.

Of course, it was necessary to work with the staff to reduce unnecessary and irritating interruptions, like people going to the coffee machine or refrigerator or using the washer and dryer. A sign on the door was helpful and included information about when the room would next be accessible.

But on the whole, much to my surprise, the kitchen turned out to be the location of choice for inpatient art therapy groups in this particular institution. Even a well-equipped art studio would have presented significant problems since the majority of patients were restricted to the units and would not have been able to participate. In addition, there would also have been constant scheduling conflicts among the art therapists who were serving this large hospital.

The lesson I learned is that you need to be open minded about space as well as about time, to be flexible in your thinking in general. However, paradoxically, you also need to be firm about your minimal needs—such as sufficient light, work area, storage space, and time—for art therapy to be possible.

Setting up the Working Environment

Once time and space have been agreed upon, the most critical artistry of stage setting occurs: the actual arrangement of furniture, easels, and art supplies within the available space. This should be done thoughtfully and as consistently as possible from session to session. While I was revising this chapter (January 2010), a lively discussion on "the art therapy space" evolved on a LinkedIn group, the Art Therapy Alliance. Although it may no longer be accessible by the time this book sees print, the fact that there were 24 responses within a month from people sharing ideas about how they had arranged their working spaces reflected a strong interest in the topic.

In general, the space should be arranged in such a way that the patients can most easily do what it is you want them to do. The precise decisions about the setting of each specific art therapy "stage" depend on the goals of the particular session as well as on the capacities of the persons involved—developmental level, degree of pathology, and so on. The ideal is an environment that is both orderly and stimulating, which looks and feels safe, as well as inviting. Clean and organized is always more appealing than dirty and disorganized, even when it is the same chunk of clay or box of watercolors.

Having observed a good deal of art therapy in a wide variety of settings, I am convinced that even greater attention could be paid by most art therapists to the "re-creation" of the physical environment in which they work. There are, of course, many situations in my experience for which the thoughtful arrangement of space and supplies was most impressive.

But in other instances, especially when the space used for art therapy must be shared with other service providers (as is so often the case), the clinician is often remarkably casual about how things are set up physically, as if it really did not matter. I have the impression that while it may matter more early in the treatment process than later, the physical stage set by the art therapist has a much more significant effect on what happens during the session than is generally supposed.

An example of one session comes to mind, in which the art therapist, who was highly skilled in relating to her elderly psychiatric patients, had pushed four small tables together—creating a nice, large working surface about 8 feet square, where each group member could easily see and relate to the others. So far, so good. The surface and setup were conducive to creative work and socialization.

However, she had also selected the largest size paper to give each of the eight patients sitting around the table, despite the fact that there simply was not enough space available for everyone to use such a big sheet (18 × 24 inches). For these disturbed older people, this presented a serious problem, solved by a few who figured out that they could fold the paper in half or quarters, but for the others, it frustrated their efforts to paint throughout the session.

Although this dilemma sounds minor, the art therapist was so focused on her presentation to the group, which was meant to motivate them to paint, that she was unaware of the frustration she had unwittingly stimulated. Had she simply offered a smaller size of paper, concerns about working area would not have interfered as they did for almost all of the patients, unnecessarily draining mental and physical energy from their creative task. Although it is helpful to expect and promote independence in creative work when feasible, for those whose energy resources are already limited, it does not make much sense to divert any of it from the art activity, where it needs to be invested.

Even when the space is sufficient, I have often observed art therapy situations in which the working surface was unnecessarily complicated by multiple supplies and extraneous items, which inevitably distract and may even interfere with patients' ability to get started or to stay focused.

If art therapists were to think about the arrangement of space and supplies as a creative task, one to be approached with as much care and artistry as layout on a page or placement within a collage, the resultant order would probably have a significant effect on people's ability to be creative. Therefore, although a facilitating physical framework can offer options in space and materials, it should also provide uncluttered and undisturbed possibilities for concentration on the art activity.

Setting the stage for different kinds of art therapy sessions will naturally reflect their distinctions. Certainly, there are different requirements for a group setting designed to evoke independent decision making and one where the art therapist wants to present a specific task to motivate and engage the group in thinking about a particular theme or activity.

If you want individuals to make a personally syntonic choice, a variety of media need to be available, set out in a clear and organized fashion, and there should be uncluttered work spaces with options for privacy or closeness to others. However, if you want to engage the attention and interest of a group in a motivation, seating everyone around the same table with no distractions on it makes the most sense, at least as an initial configuration.

Similarly, if you need to observe closely the process of a someone's work with materials, then it is logical to set up the space so that observation is possible—for example, to make sure that the person will be sitting and working within your view, whether or not there are choices of seating or working location. Or, if you want to observe subgroups and alliances within a family, it is helpful to have things set up to allow movement in space so that customary interaction patterns can be easily manifest in a natural way.

Setting the stage for the motivation portion of an art therapy group session might be quite different from the setting offered for the working time in the same session. A group first seated around a table for an introduction to a task might well be invited to move to any appealing working space, at alternative tables or easels, to make the creative process most comfortable for each individual.

In a family art evaluation for which the first task is individual scribble drawings followed by individual family representations, I found it worked well to start at a round table for the first task and then to offer options of where to work for the second one.

On the other hand, if socialization is the main goal for a particular group, then keeping people around the same table during the working time is more likely to promote informal interchange while they create. This was certainly the case for a group of women with whom I worked at a community arts center. They were all in a substance abuse rehabilitation program, and they were learning about themselves through verbal group therapy and education.

Being together in a different sort of therapy group added a new dimension to the program. For one, they could each "speak" through their art simultaneously. They could also "see" and hear each other by observing what each was doing with the materials. Although each woman worked individually for most sessions with a medium or theme suggested by the leaders, the verbal and nonverbal interaction within the group both during and after the making phase was part of the therapy process.

Of course, setting the stage for the discussion and reflection segment of any art therapy group might well be different from that which best suits either the motivation or the working period. I once observed a group in a fascinating setting created by a colleague in a psychiatric hospital. Because there were then few drugs that worked well for psychosis, the patients could focus more easily when not talking with or looking at each other. In Bernie Stone's studio in Zanesville, Ohio, each patient worked at a wall easel on his individual painting, the physical setup facilitating individual involvement in the work with minimal interaction. When they were finished, the patients brought their paintings to another section of the room, tacked them up on the bulletin board wall, and sat in a semicircle of comfortable chairs, where the discussion took place when all were assembled. This arrangement made it possible to view all of the products at once and to focus on individual pictures in the course of the discussion, sensitively led by the art therapist.

As with other phases of an art therapy session, there can be a surprising lack of attention given to creating an optimal viewing or reflecting situation. Holding up pictures individually is awkward and frustrating since the artist cannot simultaneously show his work to others and see it himself. An easel at the side of the table is one possible solution if it is considered best to view each product independently of the others for discussion purposes. If it is seen as more productive to have all of the pictures simultaneously visible, then some kind of larger surface makes more sense, such as a movable blackboard, display wall, or bulletin board wall.

Of course, it may be necessary to modify the seating of some or all patients so that all products can easily be viewed by all members of the group. While this may sound unnecessarily fussy, I believe that the therapeutic effectiveness of each facet of the art therapy session is, at least in part, a function of the environment and its facilitating or inhibiting effect on the desired behavior.

Setting the Stage Psychologically

Finally, an important part of setting the stage with any new clients is to explore openly any expectations—wishes as well as fears—about the art therapy session. What do they imagine will be "seen," and what do they think will be asked of them? It is important to encourage any questions they might have as well as to elicit their fantasies about why they are there and what is the purpose of this event.

Although I always ask for their ideas first, since what they imagine is so useful diagnostically, I also answer—as honestly and openly as I feel is feasible—their very legitimate questions about what is going to happen and why. This is especially important if they have not participated as fully as they might have in the decision making about coming for art evaluation or therapy.

Probably the most common anxiety is that the art therapist will be able to "read" things about them from their artwork, things of which they are not aware. The popularization of the use of projective drawings and the many cookbook approaches to art interpretation certainly encourage this misperception. I believe quite sincerely that there is no truly valid "meaning" to be gleaned from patient art without clarification and confirmation by the individual's own associations.

I can therefore say honestly that, despite their understandable fears, I am really unable to decipher their art without their own active participation. I tell them that understanding the meanings of what they produce will always be a collaborative effort in which their own thoughts and associations must play a central role. I also say that I will share with them as openly as possible any notions I may have, which are based not only on what I "know" about visual symbolism but also on what they have said about what they have created.

Of course, hypotheses that might seem too threatening are not conveyed to anyone prematurely, before you feel they are ready to hear that particular hunch. With this possible exception, then, you can honestly reassure patients about your inability to "see through" them on the basis of their creative products.

Like any other kind of reassurance, of course, this may be minimally successful, in the sense that someone might still be suspicious and fear being unmasked. Of course, a client might at the same time *wish* that the therapist would have all the answers and be able to translate in some facile way the underlying meaning of drawings, dreams, or symptomatic behavior.

Another common concern for clients beginning an experience with art therapy is that they are incompetent, untalented, and just "can't draw a straight line." While very young children are usually confident, as are those of any age who see themselves as gifted in art, most people feel like klutzes when they take marker or paintbrush or pencil in hand—awkward and "dumb"—even though they might feel intelligent in other realms. It is important, therefore, to bring this common anxiety into the open and to empathize with the difficulty of communicating in such an unfamiliar modality. You can tell them that making art in therapy is really different from doing it in an art class, even though it is true that no matter how you frame it people will naturally judge whatever they produce.

It is important from the outset—and periodically when anxiety or shame arise in response to products—to state clearly that the usefulness of art therapy does not depend on someone having talent in art. In fact, in my experience, being a serious artist can sometimes make it harder to be genuinely "free" in visual expression. It also helps to acknowledge the inevitable feelings of discomfort or self-criticism that go along with feeling inadequate as an artist and to sympathize with that.

But, I believe that you can say, with sincerity, that it really does not matter since art in therapy is art for another purpose than art itself. It is a way of understanding more about yourself and feeling more in charge of all of your resources, including your creativity. Depending on the age level and type of disorder, you can also try to explain in language that makes sense to the person the usefulness of the creative process as a paradigm of everyday experience, in addition to the value of visual expression as symbolic speech, saying things for which we may have no words. Since I believe in art *as* therapy as well as a vehicle *in* psychotherapy, I feel comfortable trying to "sell" a client on both of these values, neither of which demand talent, skill, or experience in the visual arts.

In addition, while clients fear looking inadequate and lacking in skill, most adults and adolescents are uncomfortable with anything that appears childish or infantile. One way of dealing with this understandable resistance to regression is to select materials that clearly look more "grown-up," like charcoal, good-quality pastels, oil crayons, colored pencils, ink, acrylics, or stone. Even when you want to offer media that can also be used by children, it is helpful to present materials in a way that looks and feels more adult.

Thus, one brand of watercolor marker is better placed in neutral containers rather than in its original box, with its grinning childlike cover. You can also choose brands and types of crayons that look as if they were designed for use by artists, as opposed to others that, while usable by anyone, are associated with grade school and childhood.

Despite care in the selection and presentation of materials, you must often deal more directly with patients who object because the activity seems babyish. As with other kinds of anxieties, it is helpful to encourage them to elaborate just what it is about art that seems childish and what might be their worries. After exploring their thoughts and associations and empathizing with any anxiety they might have about regression and potential loss of control, it is also useful to explain that the "childish" part of creating art is not necessarily incompatible with being a mature adult.

Depending on the client, I sometimes suggest that being in touch with your playful self, your silly self, and even your whiny or angry self, can be helpful in the ultimate goal of gaining access to all of your resources and feeling more completely in charge. Moreover, whether the goal is felt by the client as getting rid of that childlike part of the self or having easier access to their playful parts, the regressive aspect of art media and processes may turn out to be useful.

Although some art therapists worry about people becoming disorganized by using what are often termed "regressive materials," I do not agree. After 48 years of doing and supervising art therapy in both outpatient and inpatient settings—including acute care and nursing homes—I have not seen that happen. I believe that it may happen when you do not offer options and suggest that someone use, for example, paint or clay. But, as long as people are given a *choice* of media, in my experience, even psychotic, demented, and profoundly retarded patients still have defenses and will steer away from and not choose or not continue to use art materials that provoke too much anxiety.

In general, I believe that it is foolish, shortsighted, and generally untherapeutic to attempt to circumvent resistances, such as those caused by these common anxieties. Perhaps some art therapists have translated the writings about the ability of visual imagery to bypass mental censorship as an invitation to attempt to "cut through" defenses in general. Although it is true that people often do not subject visual imagery (mental or artistic) to the same defensive maneuvers as verbal communications, art is still much like a dream—a compromise formation between an impulse and a prohibition. So, it is naïve to think that drawn or sculpted work can ever be without defense or compromise.

It is similarly naïve to think that it would be good art therapy to succeed in getting patients to use media without acknowledging anxieties and resistances. You will get much further, in both the long and the short run, if you pay attention to anxieties and inhibitions and the fears behind them rather than attempt to seduce or pressure clients into creating in spite of them.

Why Setting the Stage Matters

Now, you may wonder why I have put so much time and energy into describing the importance of setting the stage, as if a well-set stage will help to overcome normal, expectable anxieties and inhibitions. The two are related. Creating a situation that makes art evaluation or therapy most possible pragmatically and least stressful psychologically is as much a part of being an effective art therapist as knowing art media or having excellent interviewing skills.

It is also true that setting things up in a facilitating fashion will help clients to feel less anxious and usually less confused. But, it will not take away the fear of being seen through or the worries about looking inadequate or feeling infantile. Such concerns are almost always present with adolescents and adults, and even with many children, including some who ought to feel good about their art—but who are afraid to perform badly or to lose control and can be as inhibited as older patients. These worries, in people of any age, need to be examined and to be addressed as carefully and clearly as the setting of the physical stage. Dealing with them openly is also likely to lead to more comfort in subsequent work.

Of course, any anxieties and inhibitions people may have at the outset will be present for some time. You will not make them go away instantly simply by getting them out in the open and exploring them. And, they will be there, for most people, throughout not only the first session but also later ones.

I believe it is vital to invite people in art therapy to tell you whenever they are feeling uncomfortable or upset about anything you or someone else has said or done. Such anxieties need to be taken into account, not only in setting the stage, but also in the next major component of the art therapist's task, evoking expression, the subject of the following chapter.

Recommended Readings

Case, C., & Dalley T. (2006). *The handbook of art therapy* (2nd ed.*)*. London: Routledge.
Milner, M. (1957). *On not being able to paint*. New York: International Universities Press.
Rubin, J. A. (2005). *Child art therapy* (3rd ed.) New York: Wiley.
Winnicott, D. W. (1971). *Playing and reality*. New York: Basic Books.

"Warm-up" activities, like passing a lump of clay around a circle and working on it quickly in turn, can help a group to relax.

The art therapist describes the next task to the group and checks to be sure they understand what she is asking them to do.

CHAPTER **9**

Evoking Expression

Deciding What to Do

Evoking or stimulating expression involves inviting the client or group to make something, whether it is to choose freely or to do a specific task. The most difficult issue for many art therapists seems to be the question of *what to do,* what sort of opportunity, stimulus, or task ought to be suggested at any particular session.

The usual tendency in art therapy is to classify techniques according to the materials used, the nature of the task, or some other descriptive concept. Such approaches can often be helpful, as in Kagin and Lusebrink's conceptualization of an "expressive therapies continuum" (Hinz, 2009; Kagin & Lusebrink, 1978; Lusebrink, 1990), which offers a comprehensive frame of reference regarding both materials and tasks.

In addition, there are lists of art activities provided by a growing number of clinicians (Buchalter, 2004, 2009; Craig, 2009; Darley & Heath, 2008; Furrer, 1982; Liebmann, 2005; Makin, 1999; Martinovich, 2006; Paraskevas, 1979; Pearman & Abrams, 2007; Pearson & Wilson, 2009; Robbins & Sibley, 1976; Silverstone, 2009; Simmons, 2006). Most are organized according to the objective or goal, which makes a good deal of sense since that is where deciding what to do usually starts.

Activities, exercises, and "directives" that others have found to be useful are potentially helpful in stimulating your own creative thinking. I believe that each art therapist, however, needs to be clear about the steps involved in deciding what to do and the variables you need to consider in making the final decision. Just as there are certain reality constraints (like time, space, or furniture) influencing the setting up of the physical space or economic limits on what and how much can be offered, so there are similar conceptual guidelines that form the context for decision making about activities.

The most important question, which needs to be answered as clearly as possible, is the *objective* of the particular art therapy session. Once that is evident to you, the sorting and brainstorming necessary for creative decision making about *what to do* have some direction. For example, if the goal of the activity is primarily *diagnostic,* you will want to maximize the likelihood of gaining whatever information you may desire in the shortest period of time.

Thus, if you want to find out how someone perceives his or her family in an individual interview, asking for a *representation of the family* makes good sense. If you are aware of some of the modifications others have thought of to amplify this theme, you will have them available as needed to facilitate the client's ability to comply with the request. Knowing or thinking of alternatives to make it most possible to accomplish your objective is helpful. I think of it as part of my mental storehouse or bag of tricks that can be accessed as needed.

For example, thanks to Kwiatkowska (1978), I often suggest an Abstract Family Portrait for those who are uncomfortable with drawing the human figure. Or, thanks to Burns and Kaufman (1970), I may suggest that the family be shown *doing something* (the Kinetic Family Drawing) to get an idea of the nature of the interaction within the group. And, for someone who likes modeling better than drawing, I might use Keyes's (1983) idea of a Family Sculpture.

If I sense a good deal of defensiveness and think it likely that some disguise will be useful, I may offer the possibility of drawing an animal family or the use of fruits or some other category intermediate between representations and abstract shapes. The media offered will depend on the time available and the nature of the clients, although it is always best to have some choice (of medium, paper size, or clay color) so that each individual can work in the way that feels most comfortable to them.

If you want to assess someone's ability to function independently, however, a completely free-choice procedure, with no instructions except to choose, would naturally provide the most relevant information. The number of choices offered would again be a function of the time and space available as well as the age level and diagnostic classification of the particular individual.

On the other hand, you might want to evaluate how someone works with others, such as their family or a group of peers. In that case, it would make sense to ask people to make something together, possibly to discuss it first, then to do it as a group. Or, you can ask a family or group to make something together *without talking*, another kind of task that provides yet another experience and view of interpersonal interaction.

Whether you limit space, size, location, time, medium, or topic will depend on variables such as what is available pragmatically and what you think matters most in understanding this particular group. You might end up specifying the medium, as I have often done in family art evaluations for practical reasons; for example, thick poster chalks work well because they can be used to cover large surfaces in a short period of time. Or, you might specify a topic because you want to see not only how the group interacts but also how they respond to a particular theme, such as asking a group of inpatients to create a mural about the hospital.

If you are clear about what it is you want to find out diagnostically, it is not so hard to decide what to do. Obviously, a request to determine whether a patient has some organic impairment would suggest a different kind of art interview than a request to find out if he has a neurotically distorted body image. While the answer to either *might* emerge from an unstructured art session, I would probably utilize some specific tasks, especially those that make sense in regard to the questions raised—like a copying or clock-drawing task for organicity or a self-portrait for body image.

If the request is more global and you want to find out in a broader way just what conflicts a person is struggling with and how he or she is coping, then an unstructured art interview (giving the patient a choice of media and topics) seems to work best, at least for me. I suspect others may be more comfortable with more structured tasks or sequences, and I cannot deny that such interviews are more easily comparable from one individual to another. However, the more unstructured interviews you do, the more these also can be compared and will yield the richest lode of data for most patients.

What matters is that you be clear in your own mind about what it is that you want to find out, whether for your own purposes or at someone else's request, and whether at the outset of treatment, in the middle of the process, or at the time of termination. When the question is clear, and if you have stored in your mental "grab bag" an awareness of materials, ways of using them, and what you can tell from different kinds of tasks, then it is really a lot of fun to think of how to answer the diagnostic inquiry at hand. Usually, there is no one *right* answer. The one that ends up being chosen is the one that not only seems appropriate to the circumstances but also feels most comfortable to you.

Knowing Yourself as a Clinician

Knowing yourself as a clinician matters much more than you might think for I am convinced after a number of years of observing and training others that no one can "put on" an approach that does not "fit." Like clothes on a rack, there may be a number of activities (of the right size) that fit the needs of the client and the question at hand. The one chosen, then, should be, whenever possible, the one that is most appealing and comfortable for the individual art therapist who is going to do the actual work.

As with clothes, you are often appropriately concerned with the responses of significant others. Just as I might search for a dress that both fits me and appeals to my husband, so, too, I usually use an approach in art assessment or therapy that is not only comfortable for me but also acceptable to others whose support is necessary for the ongoing work. This, of course, is as true for treatment as it is for diagnosis. Therapy, too, cannot be conducted in a way that is dystonic with your own style or aversive to others involved in the treatment. Given those necessary requirements, you can think of the decision making about what to do in art therapy when the goals are *therapeutic* as similar to that used for *diagnostic* aims.

For example, if your objective is to help someone to loosen up, you might consider arm or body movements, perhaps in preparation for doing a Scribble Drawing, as in the approach described by Florence Cane (1951). Or, you might think in terms of media and encourage a patient who always uses "clean" materials to try paint, finger paint, or clay, perhaps with a brush or a tool as a first step.

To relax people, you can also use any of a number of warm-up activities, a variety of which have been described by numerous art therapists (cf. Rubin & Levy, 1975). In addition to considering approaches via the body or the materials, you might explore topics or themes that would encourage playfulness and looseness.

On the other hand, you may have another kind of goal, such as increasing self-esteem, in which case tasks or materials with a high potential for success would be selected. I do not, by the way, mean paint-by-number pictures, molds, kits, or any such impersonal and restrictive approaches. Not only are they *not art* in the truest sense, but I also believe that, despite their popularity with patients and staff, to put together someone else's creation can never give a person the same feeling of satisfaction and of self-actualization that is available from authentic work, no matter how crude.

There are, however, materials that are themselves intrinsically beautiful, like the exciting hues of cellophane or tissue paper, as in the collages used in her work by Jungian analyst/art therapist Edith Wallace (1990). Cut or torn and glued on a white paper surface, it is almost impossible for either to appear anything but attractive. Similarly, carefully chosen oil-based clay (plasticine) can promote a "successful" outcome because of the beautiful, varied colors of the easily pliable medium, which look attractive whatever is done to or with them.

If you feel that the individuals with whom you are working need to make something "useful" to impress others or to feel good about themselves, then it makes sense to teach fairly foolproof techniques, like coil or slab pots or contour drawings. If clients are so demoralized about their ability that it seems they need some kind of preformed "crutch," then the challenge is to find one that will make them feel better about what they produce but will not interfere with the product being their own.

For example, plain white precut kites and Frisbees (which really work) were extremely popular on the adolescent unit of the hospital, yet each teenager's decoration remained a personal picture or design. Another popular activity among my child patients was to draw a marker picture on a round piece of paper, which I then sent to the manufacturer; for a minimal cost, it was made into a real (dishwasher-proof) plastic plate. A similar project involves drawing on a smaller round piece of paper, which is then made into a metal badge the person can pin on his or her chest, or on a rectangular shape that is then made into a mug. In all of these instances, the artwork involved is entirely original for each individual. And the final product is almost always a source of pride because it has a kind of utility (and therefore value) that a drawing or painting has in few households, and unlike many "homemade" items, it works.

Another common objective in art therapy is to help patients to express or release strong feelings, like aggressive impulses. While catharsis alone is never enough, genuinely experiencing the expression of any strong affect and discovering that it can be controlled and need not be destructive is a useful learning experience. It is one easily provided in art therapy, for example, by wedging clay—slicing it and slamming it onto a plaster surface—as part of preparing to make a sculpture. At a symbolic rather than a motor level, you can also suggest a drawing or painting of a time that the person was angry or upset about something.

If your goal is to uncover repressed material, it is likely that easily expressive media will work better than those that require more time and deliberation. With high-functioning "normal neurotics," I have sometimes suggested a kind of "free association in images" (Rubin, 1982). This involves going from one creation to whatever comes next, trying not to be deliberate or concerned about any kind of logical progression—a procedure based on the verbal free association of classical psychoanalysis. With this kind of objective, as with helping individuals to articulate their identity, a choice of unstructured media seems most likely to allow people the necessary self-definition and authenticity consistent with the aim.

On the other hand, you might have a specific goal in mind that would call for a narrower and more focused approach, such as helping an individual consider how he sees himself in relation to others. In this case, a picture of his "life space" at that moment in time might be appropriate. If you want to help a patient lost in delusions to focus on reality, it may be appropriate to suggest that he draw the still life placed before him or do a portrait of the patient opposite him. Conversely, if your objective is to better understand the content and symbolism of a patient's hallucinations, you can ask him to draw or paint what it is he sees or hears at delusional moments (Wadeson & Carpenter, 1976).

In working with a couple on becoming more aware of their communication patterns, you might suggest that they draw together on the same sheet of paper without talking and then discuss afterward all that they thought and felt in the course of the exercise. Or, if you want to help two people become aware of their misperceptions of one another, you might ask them to draw each other "privately" on opposite sides of an easel. They can then look at their partner's portrait of themselves and modify it as they wish, followed by a discussion of their perceptions, both of themselves and their partner—both techniques inspired by Harriet Wadeson (1973) and her art assessment for couples.

Similarly, if you think that parents each perceive their troubled child in mutually incompatible ways, a request to represent that youngster independently and then to compare the portraits can be illuminating. All of these tasks are things I have done with clients, usually decided on in response to a felt need during the treatment.

Perhaps the goal is not one of changing perceptions or promoting awareness, but rather of facilitating some kind of needed *experience* that an individual or a group might be avoiding. Whether it is being playful and having fun or being able to express aggression openly and directly, there are many possible activities using art media that can enable clients to have an enriching experience. As with all of the examples so far, once the goal is clear in your mind, you can use what you know about art and therapy and the people involved to create or decide on a relevant activity.

But, what if the therapist is not certain about what is needed at any particular moment in therapeutic time? Perhaps it is because I am rarely sure that I can always know best what patients need to see or to experience that I am personally more comfortable with an open-ended approach in which the choice of both materials and themes is left up to the individual most of the time.

The times when I have decided to suggest something specific are infrequent, usually in response to what is going on at that particular moment. On even more rare occasions, I have planned ahead, out of a strongly felt need regarding the clients, often based on the immediately preceding session. Planning ahead, however, seems risky since you never know "where" any individual, family, or group is going to be in advance of any particular meeting, no matter how long you have been working with them.

What I am more likely to do is to have some thoughts about where the individual or group needs to go and some ideas of how to help them to get there. If anyone is unable to get started successfully, even with my help, I might then suggest as an option a particular medium, theme, or exercise related to the "plans" in the back of my mind.

The only exceptions to this way of operating that make sense to me are diagnostic sessions and time-limited or theme-centered art therapy. In the last two, the inherent constraints make it more appropriate to zero in on whatever limited goals seem possible rather than wait for a more natural course of therapeutic events to occur.

While it seems to me that the structured approaches to art therapy, which are sometimes called "art therapy techniques," are often clever, creative, and probably harmless, I worry that in preventing people from finding their own creative way with materials, we are also depriving them of the essence of a genuine art experience. I would like to be able to believe that the many delightful and stimulating activities that are so popular serve mostly to enhance people's abilities to be creative and communicative.

I feel some concern, however, about what seems to me a kind of arrogance on the part of many clinicians who decide for clients what is *best* for them at any point in treatment. Such omniscient art therapists also have a regrettable tendency to specify themes and manner of working at moments when I would prefer giving individuals more options.

But, many would say, "Isn't that part of our job? Aren't art tasks the medicinal resource of the art therapist, who has a responsibility to choose from among the many creative activities available the one that is most needed by the client, just as the medical doctor is obliged to prescribe thoughtfully for his patient?" While those who subscribe to this position believe it to be their responsibility, I feel it is a perversion of the medical model and am astonished at the certainty of those who practice in such a prescriptive fashion. The recent popularity of the term *directives* for structured art activities makes me really uneasy.

As noted above, there are times when choosing or creating a specific task makes good diagnostic or therapeutic sense. But whether you value the art primarily as sublimation or as communication, authentic artwork by anyone requires independent decision making about as many aspects as possible.

I do not think I am a rigid art therapist in most respects, yet I feel stubborn about the importance of safeguarding personal choice in regard to art whenever people are capable of exercising such options. Parenthetically, it has been my happy experience that even severely impaired populations can be enabled to learn to make their own decisions with the right kind of help. Of course, there are times when the limited time or work space available makes it difficult—or maybe even impossible—to offer any kind of choice at all. But, I feel convinced of the morality of the issue, that any human being has a *right* to make his own choices, especially in such a personal realm as art.

Art therapists have many choices available in regard to media, task specificity and structure, and the nature of their own involvement. To achieve whatever objective is primary at the time, we have options in regard to the *medium:* you can offer an open choice from two or more alternatives, specify the use of one class of material (e.g., drawing, painting, or modeling), or designate a specific one to be used.

We have a similar range of choices in regard to the *theme* or topic, which can be quite open or more or less specific. We can request the drawing of a feeling or specify one like sadness or anger. We can also be more or less specific about the *manner* in which the task is to be done. You can ask someone to represent a feeling by using abstract shapes and colors or by showing people expressing it and so on.

There is always a variety of ways of combining medium, theme, and manner into a task for any particular situation. The objective might be helping patients to work together cooperatively. However, the particular group involved might not yet be ready to discuss and create a mural together without severe tension and probable fighting. The challenge, then, is to decide what degree of cooperation they are capable of and to lead them in slow steps toward the desired goal—the method of "successive approximation."

For example, a group of disturbed youngsters wanted to work together but were unable to do so when provided with the opportunity. The challenge was to help them in a gradual way to learn to work together successfully. The first step was for them to make a mural in which each child created his own building independently, cut it out, and placed it—one at a time—on a common backdrop. The children then took turns drawing the "environment" around their individually created houses.

Essentially the same approach was subsequently used with a three-dimensional group project, each child creating a plasticine animal and placing it on a cardboard "ground," which was later defined with markers. During the discussion of each activity, attention was given to whatever open disagreements or silent hurts might have been present during the minimally shared aspects of the task.

The next step was for each child to work with one other person on a joint picture, with adult assistance when necessary in both the decision-making and doing phases. Since the children were able to do that with some success, it was decided to try increasingly larger groups, each time paying attention during the discussion to the working process, where it was hard, and what alternatives might have been successful. The focus was on the interaction among team members, rather than on the product, which was primarily present as a concrete reminder and reflection of that interaction.

Quite a few sessions were needed to help this group of troubled youngsters, who had really poor impulse control, to get to the point at which they could work together in groups of four on the planning and execution of a joint project. They then exercised their teamwork on both two- and three-dimensional products and, by the time the series of sessions was over, had grown a good deal.

What they learned had less to do with art and more to do with social skills, but their pride in the joint creations they were able to produce was great, and the amazement and admiration of the staff was genuine—especially since these same children were much less cooperative in most other situations on their inpatient psychiatric unit. This limited experience exemplifies how the relevant variables—in this case, the degree of disturbance in relation to the goal of cooperation—influences the decision making about what is offered or suggested in art therapy.

These decisions are not really so hard to make if you truly understand the *who* and *why* of the patients and the *what* of growth needs. The challenge, then, is to provide the kind of artistic activity that will best meet those needs at any particular moment in time. It is clear that you cannot make such decisions about what to do or how to do it without a wealth of background understanding and knowledge about both art *and* therapy. Otherwise, there is a temptation to latch on to cleverly creative activities provided by others and to use them in an imitative way without fully understanding either their original intent or the needs of the clients to whom you are responsible.

I am not, by the way, suggesting that you should never use the ideas of others. Using someone else's idea in a way that is synchronous with its original purpose and meets your own treatment needs is indeed "a sincere form of flattery" and highly appropriate. Equally relevant, however, is feeling free to modify a good idea to suit your particular situation when the original format does not quite fit the new context. Perhaps most pleasurable for the creative art therapist is dreaming up needed ideas as required in your own clinical work.

I feel we do our clients an injustice to approach them blindly, without knowing why we are doing what we are doing and without a clear sense of how to deal with whatever arises from our evocation of patient expression. I am concerned that the use of stimulating materials and cleverly structured activities may sometimes mask an underlying confusion on the part of the art therapist about what is happening.

Of course, patients often need help to get started, and some patients do need more help than others. No one expects a retarded, depressed, or confused client to be as self-motivated or independent as a neurotic one. But you do not necessarily have to deal with a lack of motivation by using lots of "turn-on" techniques. Yes, it is necessary to "wind up the mainspring" (Linderman & Heberholz, 1979) more actively with some individuals or groups before they are able to work productively. But there is a tendency to do this more often than is really necessary or helpful, in my opinion.

An experience with geriatric groups in a psychiatric hospital again convinced me of the power of self-motivation when the right kind of stimulating stage is set for art, despite the very real effects of age and confusion. The art therapist, who had assumed for several months that these older patients required a great deal of structure (being told what to use, what to represent, and how to do it), was asked what she thought would happen if she offered them the same kind of choice she was making available to the substance abuse group, a younger and more independent population.

She assumed they would do nothing. She was pleasantly surprised when she found that most of the older patients could decide for themselves, although they did need more help from her to make decisions about what to use and what to make and often needed assistance in actually starting to work. Given such support, however, these patients made impressively varied products, which were much more personal and expressive than those they had done in response to the therapist's carefully designed "lesson plans."

If I have a bias in the area of what to do, it is for *flexibility*. Given my conviction that an open choice is best for most therapeutic and diagnostic purposes, I also see the advantages, at times, of assessment, short-term therapy, and theme-centered work of more specific task structure. I can even acknowledge the rare but real moments during work that is primarily open ended when it is best to suggest a specific medium, theme, or task. One of the most critical aspects of presenting the idea (whether open or structured) is the therapist's manner of doing so. How patients are invited to choose or to do may affect whether they are able to follow through more or less easily.

In general, the more comfortable and confident you are in issuing the invitation, the more positive will be the patient's expectation of his ability to accept it. My own conviction is that, one way or another, it is possible for any person or group to use art media creatively. It may be necessary to shift gears several times to help someone get started or to assist them through the steps of the decision-making process, but with the conviction that everyone can find something that feels right for them, it is usually possible to enable that to happen.

Perhaps most important, there is no need to feel any great rush or pressure about how quickly that should occur. Often, patients in art therapy groups will spend a significant period of time observing, talking, looking around the room, or watching others before being able to plunge in themselves.

At moments like that, I have sometimes adopted a "Pied Piper" approach in which I use myself as a model, attempting to engage people in creative activity by doing so myself with evident pleasure. I rarely have to put into words the invitation to others to use the materials I have chosen; I just make sure that the equipment is accessible to them, and my activity itself seems to act as sufficient stimulation. Whether those who "follow" do so in a submissive, competitive, or imitative fashion is not the issue; what is important is that it is a most useful way of using one's artist self in the service of a pivotal task in art therapy: evoking expression.

It is important to be clear about the request and, if it seems indicated, to be firm—not to ask the patients if they would *like* to do something but to expect that they *will* do it and to offer to help them begin if they have any difficulty. Although some diagnostic or therapeutic goals might lead to a less-supportive structure, there is little to be gained by making it unnecessarily hard for people to get started.

You can always be helpful, especially when the task is a fairly threatening one. Moreover, presenting tasks or offering theme ideas can be done in an artistic way almost as easily as a heavy-handed one—it just takes time and thought to do so. But to my mind, it is the same as creating an inviting set of media and working spaces; it is part of an art therapist's overall job of evoking creative expression.

Of course, that is just the beginning of the creative process. Setting the stage, deciding what to do, and helping people get started are the necessary events that initiate the central core of art therapy: the work with art materials. While people are working, whether individually or in groups, you are still present and have an important and equally critical task: to enable the artists to make a creative statement. The complexities of this role, how it shifts and fluctuates in the course of a session as well as over time, are the subject of the next chapter on facilitating creation.

References

Buchalter, S. I. (2004). *A practical art therapy.* London: Kingsley.
Buchalter, S. I. (2009). *Art therapy techniques and applications.* London: Kingsley.
Burns, R. C., & Kaufman, S. H. (1970). *Kinetic family drawings.* New York: Brunner/Mazel.

Cane, F. (1951). *The artist in each of us.* New York: Pantheon Books.

Craig, C. (2009). *Exploring the self through photography.* London: Kingsley.

Darley, S., & Heath, W. (2008). *The expressive arts activity book.* Springfield, IL: Thomas.

Furrer, P. J. (1982). *Art therapy activities and lesson plans for individuals and groups.* Springfield, IL: Thomas.

Hinz, L. D. (2009). *Expressive therapies continuum.* New York: Routledge.

Kagin, S., & Lusebrink, V. (1978). Expressive therapies continuum. *Art Psychotherapy, 5,* 171–180.

Keyes, M. F. (1983). *The inward journey.* (Rev. ed.). LaSalle, IL: Open Court.

Kwiatkowska, H. Y. (1978). *Family therapy and evaluation through art.* Springfield, IL: Thomas.

Liebmann, M. (2005). *Art therapy for groups* (2nd ed.). London: Routledge.

Linderman, E. W., & Heberholz, D. W. (1979). *Developing artistic and perceptual awareness* (4th ed.). Dubuque, IA: Brown.

Lusebrink, V. B. (1990). *Imagery and visual expression in therapy.* New York: Plenum.

Makin, S. R. (1999.) *Therapeutic art directives and resources.* London: Kingsley.

Martinovitch, J. (2006). *Creative expressive activities and Asperger's syndrome.* London: Kingsley.

Paraskevas, C. B. (1979). *A structural approach to art therapy methods.* New York: Collegium.

Pearman, H., & Abrams, H. (2007). *Art therapy for children of all ages.* Denver, CO: Outskirts.

Pearson, M., & Wilson, H. (2009). *Using expressive arts to work with mind, body and emotions.* London: Kingsley.

Robbins, A., & Sibley, L. B. (1976). *Creative art therapy.* New York: Brunner/Mazel.

Rubin, J. A. (1982). Art and imagery: Free association with art media. In A. E. Di Maria (Ed.), *Art therapy. A bridge between worlds.* Falls Church, VA: American Art Therapy Association.

Rubin, J. A., & Levy, P. (1975). Art-awareness: A method for working with groups. *Group Psychotherapy and Psychodrama, 28,* 108–117.

Silverstone, L. (2009). *Art therapy exercises.* London: Kingsley.

Simmons, L. L. (2006). *Interactive art therapy.* Binghamton, NY: Haworth Press.

Wadeson, H. S. (1973). Art techniques used in conjoint marital therapy. *American Journal of Art Therapy, 12,* 147–164.

Wadeson, H., & Carpenter, W. T. (1976). The subjective experience of schizophrenia. *Schizophrenia Bulletin, 2,* 302–316.

Wallace, E. (1990). *A queen's quest.* Santa Fe, NM: Moon Bear.

Recommended Readings

Klorer, P. G. (2000). *Expressive therapy with troubled children.* New York: Aronson.

Malchiodi, C. A. (2006). *The art therapy sourcebook* (2nd ed.) New York: McGraw-Hill.

Nucho, A. O. (2003). *Psychocybernetic model of art therapy* (2nd ed.). Springfield, IL: Thomas.

Rhyne, J. (1995). *The gestalt art experience* (2nd ed.) Chicago: Magnolia Street.

Rubin, J. A. (2005). *Artful therapy.* New York: Wiley.

A boy who is mentally challenged, cerebral palsied, and legally blind can mobilize amazing energy and control when he has the chance to build with wood scraps and glue.

The art therapist helps an elderly patient by being interested in what he is doing and assisting with any technical problems that may arise in the course of his technical work.

CHAPTER 10

Enabling Creation

The Importance of Observing

Enabling art expression goes on from the moment the client has started to work until he is finished, whether you take an active or a receptive position. And from the time of getting started, to doing all along the way, to deciding when to stop, a person may be more or less independent. Those who can function well and creatively on their own need to have their autonomy, working space, and time respected by lack of intrusion.

In this regard, it appears that some art therapists do not think they are doing their jobs if they are simply sitting and observing. But, if you can learn to be comfortable being on your observational toes, there is a huge amount of information to be gained from watching facial expressions, body language, and the sequence in which things are created. Quiet, focused observation is a skill that, when learned, is deeply rewarding.

Although there is so much to observe that it is not possible to detail all of it here, it might help to note some typical aspects of a person's encounter with art media, whether seen individually or in a group. It is especially interesting to note how the individual makes his selection of medium and just how he takes the first step with the materials. Is he slow and cautious, or does he plunge right in? And, if he starts quickly, is it impulsive or deliberate? Does he seem selective or haphazard in his use of materials? Does he seem intent on making something, or is he more interested in manipulating? How involved does he become with the material, and does that change over time? How absorbed is he in the working process? Does he seem to pay attention to the environment and to other people, or does he seem lost in his own thoughts? How intense and how long is his concentration span? Does he seem distractible, and if so, when and by what? Does the art activity seem to be a means to gain approval, to engage in social contact, or is it perhaps an end in itself?

While someone is working, you can observe whether he works at a fairly even pace or uses a lot of energy in manipulation of the material, body movements, or verbalization. What is his working tempo? Does it change over time, and if so, how? How much or how little energy does the person seem to have available over the course of the session? In the course of doing his art, does the person become progressively more free? Does he start in a disorganized fashion and gradually become more controlled? Or does he stay the same throughout?

Is there any change in body movement, speech, or mood in the course of the work? What kinds of movements does the person use with the materials: Free or tense? Careless or careful? Large or small? Jerky or smooth? Are his body movements in general sure or unsure? Rigid or relaxed? Steady or uneven? Slow or rapid? And on and on—there is so much rich nonverbal data available when you learn how to observe.

If someone talks while working, what kind of voice tones does he use? How articulate is his speech? And to whom does he speak: the art therapist, other clients, or himself? Even apparently unrelated spontaneous verbalization during the working process is important to note since it is inevitably connected with what is being done with the materials.

If the person wants to describe or talk about the product or process while working, you need to listen with respect and be careful not to intrude on his creative work space. Observing what is actively rejected, as well as what is selected, and watching as closely as possible the sequence of steps on the way to the final product are both important in understanding the individual and his art. This is especially critical if someone is using materials that permit "undoing" (like clay or finger paint) or covering over (like tempera paint), where the messages visible in the process can easily be partially or even totally obscured in the final product.

If, When, and How to Intervene

With all there is to observe during the art process, there should be no need to initiate intervention for its own sake. After all, to intrude on a creative process is to disrupt the very event for which you have so carefully set the stage and prepared the client. On the other hand, if someone is asking, either verbally or nonverbally, for help at any moment, you should first try to figure out what kind of help is being requested and then offer assistance, but in the least intrusive fashion possible.

It is ideal if the help can be given in a way that enables the person to discover the answer himself. The challenge is to act in such a way that the individual can find the problem or the solution. This may require a nonverbal action, like turning a picture upside down to help someone decide if it feels balanced, or it may require a verbal intervention, like a comment or question that can catalyze some new awareness on the part of the individual.

For example, a person might express despair or frustration about his artwork, that "it's not turning out right," or "it doesn't look good." Before you can help in any meaningful way, it is necessary to help the individual to clarify the source of his distress. You might therefore ask the patient to tell you, as specifically as possible, just what it is that he finds distressing about his work. Once that has been defined, then the art therapist can ask other questions or engage in other actions, which will eventually enable the client to decide how best to remedy the problem.

On the other hand, there are times when you might know some technical tip of which the client is unaware. When it seems that the naïve artist's life would be made easier by the sharing of that knowledge, it seems inhumane not to do so. However, if respect for the person as artist is sincere, the technical tip will be offered as an option, not an instruction or a command.

It is difficult not to insist that a person use a smaller brush or a stronger glue when you know that his chances of ultimate success are minimized by what he is using or doing. While it is an art therapist's responsibility to let the patient know the probable consequences of one procedure or another, it is also important to permit each individual to make the final decision for himself.

You cannot prevent frustration for clients any more than you can protect your children from pain. In fact, as with your offspring, it is probably ultimately more useful for people to fully experience some negative consequences in order to be able to freely change their own behavior. What goes on between therapist and client in art therapy in regard to technical procedures is much like real-life learning experiences. But these occur in a protected situation in which the person can safely find out what happens if he submits, opposes, or responds in some other way to the therapist's suggestion of an alternative way of working.

Using Yourself to Facilitate Another's Process

Facilitating another person's creative behavior is a delicate matter. Whether to be active or passive, to be physically near or far, to be psychologically close or distant, to act warm or cold, to comment or to stay quiet, to look or not to look—these are the difficult decisions that have to be made from moment to moment in clinical work. In making such decisions about when to intervene and how, you must be not only artistic but also knowledgeable.

It is in making these kinds of decisions that knowledge about both art and therapy becomes essential, especially your understanding of appropriate goals for the individual(s) involved. Intuition is simply not enough. Therapy is not something that can be done "by the seat of your pants," at least not well. The challenge is to make your knowledge about art and therapy so integrated a part of yourself that it is fully available in a spontaneous way. Clinically informed intuition is different from following your impulses; the former can usually be trusted, so that you are free to act on hunches. Later, when there is time, you can think about it deliberately and reflect critically.

Whatever the nature of your intervention, whether initiated or in response to an overt request, facilitating client art making can be thought of in general as the provision of what has been called an "auxiliary ego." That means lending your own ego (your knowledge or organizing capacities) to the client when you feel that it would help him to actualize his creative intentions. Sometimes, lending your ego is optional, and sometimes it is essential, as with severely disabled or disordered patients. But in either case, it is different from dominating, deciding, or doing *for* the person, especially if he is capable and simply needs some help to be able to think or act on his own.

Being respectful of individual choice and artistic preference is essential—a reflection of respect for other people, no matter how confused the state in which they are seen. Such an attitude is also consistent with any kind of genuine creative process, which has to be ultimately from the person if it is to be truly his own. This is true whether you believe in art *as* therapy or art as a means of communication *in* therapy. The more authentic the art from the person, the more likely it is to be a true sublimation or an honest communication.

Whatever you do, from the beginning to the end of the working process, a guiding principle for me is that of the "least-restrictive intervention." This is a paraphrase of a contemporary term in special education—the "least-restrictive environment." As with the latter, what is unstated but implied is that you should provide the "most facilitating" intervention or environment for that particular individual or group.

It does take skill, artistry, and tact to find the least-restrictive or least-intrusive way to support a person's creative efforts. Perhaps what is most needed is a wordless "gleam" in your maternal eye (Kohut, 1971) or an approving comment about the artwork itself, or about the client's behavior during the process. Sometimes it is necessary to offer or to give more active assistance with the work, usually in response to an overt or subtle request. This is a delicate and demanding task since your job is to promote the individual's autonomy and to do so with respect.

However, if things are threatening to get out of hand, you do need to intervene without being asked, to set limits on action or words, and to help anyone losing control to regain it. Even this kind of intervention is best done in the least-restrictive or least-intrusive way possible. You may be able to settle things down with just a glance, perhaps a gesture, or a few softly spoken words. Or the situation may require that you take charge in a more active way.

This kind of limit setting need not be seen as restrictive, however, despite the fact that you are probably literally restricting one or another sort of behavior. Rather, the limit setting should be viewed as a re-establishment of the very *framework* for free functioning that you have worked so hard to create. Whether silent or assertive, you need to maintain an ever-watchful eye and presence throughout all moments of any art therapy session in order to use what you know to help those in your care to experience both creativity and consciousness in a safe and secure context.

When you intervene, you will hopefully strive to be not only correct but also artistic in how you do it. It is probably in the *how* rather than the *what* of intervention that artistry is distinguished from mere competence, more a matter of style than of substance. Perhaps one reason you can make a fair number of mistakes and still help patients to get better is that your manner conveys the sincerity of your wish to assist, even if the content or form of what you are doing or saying is widely off the mark.

Your behavior in the course of the working process is critical to the success of your clinical work, but it is oddly ignored or minimized in discussions of technique. As with stages in therapy, much attention is paid to the beginning phase (evoking expression) and to the final one (looking and learning), but what goes on in the middle is often a muddle. The range of possibilities for intervention is so great that it is difficult to make generalizations. Whether you are seeing an individual, a family, or a group, what you do and how you do it depend on an almost infinite number of variables, which are overwhelming to list, let alone quantify.

But the kind of thinking that is relevant for setting the stage and evoking expression is also relevant for the task of facilitating the creation of art in therapy. That is, you ought to do what seems most appropriate at that particular moment in time for that particular person or group in order to move the treatment along toward your goals and objectives. And, in accord with the principle of least-restrictive intervention, it should be done in the most subtle way, one that is likely to enable people to reach the objective of the moment as well as the long-term goals that you have decided make the most sense.

Knowing Your Limitations

It is always necessary to disentangle patient needs from your own—a task most easily accomplished if you have achieved some degree of self-knowledge—and to engage in continual self-monitoring. For example, it is important not to let your need for finished or attractive products interfere with the client's use of art media in the fashion most helpful to him at that moment in time.

This may mean manipulation or even destruction, rather than a formed creation. For an artist, it is not easy to sit quietly by and observe something that seems to be moving toward form begin to disintegrate. Although there are times when I would intervene, there are others when I would not, guided much more by my therapist-self than my artist-self.

If, as Kramer (1958) has suggested, an art therapist combines in one person the ability to be artist, therapist, and teacher, then one of the issues during the working process is how much you should use any particular aspect of yourself at any moment in time. My own preference is for flexibility in this area, as in others. What is nice is to have options; what is hard is to decide which to access.

I am convinced that the pendulum swings for most individuals in art therapy from an emphasis on the art as sublimation to an emphasis on the art as communication, sometimes in the course of a single session, sometimes at greater intervals. I therefore feel a frequent need to shift gears, at times using more of my teacher-self in the service of a meaningful product, at others using more of my therapist-self in the service of understanding the messages therein. In both, I hope that my artist-self is available to facilitate and respond to the patient's creative work.

You can use your artist-self in a variety of ways in art therapy. Perhaps the most important is in empathizing with what the client is going through in the course of the creative process, from the initial decision-making moments, through the ups and downs of the work, to the time when he feels "finished."

As noted in the chapter on materials, this means actually having worked with all media offered to clients, allowing yourself to become engaged and to experience the peculiarities of each medium, tool, or process so that you can genuinely "feel with" a client's attempts. Although I believe that you do not need to be an exhibiting artist to be a good art therapist, it is necessary to allow some time and space in your own life to work with materials, whether for recreation or more serious aims.

It is also helpful to use your artist-self as a tool for reflecting on what you are experiencing in response to any particular client or group. Using art media yourself to represent the individuals or the feelings and fantasies they evoke is a most powerful way of reflecting on your inner experience. Whether or not you sense some countertransference reactions, you should always try to keep in touch with whatever is stimulated by clients. It is not only a source of further self-knowledge but also a source for better understanding the people with whom you work. Whether you use paint, chalk, clay, or cut paper matters little; what is important is the use of all aspects of yourself, including the artist inside, as a means of helping the others whose growth you are trying to promote.

Using Your Artist Self as a Therapist

Perhaps the most common appearance of the artist-self in art therapy is in the use of media with clients for one or another purpose. The "Pied Piper" technique described as a way of stimulating others to use art materials is one possibility. Another reason you might choose to work alongside people is to reduce their self-consciousness about being watched. Yet another is to demonstrate what you are requesting to be sure that they understand.

I often do a scribble drawing, for example, as a way of explaining the technique, and sometimes I continue and develop the scribble to promote interaction with a reluctant individual or to help family members in an evaluation feel less uncomfortable. For similar reasons, I might casually manipulate a material that someone else has chosen, not so much to stimulate or even to demonstrate possible uses, but more often to reduce the tension many people feel when they are working and the art therapist is sitting and staring at them. Observing unobtrusively is a real art, but you can develop it over time.

Another way in which you can use your artist-self is in actually drawing (or painting or sculpting) with the patient. One such possibility is literally working together, as in the "nonverbal dialogues" used by several therapists with severely regressed and withdrawn patients (Horowitz, 1983). The only time I found myself wanting to become involved in a pictorial dialogue with a client was in work with an elective mute—in an attempt to connect with her, despite her intense resistance. This same patient also evoked in me an uncharacteristic desire to create several portraits of her, probably another attempt to establish a relationship.

On equally rare occasions, I have found myself using drawing as a way of clarifying an interpretation, such as showing someone that he has put a "wall" between us or has "boxed" himself into an isolated space. In ongoing family art therapy, I have occasionally drawn an image of how I see the family's interaction patterns, which is more eloquent and probably closer to the truth than I could achieve with words alone.

Also on rare occasions, it has seemed useful to work with a client on a creation, usually when I feel that my involvement can make possible a kind of artistic statement that the person is too insecure to make without active support. There is yet another usage of the artist-self I have occasionally employed—a technique called *closure,* which art educator Viktor Lowenfeld (1957) developed in his attempts to reach children with severe disabilities. It involved beginning something (like a clay sculpture) by partially doing it, then giving it to the child to complete. It is a kind of "starter," which may be necessary for a person who is unable to organize materials completely on his own.

A similar kind of starter approach can be used to help inhibited individuals to begin, although most often it is possible to help them to create their own scribble lines or ink blots. For some, however, a dot or line or shape on the paper supplied by the therapist seems to enable them to get started more easily. Whether it is related to a need for permission, a desire for oneness, or some other cause, it is an additional way in which a therapist who is also an artist can use those specialized skills in the service of treatment. Edith Kramer's (2000) description of using the art therapist's "third hand" offers yet another way to think about the use of your artist-self in your work.

Another possible use of yourself as artist is in following instructions to create as given by the patient. While I see this kind of technique as something of a last resort to be used when all else fails, it is really analogous to following a patient's directions in dramatic play, role-play, puppetry, or psychodrama. That is, given the fact that you have decided to use art media yourself with someone who for the moment refuses, it makes more sense to me to use it in a way dictated by the client than according to your own impulses or whims.

For example, a child I was once seeing wanted very much to be my "boss" in many ways. I suggested that we could play school. So, he pretended that he was a teacher, instructing me in how to draw a particular cartoon character. Not only did I get an A, but we both experienced what a demanding and critical boss he was, which he then related to disciplinary experiences with his own punitive mother.

One of the most exciting uses of your artist-self with clients has been reported by art therapist Mildred Lachman-Chapin (1983). Her technique involves drawing or painting in a spontaneous fashion during the time when the patient is involved in doing his own work. Since the artwork for both follows an initial period of discussion and a decision about the theme for the day, each person is presumably focusing on that topic and its meaning for the patient. It represents another way of using your preconscious thinking as a therapist and reminds me of the mental images that run through my mind when I am with a client or the doodles I draw in my notebook while an analysand is on the couch.

However, such a technique could be abused by those with insufficient self-awareness. Like Winnicott's (1971) use of "squiggles" with child patients, in which he and the youngster took turns elaborating simple scribble drawings into images, it is something that seems appropriate only in the hands of a very experienced clinician.

Nevertheless, given a sophisticated art therapist and an agreeable client, the approach has considerable potential as a way of using your artist-self in an authentically creative fashion in your work as a therapist. One of the best discussions of this complex and challenging topic is in Cathy Moon's (2002) book *Studio Art Therapy,* which is actually subtitled *Cultivating the Artist Identity in the Art Therapist.* I hope that all art therapists will strive to be as thoughtful and self-aware as Chapin and Moon in using this powerful tool in our artist repertoire (cf. also Moon, 2007).

Using Your Teacher Self as a Therapist

There has been considerable focus on the use of the artist part of yourself, largely because that is what is unique to art therapy as opposed to other modes of treatment. The educational function in art therapy may also be seen as distinct if viewed specifically as teaching the patient how to use art media or how to look at and think about art products.

Yet every kind of treatment requires some education of the patient on the part of the clinician, whether it is explicit, as in cognitive therapy, or implicit, as in client-centered or existential therapy. Whatever the "game" played by the particular therapist, the client needs to learn its "rules" and how to play it.

One question that is relevant in art as well as in other therapies is how explicit to be about what is happening and why. Although I began in my work saying little and hoping that people would grasp the essence of art therapy by experiencing it, I have gradually become more open with patients, especially in first encounters. This parallels an increasingly direct way over the years of dealing with issues in general, such as asking a reluctant child why he thinks he has been brought to a therapist and what he sees as his biggest problems. It seems equally relevant for you to tell him or a group why you are offering them art media and why you are inviting them to choose or to do something in particular. Not only is such an open approach more honest and ethical, but it is also quite helpful to people of all ages and diagnostic classifications.

The educational role of an art therapist should not, therefore, be limited to helping people use media or look at art; it should include helping them to understand the essence and purpose of art therapy, for them and for their growth and development. The natural resistance of most adults to using materials is more easily overcome if they are presented with a meaningful reason why such an activity will be helpful to their recovery. They can then allow themselves to regress, play, and create because they can see the serious purpose of the activity and are less likely to be overwhelmed by feelings of foolishness or embarrassment.

One of the most difficult aspects of this educational task is finding nonthreatening but understandable language with which to present the purpose of art in evaluation or therapy. Part of the "art" of being an effective therapist is being able to "tune in" to people of different age levels and views of the world and to communicate comfortably and effectively through words. One of the assets of art therapy is that it gives you and the client yet another mode of communication, one that can be carried on in complete silence and, as described, can be used to confront, to mirror, or in some other way to communicate with each other.

The art educator aspect of the art therapist is that of a teacher who knows a lot about materials, tools, and processes, as well as looking at and learning from creative products. In teaching the use of materials, my preference is to do so only when necessary. For most people, little or no formal instruction is required to use basic art media. For many, a minimal statement or demonstration may do the trick.

In groups and families, individuals often learn from other members how to do something in art. An art therapist is not primarily a teacher, although clinicians in certain settings have offered formal art classes to patients with success, and that seems like a fine idea, as long as it is made explicit. In art therapy, the teaching of techniques seems relevant to me only when it is essential for the client to be able to use the materials to say what he wants to say. Teaching in art therapy is another way of helping someone to find their own artistic voice.

Thus, it is a means to an end rather than the central focus of the work. It is important to remember that the end is not art, but therapy, so that any teaching about art is always in the service of its therapeutic usefulness. For some clients, this may mean skill development in the use of a medium, learning specific techniques that enhance their comfort and facility with the material.

But, the goal is rarely to make them into artists, even if that may be a happy secondary gain. When it happens, it seems to me to be a wonderful fringe benefit. It is more likely that the goal is to help them to feel like competent individuals or to understand more about their inner selves. From my perspective, only if the creation of increasingly refined products would seem to promote either goal does it make sense for an art therapist to use her teacher-self.

Having minimized the role of art instruction in art therapy, I also remind the reader that the first portion of this book is called "The Art Part." I do feel strongly that no one can be an effective art therapist without knowing materials, tools, processes, and products—without knowing enough, in other words, to be able to teach any patient at any time what he needs to know to say what he wants to say in art therapy.

The artistic component of this role is in being selective, in using yourself as a teacher only when necessary, and in providing there, as elsewhere, the least restrictive intervention. If you can help a patient to help himself, even on a technical matter for which you might have a quick-and-easy solution, it will be a better learning experience for him and will promote his eventual autonomy as a person and an artist.

Using Your Therapist Self

How does the therapist aspect of your role become visible during the working process, when the main task is facilitation of the patient's creative artwork? On the surface, it might appear that the artist and educator facets are more central, especially during the time when people are involved in creating. But, as with many other things about the art of art therapy, it is not that simple.

In addition to the active observation noted as an important part of the working time for the therapist, your primary identity as a clinician should really infuse everything you do. That is, when observing clients at work, it is with a clinically trained eye, one that sees behaviors with art materials and with other people primarily in psychological terms. Someone looking in the room during the middle portion of an art therapy session might easily think it was an art lesson or a recreational activity. While both learning and fun may well be part of what happens, neither is the primary aim, except as they relate to the goals of therapy.

Whether to interact with a client and how to do it during the working process—whether to initiate, how to respond—these are the difficult clinical questions that are always present in art therapy as well as in other forms of treatment. It is only the *therapist* part of your identity that can answer them, hopefully a well-trained and self-aware one that can do so in a thoughtful way.

I believe that there are two main variables to be considered in answering these questions at any moment in time with any client. The first has to do with the goals and objectives you have set for the individual, both short and long term, and how best to reach them. If, for example, you have determined that a person needs to work on some reality problems that he is not representing in his artwork, then casually talking about them while he is working might be appropriate.

The second variable concerns the readiness of any client at any time to move in the direction you see as relevant in some specific way. While some might be comfortable talking while they work and it might even enhance the freedom of their art, others find their creative process seriously inhibited by simultaneous conversation. But, you cannot usually know or even guess in advance how an individual who has not initiated it spontaneously will respond to talking while working. You therefore need to try it out and see what happens.

This kind of trial and error is a necessary mode in any work as delicate and multileveled as art therapy. Many clinicians seem afraid to fail. Indeed, one of my most common supervisory tasks is to support therapists in trying things they fear will backfire. In most cases, the worst that could happen is that the person will not respond at all or will do so with anger. Neither of these is disastrous, although it is wise to be cautious with those who have problems controlling physical aggression.

Making mistakes is inevitable, in therapy as elsewhere, and I am not advocating impulsive action. But, I am suggesting that fear can be paralyzing, and that trial and error is the best mode for testing the waters of someone's receptivity at any point in therapy. If your anxiety about failing can be overcome, and you try something that does not work, you will learn from the experience and will go back to your mental drawing board, looking for yet another way to achieve the same goal.

If, for example, the client who needs to discuss a reality crisis cannot talk while he draws and does not bring up that topic when discussing his art, you need to think of other options, like separating such "news-of-the-week" discussions in time from the rest of the session, either at the beginning or at the end. In other words, there probably is a workable way to help people to discuss crucial issues; the challenge is to figure it out through trial-and-error thinking and action.

Or, if you feel that an important short-term goal is helping a client to become freer and less stereotyped in his art, which has stayed largely defensive for some months, you will try all kinds of approaches until you find one or more that "click" with the particular person. It might be doing a scribble drawing; it might be using a fluid medium; it might be thinking of mental imagery before using media—but whatever it is, the important thing is to keep on trying, to be open minded and inventive in your thinking about what might help to facilitate that person's growth.

On the other hand, you might try everything you can think of either to get someone to loosen up or to discuss reality concerns, and still nothing works. So yet another part of your job is realizing your limitations, your lack of omnipotence, the need for consultation with a colleague, and the ever-present possibility of failure in this delicate discipline of therapy through art.

Deciding to give up, whether permanently or for the time being, is not always because of failure, but more often, I hope, because of success. For any client who is actively working with media, there is also the need to decide when any particular artistic product is done, finished, complete. For some this is easy, intuitive, and unconflicted; for others, it is the focus of an intense, obsessional debate or block. For many, at least at first, it is an area in which they feel inadequate because of their limited experience with art. Clients often ask you to tell them not only how they are doing, but also whether something looks finished.

As with other judgmental questions, my own preference is to help the person to make their own self-evaluation. You can be active in noting things to think about or ways to look at a product to decide if it is all right and if it feels "done," without ever making an explicit judgment. The artist in you may have to bite your tongue at such moments since it is impossible to avoid having an aesthetic response to a client's work. But a good teacher, as well as a good therapist, can promote more growth by helping the person to evaluate himself than by doing it for him. In learning how to be his own critic, the individual also learns at various steps along the way how to perceive his artwork in an informed fashion.

The final step in most art therapy sessions, whether individual, family, or group, is looking at and reflecting on the product and the process behind it. The therapist's task in this activity is helping people to do this so that both therapist and client may better understand and learn. This is the subject matter of the following chapter on looking at and learning from art.

References

Horowitz, M. J. (1983). *Image formation and psychotherapy.* New York: Aronson.

Kohut, H. (1971). *The analysis of the self* (The Psychoanalytic Study of the Child, Monograph No. 4). New York: International Universities Press.

Kramer, E. (1958). *Art therapy in a children's community.* Springfield, IL: Thomas.

Kramer, E. (2000). *Art as therapy: Collected papers* (L. A. Gerity, Ed.). London: Kingsley.

Lachman-Chapin, M. (1983). Empathic response through art: The art therapist as an active artist in the therapeutic relationship. In L. Gantt & S. Whitman (Eds.), *The fine art of therapy* (pp. 80–81). Alexandria, VA: American Art Therapy Association.

Lowenfeld, V. (1957). *Creative and mental growth* (3rd ed.). New York: Macmillan.

Moon, B. L. (2007). *The role of metaphor in art therapy.* Springfield, IL: Thomas.

Moon, C. H. (2002). *Studio art therapy.* London: Kingsley.

Winnicott, D. W. (1971). *Therapeutic consultations in child psychiatry.* New York: Basic Books, 1971.

Recommended Readings

Malchiodi, C. A. (Ed.). (2003). *Handbook of art therapy.* New York: Guilford Press.

McNiff, S. (1998b). *Trust the process.* Boston: Shambhala.

Robbins, A. (Ed.). (1998). *Therapeutic presence.* London: Kingsley.

Rubin, J. A. (Ed.). (2001). *Approaches to art therapy* (2nd ed.). New York: Brunner-Routledge.

Schaverien, J. (1992). *The revealing image.* London: Routledge.

Wadeson, H. (1987). *The dynamics of art psychotherapy.* New York: Wiley.

Working silently together and later discussing it can be a powerful learning experience about both art and human interaction.

Suggesting that the child look at, consider, and decide what to do next with his mobile allows him to begin reflecting while still engaged in creating.

CHAPTER **11**

Facilitating Reflection

The Value of Reflecting

No matter what the age of the client, there is value in both doing and reflecting in the visual arts. One of the ways in which art in therapy differs from art in other situations is that there is almost always some kind of reflection on the art experience as well as the work that emerges. Depending on the age of the people involved and the context of the work, it may be brief or fairly extensive, but it is an important component.

Reflection may be more critical for those who see the art primarily as a form of communication and less central for those who primarily value the potential for sublimation through art. But even clinicians who subscribe to the *art-as-therapy* approach are interested in how people respond to the experience and the products they create.

My own preference is to invite people to reflect not only on the *product* but also on the *process* of making it. This component of reflecting seems often to be neglected, but in my experience this aspect is also a rich source of learning. Whether it is an individual reflecting on working with the medium and trying to express his ideas or a couple, family, or group reflecting on the task of working together, exploring reactions to the process of creating is as important as responding to the art itself. It is ironic that art therapists, who often state that their work focuses on the process rather than the product, so rarely help clients to explore that aspect of the experience.

The reflection on the *image* itself can be nonverbal as well as verbal. This idea was first proposed by Jung (Chodorow, 1997), who suggested that "active imagination" could involve moving or writing in response to the image (Fay, 1994) or letting the image "speak" to its maker. Art therapists Shaun McNiff (2004) and Pat Allen (1995, 2005) have suggested a similar kind of dialogue with the image to be carried on in a meditative state. In Allen's "open studio process" (OSP), the initial response is called "witness writing" and is done quietly and reflectively by the individual rather than orally. In contrast to most group art therapy, in which other members are invited to respond to another member's artwork with their own associations, the OSP includes a "no comment rule" (http://www.patballen.com/pages/process.html). As developed by Allen and her colleagues, it is a powerful approach (http://www.openstudioproject.org).

Nevertheless, most art therapists do invite clients to respond to images in ways that require an oral dialogue with the therapist. Some begin with a phenomenological inquiry, such as that proposed by Mala Betensky (1995): "What do you see?" While helping the client to regard his art, to focus on looking in the fullest sense, the expectation is that what is seen will be described in words, and there is in fact a conversation that ensues, stimulated by viewing the product and reflecting on it.

Helping clients to reflect on and learn from either process or product seems to be the most difficult aspect of art therapy for the novice. Since most art therapists have a good deal of the artist in them, setting the stage and evoking and facilitating expression seem to come more naturally than looking at and talking about what has happened. Stepping back and reflecting verbally or nonverbally on either product or process is a new experience, not only for the clients but also for art therapists in training, and requires learning new skills and sensitivities. Since defenses are such powerful forces, even though they may be partially bypassed in art, most clients make it difficult for the interviewer to elicit really meaningful comments about their work. As with all of the other roles you play, an adjustment must always be made to the disability and functioning level of the individual.

It is especially tricky to find the right "language" with which to enable different people to talk about their art or the experience of making it. Creative interviewing is, like much in therapy, an ongoing trial-and-error process in which you need to be willing to encounter many blind alleys and frequently frustrating responses. The challenge is to maintain your enthusiasm and optimism, to continue trying hard to find a way that is comfortable and compatible, and to help every individual to reflect meaningfully on the art experience.

You need to be willing to try not only different verbal avenues but also different expressive modalities. Dramatization with or about the art product, for example, can be a way to help a person to associate when other approaches have failed. In a videotape of a diagnostic art interview I did many years ago, I see myself practically turning verbal somersaults while trying to get something meaningful in the way of associations out of a resistant girl of 10. I confess that it is mildly embarrassing to show the tape, and that I usually excuse myself by telling my audience that I was under pressure because of the many observers who were watching this demonstration interview.

But, the fact is that a child or adult like the one involved always requires more activity on your part to elicit significant responses. Just as it is most artistic to ask the fewest and most open-ended questions of a fluent, freely associating client, so it is equally artistic to move in with action and drama when encountering resistance. Perhaps it is analogous to the sculptor's task: to chisel and chop with vigor when that is required by the material but to sand and smooth with caution when working with another medium or at another stage of the process.

Lest you think I am comparing patients in art therapy to an artist's medium, to be molded or shaped according to the clinician's desires, let me restate the importance of each individual and his own authentic creative unfolding. So, perhaps a better analogy than sculptor would be gardener—providing the proper environment, nurturance, and care to enable the person to flower best in his or her own fashion.

This imagery can also be applied to the tasks of setting the stage and evoking and facilitating the client's artistic expression. It may be a bit more difficult to see its relationship to the task of helping someone to learn by looking at and talking about his art. But I believe that they are similar since the challenge of creative interviewing is to help the person to say what is truly on his mind, to bring out into the open what is inside of him, just as in the art process one hopes to evoke the individual's own personal imagery and help him to give it concrete form.

Discovering meanings in client art and behavior goes on throughout the art therapy session. Observing selections, avoidances, images, sequences, and so forth requires that you learn to "watch with the third eye." You need to observe, as closely as possible, the manner in which each individual proceeds and how he works. This includes *all* steps on the way to the final product. It also requires learning to "listen with the third ear" (Reik, 1948), especially to what may seem to be unrelated spontaneous verbalization during the working process. Nonverbal expression can also be eloquent, like the pleasure in a patient's face as he smashes a piece of clay with his fist. Sometimes, a person wants to describe or discuss the product or process while he is working. It is important then not only to be receptive but also to listen without intruding.

The really fascinating exploration of the product and the patient's responses to it, however, usually take place after the working time is over, during the reflecting part of the art therapy session. While looking and associating and discussing products can, of course, occur during the *doing* phase of a session, I believe that it is helpful to separate the two kinds of behaviors in time and, if appropriate, in space.

As noted in the chapter on setting the stage, creating a physical situation in which an individual or group members can look at the artwork with some aesthetic and perhaps psychic distance makes possible a deeper and more focused kind of learning from the experience. Placing the artwork in a location that minimizes the need for eye contact with the therapist (or other group members) can help greatly in reducing self-consciousness during the interviewing process. Whether the product is on the wall, an easel, the table, or even on the floor matters little. What is important is that all those involved be able to see it easily and that they can, if they so choose, look at the art rather than at each other.

From a visual perspective, it is important to set things up so that the art produced in a group or by an individual can be viewed clearly and coherently. Finding a location that is neither too close nor too far, as well as one that is central to the viewers, is of course essential. Another useful aid is some kind of "framing," whether temporary or permanent. This need not be elaborate and can easily be done by simply suggesting that the client find a piece of colored paper of the next larger size on which to mount the picture, choosing from among assorted hues the one that most appeals. Another possibility, less colorful but more professional in appearance, is to use a precut mat of the appropriate size, which immediately gives a rather finished look to the artist's creation. What is most important here is separating the art product clearly from other visual stimuli so that the client can really focus on it.

The same considerations are true for three-dimensional work as for that on a flat surface. Creating an attractive setting on which to display someone's sculpture can help immeasurably to enhance the viewing/reflecting/discussing part of the process. Sometimes the best "stand" is simply a piece of colored construction paper, setting the sculpture off from the table surface and the surrounding stimuli through shape and tone.

Sometimes greater separation is needed, so that a tray of a size and shape appropriate to the product is best, perhaps on a raised surface; a modeling stand draped with a piece of cloth, for example, makes an attractive and easily available sculpture mount. In some cases, it helps to present the three-dimensional work against a solid-color background, light or dark, like a wall or board covered with some color of paper. Putting a folded piece of construction paper at right angles to both wall and table at the point where they join makes a quick, attractive, and visually clear background for most work in clay, wire, or wood.

The next challenge, of course, is in how to invite reflection since a request to talk about the art may easily get no reaction or a negative one. Although you should always respect a client's right *not* to talk about his work, just as you should respect his right not to use art media, you can also try to encourage some reflection, just as you would attempt to stimulate some creative activity. The person might want to talk about someone else's picture if he is in a group, or he might prefer to reflect on the experience of using the medium rather than on the product. Either of these alternatives should be acceptable to you, and if they are okay with you, that will help him.

The message that should be given in the discussion portion of a session is similar to what needs to be sent when evoking expression: that you expect and feel confident that each individual has something to say (verbally or creatively), and that your job is to find a way to make it comfortable for him to say it. It probably does help if the initial request is simply to look, to take as much time as is needed, and to see what thoughts and ideas emerge. It also helps to leave the invitation to reflect as open ended as possible, so that different people can use the opportunity in the way most comfortable for them at any moment in time. Although you could suggest a specific focus on the process of creation, on the art elements, or on the representational messages, it seems more valid in this area (as in art expression) to allow the direction to come from the client if at all possible.

It is for this reason that the initial question or invitation should be as unstructured as seems feasible, leaving considerable leeway to the respondent, such as: "Would you please tell me [the group] about your picture [sculpture]?" Or, "Does that have a story to go with it?" For some highly verbal patients who want to share and who enjoy this kind of exhibitionism, an open invitation to talk may be enough to stimulate a veritable flood of descriptive or associative material.

The Creative Challenge for the Art Therapist

For most clients, however, more creativity is needed on the part of the interviewer to help them to clarify and extend the ideas inherent in or stimulated by their art. This is more difficult than it may sound since you have your own projective reactions to client art. So, you need to guard against asking questions in such a way that you intrude your ideas or in any way pressure the patient to agree or disagree with how you see the artwork. The individual may have a need to be compliant or oppositional or can respond relatively freely. In any case, the goal is to avoid any kind of implicit suggestion about the response on your part, which requires continual self-scrutiny as well as clear focus on the other.

The difficult but also pleasurable challenge, then, is to find ways to help people to talk about their artwork that are comfortable for them yet do not in any way influence what they are able to see in or say about their products. There are, fortunately, a number of specific questions you can ask that do not give the answer or even suggest it, but that do help clients to be more articulate about what they have made.

If the artwork is abstract, for example, you can ask if it *reminds* the artist of something or what it *looks like*. If there is still blocking, turning the picture or sculpture around so that it can be viewed from different perspectives may help to stimulate some additional projections. Sometimes covering a portion of the artwork helps a client to focus on one part and to deal with it more effectively. Indeed, such visual techniques should always supplement verbal ones throughout the evocation, facilitation, and discussion phases of an art therapy session.

If the artwork is representational but the content is still not clear to you, it is safest to be open about that and to ask for clarification. To guess incorrectly can be distressing to the client, who thought that the picture or sculpture looked like what he had in mind. While it may wound his narcissism to know that you cannot identify what he has made, it is probably less painful than if you thought it was something he never intended.

Not knowing all the time what a person means to say visually is really human, and in the long run admitting it is more helpful to a client than trying to be omniscient. This last quality, while often feared, is also desired by most patients. Most yearn for a therapist who not only knows it all but also is omnipotent, magically able to make their troubles go away. While people might wish that you could read their minds without them having to put things into words, that is also a pretty frightening thought. Confessing that you sometimes do not understand a picture, just as you sometimes cannot understand what a person is trying to say in words, is really helpful to the client, who needs not only to see you as less than perfect but also to be able to accept his own limitations. Indeed, it is usually more of a relief than a letdown for most clients to see a therapist's feet of clay.

Once you have some idea of what is represented in or projected onto the artwork, you can try to engage the client in the potentially pleasurable activity of getting ideas from what he has made, taking yet another creative journey with guidance and support. Ideally, interviewing someone about his artwork is an adventure for both clinician and client, a voyage through associations and ideas that often leads to unexpected realms.

When trying to involve someone in this process, you ought to give it validity by justifying its usefulness and relevance to treatment, just as you should be able to justify using art materials in therapy, especially with a reluctant or resistant individual. I feel comfortable telling anyone of any age that talking about art is an interesting way to find out more about themselves, and that it is also fascinating since the thoughts can lead in so many unanticipated directions.

Whether you stress the creativity involved or the importance of understanding symbolic communication will depend on the person's age and anxiety level. It is never appropriate to be dishonest, to pretend that the story a client tells is *not* related to him, for example. But, it is equally important to meet him where he *is,* which may mean respecting a good deal of disguise and distancing in his art or in his spontaneous associations to it.

Creative Interviewing

The most useful initial questions, as noted, are open ended, allowing maximum leeway to the interviewee. However, it is also true that these often elicit either no response or a minimal one, so that you are then challenged to use your creative resources without influencing the client's ideas. If there is a constant self-monitoring process going on, the risk of intruding your own projections is minimized, and you are then free to explore different associative avenues.

What probably matters more than anything else in this endeavor is being both optimistic and persistent. This combination of attitudes, if held sincerely, works as well for the interviewing activity as it does for the creative one. If you approach the discussion with the expectation that everyone has something to say about the product, the process, or both, you will be able to work hard to find a way for each person to do so. If you do not get discouraged by blind alleys or dead ends, you will continue to explore new avenues of discourse—to find a workable "wavelength" for any particular client at any moment in time.

Of course, you may sometimes have to give up. But, it is my honest impression that many clinicians give up far too often and far too easily during the interviewing process, much more than they do in regard to the creative activity itself. Perhaps it is because they are more comfortable with art than with words. Perhaps it is because they see their primary task as the provision of a creative experience, with reflection as secondary and optional.

My own conviction is that it is the *combination* of doing and reflecting that gives art therapy its special potency … that we do really engage both hemispheres of the brain in the expressing and thinking aspects of treatment, thereby enabling integration and synthesis. Moreover, we not only encourage the ego to use its full capacities to select, organize, and synthesize in the creative process itself but also promote the development of its observational skill (observing ego) in the looking-at and reflecting process involved in viewing and discussing the art.

Having emphasized optimism and persistence, I should like to add creativity to the list of qualities necessary for the art therapist as interviewer. There are many possible ways to elicit projective ideas through art, limited only by your ingenuity and the client's resistance. For example, if a piece of artwork represents a scene of any sort, a question about what is *happening* there or where the person would *be* if he were in that place can lead to rich associations. Or, if there is a representation of a living creature, you might ask what the character would say if it could talk, eliciting either telling about it or actual role-taking. It is even possible to suggest that inanimate objects might talk and to ask what they would say if they could speak.

It is also useful at times to suggest that the client imagine something moving or changing in the picture and ask how it would then be, for example, if the person came out of the house or if we could see inside. A broader question of a similar nature involves what happened just before the depicted or described scene or what is likely to happen next. A person can also be invited to say the first word that comes into his head as he looks at different components of a work of art, perhaps with the therapist pointing to one at a time (the "pop-into-your-head game" approach to free association). Or he can be asked what he is reminded of or is made to think about by a particular shape, color, or object.

If talking *about* something seems too threatening, it is often the case that talking *for* it is less so; this is especially true with children, who frequently prefer talking *as* a character to telling *about* it, taking the role of a creature they have made with abandon and expressiveness. For those who have exhibitionistic tendencies (true of most who are not inhibited in this area), making a radio or television "show" out of the interviewing process can be most useful, with a paintbrush or other suitable object as the microphone, and an invitation to the "artist of the week" to tell the listening/viewing audience about what he has done or made.

Another approach to interviewing the reluctant client is to offer a choice between logical alternatives, which enables the person to further clarify and elaborate his ideas. For example, if someone has drawn a human being and responds with the statement that "It's just a person," you can ask what gender, what age (or age group), and what the person is doing or thinking. It is then more natural to ask questions about how the person (now defined by age, gender, and activity) is feeling, where he is going to or coming from, what he might be thinking, or what he would say if he could talk.

The more articulated the fantasy, the easier it is to follow it and for the individual to further elaborate it. Again, the tricky part here is not to impose or suggest your own ideas but to ask the kind of characterizing questions that help someone to create his own story and to always follow his lead as closely as possible.

Other adjuncts to successful interviewing are such props as real microphones and tape recorders, with the possibility of listening to yourself (and to others in a group) and reflecting at yet another level on the event. For many years, I had in my art therapy space a Dictaphone with both built-in and handheld microphones, either of which could be used for recording interviews about art. An especially useful feature was the playback, which could be private if set on low in the mike and held to an ear, or on the speaker playback, for which I could vary not only the volume but also the tone and the speed.

Even without such fancy gadgetry, I found, especially with children and some adults, that a portable tape recorder, with a microphone they could hold while they spoke, could enable a much more fluent description of the product and of associations than seemed possible without such an aid.

Some, on the other hand, find it easier to *write* than to talk out loud. Indeed, *titles* are probably the simplest kind of initial association or reflection on a creative product. They are also rather easy for most clients to produce, especially if you are supportive of artistic titles that do not have to make a lot of sense, but that come into someone's head as he regards his artwork. If the person can say it but cannot write it himself, that becomes the job of the therapist, parent, aide, or another client—whoever seems clinically most appropriate.

Poetry, which can be free flowing and unrhymed, is another way to elicit verbal associations of a nondiscursive nature. Like a title, poems can be written down or dictated. Another approach is to simply encourage clients to write—on the artwork itself or on another piece of paper—words that seem to them to go with or describe the art, the process of doing it, or the product itself.

Stories are probably the most elaborate kinds of verbal associations of a literary sort and are congenial for people of all ages. Group storytelling, perhaps of the round-robin variety, is easily stimulated by art produced by one or more members and can be playful as well as productive.

With children, puppets or miniature life toys come in handy and can even be used with some adults who are either intellectually childlike or comfortable being playful. The puppet or small figure of a person or animal can become the interviewer and is sometimes much easier for the client to answer than the more threatening therapist. Or the dramatic play prop (puppet or figure) can be the one who answers the questions, posed by either another such character or the therapist.

One little boy and I did a good deal of work during a resistant period in his analysis by using an owl puppet, who was quite willing to answer questions about his artwork and other topics when he himself was not. This same owl was also able to pose useful questions to me and to other puppets about the boy's symbolic productions, which reflected his concerns in yet another way.

There are countless ways to evoke people's associations to their artwork, limited only by the imagination of the interviewer. This is a similar situation to that which exists regarding activities, which are also probably infinite and require the spontaneous ingenuity of the individual art therapist. It may be that many art therapists do not trust their own creativity—their capacity to either design a relevant activity or to evoke meaningful comments. Given the necessary knowledge and understanding, however, and a substantial amount of flexibility and creative thinking, you can be as good a facilitator of verbal expression as you are of visual expression.

With both, you need to be careful to always maintain your focus on the patient, your primary task being to bring out what is already inside of or potential in that person. Even if you also see your job as adding to or filling in (e.g., building structure or making up for deficits), your actions should still be undertaken in the service of what seems to be the most legitimate aim of art therapy: the development of the creative power and self-control of the individual client.

To be a good interviewer, I think it helps to be something of a chameleon. This does not mean that you ought to imitate or mimic the person with whom you are conversing; it is not helpful to lose your own identity in that of another. Rather, to get on a workable "wavelength" with another human being, you always have to feel your way and even take on some of the coloration of his communicative mode. You may be unconsciously echoing the rhythm of a client's speech, mirroring his body language, using some of his more colorful vocabulary, or in some other way trying to be sure that you are both hearing and being heard.

This is vital because only when the client feels heard can he begin to feel understood. Many bright clinicians, who in fact comprehend what a person is trying to tell them, fail in communicating that understanding. The individual in turn does not feel that his message has been received, let alone understood, because the therapist's language and mode are so incomprehensible to him.

Such chameleon-like activity on the part of the therapist is part of a total attempt to empathize with the patient. You need to be comfortable enough with yourself to do this, to let go of your usual controls and even some of your characteristic style, to make real contact in verbal communication with another person who may be very different from you.

Fortunately, the discussion phase of any art therapy session is preceded by the evoking and facilitating of expression, both of which entail much nonverbal, and probably some verbal, interaction between you and the client. By the time you start to talk formally about product and process, you have already established some sense of each other and it is hoped found some workable ways to communicate. Making sure that you touch base with each person in an art therapy group, therefore, whether with eyes, hands, or words, is probably closely related to your eventual success in evoking a spirited and lively discussion among all of the members.

One of the biggest questions on any interviewing art therapist's mind is whether to try to relate any of what the client is saying about his art to him as a person. Sometimes the answer is provided by the person, who spontaneously remarks on how a drawing or sculpture reminds him of something in his own life or how his way of reacting to the disappointment he feels about his product is typical of him.

But more often than not, the painting or sculpture is discussed on its own terms, as a separate object, which is actually one of the great assets of art in therapy. The art product becomes an intermediary object, perhaps transitional at times. It is always a concrete something, with meaning to both therapist and client, on which each can focus in both the doing and discussing phases of a session. The difficult part for many therapists lies in the question of making a bridge or connection between the art and the patient's reality.

One simple rule, which makes good psychological sense to me, is to stay at the metaphoric level for as long as possible in discussing any particular product. It is best to stay with the disguise in the imagery and associations, to talk about what is in or projected onto the artwork, and to go as far as you can at a symbolic level. This is true because the more disguised the images, the more the patient will be able to safely and comfortably reveal. Only after you have, in a sense, "milked" the imagery, via storytelling or associations, does it seem sensible to explore in any kind of open fashion the possibility that it might represent something related to the client.

As soon as a person becomes aware that he is talking about himself through his art imagery, he naturally becomes more self-conscious and is only able to reveal that which is currently tolerable to his ego. You may, of course, introduce the notion that there might be some connection, as in asking whether he sees any relationship between what he has said about his art and himself. If his response is negative, that is usually a clear signal that he is not yet ready to see the connection, and the best therapeutic response is to gracefully withdraw. On the other hand, the question may evoke a positive or quizzical reaction, in which case you are invited to pursue the notion, always asking questions in an open-ended way that allows the client to be in control, take the lead, and be in charge.

Just as art therapists sometimes seem unnecessarily timid when pursuing the asking of creative questions about someone's art, so they can also seem unnecessarily intrusive when they finally get into the interviewing mode. This may be due partly to a certain naïveté about defenses, which are very "real" psychic phenomena. Frequently, what a person has said about his symbolic creation is so blatantly revealing to the art therapist that it seems inconceivable that the client really did not know that he was talking about himself.

But that, after all, is what symbolization is all about, A true symbol, in most depth psychologies, expresses in a disguised form an impulse that is not known by the artist. Its adaptive (defensive) power derives, in large part, from the fact that the forbidden or ineffable ideas it represents remain unconscious to the artist (Jones, 1916; Petocz, 1999).

This kind of symbolism is, of course, quite different from the patient's conscious labeling of colors, forms, or representations as standing for some person or feeling. I am not suggesting, by the way, that such deliberate use of the symbolizing properties of art is invalid. I simply wish to remind you that, with the exception of someone in the acute phase of psychosis and incapable of repression, for most people those kinds of conscious connections are different from the deeper meanings that remain less available to awareness. What can be elicited through interviewing and brought to consciousness are only those thoughts, ideas, and feelings that are "preconscious"—not fully repressed, but not necessarily in awareness at all times.

If you understand enough about symbolization and the workings of the wide range of possible defense mechanisms, a good background in development and dynamics can enable you to hypothesize the unconscious messages disguised in client art, just as an experienced analyst can often guess correctly the concealed meanings of a person's dream imagery. With both, despite the reality of certain so-called universal symbols, whose likely significance may be hypothesized within a fairly narrow range of possibilities, it is essential to look at the individual's own associations to obtain any kind of valid understanding of the imagery.

Even if it turns out that your initial guess about meaning was correct, you should not assume that any image "always" means something specific, or that its significance is the same over time for any particular patient. Because of such unconscious defense mechanisms as reversal, condensation, displacement, and symbolization, visual imagery is usually multiply determined, like other mental products. This very richness and multileveled quality of visual imagery is part of what gives art therapy its potency, and it is something you must keep in mind, especially when you feel some pressure to find a nice, simple translation of meaning.

This multifaceted nature of visual symbols can also be taught to clients, some of whom learn to enjoy with you the mental game of generating a variety of associations and attempting to make sense out of them. This leads me to think of "interpretation," something misunderstood by many art therapists in concept as well as in their work with patients. One reason for the confusion is that there are at least two important meanings of this term, which are not identical but are related. One is more narrow, confined to the art product, and has to do with interpreting the meaning of his *art* to the patient. The other is broader and includes any statement of an explanatory nature regarding patient dynamics, which ideally includes some genetic (historical) component as well.

Even in psychoanalysis, in which interpretation is considered a primary therapeutic tool, it is used rarely. Most of the analyst's comments are of a preparatory nature, such as "running commentary" or a "restatement" in a clarifying fashion of what the patient has said. Similarly, in a client or person-centered model, "reflection" to the patient includes making explicit those feelings or attitudes that have been implied but not stated. And, if one feels that what the person needs at a particular moment is support, then such statements are also appropriate and are common in art therapy when you are reinforcing the patient's creative behavior or art product.

But none of these are "interpretations," which in insight-oriented therapy usually include explanation, not simply translation. In well-conducted analytic psychotherapy or psychoanalysis, such interpretations are not made until the analyst is quite sure that the patient is ready to accept them. Most clinicians offer interpretive statements as possibilities, sometimes as probabilities, but rarely as certainties. They usually invite the patient to consider the connections suggested but never insist that they are correct without some confirmation from the patient.

Unfortunately, defenses being what they are, confirmation is rarely a simple, calm affirmation; and negation is not necessarily an indication that the interpretation was wrong. The only valid index, which makes as much sense in art therapy as in psychoanalysis, is to be found in the subsequent material—in that session and in later ones. If it reveals a clarifying of the conflict or a loosening of defenses, then you can be pretty sure that you are moving in the right direction, no matter what the client says. Of course, in art therapy, the subsequent material includes the art as well as the verbal behavior, which is often less disguised and more rapidly revealing of the person's unconscious response to what has been suggested.

Your verbal interventions during the discussion of art products and processes are perhaps more loaded for clients than those that occur during the evoking and facilitating phases of the work. Words, after all, are still the common currency of communication, and people tend to respond strongly to them. This is especially true when you are talking about a client's creation, which is felt as an extension and often a part of himself.

Because of this narcissistic aspect of everyone's art, it is especially important to be acutely attuned to potential sensitivities when discussing client products. So in addition to being creative and persistent in the pursuit of associations and being clear about how and when to help someone to discover the meaning for him of his own art, you also need to be tactful.

Such tact is essential in all facets of art therapy, but the lack of it is more visible and perhaps more toxic during the discussion phase of a session. Getting anyone to receive any kind of message requires putting it into a form that is both comprehensible and acceptable to the other person. If it is also relatively more appealing and relatively less threatening, then it is much more likely to be heard and considered.

It is a little like extracting a splinter. It is best done carefully and gently, thereby causing minimal pain and maximizing the likelihood that the wound will heal safely and well. Whether you consider this to be "sugarcoating the pill," overcoming resistance (which is inevitable), or simply doing your therapist job as artistically as your artist job, I should like to put in a strong plea for artistry in art therapy, which is the subject of the next chapter.

References

Allen, P. B. (1995). *Art is a way of knowing.* Boston: Shambhala.

Allen, P. B. (2005). *Art is a spiritual path.* Boston: Shambhala.

Betensky, M. G. (1995). *What do you see?* London: Jessica Kingsley.

Chodorow, J. (1997). (Ed.) *Jung on active imagination.* London: Routledge.

Fay, C. G. (1994) *At the threshold.* Houston, TX: C.G. Jung Educational Center.

Jones, E. (1916). The theory of symbolism. In *Papers on psycho-analysis* (5th ed.) (1948). Baltimore: Williams & Wilkins.

McNiff, S. (2004). *Art heals.* Boston: Shambhala.

Petocz, A. (1999). *Freud, psychoanalysis and symbolism.* Cambridge, U.K.: Cambridge University Press.

Reik, T. *Listening with the third ear.* New York: Farrar, Straus, 1948.

The art therapist helps the group to discuss their individual creations thoughtfully and respectfully, learning from their own work as well as from their responses to the work of others.

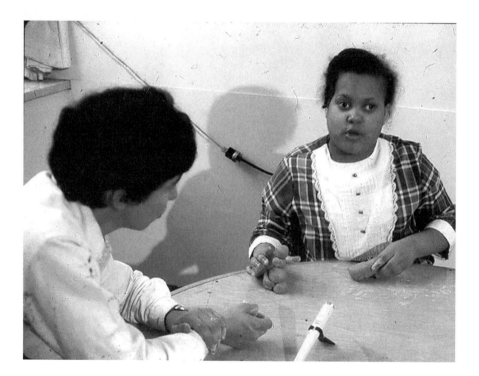

When this girl talks about her tired, angry clay "horsie," the art therapist understands that she is also talking about herself.

CHAPTER 12

Working Artistically

Introduction

Although I thought of this book originally as describing the *art* of art therapy, what also became apparent during the writing was the need for *artistry* in doing your work. While this may seem to be a fine distinction, it is an important one because it is possible to master the art of many things, such as piano playing, gourmet cooking, crewel embroidery, and to do them well (i.e., skillfully or competently). But, to do them in such a way that people sigh when they hear your sonatas, eat your mousse, or view your wall hangings requires something above and beyond mastery of the art form itself—something best identified as artistry.

You might argue that outstanding performance in any area is usually attributed to the possession of special gifts or talents. It may well be true that there are natural clinicians, individuals who already have so many of the personal prerequisites for successful work as therapists that they seem to develop the necessary skills effortlessly. However, such natural capacities (like warmth, empathy, sensitivity, and intelligence) are limited in value if they are not harnessed to therapeutic work that is also well understood. That is, such personal qualities are worth less than they might be if you do not also possess the necessary understandings about both art and therapy outlined so far. When such knowledge is integrated and used by someone who takes to the work with comfort and pleasure, then there is the possibility of true artistry.

There can never be a good reason to be careless or sloppy in your work as an art therapist. There is no excuse for being heavy-handed, with the possible exception of lack of experience. What is impressive about art therapy, however, is that, even when it is done in an awkward, clumsy fashion, it is still a potent diagnostic and therapeutic modality. This is most apparent when students in training begin their supervised work. One can only imagine what is ultimately possible when the powerful tool of art in therapy is handled with the utmost exquisite and knowledgeable care.

Perhaps even more important, as an artist turned therapist, I have found that I have gotten great pleasure out of doing my work creatively, even though it has been people who are my concern rather than products. Whatever satisfactions accompany the creative process in other realms must also attend when doing creative work in human services. I have derived satisfaction not only from seeing people get better but also from the aesthetic pleasure of trying to help them do that in an artistic and inventive way.

Maybe it is the artist in me, after all, that prompted the writing of this book. Perhaps the question ought not to be, as one of my favorite colleagues posed it years ago, "Are you an artist *or* a therapist?" (Ault, 1977). Rather, it should be, "Are you an artist *and* a therapist?" Or, better yet, "Are you an artist *as* a therapist?"

It seems to me increasingly clear that good therapy, especially through art, is always a creative adventure. That is probably why, although I have sometimes been bored by teaching or lecturing or even supervision (which is also a change and growth process), I have never gotten bored with art therapy—and I have been doing it for almost five decades. The creative challenge of the work, the puzzle of each new client, and the delicate task of figuring out how to help each person move toward better adjustment—all of these have been unpredictable, stimulating, and endlessly fascinating.

In all, through the people, their problems, and the therapeutic process, I have felt as if I were continually learning and discovering something new. Despite the universality of certain human problems and of some artistic symbols, the variety in people and their imagery is endless. The particular twists and turns of any therapeutic journey have been sufficiently unpredictable and unique that it has almost always been fascinating, whether I ended up feeling successful or frustrated.

Of course, I know that I also have gotten satisfaction for a variety of personal reasons from many aspects of the work, from "rescuing" others, to "peeking" at their secrets, to the occasional feelings of heightened aliveness that can occur in art therapy. Needless to say, there are also the less-attractive aspects of the work, like carrying heavy supplies, cleaning up sloppy messes, or being on the receiving end of a violently negative transference that expresses itself in a particularly irritating way. As I got older, I found that the high energy level and occasional destructiveness of younger children was more often distressing and less often delightful, and that someone who refused to engage with media or me could strain my patience, especially if I were fatigued or upset.

But, despite the many intrinsic frustrations of doing art therapy with disturbed people, it has generally been such fascinating fun that I actually looked forward to each day of work and frequently felt a sense of excitement while I was with a patient, usually in response to an aesthetic achievement or some other long-awaited sign of progress. I hope that is true for every art therapist. I suspect that it must be so since the work is so physically and psychologically demanding that you would need to derive some ongoing satisfactions to stay with it. This is especially true since the financial rewards are rarely substantial, and most art therapists get much more significant reinforcement from their work than from their paychecks. I have suggested here that one reason it can be so gratifying is that doing art therapy can be experienced as a creative venture, one that can be carried out more or less artistically.

I submit, although without any hope of ever being able to control the variables involved sufficiently to prove it, that the client's ability to grow through art therapy is directly proportional to the artistry of the therapist. And, whatever the limits on the person's potential growth, the more knowledgeable you are, the more artistic you can be.

In work with clients of all ages and in all settings, art therapists use what they know about art and therapy to help people to prevent or to overcome mental pain. If they can use that knowledge in a well-synthesized way, then they have mastered the *interface*—the area where art and therapy meet. If that well-synthesized and fully integrated knowledge is then utilized in an *artistic* way, they are much more likely to be effective than if they are heavy-handed or careless in style or manner of work.

The difficult question of how and when to intervene requires a kind of continuous tracking, a constant alertness on the part of the art therapist, who tries to stay "tuned in" (i.e., attuned) to the individual, family, or group as empathically as possible. On the basis of such observations, you sometimes get the feeling that it would be good to intervene in some way, verbally or nonverbally, but deciding exactly when and precisely how is not easy. Indeed, it seems to me to be the most challenging aspect of doing any kind of therapy, including art therapy.

The decision about whether to move in is probably made largely on the basis of cognitive awareness (that is, some understanding of the vicissitudes of the therapeutic/creative process in relation to the client's needs). But the *how* (the form the intervention takes), the *when* (the precise timing and tempo), and the *style* (the specific manner of action or words involved), these are as much artistic decisions as clinical ones. Unless they fit comfortably or aesthetically into the client's space at that moment, they will not be effective. Even if uncomfortable, as is true with most confrontations, how and when they are made have a great deal to do with the nature of the person's response.

The Relationship to Other Art Forms

It may help, for a moment, to think of the relevance of other art forms to the issues involved in the questions of timing and mode of an art therapist-initiated intervention. The tracking referred to is largely visual; it requires looking at not only details (e.g., facial expressions or hand movements) but also the larger picture, continually shifting lenses like a photographer from close-up to telephoto, especially with a group. It is something like being present at the performance of a symphony, an opera, a play, or a dance recital.

Your gaze constantly shifts from particular parts to the whole, just as your overall sensory consciousness includes not only the visual input but also the sounds, the words, and the movements of bodies in space. What is different about a therapy group is that it is more like a chamber music concert in your living room because of your closeness to what is observed. It can also feel sometimes as if you are the conductor of such a performance, constantly alert to each player's music as well as to the sound of the ensemble, offering leadership, guidance, and support for the efforts of both individuals and the group.

One must not stretch these analogies too far. A therapist does not, except in the most structured kind of clinical work or necessary limit-setting, need to use the kind of authoritarian control required of a conductor. But a listening, watching, feeling art therapist *is* aware of the music between herself and an individual, as well as the vibrations between members of a family or a group. She can sense whether things are synchronous or dyssynchronous and might even try to help people to harmonize at times, especially with those who need to learn socialization.

She might wish at times to echo a patient, at others to blend, and at others to work together in a related but more differentiated way, as in counterpoint. She might even see it as useful to the patient to present herself as very different, in a dissonant way, as in some contemporary music. Similarly, she might want to get into the patient's rhythm, to respond to it, or to change to a different one that challenges and confronts.

More often, the therapist is the interpreter of the patient's music (often as yet unwritten)—his internal strivings toward actualization, and the tensions and dissonances that must be lived through to reach a harmonious finale. The process of therapy can also be seen as similar to a symphony, with a series of fairly separate movements or phases, yet a common underlying set of themes, often repeated in various guises, and a central unifying motif or key.

As with symphonic movements, it is best if each aspect of the client or stage of the process can be permitted its full development, possible only when there is no time limit on the treatment. With ample time, the full range of each musical idea (conflict or part of the personality) can be explored, developed, and allowed to come to a natural denouement in the course of the overall work. The finale, of course, may include a replay of earlier themes and may be stormy as well as calm; endings in music usually involve both crescendos and decrescendos, just like terminations in art therapy.

The treatment process is largely one of improvisation, as opposed to a scripted or fully composed score or drama. As in all improvisational work—in music (jazz), drama (street theater), or art (free painting)—the artist/therapist's job is, like that of a director, to help people give form to whatever emerges.

With an individual, your energy can go into facilitating the form-finding and refining processes. With a group, some energy is also needed to help people to stay in some coherent aesthetic relationship to one another. Whether this seems geometrically organized like a Mondrian or fluidly ordered like a Pollock is not important. What does matter is that the participants experience the organizing principle involved as something present, constant, and integrating for them individually as well.

Since the art should be the patient's own, the therapist needs to be the kind of teacher who helps a musician to fully develop a personal style of interpretation, even though the composition may come from another. Similarly, a group or family art therapist often feels like the choreographer of those in the room, although in a much more subtle and responsive way than is usually thought of in regard to that role.

She responds to the hints of movement in the patients; she helps each to carry them further and to shape them in whatever direction seems artistically and psychologically right for each person at that moment. When the art therapist puts connections into words through interpretations, they are meant to clarify and to explain, much as a ballet master might do with a dancer. As with any art form, such thoughtful connection making is also a way of giving relevant emphasis to important components and creating an overall sense of order out of something that was previously confusing.

The ideas of aesthetician Suzanne Langer (1953) are most congenial to art therapists. She proposed that the arts are tangible forms of human feeling, which is often inexpressible in words. The art therapist helps the patient not only to capture and express feeling through art but also to feel in touch and in charge through nonverbal behavior (smiling, crying, frowning) as well as words.

Words that name significant ideas are like artistic forms—they relieve tension because they provide an externalization that is concrete and discrete. And, like more complex verbal constructions or visual creations, words provide containers for all of the complex feelings, thoughts, and images they are trying to convey. When you can use *both words and art* to help clients with the task of expressing and containing their feelings, you are then better able to assist them in channeling their life energy into a coherent and satisfying existence.

Drama is an art form that involves words much more than art, music, or dance. I often find myself thinking of a therapy session itself as a dramatic event or of a course of psychotherapy through art as a kind of drama. However, the visual arts, which are static, cannot capture (except in a series of sequential images) the feeling of development over time that is so well represented in drama. Thus, the unfolding of the therapeutic drama of any person or group is like what happens in a play, beginning when areas of conflict and concern are laid out, followed by the heightening of tension and the working through of conflict, ending with the denouement and resolution of the plot. In the process, the tension builds, often leading to one or more climactic moments.

In any art form and in any therapy, it may take some time to express, to clarify, and to focus on those major themes. Only after that has been done is it possible to work toward either elaboration or development, and only after those have been accomplished is it possible to work toward climax and resolution.

In the moment-to-moment interchange of a therapeutic encounter, you are also engaged in a kind of dance with the client. This is especially visible in individual therapy but is also present in groups at a more complex level. In the therapeutic dance, the challenge is to engage with the person when necessary and appropriate—for instance, when it is clear to you, although not always to the client, that he could use some help with the art process, or when you want the client to see or consider another way of thinking about his symbolism.

On the other hand, you also need to know when it is best to disengage, to give a client the kind of space and freedom necessary for him to truly develop his own step, rhythm, and form (work of art). The necessary total disengagement at the end of each session is difficult for many clients, especially as the transference develops. Some need more help to connect, and others require more assistance to disconnect. But in either case, one thing that facilitates the differentiation (separation) process is the art therapist's role as critic.

Like the person who writes art, drama, film, and music reviews for the newspaper, the clinician uses her expertise with art therapy to help people learn what to look *for* and what to look *at*. She also helps them to gain a sense of perspective, to step back and look at the painting or performance in a larger context, just as she helps each person to look at his art and himself in therapy, in the matrix of his entire life space. Just as a good critic educates the public by showing connections between the art of the past and that of the present, so a good art therapist helps clients to see relationships between the immediate past and the present (e.g., what they have been drawing or painting over the course of the preceding days or months of treatment). Perhaps even more important, she helps them to see connections between their art in the present and what happened in their personal, social, cultural past since their art and associations so often refer to issues or memories from earlier periods in their lives.

The Role of Insight in Art Therapy

This chronological, historical, genetic framework is as useful to clients as psychodynamic or learning constructs. All three perspectives are important, and synthesizing them is ultimately necessary for the fullest understanding by both therapist and patient. I am, however, skeptical about the value of insight for many patients, especially when conceived of in too limited a fashion, as a linear, verbal, explanatory kind of "knowing."

I am convinced that therapeutic change has a strong experiential component that also involves a kind of learning, which does not get verbalized or explained but is most powerful when felt genuinely and strongly. If the client is able to further grasp and comprehend the art therapy experience through language that explains (e.g., insight), he can achieve an even greater sense of control.

But insight is not possible or essential for many clients, and if it is overemphasized as a goal in treatment, that in itself can detract from the power of direct experience. Insight alone is too intellectual; like *knowing* about art and therapy without *believing* or *being*, it is flat and one dimensional. This is another reason why I think art therapy is so powerful. It combines a deeply involving experience with a distancing, organizing perspective. Through both vision and words, the looking at, considering, capturing, and comprehending of the experience become possible ... a true "in-sight" ("seeing in").

Rudolf Arnheim (1982) once suggested that man and art view the world either from the center (like a bull's-eye) or from a distance (like a grid). In the doing part of art therapy, patients do not talk *about* feelings or relationships from a distance (the grid), but they get *into* them and feel them, as if at the center of a target or a whirlpool. In the reflecting part, there is the possibility of both distance and perspective.

The availability of both kinds of experience in art therapy, as part of the total composition or script, provides a multidimensional kind of "knowing" for a client. When the distant view of cognition can be integrated with the close-up of affect, the person is able to gain a genuine and full understanding of what goes on inside himself and in relation to others.

I believe that it is the presence of both components, the involvement and the reflection, that makes for maximally useful art therapy. Thus, it is not the catharsis alone that is valuable, but the experience of strong affect in a controlled context that makes it safe, bearable, acceptable, and knowable. And, it is not insight alone that is curative, but "seeing-in" after "being-in," understanding and grasping (feeling, owning, controlling) previously feared impulses, ideas, fantasies. There are times when such a perspective can be attained with few or no words, but with the kind of reflective distance and consideration of process and product described.

When sublimation is successful, it must partake of intense involvement, as well as the taming and forming required to make the product attractive to self and others. The act of containing forbidden impulses and ideas in an aesthetic form may provide a sense of mastery, similar to the more intellectual act of understanding what is hidden in the art. Sublimation is a most useful defensive/adaptive mechanism for otherwise unacceptable impulses, permitting as it does both gratification and disguise in symbolic form. I am uncertain whether the capture of such wishes on paper or canvas is as clinically useful as knowing about and accepting them in full consciousness. Some studies suggest that neurosis interferes with the creative process, which requires conflict-free energy for its work, while others insist that it is conflict or tension that must fuel creative activity. As with most observations about man and the arts, there is probably truth in both positions.

What does seem true is that some people improve in their mental health following involvement in creative activity with minimal reflection, so that the healing element probably is sublimation or some other aspect of the creative act itself. On the other hand, it is also true that for many people genuine creative involvement seems difficult or impossible to achieve. And for others, despite such involvement, the art process provides only a temporary respite from crippling tensions and feelings of despair.

Yet, many of these people can achieve significant psychological growth through an art therapy in which as much attention is given to the reflective as to the productive components of making art. Their reflection is not always on the level of awareness that many would call "insight," yet there is usually some degree of understanding more and of getting a better perspective on themselves through looking. It is my impression that, if linked closely in time with the doing and feeling part, this component of art therapy is a richly fruitful area, requiring knowledge and artistry to reach its fullest potential.

I believe this to be true for all aspects and phases of art therapy with any client, in any setting, and at any time. The more artistic you are about the way you apply what you know about art and therapy, the more effective you are likely to be. One sign of such artistry is in your ability to really follow the client, whether it be "feeling with" his creative activity or staying with the "red thread" of the key themes that he is expressing, usually in a variety of ways.

There is a constant tension throughout any session between following the lead of the client and deciding whether, when, and how to intervene. In truth, there are always multiple leads, verbal and nonverbal, symbolic and direct, and the challenge of selecting which to follow is best met through being deeply knowledgeable about both art and therapy. To intervene in a way that is most effective is to do so artistically, as if you were an experienced conductor or director.

In choosing which of the many possible directions to follow, a therapist needs to select one that seems both critical to the person's problems *and* most accessible at that moment in time. Any artwork, for example, contains imagery with both manifest and latent meanings. While the manifest content may be a disguise, it is but a partial one, so there is always something to be learned from its consideration. And, in terms of accessibility, you can always be sure that it is more acceptable to the patient's ego since it was actually represented.

You cannot intervene effectively, however, if a client is not ready to deal with an issue. Even if he seems ready, critical areas are likely to be tender or sore, and the more delicately and artistically you work, the more likely the person is to be able to see and hear what you have to convey. The skill (the *art* of art therapy) lies primarily in knowing enough about your work (art *and* therapy) to be able to make clinically appropriate decisions most of the time. The *artistry*, which goes beyond mere competence, lies in being able to implement those decisions in a way that works clinically, just as a brilliant interpretation of a sonata works musically.

So, I should like to put in an invitation—no, a plea—for greater attention to *artistry* in art therapy. While some of the human talents involved may seem natural and inborn, they are latent in most people and capable of development in a facilitating supervisory relationship. I also think that many clinicians who are vaguely aware may improve by simply monitoring themselves in regard to the artistry of their work.

As the artistry in your art therapy grows, you will experience increasing positive reinforcement in your clinical work—from clients, from their families, and from your colleagues. As someone once said, "Nothing succeeds like success." The reinforcement derived from doing artistic clinical work is itself highly motivating, serving as intrinsic gratification, as well as a stimulus for external rewards.

As with creating a beautiful painting, doing effective art therapy can be gratifying in and of itself. Like painting, the work is often slow, frustrating, difficult, painful, and boring, and it is also at times stimulating, pleasurable, and exciting. Both experiences can be immensely rewarding in an infinite variety of ways, and in both it is always true that the more artistic, the better.

References

Arnheim, R. (1982). *The power of the center*. Berkeley: University of California Press.

Ault, R. (1977). Are you an artist or a therapist? A professional dilemma of art therapists. In R. H. Shoemaker & S. E. Gonick-Barris (Eds.), *Creativity and the art therapist's identity* (pp. 53–56). Baltimore: American Art Therapy Association.

Langer, S. K. (1953). *Feeling and form*. New York: Scribner's.

Recommended Readings

Robertson, S. (1963). *Rosegarden and labyrinth.* London: Routledge & Kegan Paul.

Rogers, N. (1993). *The creative connection.* Palo Alto, CA: Science & Behavior Books.

Winnicott, D. W. (1971). *Therapeutic consultations in child psychiatry.* New York: Basic Books.

Rubin, J. A. (2005). *Artful therapy.* New York: Wiley.

Winnicott, D. W., Winnicott, C., Shepherd, R., & David, M. (Eds.). (1989). *Psycho-analytic explorations.* Cambridge, MA: Harvard University Press.

An art therapist helps two blind children to enjoy creating and to share that pleasure with each other as well as with her.

Art therapy with disabled populations often requires adaptations. This girl with spina bifida must lie prone in her crib, but she can make a collage when the art therapist puts the materials in a bowl in front of her.

PART 4

Applications

The first three parts of this book are concerned with the basics underlying the art of art therapy: the art part, the therapy part, and the interface where the two come together in the actual clinical work. This section deals with the *application* of these basics to the doing of art therapy in different contexts. Although this book is not the place for detailed examples of work in art therapy, either direct or indirect, it seems important to include some of the key issues involved when using art therapy with different *populations*, in different *settings*, and in different *modes*.

Happily, art therapy can be used with almost all sorts of people needing help, although its potential and direction will naturally differ with diverse groups. Issues to consider when dealing with people at different levels of development, with different types of psychopathology, and with different kinds of disabilities are noted, as well as particular problems related to art therapy.

Settings, the subject matter of the second chapter in this section, include all kinds, for there, too, art therapy is adaptable. It is now used in almost every sort of human service institution imaginable, but although it has moved more into the community than when the first edition of this book was written, it is still used most often in hospitals, clinics, rehabilitation centers, and schools.

There are also many other settings where it has also been found useful, from community centers and art schools to prisons and hospices. The chapter deals with some of the key issues an art therapist needs to be aware of in regard to the setting, the general type as well as the particular place. Most central are the development and definition of the role of the art therapist and the place of art therapy within the institution.

Since the publication of the first edition of this book in 1984, more and more art therapists have gone into private practice. In addition to seeing individuals, groups, and families in therapy, many offer workshops and personal growth groups for a wide variety of interested clients. There are many reasons for this development, but the issue of the setting for an independent practitioner is more intimately related to the considerations noted in the chapter on "setting the stage" inside the space and in the "neighborhood."

The latter includes both the physical neighborhood (the other people whose offices are on the same hall or in the same city block) and the more intangible neighborhood—the community of others with whom the art therapist works and relates, who may be provider colleagues, fellow artists, administrators, and the public. Although the focus for most is on their local community, for many there is also a relationship with the wider community of art therapists or other related professionals. Because of the significant increase in the number of independent practitioners since the first edition, I have added a separate section on the importance of paying attention to the community "settings" within which they do art therapy.

By *mode*, I refer here to the different possible configurations used in art therapy today, of which the main ones are individual, group, and family art therapy. There are also other possibilities, such as working with couples or multiple family groups, as well as the larger groups one finds in homeless shelters, workshops, or school classrooms.

In addition, there are many potential variations, like using works of art or photographs as stimuli for discussion rather than asking for art production per se. Considerations relevant for each of the major modes of treatment are discussed, such as the frequency and length of sessions and the particular goals that seem appropriate, which will determine the choice of mode when that is possible.

Another way of working is in collaboration with another clinician, whether parallel with individuals or as cotherapists with a family or group. This person might be an art therapist or someone from another discipline, which could be a traditional mental health field, another one of the creative arts therapies, another service profession like nursing, an educator, an artist volunteer, or someone else.

The issues of collaborating with others in community or medical settings are dealt with more fully in the chapter on consultation in Part V. In this chapter on different modes of working, some of the special issues involved in clinical collaboration and cotherapy are noted, with particular attention to ways of combining skills,

To best apply what you know about art and therapy—the basics as well as the extras—you must really understand each of the subjects discussed in this section: the populations, the settings, and the modes in which you work. Without considerable information as well as some awareness in all of these areas, even an art therapist who knows a great deal may be unable to apply it successfully because she does not know enough about the particular soil in which she hopes to plant her art therapy seeds.

I suppose that, if she is as "artistic" as I would wish, she would be creative and sensitive in the way she deals with institutions, other professionals, and patients of any age or diagnosis, using any form of art therapy. But, as noted, for artistry to be possible, it must be based on knowledge, and there are some things you need to learn if you are to work with any particular population in any particular setting and in any particular mode.

Awareness that such learning is needed is just the initial step; finding out where to get it is, of course, the necessary next move. Rarely is it handed to anyone on a platter, and never is all of it available "by the seat of your pants." Inquiring and finding out where and how you can learn what you need to know, to function most effectively in any particular situation, becomes a continuing part of professional growth. Your search must be within the constraints of reality for the best kind of learning that is available and accessible. But with a will, there is usually a way, especially if you can think and act with flexibility.

Art therapy in the community can be for people of all ages. This woman and her grandson are working side by side with clay. When the art activity was over, the boy went to play with other children, while his grandmother met with the other adults for a group discussion of the experience, extending its educational value. This multigenerational art session took place in a public school during the summer.

A resident is deeply involved in creating her drawing during an art therapy group in a nursing home.

CHAPTER **13**

Different Populations

Introduction

The first and most important thing to remember about different populations is that all human beings, whatever their age or disability, can do something creative with art materials. One of the most distressing attitudes I have all too often encountered is a negative or skeptical one in regard to the ability of a particular group to use art media constructively. I can hardly think of an age level or disability for which at one time or another someone—usually a knowledgeable professional, sometimes an art therapist—has not expressed the opinion that people in that group were incapable of doing anything meaningful in art.

The reasons given always sound rational, and the experiences or literature on which such negative expectations are based usually seem legitimate. But, the effect of expectations on people's ability to perform is so powerful, as demonstrated in the Harvard study recounted in *Pygmalion in the Classroom* (Rosenthal & Jacobson, 1992), that even extensive documentation of failure with one or another type of client is not sufficient reason for giving up in advance.

The famous experiment by an Iowa third-grade teacher in which blue-eyed and brown-eyed children were told that first one group and then the other was "superior" has been replicated many times with many age levels (*Frontline*, 1985). Stimulated by an Iowa teacher's concerns about racism following the assassination of Martin Luther King, it demonstrated vividly the impact of perception on both self-image and how one is viewed by others.

It is my sincere conviction that almost anyone is capable of creative expression, with few (if any) exceptions; the critical variables are your optimism and creativity. Both are important since positive expectations alone will not solve all of the problems some people will have in using art media. Whether those problems are primarily sensory, physical, mental, or behavioral, an inventive approach to solving them can be successful, especially when it is combined with a sincerely optimistic attitude about the outcome.

Often the negative expectation is not applied to the group as a whole but rather to subgroups or individuals; the principle, however, is the same. The challenge for the art therapist is to find a way, given the physical and mental condition of each individual, for that person to be able to create. Whether you need to devise a mechanical contraption or to use your own ego in an auxiliary fashion, whether you need to design the least-distracting setting

143

or the most stimulating motivation, the challenge can be met if approached with optimism and creativity.

Developmental Factors

Having delivered the polemic that no one should be denied the opportunity to participate in art therapy because it seems to someone that an individual is incapable of creative behavior, let us look more closely at the most significant variables in regard to different populations. The first and most obvious is age since art therapists can work successfully with toddlers through people who are very old, but the approach naturally needs to vary for different developmental levels.

Both chronological and mental age are important, the former because of the likely physical maturation and interests, the latter because of the issue of emotional maturity and developmental capacities. When there is a significant discrepancy between the two, as in cognitive impairment, you need to pay attention to both. Knowing a good deal about normal development is clearly one major key to understanding and dealing in a meaningful way with people at different stages of life.

In addition to the expanded range of skills and understandings that become possible during the years from early childhood through adulthood, there is also a corresponding change in the life or growth tasks that are primary at each developmental stage. The therapist becomes less and less of a caretaker as children get older, while needing throughout to maintain both support and the setting of limits. Of course, you must talk differently to a 3-year-old than to a 10-year-old and differently to a teenager than to an adult. It seems that knowing about development, however, is only part of what is needed if you are to do successful art therapy with different age levels.

It is also necessary to be able to relate with comfort and pleasure to people at varying stages of life, and not everyone can do so with equal ease. I have elsewhere (Rubin, 1982) stressed some of the special qualities needed for work with children that, while desirable, are somewhat less critical for success with adults—for example, a sincere enjoyment of the young, playfulness, and the ability to set limits on destructive behavior in a calm and confident manner.

People at different life stages can evoke different kinds of responses in clinicians, depending in part on the therapist's own stage of development as well as on her past experiences at different stages and with individuals in each age group. Someone who has had a close relationship with a grandparent, for example, will probably be able to relate more effectively and more comfortably to elderly clients than someone whose only contact was distant or aversive. Someone who has been a parent can empathize with a mother and father's problems in a way that a childless clinician cannot.

What matters most is that you be as honest as possible with yourself and your employer about which developmental levels are most appealing to you, and that you try, if at all possible, to work with the stages with which you are most comfortable. When that is not feasible, and you find yourself working with an age range that makes you feel uneasy, you have a responsibility not only to obtain fuller information about that developmental level, but also to do some therapeutic or supervisory work on yourself to try to overcome the aversion, which is more often based on emotional than intellectual factors.

The implicit as well as the explicit demands made by individuals at different developmental levels vary tremendously; and the dependency of a young child or an adult with mental retardation may be quite threatening to an insecure art therapist and quite rewarding to a nurturant one. Similarly, the distancing and sparring so common with adolescents, who are necessarily ambivalent about developing intimate relationships with adults (working as they are on separation from their parents), may be great fun for some clinicians and quite distressing for others. Active children can be experienced as a joy or a nuisance, depending as much on the emotional response of the art therapist as on any qualities inherent in the youngsters.

While examining the sources of any response in yourself should be part of good supervision (and your own therapy, when necessary), learning more about the particular developmental level involved can sometimes make a big difference in how you react to clients. Such learning, like any other, is always best when it can be confirmed by others, so reading books or articles on different developmental levels encountered can be surprisingly helpful. In addition to textbooks, I have often recommended novels, such as *The Catcher in the Rye* (Salinger, 1951) or *Look Homeward, Angel* (Wolfe, 1929), for work with adolescents or films, like *Wild Strawberries* (Bergman, 1957) or *On Golden Pond* (Thompson, 1982), for work with the elderly.

In addition to being relevant for art therapists working with patients of any particular age range, such knowledge can also help those whose patients may be at any chronological level but are stuck on difficulties related to earlier developmental tasks. Readings on separation-individuation, for example, can be useful to art therapists seeing adults with borderline personality disorders, as well as to those working with preschoolers and their parents (Mahler, Pine, & Bergmann, 1975).

There are some implications here for training in art therapy. Any trainee at the master's level should have experienced, either as observer or worker, art therapy with people of all age levels—from early childhood through old age. Of course, an in-depth experience with each stage is not possible, but a look or a brief practicum is, and can be, one goal of any serious training program.

The same recommendation makes sense regarding different types of disability—from mental (retardation, brain damage) to physical (palsy, blindness, deafness) to psychological (neurosis, psychosis, personality disorders), each in as many forms as possible. Exposure via observation is a minimum requirement. No amount of reading about diagnostic classifications or exceptionalities can compare with even a brief live observation or interaction with someone who fits the description.

I have been stressing the art therapist's comfort or distress with different age levels, as well as the need to know about normal developmental tasks and capacities. The same is true of disabilities. It is important to know about and to have at least some experience with all of the major kinds, and it is equally important to be aware of your own subjective response to patients in different diagnostic categories. A combination of learning about the group and examining the emotional roots of your own reactions is probably ideal. Both can be really helpful in accepting the common feelings of disgust, helplessness, and aversion, as well as overwhelming pity or excessive attraction.

You may now be wondering when I am going to tell you what to *do* with different age levels or with different diagnostic groups. It would be nice if there were a way to classify approaches in art therapy according to either developmental levels or disorders. It is, of course, possible to attempt to build a treatment program on what people normally do sequentially with art media, as in the "developmental art therapy" approach proposed by art therapist Geraldine Williams and special educator Mary Wood (1977). It is also possible to generalize, at least statistically, about the frequency of one or another formal or thematic characteristic in the art of patients with different diagnostic classifications or degrees or types of pathology.

However, while behavior and art creations can indeed reflect development and deviations from a normal course, this does not mean that there are significantly distinct and predictable *approaches* that can be generalized for different age levels, specific disabilities, or types of pathology. There is so much inter- as well as intraindividual variability in art behaviors that I have yet to find a generalization that works for any single population.

The only one that makes sense to me, after 48 years in the field, is that it is always a trial-and-error process, and that an open choice along with active support is probably the best way to find out just where anyone "is" in art, no matter what information you may already have about age, IQ, or diagnosis. I would be remiss, however, were I not to acknowledge that some professionals feel that you can prescribe therapeutic art activities for certain groups of people, like individuals with Asperger's syndrome (Martinovitch, 2009) or children with autism (Martin, 2009). While there is no doubt something to be said for proposing activities that relatively low-functioning clients can master, I always find myself remembering the psychotic patients I observed at a state hospital in the 1960s pouring clay into molds because the occupational therapist was convinced that was the most they could achieve creatively. A later art therapy program demonstrated that they were far more capable than anyone imagined.

Almost as toxic as negative expectations about particular populations are rigid attitudes and expectations about what one *ought* to do with specific groups, however that is defined. As with overly simplistic generalizations about symbolic meaning, there is probably some validity in all of the more commonly accepted maxims. It does make sense, for example, to focus on the developmental tasks of any age level when you are using a theme-centered approach, so that "life review" for the elderly is appropriate, as is "identity" for the adolescent.

And, of course it would be frustrating to invite anyone to use a tool or medium that he could not possibly manage physically, despite adaptational efforts. But, it is still more common to *under*estimate than to *over*estimate patients' abilities in that regard, as well as in the degree of cooperation, concentration, or reflection of which they are capable. I have had numerous experiences of having to persuade administrators that children with severe disabilities or cognitively impaired elders would be capable of creative work in art. Even though I had profound learning experiences about the difference between expectations and possibilities early in my art therapy career, I continued to have further pleasant surprises about people's capacities many years later.

In the 1980s, a drama therapy colleague and I were asked by the chair of the Psychiatry Department to initiate a Creative and Expressive Arts Therapy program in a large teaching hospital. In the course of administering that program and supervising the art therapists, I learned even more about what patients could do despite low or negative expectations on the part of those running the units as well as, I confess, myself.

An experience with acutely ill schizophrenics was a case in point; no one would have predicted either their ability to become focused and absorbed in the creative process for up to 2 hours at a time or to carry on a group discussion, demanding distance and reflection, for an hour or more regarding their productions. Yet, it did happen—art therapy groups of over three hours in length. While there is no doubt that this phenomenon was due in part to charisma and skill of the particular art therapist on that unit, this amazing finding contradicted many assumptions, including my own.

I had many other surprises as well in that hospital, such as the ability of children with severe conduct disorders to function much more cooperatively than I had anticipated in small art groups with minimal structure. I was also astonished by the capacity of some of the geriatric patients to write eloquent poetry about their paintings despite being in a group led by a woman with no special training or facility in that art form.

I was also impressed by the refusal of those with major affective disorders to paint or draw in the way that depressed patients are supposed to do. While there was some dark, bleak, and constricted work, there was also much that was bright and cheerful. Of course, this is likely to have been primarily defensive, but nonetheless what stood out for me was that it did not meet the usual criteria or expectations.

And, I have often had such surprises about therapists as well, like the capacity of a rather shy, white, middle-aged woman to evoke impressive artwork from angry black males, who would normally not relate positively to such a proper, middle-class lady. Yet, this woman was able, in her art therapy groups, to help these patients to find hidden talents and to release some of their most poignant, sensitive images and thoughts, flying in the face of all my expectations of both the patients and the therapist.

Knowing Disorders

Am I saying, then, that there are no guidelines at all about what to offer or how to deal with patients from different populations? Not at all. What concerns me is that many art therapists accept the largely anecdotal literature by other art therapists about what to do with Group A or what the art of Group B means. To be able to work effectively with different age or diagnostic groups, you need to learn about both the general and the particular.

Regarding general information, the first step is to become familiar with the characteristics and needs of people at different developmental levels, of different socioeconomic or cultural groups, and in different diagnostic classifications. The more you understand the psychobiological nature of adolescence, the better you will be able to do art therapy with teenagers. The more you comprehend about the nature of how the mind works in schizophrenia, the better able you will be to do art therapy with schizophrenics. You will then be in a reasonable position to evaluate the available clinical literature, such as another art therapist's report of a particular methodology or finding with any population.

The *Diagnostic and Statistical Manual of Mental Disorders* (*DSM*) classifications that have been used in psychiatry for almost half a century (e.g., the text revision of the fourth edition, *DSM-IV-TR*; American Psychiatric Association, 2000) are largely descriptive, as are contemporary ways of identifying types of exceptionality. An art therapist who is to work in a meaningful way with any population needs to go beyond a description of how that group functions or looks to some coherent way of understanding why those people are the way they are in a more existential sense.

Even if the condition itself is not modifiable (like blindness or schizophrenia), the subjective attitude and experience of it may well be altered. This is not to suggest that we eliminate or disregard classification or categorizing, for communication without them would be unnecessarily difficult. More simply, what I am saying is that knowing at a descriptive level is only a first step; understanding at a deeper level is essential for meaningful work with any population.

My own reluctance to think in terms of labels sometimes backfires, however. I remember sitting on the doctoral committee of a bright art therapist who had studied with me and who knew my writings well. In her competency paper, she noted the paucity of reports on art therapy with mental retardation. I was surprised and mildly offended that she did not think of quite a few children I had described in a book I had written on *Child Art Therapy* (Rubin, 2005).

But then, I realized that in most of my writing about these youngsters I had either omitted or minimized the fact of their retardation, so it made sense that she would not be likely to think of them as belonging to that category. In stressing their capacities and their ability to use art therapeutically like children of average intelligence, I had disregarded the actuality of their mental retardation, a very real cognitive disability.

This was a useful learning experience for I have always had a tendency to focus (perhaps defensively) on capacities rather than on deficits. While it may be a useful attitude in helping people to create and to get better, it is not helpful to students or to practitioners at any level to deny the existence of such disorders as mental retardation, brain damage, or psychosis when they are present.

Labeling can, in fact, be useful in thinking about patients. It can also get in the way. It is done, in most psychiatric and special education settings, partly because it is necessary to receive funds. The more I have learned about diagnostic labels, even with the careful decision-making system used in *DSM-IV-TR* (APA, 2000), the more skeptical I have become. Like statistics, they can be used by a sophisticated clinician in a variety of "legitimate" ways, each of which can give manifestly different impressions. Eventually, you need to become knowledgeable enough to understand the kind of reasoning behind primary versus secondary diagnosis, or personality versus developmental disorder, in order to translate diagnostic terminology in a sensible way (Millon, Krueger, & Simonsen, 2010).

Despite the many sincere efforts at creating objective psychological tests and identifying neurobiological markers, there is ultimately a good deal of subjectivity in any kind of psychological assessment. Even with all of the progress that has been made by neurologists, psychiatrists, and epidemiologists in the decades since this book was first published, this is still the case.

Given the current stage of development in the art of one human being understanding another to help and to treat, that seems inevitable. As with physical medicine, there is considerable overlap between psychiatric disorders—anxiety can be part of depression and vice-versa, for example. The use of symptom clusters and mental status examinations to determine how to classify someone is an ongoing task for those on the front lines in mental health.

On the other side of the coin, when labels help the therapist to better understand the nature of the patient's disorder, they also help to indicate appropriate forms and methods of treatment. Art therapy, as indicated in previous sections, can be more or less structured, more or less intense, and can be aimed primarily at building psychic structures or at undoing defenses. A clear understanding, not so much of the *name*, but of the *nature* of a patient's problem, can be immensely helpful in decisions about the appropriateness of art therapy and the general as well as specific approach that is likely to help.

Assessment in the broadest sense is an important part of treatment, and there is no question that developmental and dynamic evaluation (as well as analysis of the family system) seem to have at least as much relevance as specific nosological labels. If both can be done thoughtfully, with attention to etiology and underlying mechanisms, then they can be of great assistance in the always-murky work of psychotherapy through art.

Parenthetically, art products can sometimes be useful in the difficult task of differential diagnosis since neurological damage is sometimes evident in the formal aspects of a drawing, for example, when it is not always or yet apparent in behavior. The well-known Clock Drawing Test (Shulman, Shedletsky, & Silver, 1986) has been used for many years to assess cognitive functioning in elderly patients

Understanding Those Who Are Different

One important aspect of understanding populations was alluded to in relation to being aware of your own responses to different age groups and has a significant impact on your ability to empathize with those who are really different. This is the simple fact that, while we all have been children once and some of us have been parents, few art therapists have been schizophrenic, blind, or retarded. While all of us are what I would call "normal neurotics" and are able to empathize with most feeling states stemming from anxiety, the majority of disabilities and disorders are foreign to our personal experience and must remain so.

Thus, it is no surprise that many art therapists have found that working with "wellness" groups, like those popular during the heyday of the "human potential" movement (Hieb, 2005; Rhyne, 1995) is more comfortable for them. After all, the people who tend to come to the increasing number of self-help and growth workshops offered by art therapists tend to be more like us and their struggles more familiar.

For myself, in addition to what I have learned from patients themselves, reading books by individuals who have lived with a serious mental illness or a physical disability has helped me to get some sense of what life is like for someone so afflicted (Barnes & Berke, 1971; Beers, 1908/2009; Chilvers, 2007; Cohen, Giller, & Lynn, 1991; Cutsforth, 1951; DeLoach, 1981; Grandin, 2006, 2008; Greenberg, 1964; Hunt, 1967; Jamison, 1995; Kaysen, 1993; Klein & Kemp, 2004; Miller & Miller, 2008; Plath, 1971; Sechehaye, 1951; Styron, 1992; Wagner & Spiro, 2005).

Since the millenium, there have been several attempts to create a simulated experience of schizophrenia and to study its effects on volunteer subjects (Yellowlees & Cook, 2006). In an excerpt from a report by *NPR*'s Joanne Silberner in 2002, one project's psychiatric consultant described his own reaction of terror:

> Dr. Sam Keith, medical advisor on the virtual reality project, is a veteran psychiatrist who's heard thousands of patients describe schizophrenic episodes. Still, after trying the simulation, Keith said, "When it's real, it's different—it's very frightening, it's very scary." [The technical director] said that's precisely the effect he hoped to achieve. After years of the illness being misdiagnosed, mismanaged and stigmatized, he says, "People should understand what it's like to go through this."

There is probably resistance in all of us to the thought of actually experiencing life from the perspective of a deaf or paranoid individual. It is frightening even to think about, and the normal human reaction is one of relief at being free of the burden, whatever it is. Yet this resistance needs to be overcome if you are to be an effective art therapist. To have real empathy for another person, you not only need to connect mentally with the human experiences you have in common with a patient. You also need to *imagine* what it is like to see or feel or think like that person, with full recognition that you can never fully put yourself in someone else's shoes.

It is an exercise primarily of the imagination, one at which art therapists, usually comfortable with fantasy, ought to do well. Sometimes you can learn from a concrete exercise, such as blindfolding yourself for a period of time in a familiar locale and trying to go through your usual activities without sight. Such attempts to "feel with" and "into," while difficult and sometimes frightening, are probably more important in the long run in understanding different populations than any amount of book or classroom learning.

It is especially helpful to try to imagine what the *art therapy experience* is like for a particular individual or member of any group—how the space looks and feels, how such a person might react to the other people or the therapist, how he might understand and feel about the request to create, and how the creative task itself might appear to him. This seems self-evident, yet art therapists, like many other clinicians, often distance themselves in a defensive fashion from too close an involvement with the disabled or "crazy" patients with whom they find themselves working.

The phenomenon of "burnout" in work with difficult patient populations is very real. It is my impression, however, that it may be less common among art therapists than among other mental health professionals. Perhaps that is a result of our schedules, which tend to require periodic rather than continuous contact with any single patient or group. It may also be related to our capacity to tap the strengths and creativity in people, which can be exciting for us as well as for them. Recent developments in "positive psychology" (Peterson, 2006; Peterson & Seligman, 2004; Snyder & Lopez, 2005) appear to have been especially appealing to art therapists, no doubt for this reason.

Perhaps art therapists have an easier time with empathy due to our comfort with imagination and fantasy and what I think is an ability to flow with patients in all their craziness and confusion. I am quite convinced that art therapists are more comfortable with primary process thinking than are most clinicians, that we often find the free-flowing fantastic aspects of psychotic thought rather appealing, even fascinating. And, most important for work with different populations, we may not be as afraid as some to "feel with" people who think strangely since that is such a familiar state from our own creative activity in art. Similarly, the lack of logic of a retarded or brain-damaged individual is probably relatively congenial for us because we are comfortable with an illogical, primary process mode of thought as part of creating.

I do not think I am being naïve about art therapists in my optimism about our capacity for entering alien mental/perceptual worlds. Art therapists are often successful with groups who do not usually respond well to treatment, in part I believe because of this enhanced capacity for empathy. It is usually thought and said that we succeed because we offer a modality that resistant or nonverbal patients can use to express themselves. While that is true, it is also true that we offer ourselves to both support and understand the individual's struggles with self-expression.

In recent years, art therapists, like other clinicians, have become attuned to the importance of cultural and racial differences between and among themselves and their clients. While it was appealing to think that we as a group were "color blind," the truth is that, as part of the societies in which we live and work, we unconsciously accept all kinds of stereotypes and prejudices without even being aware of them.

Fortunately, now that our consciousness has been raised, some art therapists have begun to tackle this sensitive area in their articles and books (Betts, 2003; Campbell, Liebmann, Brooks, Jones, & Ward, 1999; Dokter, 1998; Hiscox & Calisch, 1997; Junge, 2008; Stepney, 2010). Because of our growing awareness, "multicultural/diversity competence" is now part of the American Art Therapy Association (AATA) Code of Ethics. It has also for some time been a required component of graduate degree training programs.

In this aspect of our task, as well as in reflecting on what has been expressed, we must call on our empathy, which must also be felt by the other person if we are to be really effective. It probably does not matter how many books or courses you have under your professional belt about any particular population; if you can imagine what it feels like to be that way, you are well on the road to an art therapy that works.

References

American Art Therapy Association (AATA) Code of Ethics. http://www.americanarttherapyassociation.org/upload/codeofethics.pdf

American Psychiatric Association. (2000). *Diagnostic and statistical manual of mental disorders* (4th ed., text revision). Washington, DC: Author.

Barnes, M., & Berke, J. (1971). *Mary Barnes: Two accounts of a journey through madness.* New York: Ballantine Books.

Beers, C. W. (2009). *A mind that found itself: An autobiography* (5th ed.). Charleston, SC: CreateSpace. (Original work published 1908)

Bergman, I. (Author/Director) (1957). *Wild strawberries.* Sweden: Svensk Filmindustri.

Betts, D. J. (Ed.). (2003). *Creative arts therapies approaches in adoption and foster care.* Springfield, IL: Thomas.

Campbell, J., Liebmann, M., Brooks, F., Jones, J., & Ward, C. (Eds.). (1999). Art therapy, race and culture. London: Kingsley.

Chilvers, R. (2007). *The hidden world of autism.* London: Kingsley.

Cohen, B. M., Giller, E., & Lynn, W. (Eds.). (1991). *Multiple personality disorder from the inside out.* Baltimore: Sidran Press.

Cutsforth, T. D. (1951). *The blind in school and society* (rev. ed.). New York: American Foundation for the Blind.

DeLoach, C. (1981). *A metamorphosis. Adjustment to severe disability.* New York: McGraw-Hill.

Dokter, D. (Ed.). (1998). *Arts therapists, refugees and migrants.* London: Kingsley.

Grandin, T. (2006). *Thinking in pictures: My life with autism* (2nd ed.). New York: Vintage Books.

Grandin, T. (2008). *The way I see it.* Arlington, TX: Future Horizons.

Greenberg, J. (1964). *I never promised you a rose garden.* New York: Holt, Rinehart & Winston.

Hieb, M. (2005). *Inner journeying through art journaling.* London: Kingsley.

Hiscox, A., & Calisch, A. (Eds.). (1997). *Tapestry of cultural issues in art therapy.* London: Kingsley.

Hunt, N. (1967). *The world of Nigel Hunt: The diary of a mongoloid.* New York: Garrett.

Jamison, K. R. (1995). *An unquiet mind.* New York: Random House.

Junge, M. B. (2008). *Mourning, memory and life itself.* Springfield, IL: Thomas.

Kaysen, S. (1993). *Girl, interrupted.* New York: Vintage Books.

Klein, S. D., & Kemp, J. D. (Eds.). (2004). *Reflections from a different journey: What adults with disabilities wish all parents knew.* New York: McGraw-Hill.

Mahler, M. S., Pine, F., & Bergmann, A. (1975). *The psychological birth of the human infant.* New York: Basic Books.

Martin, N. (2009). *Art as an early intervention tool for children with autism.* London: Kingsley.

Martinovitch, J. (2009). *Creative expressive activities and Asperger's syndrome.* London: Kingsley.

Miller, E., & Miller, K. (2008). *The girl who spoke with pictures.* London: Kingsley.

Millon, T., Krueger, R., & Simonsen, E. (2010). *Contemporary directions in psychopathology: Scientific foundations of the* DSM-V *and* ICD-11. New York: Guilford Press.

Peters, W., & Cobb, C. (co-writers) (1985). A class divided [Television series episode]. Produced in New Haven, CT: Yale University Films for *Frontline* by WGBH in Boston, MA.

Peterson, C. (2006). *Primer of positive psychology.* New York: Oxford University Press.

Peterson, C., & Seligman, M. (2004). *Characters strengths and virtues: A handbook and classification.* New York: Oxford University Press.

Plath, S. (1971). *The bell jar.* New York: Bantam Books.

Rhyne, J. (1995). *The Gestalt art experience* (2nd ed.). Chicago: Magnolia Street.

Rosenthal, R., & Jacobson, L. (1992). *Pygmalion in the classroom.* New York: Irvington.

Rubin, J. A. (1982). Special personality traits of child therapists. In I. Jakab (Ed.), *The personality of the therapist* (pp. 111–116). Pittsburgh, PA: American Society of Psychopathology of Expression.

Rubin, J. A. (2005). *Child art therapy* (3rd ed.). New York: Wiley.

Salinger, J. D. (1951). *The catcher in the rye.* Boston: Little, Brown & Co.

Sechehaye, M., & Renee (pseud.). (1951). *Autobiography of a schizophrenic girl*. New York: Grune & Stratton.

Shulman, K., Shedletsky, R., & Silver, I. (1986) The challenge of time: Clock drawing and cognitive function in the elderly. *International Journal of Geriatric Psychiatry, 1,* 135–140.

Silberner, J. (2002). The sights and sounds of schizophrenia [radio broadcast]. Washington, DC: National Public Radio. Retrieved February 2010 from http://www.npr.org/programs/atc/features/2002/aug/schizophrenia/

Snyder, C. R., & Lopez, S. J. (Eds.). (2005). *Handbook of positive psychology*. New York: Oxford University Press.

Stepney, S. (2010). *Art therapy for students at risk* (2nd ed.). Springfield, IL: Charles C. Thomas.

Styron, W. (1992). *Darkness visible: A memoir of madness*. New York: Vintage Books.

Thompson, E. (Author) (1981). *On golden pond* [Motion picture]. United States: Universal Pictures.

Wagner, P. S., & Spiro, C. S. (2005). *Divided minds*. New York: St. Martin's Press.

Williams, G. H., & Wood, M. M. (1977). *Developmental art therapy*. Baltimore: University Park Press, 1977.

Wolfe, T. (1929). *Look homeward, angel*. New York: Scribner's.

Yellowlees, P. M., & Cook, J. N. (2006). Education about hallucinations using an internet virtual reality system: A qualitative survey. *Academic Psychiatry, 30,* 534–539.

Recommended Readings

Art Therapy With Children, Adolescents, the Elderly

Abraham, R. (2004). *When words have lost their meaning: Alzheimer's patients*. New York: Praeger.

Betensky, M. G. (1973). *Self-discovery through self-expression*. Springfield, IL: Thomas.

Campbell, J., & Waller, D. (Eds.). (2007). *Arts therapies & progressive illness: Nameless dread*. London: Brunner-Routledge.

Case, C., & Dalley, T. (Eds.). (1990). *Working with children in art therapy*. London: Tavistock.

Case, C., & Dalley, T. (Eds.). (2008). *Art therapy with children*. London: Routledge.

Evans, K., & Dubowski, J. (2001). *Art therapy with children on the autistic spectrum*. London: Kingsley.

Klorer, P. G. (2000). *Expressive therapy with troubled children*. Northvale, NJ: Aronson.

Kramer, E. (1971). *Art as therapy with children*. New York: Schocken Books.

Kramer, E. (1979). *Childhood and art therapy*. New York: Schocken Books.

Magniant, R. C. P. (Ed.). (2004). *Art therapy with older adults*. Springfield, IL: Thomas.

Moon, B. L. (1998). *The dynamics of art as therapy with adolescents*. Springfield, IL: Thomas.

Riley, S. (1999). *Contemporary art therapy with adolescents*. London: Kingsley.

Rubin, J. A. (2005). *Child art therapy* (3rd ed.). New York: Wiley.

Art Therapy for Specific Disorders and Disabilities

Brooke, S. L. (1997). *Art therapy with sexual abuse survivors*. Springfield, IL: Thomas.

Case, C. (2005). *Imagining animals: Art, psychotherapy and primitive states of mind*. London: Routledge.

Gerity, L. (1999). *Creativity and the dissociative patient: Puppets, narrative and art in the treatment of survivors of childhood trauma*. London: Kingsley.

Hagood, M. M. (2000). *The use of art in counseling child and adults survivors of sexual abuse*. London: Kingsley.

Hogan, S. (Ed.). (2003). *Gender issues in art therapy*. London: Kingsley.

Horovitz, E. G. (Ed.). (2007). *Visually speaking: Art therapy and the deaf*. Springfield, IL: Thomas.

Makin, S. R. (2000). *More than just a meal: The art of eating disorders*. London: Kingsley.

Milia, D. (2000). *Self-mutilation and art therapy: Violent creation*. London: Kingsley.

Murphy, J. (Ed.). (2001). *Art therapy with young survivors of sexual abuse*. Philadelphia: Taylor & Francis.

Rees, M. (Ed.). (1998). *Drawing on difference: Art therapy with people who have learning difficulties*. New York: Routledge.

Safran, D. (2002). *Art therapy and AD/HD*. London: Kingsley.

Seftel, L. (2006). *Grief unseen: Healing pregnancy loss through the arts*. London: Kingsley.

A legally blind boy with partial vision must get close to the paper to create his drawing, but given sufficient time and support, he is able to make a picture of his favorite character, Winnie the Pooh.

A boy in a public kindergarten is deeply engrossed in his drawing during a session of "Art for Self-Awareness."

CHAPTER **14**

Different Settings

Getting to Know the Place You Work

Working in diverse settings can be as different as working with diverse populations. Like the latter, it requires getting to know about the settings in which you find yourself. And, as is also true for populations, you need to understand the type of setting in general as well as the particular one involved.

You might think that knowing different kinds of settings is simpler and more straightforward than getting to know different populations, a complex task with many subjective components in both the definition of the group and the response of the art therapist. However, settings and institutions also have personalities, and they can look one way on the surface and another if you probe more deeply. Indeed, analyzing a system is as complicated and demanding as analyzing the dynamics of a family—perhaps more so because of the many subsystems and the larger number of people involved.

In any case, the art therapist who works in a school is in a very different kind of situation from the one who works in a clinic, and both are in settings vastly different from an inpatient hospital unit or a drug rehabilitation center. It is still not uncommon for an art therapist to be the first and only one of a kind in a particular place, which means that, in addition to getting to know the setting itself, she must also define her role within it from scratch. That task, of course, is greatly affected by the expectations of art therapy, on the part of the institution, that are rarely consistent from person to person within any single setting. The art therapist's perception of how best she can be used is also a significant variable, which depends very much on getting to know and understand the needs of the particular setting as well as her own experience and strengths.

As with any therapy, there is usually no choice but to start "where they are"—where the institution wants you to begin. Even in a setting that has already found ways of using the skills of one or more art therapists as students or staff, it is always best to work with those in charge toward flexibility in role definition. Although it may take a good deal of time before an institution and an art therapist learn how best to use the skills of the one in the service of the other, such an organic kind of program development is less likely to occur if the art therapist herself is not thinking imaginatively from the beginning.

As with the other roles you play, you need to be patient and to assess strengths, weaknesses, and dynamics in addition to needs—all the time incubating ideas about how art therapy can be utilized in the particular setting. When and with whom these ideas are shared will depend, as in doing therapy, on the art therapist's judgment of the readiness and receptivity on the part of others, as well as on an assessment of who is likely to be helpful in effecting the modifications seen as appropriate.

The need to understand the covert as well as the overt values and power structure of an institution cannot be overstressed. Many a good idea about using art therapy in a particular setting has never been implemented, not because no one thought of it, but because the art therapist went about trying to "sell" it unsuccessfully. Perhaps she went to the wrong person, perhaps it was the wrong time, or perhaps the time and the person were all right but the method of presenting the idea was poorly conceived and not persuasive. Sometimes, the art therapist goes to the right person (as defined by charts of administration) but fails to inform or to obtain the support of significant others, who may be offended by not being included and who might have been critical allies. Navigating the waters of any institution requires preparation, patience, and persistence.

To use yourself in an optimal way in any setting, you must be constantly alert to possibilities for service, research, or some other role. To take advantage of opportunities as they present themselves, you also need to have a fairly clear internal agenda of relevant ways to develop the role of art in the institution. Then you are much more likely to see opportunities when they arise, and you will be more likely to utilize a change of administration, a new program, or any other perceived "opening" in a creative way. Without ideas that have been germinating and becoming clear for some time, it is unlikely that the opportunity for development will even be perceived, let alone utilized.

It may seem strange to begin a chapter on work in different settings by emphasizing role and program development. It is my conviction, however, that if art therapists do not participate actively and creatively in this aspect of our work in most settings, we are likely to be placed in pigeonholes that make sense to some administrator but are often not the best use of our skills. In attempting to get those in charge to support program development, it is useful to be able to point to relevant models—reputable places of the same sort—where the kind of program you are suggesting has been implemented with success.

Of course, the more you know about art therapy programs in other institutions similar to your own, the more ideas you will be introduced to vicariously about possible directions for development. Some of this information is available in the published literature, primarily in journals. Much more is available through professional organizations, both national and local, in their newsletters and at conferences. It is a waste of precious time and energy to reinvent the wheel in my opinion. Good models are good inspiration and also show that something works. Knowing about art therapy in any particular kind of setting is as useful for healthy program development as knowing about the populations you serve.

Knowing about the type of facility is, of course, necessary if you are to become familiar with its mission and its goals. As in other attempts at understanding, knowing the history of the *kind* of facility is almost as helpful as knowing the history of the *particular* place. While not absolutely essential, I have found such knowledge to be more helpful than you might imagine in conceptualizing the possible role of an art therapist in any institution.

Each of the kinds of settings where you are likely to work has its own fascinating history as a type and as a specific example. If you are to become a well-integrated part of the institution, it does help to become familiar with its "family background" as one way of getting oriented.

Getting to Know Your Coworkers

Of course, the real challenge in becoming integrated is finding ways to become an accepted and respected part of the particular institutional family. As with entering any existing group, this requires the careful avoidance of stepping on anyone's toes or territory, as well as becoming useful to others. Working together collaboratively is one good way to begin forming personal alliances, whether the work is in research or service, in-service training or public relations.

It is best if such collaboration involves art therapy, although serving on staff committees or joining other groups can also help you to become part of the family. As you begin to develop ideas about further uses of your talents as an art therapist in this place, you will be able to use the connections you have formed for advice and assistance in accomplishing specific goals.

It is not always so easy for an art therapist to be integrated into a setting, especially one that has never before employed such a person. Many individuals will be skeptical, some may be fearful, and others may be critical of spending always-scarce resources in this particular way. "Arty" people are always a little threatening to nonartists, so that dressing and behaving according to the conventions of the institution may help to allay any anxieties that the art therapist will be strange or flaky.

Certain concerns are common—that an art therapist might overstimulate patients who are fragile, create unbearable messes, or engage in activities without accomplishing anything substantial—these are inevitable and are sure to be present in almost any institution, whether a school, a hospital, or a clinic. As with the inevitable defenses and resistances you encounter in patients, such expectations and anxieties need to be identified and ways found to modify them if you are to be accepted.

One technique I found useful in my early days in a child guidance center was to invite other clinicians to observe individual art evaluation or therapy through a one-way vision glass, as well as offering to work alongside others with families or groups. In this way, many staff members got a look at what this strange new thing was. They had a chance to discuss it following the session and were able to modify distorted notions they may have had about art therapy. By encouraging them to ask questions, I was able to become aware of misunderstandings and concerns that might not have occurred to me.

Another useful approach is to offer in-service training or consultation to anyone who is interested, either short or long term. Presentations to the various discipline groups about art therapy and consultations with clinicians on drawings from their own patients were also helpful icebreakers in those early days. At the psychiatric hospital where I later co-directed a creative and expressive arts therapy program, I and my art therapist supervisees used many similar approaches to introduce the program and to assuage staff anxieties, differing as needed from one unit to another.

Even though no one in the administration of the hospital or of the units, for example, required the art therapists to attend team or unit meetings, I urged them to do so as much as possible from the beginning of the program. I also suggested that they bring along the artwork of those patients who might be discussed and offer to show and explain it to the others.

I knew, from my own previous experience as an art therapist on an inpatient unit in the same hospital, how helpful this could be for all parties. In fact, it paid off handsomely, with an increase from half-time to full-time employment for all of the art therapists within less than a year as well as requests for additional services like diagnostic evaluations of individuals or families, leadership of low-functioning groups, and individual work with nonverbal patients.

While all of these options were offered at the initiation of the new program, none were actually requested until the administrators on each unit came to recognize and respect the individual art therapists. This happened because of their successful work with groups, which was reflected in their helpful contributions to the team meetings.

Throughout my time as codirector of this program, seeds were constantly being planted by myself as supervisor and the art therapists as well for possible ways to expand and enhance their services. Although it often takes months for ideas to germinate, planting them in the right places can bear surprising fruit, sometimes more rapidly than you would anticipate. Within 1 year of initiating the program in this hospital, three more art therapists were hired, and within several more years, the expressive arts therapies staff size was actually doubled.

One of the most difficult aspects of role definition and development involves our close relatives in other disciplines, mentioned in Chapter 7 on developing your identity as an art therapist. When someone already in the system is doing something even superficially similar to what an art therapist might do, then issues of competition and territory become critical and, the risk of tension is inevitable.

One way to minimize such problems is to be aware of their likelihood and to try to develop alliances from the beginning, informally if not formally, with those in related fields doing similar work with patients or students. If you can work together to refine and define your respective roles, so that neither is felt as a threat to the other, things can work out well. If you are not able to work collaboratively, you may collide head-on at some point in time, with possible injury to one or both of you.

When I first arrived at the child guidance center, the clinical psychologists routinely requested drawings during their diagnostic evaluations, most clinicians used some art supplies in play therapy with children, and the social group workers included many crafts in their activity groups. Sensing that collaboration would be more fruitful than the competition that seemed possible if not likely, I initiated work with the interested psychologists on drawing analysis studies. I also offered to consult with anyone who wanted to on ways of requesting art from children, the possible meanings of a child's products, and how to help youngsters to talk about what they have made.

Such activities seemed to relieve anxiety and to reassure everyone that we could share the territory comfortably. With the group workers, I offered any help they might want in ordering or using supplies, resulting in a year-long series of meetings during which they used a wide variety of art materials under my guidance and discussed how to use them with children's groups. I ended up doing co-therapy in groups with several of them, an excellent learning experience for both of us.

When a psychologist and I developed a *family art evaluation*, because of his interest in family assessment and curiosity about art therapy, others on the staff who did family therapy were curious. Some were even jealous, their remarks suggesting that they felt left out of an activity that they saw as in their territory. The psychologist, who was the head of that department and attuned to interpersonal rivalries within the center, had a good idea. At his suggestion, we invited the whole staff to a showing of a videotape of a family art evaluation, after which many indicated a desire to learn more.

We agreed to organize a family art study group, in which members conducted family art evaluations observed by other group members, discussing the videotaped sessions the following week. The group met for almost a year, and the members (from all disciplines) went on to use art with families in both evaluation and therapy. Some made presentations at their own professional conferences (in social work and child psychiatry, for example), and others wrote papers. It was a mutually satisfying learning experience for all involved.

In general, then, I believe that it is always best to be open and inclusive about what you do, especially when others have their own legitimate reasons for using art or craft materials with patients or students. On the geriatric unit of the psychiatric hospital where I initiated and co-directed an expressive arts therapy program, for example, the nurses were already teaching crafts to patients several afternoons a week when the art therapist arrived. Although it took more than a few months after her offer, because of territorial anxieties, the art therapist was eventually invited to work alongside the nurses in these groups as well as consulting to them about materials, supplies, and activities.

Had the Occupational Therapy (OT) Department not been eliminated, I am sure that the art therapists in the hospital would have faced potential conflicts with that group, which in 1980 was offering a great many arts and craft activities. It would have been vital to establish an ongoing communication mechanism, as well as a way of defining for other staff (those who refer patients) how these two kinds of activities that look so similar are really so different (Tubbs & Drake, 2006).

Although the new Chair of Psychiatry essentially replaced OT with the Creative and Expressive Arts Therapy (CEAT) program at that time, when I consulted 20 years later to the CEAT staff in the same hospital, OT had returned to the institution. Since by then the primary activities in OT were no longer arts and crafts but rather assistance with overall adaptation, as in "activities of daily living," there was less possibility of confusion or conflict.

Parenthetically, when I was working for the Department of Psychiatry in 1969, I was asked by the OT Department in this same hospital for some consultation. At the time, I was meeting with art therapy pioneer Margaret Naumburg for guidance since there was no formal training in art therapy. She advised me not to accept the request because she had faced such tremendous resistance to the development of art therapy by OT departments in her early career.

My administrative supervisor, however, overruled Naumburg, and said I should accept the invitation. So, I ended up meeting with the large and receptive OT staff for several hours a week. It was a most rewarding consultation experience, in which I was able to help them to approach their work with art materials (already ongoing) from a slightly more psychotherapeutic point of view, in regard to both doing and reflecting on the activities. Two of the staff in fact went on to become art therapists.

Another common instance of potential conflict can occur when both an art therapist and an art teacher work in a school or rehabilitation center with exceptional children. It is then necessary to differentiate the two, not on the basis of population or setting (which are identical) or activity (which can also look identical), but in terms of the primary *goal*. If the goal is primarily educational (e.g., learning about art), then the art educator is the art giver of choice. If, however, the goal is primarily psychological (e.g., assessing the child's impulse control problems), then the art therapist becomes the art giver of choice.

Most exceptional children probably could benefit from both, and ideally choices should not be made as if it were an either/or situation, just as most psychiatric patients in the early 1970s would have benefited from both art therapy and OT. When I observed Edith Kramer (1971) in the 1960s at the Jewish Guild for the Blind, it was clear that she was the art *therapist,* and Yasha Lisenco (1971) was the art *teacher.* They each understood their respective roles, as did the children and the rest of the staff.

Sometimes, because of a child's extreme deficiencies, he is not able to benefit from the usual approach to art education; then, too, the art therapist becomes the provider of choice. For example, if a youngster is severely and profoundly retarded, it may be hard (or even impossible) for a regular art teacher without training in special education to reach and teach him, while the special training and experience with deviant populations of the art therapist make it more likely that she will be successful.

Moreover, the goals, even in art, will probably be at a pre-art or sensory level, having much more to do with differentiating self from nonself than with learning about or mastering techniques. The patient who is unreachable by the nurse or psychiatrist because he refuses to speak or is unable to talk is a similar kind of case; the art therapist is called in to do the psychotherapy because she uses a modality to which such a person can respond. It is not that the goals are necessarily different in either case from what an art teacher or another kind of therapist might normally have; it is just that the means to reach them are less available to either of them than to an art therapist.

Different kinds of institutions present different kinds of problems in role definition and relationships with staff members in related fields. But whether it is the art teacher in the school, the occupational therapist in the hospital, or the recreation therapist in the rehabilitation center, a major task for the art therapist is to define the differences between her expertise and theirs, between her role and theirs.

Because of the very similarities causing the inevitable confusion and possible competition, there also exist many possibilities for cooperation, collaboration, and mutual growth. Such alliances, as in study groups or other peer learning configurations, are helpful in avoiding problems, building trust, and minimizing suspiciousness.

If the setting happens to include specialists in one or more arts therapies, the potential there, too, is for either destructive competition and envy or constructive collaboration and mutual growth. Although not always in the same department (as in the program I co-directed), I think it is always a good idea for art therapists to attempt to work collaboratively with music, dance, or drama therapists in the same institution, even if only occasionally. The collaborative work can be in assessment, therapy, in-service training, research, or some other area. For the most part, it is usually fun.

Individuals may be nervous, self-conscious, or shy about initiating such partnerships and may need to be encouraged by those in charge. As most will discover, there is a great deal to be learned as a therapist through any kind of work with another professional. In addition, such collaborative activities lessen the likelihood of too much envy or competition, which can potentially drain staff energies.

One problem that became apparent early on in the program I co-directed with a drama therapist was the relative "salability" of art therapy, compared with dance, drama, and music. Hospital staff members were more anxious about the other art forms, even before the program started, and were less eager to ask for increased time from the other creative therapies, although the clinicians were as skilled as the art therapists. Not only is art a less-threatening activity than dance or drama, both of which require moving around and performing in front of others, but it can even be less anxiety provoking than music, which seems to some patients and staff to require more skill or talent.

In addition, the visibility of art therapy seemed to be a major factor in its relatively more rapid acceptance and utilization. The often-dramatic art products, which do speak so much more eloquently than words, vivify concretely the potential of art to enhance communication. Sometimes they also help the staff to clarify the diagnosis, as well as the sources, of a particular patient's distress. Often, they demonstrate strengths as well.

In any case, the concreteness of the art product seems to play a large part in the growth of art therapy programs in institutions and should be conscientiously utilized by every art therapist. In the hospital, we requested, for example, very large bulletin boards for each unit, the size of which alarmed both the purchasing department and the head nurses, who had to decide where to put them.

But the large size made it possible to display more patient art and their written or dictated commentaries as well as to frame pictures clearly and dramatically. The artwork on the bulletin boards was useful, not only with patients in the art therapy groups, but also perhaps even more in the long run as an ever-present way of educating staff and visiting families about the values of art therapy.

An art therapist in any institution who does not use patient artwork in communications with other professionals, or who does not, when possible, exhibit those products that the artists want to have shown, is not fully using one of the major assets of art therapy. It is one of the best ways to promote art therapy both physically and psychologically in any setting. And, it is an excellent way to show its value.

So far, I have written at a general level about things you need to know, to think about, and to do in all kinds of settings. You may be wondering whether there are any specifics about inpatient versus outpatient, school versus hospital, clinic versus rehabilitation center, or shelter versus community art center that an art therapist ought to know.

Of course there are, just as there are differences between those suffering from bipolar disorder and those afflicted with obsessive-compulsive disorder or between oppositional and autistic children. But this book is not the place to go into detail about specific settings, any more than it is the place to write about specific groups. Settings, like populations, differ widely. There are types just as there are groups, and there are particular places, just as there are individual patients. In both areas, it is useful to know both the general (about the type of person or setting) and the particular (about the individual person or place).

In both instances, it also helps to know how art therapy has been shown to be useful by others. With populations, you need to know what the literature has to say about art by a particular group (diagnostically) as well as what kinds of approaches have been found to be effective (therapeutically). With settings, you need to know what other professionals have to say about the place and role of an art therapist in such an institution, what has been found to be possible as well as useful. In neither instance, however, should you stop at such findings or consider them either sufficiently or necessarily applicable to the particular person or place. But they are extremely useful as reference points and guidelines. They can offer stimulation as well as possibilities to know about and perhaps to convey to others in an effort to develop a program of art therapy for any population in any setting.

In addition to these generally applicable ways of thinking about settings and what you need to know, there are a few others that also seem similar to what needs to be understood about populations. These relate to empathy—that it is important to try to imagine what it is like to be someone so different from yourself, especially how it would feel to be that person confronted with an invitation to create art.

In regard to the setting, you need to imagine what it is like to be the patients or students in either a place where they live (dorm, unit) or come to for services (day school, clinic). It also helps to develop perspective about your coworkers, to respect the strain they are under and the tensions of their jobs, from responsibility as well as wear and tear.

It helps as well to try to be sensitive to how the institution is viewed by others, just as when you are working with a severely disturbed or disabled individual. As sometimes happens with a person who may stimulate discomfort in others, the staff members of an institution can become a little paranoid, can feel unappreciated or undervalued by its board or by the community. Conversely, they can feel grandiose, especially if there have been many successes.

Whatever the image of the institution in the community, it is helpful to try to get a sense of how the staff sees itself, especially since that has an impact on those employees with whom you must work and whose support you need for program development. If you can in some way connect what you have to offer with what individuals in power see as a primary (perhaps even neglected) role in the community, this may be yet another way to accomplish more and better art therapy.

While I do not mean to anthropomorphize institutions or settings, it can sometimes be helpful to think of them as having personalities, priorities, and an image of themselves that may be different from the one held by others. In any case, it is important at a much deeper level to empathize with the pressures that affect any institution, just as you need to do in regard to your coworkers. Without such empathy, your attempts to function and grow in any setting are likely to fizzle. Being sensitive to pressures on people in decision-making positions is part of what is involved in knowing when to take action on any personal or programmatic goal.

Being sensitive to how it feels to be a patient or pupil in an inpatient hospital or a residential school may be as difficult as imagining what it is like to have schizophrenia since you probably never had to be in such a place. It may also be hard to imagine what it feels like to be in a rehabilitation center, whether long term or short term, whether inpatient, outpatient, or partial. Similarly, it may not be easy to know how it feels for the nurses, who work 8-hour shifts with the same patients, compared to the art therapist's more common 1- or 2-hour groups.

Outpatient settings are yet another matter, from the clinic waiting room to the offices, conference rooms, and group rooms where the therapeutic action occurs. It feels different to both patients and staff to be in this kind of setting as opposed to being in one where people are separated from the outside world for days, weeks, or months at a time. In addition to consulting to a variety of places, I have also worked full time in both outpatient and inpatient settings at various times in my career.

I found a dramatic difference in the flavor of both sorts of places, in the attitudes of staff and patients, and in my own internal responses. While none of the places where I worked full time may have been typical of their genres, many of the differences between them did seem to depend on factors related to the type of setting and, of course, the type of patient and patient care appropriate to each.

Although the personnel in the two buildings also differed, many individuals worked on "both sides of the street" since the clinic and the hospital were both part of the Department of Psychiatry at the same university. But in spite of the fact that the faces in the elevator were often the same, the mood and the atmosphere were not, and over the years I have come more and more to feel that such differences are due, at least in part, to intrinsic distinctions between the two kinds of settings.

As with different patient groups, you may find yourself reacting with discomfort to some settings and not to others. It is then vital to try to understand just what it is you are responding to and how you can modify your reaction in order to work with relative comfort in that particular place. While understanding the source of your negative reaction may not eliminate it, it can sometimes help you to feel differently about where you are.

Although I have stressed the development of art therapy services and programs, such growth should ideally be consonant with your own personal development as an art therapist. So many of the same events promote both, such as collaborative work in research, service, or training. Also, in a more general way, an institution that feels well served by an art therapist is much more likely to be flexible in regard to requests that are primarily for the professional growth of the clinician.

Any time you invest in further training, it will probably benefit the setting you are in, especially if it is clearly relevant to your work there. It is of course considerate to arrange any such personal development activities in ways that least impinge on your job responsibilities and to be sure that neither the quantity nor the quality of your work suffers. If, therefore, you are sensitive to your employers in the selection and timing of further training, it is likely that they will be supportive, flexible about arrangements, and maybe even willing to pay some of the costs, if that is possible.

In any case, it is not just the setting that grows with the development of an art therapy program; it is also the individual clinician. If there is no space or time for personal development as an artist and a therapist, then your work is bound to be affected, not to mention your morale. You will find that some settings are more congenial than others, just as you may find that you prefer working with some age or type of client. But "knowing about" and "feeling with" seem as important in creating a secure place for art therapy in any setting as in doing effective art therapy with any kind of individual.

References

Kramer, E. (1971). *Art as therapy with children*. New York: Schocken Books.

Lisenco, Y. L. (1971). *Art not by eye*. New York: American Foundation for the Blind.

Tubbs, C., & Drake, M. (2006). *Crafts and creative media in therapy* (3rd ed.). Thorofare, NJ: Slack.

Recommended Readings

Betts, D. J. (Ed.). (2003). *Creative arts therapies approaches in adoption and foster care*. Springfield, IL: Thomas.

Bush, J. (1997). *The handbook of school art therapy*. Springfield, IL: Thomas.

Camilleri, V. A. (Ed.). (2007). *Healing the inner city child*. Philadelphia: Kingsley.

Gussak, D., & Virshup, E. (Eds.). (1997). *Drawing time: Art therapy in prisons and forensic settings*. Chicago: Magnolia Street.

Hartley, N., & Payne, M. (Eds.). (2008). *Creative arts in palliative care*. London: Kingsley.

Kalmanowitz, D., & Lloyd, B. (Eds.). (2005). *Art therapy and political violence*. London: Routledge.

Kaplan, F. (Ed.). (2007). *Art therapy and social action*. London: Kingsley.

Karkou, V. (Ed.). (2009). *Arts therapies in schools*. London: Kingsley.

Le Navenec, C.-L., & Bridges, L. (Eds.). (2005). *Creating connections between nursing care and the creative arts therapies*. Springfield, IL: Thomas.

Pratt, M., & Wood, M. (Eds.). (1998). *Art therapy in palliative care*. London: Routledge.

Stepney, S. A. (2009). *Art therapy with students at risk* (2nd ed.). Springfield, IL: Thomas.

Waller, D., & Mahony, J. (Eds.). (1999). *Treatment of addiction*. London: Routledge.

A girl with hydrocephaly draws using a tray in her crib at a residential school for children with physical disabilities.

A small group who had worked on a mural together then created individual representations of the group using an agreed-on color for each member. Here, they discuss their differing perceptions of the experience as represented in their color-coded pictures.

CHAPTER 15

Different Modes

Individual Art Therapy

As noted in the introduction to this section of the book, there are many possible ways of working in art therapy, whether the emphasis is diagnostic or therapeutic. At the time I first wrote this book in 1984, it was likely that most of the art therapy practiced in countless settings, regardless of the population, involved one person who was a therapist and another who was a patient or client (Casement, 1985). Almost 30 years later, I imagine that individual art therapy is still the most common mode of treatment in private practice, but I would also guess that group art therapy is more common in hospitals and clinics.

Frequency and length of art therapy sessions—whether individual, family, group, or some other configuration—will depend on many factors, including the level of motivation and the ability of the patient to participate. In outpatient treatment, weekly sessions are usually best. When I left the hospital in 1985 to go into full-time private practice, I was able to experiment with different frequencies and patterns of meeting.

Ironically, it seemed that once a week hardly ever seemed to be optimal, unless there were external reasons that imposed some constraint, such as the distance the person needed to travel, parental or client resistance to increased frequency, or the involvement of the individual in other forms of treatment.

When individual art therapy is the sole form of treatment, as was most often the case in my own practice, meeting with people twice a week seemed to me to be more than twice as effective. I had the impression that the more frequent contact accelerated the patient's involvement in the creative as well as the therapeutic process. It seemed to promote continuity between sessions and to intensify both the alliance and the rapidity of the developing transference.

It was also my impression, although never tested—and probably not testable because matching client-therapist pairs would be virtually impossible—that seeing people twice a week may have enabled them to work through their problems in fewer sessions than would have been possible in the more usual weekly contact. I was certainly influenced in this regard by my psychoanalytic training, which required me to meet with my analyst and to see my adult patients five times a week.

With child analytic patients, the minimum requirement was four times a week, so that I soon got accustomed to seeing people on a much more frequent basis than had been possible following the usual outpatient pattern of a child guidance center or the hospital outpatient pattern for adults. When I was at the guidance center, the only time I changed a child's meetings to twice a week was in response to a worsening of the child's symptoms and a feeling that the therapeutic "dosage" needed to be increased, usually to limit acting out that risked the youngster being expelled by his school.

My experience with inpatient treatment also served to modify my sense of what is best in regard to frequency since the hospital we served was one in which patients stayed for increasingly shorter periods of time, especially after the advent of managed care. To accomplish even limited goals with individuals referred for art therapy, it became essential to see them at least twice a week, sometimes more often. The latter frequently occurred because the patient was not able to tolerate long sessions at first, needing to start perhaps at 15 minutes and to gradually lengthen meetings to a half or three quarters of an hour.

Over the years, I also became more flexible about the length of separate sessions in individual work, although it is best for the client, once you have decided on a length of time, to keep it consistent—with the possible exception of some low-functioning people for whom an explicit goal is to increase their ability to work longer in art therapy. In any case, some very young children do quite well with 30- or 45-minute sessions, while some older ones can tolerate a full hour or even more. To go beyond an hour in individual work in a treatment facility, with rare exceptions, is probably not possible for most clinicians, bound as we usually are to fixed schedules.

That said, I believe that art therapists should try, whenever it is feasible, to be as flexible in their thinking about length as about frequency of sessions. There is no magic to the 50-minute hour. What may actually be magical about it is how important the time frame—whatever it is—becomes to the client, and how one can work on so many issues in relation to that aspect of the framework.

While it might be interesting to experiment with an open-ended time span (cf. Lacan, 2007) for individual appointments—scheduling a full morning, for example, for one person—it would probably only make therapeutic sense if the client was working with material or a process that required more time, like stone carving or animated filmmaking. Given the immense power and usefulness of the time limit in therapy, however, the minutes gained would probably not be worth the treatment lost. As for the frequency of appointments, I am not suggesting that you should be changeable from week to week or from session to session, but rather that you should be open-minded in deciding on the best format for any individual, couple, family, or group and acknowledge the ever-present possibility that some modification might be indicated at some point in time.

Regarding the schedule, I once had an experience that made me aware of my own rigidity about session timing, I was working with a boy who came twice a week—once during school and once after school. As a fifth grader, he was anxious about missing school too often, and the Tuesday morning time had been chosen by him because it was during a non-academic class. Because of a schedule conflict, I could no longer see him on Thursday afternoon, which had seemed to me to be well spaced in relation to the Tuesday morning time. He, however, chose Wednesday afternoon in preference to the Friday time I offered, but insisted that Tuesday morning would still work best.

I was skeptical about meeting 2 days in a row, but agreed to try it out at his insistence. Much to my surprise, the new schedule helped immensely in his treatment, in which there had been a good deal of resistance. He was much more able to continue on a Wednesday with what he had begun on a Tuesday than he had been with 2½ days in between. As has happened so often, I learned that I had been operating on an assumption that made sense logically but not clinically.

Individual work is more than a matter of scheduling, of course. What goes on between client and therapist in a one-to-one situation is more focused and often more intense than in work with groups or families. The alliance and the transference both develop rapidly, so that the management of potential transference resistance becomes a more common concern than in group art therapy.

For learning and working with art as a therapeutic modality, individual therapy is the mode I personally find the most fascinating and is the one I feel is most useful for training others in the fine points of technique. It can be conducted in a variety of ways—as can work with families or groups—with more or less support and with more or less of an attempt to uncover and to promote insight. My personal preference is to shift my approach flexibly, according to the needs of the individual client at any particular moment in time.

To assist in the development of any individual as an artist and a more comfortable human being can be deeply rewarding. It can also be extremely frustrating and distressing, especially at moments of confusion or impasse in the therapy. Depending on your goals and those of the client, individual art therapy can be brief (four to six sessions) or lengthy (4 to 6 years).

Sometimes, a youngster will terminate at one stage of development (like latency) and return for further work at another (like adolescence or young adulthood). The same is true for adults, of course, who may feel satisfied or unable to further invest themselves at termination but may later decide that there is more self-development that they would like to pursue through art therapy. What is most important is that the individual have a satisfying enough experience that the prospect of coming back for more therapy, whether with you or someone else, is an appealing one.

One of the difficult decisions in art therapy, especially with individuals, is where to position yourself physically. It is important to do so thoughtfully so that the person does not experience you as either an intrusive or a disinterested presence. Some art therapists sit quite far away from the patient, who may be at an easel or a table, so they do not interfere with his involvement in the creative process. Others sit close, either at the side of the work-table (kitty-corner) or opposite the client, which is my own personal preference, at least with those individuals who can tolerate the relative intimacy of such an arrangement.

Of course, if I get the feeling that looking at the person working is having an inhibiting effect, I might start using media myself or even move to another chair that is still fairly close. I prefer being across from the client, however, because I can easily observe facial expressions and subtle body movements, as well as hear softly spoken or mumbled comments. It also makes it easy and natural for the person to talk while he works, if that appeals to him.

Saving the artwork of individuals has always seemed important to me. Depending on the setting, there are various arrangements that have worked, from a large portfolio for each youngster on the childhood schizophrenia unit to shelves, folders, and containers of various sizes. For many years, I used a tall set of deep, wide, open shelves, on which each person had his or her own space. Most children would put their names or code on a piece of tape; most adults would prefer to keep their identities private.

Whatever storage system works best for you, it is ideal if the person's work is always accessible to him. It has always been striking to me how often a client would spontaneously look at something he had done in the past. As for me, I frequently found myself reminded of a previous creation and sometimes felt it would help to bring it into the dialogue of the session. In a more formal way, during the termination phase I have always suggested going through person's artwork, sometimes in the order in which it was created, as a way of literally re-viewing the therapy.

In addition, after many years of debate on the pros and cons—in which the cons always won—I finally decided to use a bulletin board on one of my office walls to display client art. The surface was large enough that all of the individuals I might be seeing at any point in time could have a space on it if they wished. Each was told that he could choose to pin one small-size picture up there if he wanted to at any point in time.

Whether individuals chose to display their art, and how they responded to the work of other clients, turned out to be extremely useful "grist for the [therapeutic] mill." Clients often became competitive, whether superior to or envious of others' work. I do not think I ever saw anyone of any age level who did not at some point think he or she was entitled to additional space on the bulletin board, wishing to be special.

Some clients, of course, children as well as adults, chose not to display. This decision also was useful to explore and to try to understand as part of their art therapy. In any case, having overcome my initial resistance to the idea, it turned out to be really fascinating, clinically useful, and it definitely enhanced the appearance of my art room.

Are You Solo or Adjunctive?

Before leaving the subject of individual art therapy, it is important to note that the responsibility and role of the art therapist—and probably the nature of the art therapy—are both heavily influenced by whether you are the only person treating the client or whether there are others involved. When you are working adjunctively, especially with individuals, you can more freely concentrate on the creative process itself since the primary psychotherapeutic responsibility is being handled by one or more others.

When you are the sole therapist, then all aspects of the client's problems become your concern, which often requires broadening the art therapy to include connections with the patient's real life. It may also require contacts with others who are involved with the individual, such as parents, schools, hospitals, and doctors.

When treating a child who has behavioral difficulties in school, for example, an art therapist—like any other clinician—may need to make school visits and consult with the teachers. When treating an adult who is a drug addict, an art therapist—like any other clinician—may need to be in contact with the patient's physician, as well as with any agencies involved in detoxification or rehabilitation.

Such responsibility also rests on the shoulders of any art therapist who is the sole clinician involved with members of a family or of a group who have come for treatment. In such instances, the fact that you are a therapist first and foremost, albeit of a particular type (art), becomes apparent.

Group and Family Art Therapy

There are differences, however, between individual and group or family art therapy, which exist regardless of whether the work is independent or adjunctive. Some of the issues discussed in regard to individuals also need to be considered, but the parameters become more complicated because of the need to accommodate more separate individuals. Because it is essential to know about group and family dynamics and the specific therapeutic approaches developed for both, any art therapist specializing in either has typically done intensive study in the area chosen.

The potentially superior efficacy of greater frequency, for example, while possibly true for group and family art therapy, is often not worth the effort and resistance involved in trying to schedule more than one weekly meeting when many clients are involved. In my experience, lengthening group or family outpatient sessions seemed to work better if intensifying the treatment seemed to be indicated.

Inpatient or partial hospitalization work is quite different since the group is virtually "captive" and is therefore easily available to meet more than once a week—even daily if deemed appropriate. In short-term care settings, a greater frequency of group meetings seemed in fact to be more effective.

In the psychiatric hospital where I co-directed the CEAT (Creative and Expressive Arts Therapy) program, the substance abuse patients had 2 hours of creative arts therapy every day—one in art, the other in dance, music, or drama. Another group of patients, who were functioning at a very low intellectual level, ended up receiving their daily required "psychotherapy" in an art or movement group rather than a verbal one. Open studio groups on many of the units could be attended by any interested patient and were usually available several times a week; they were often of a longer duration, allowing for more complex work with materials.

Groups in art therapy, like groups in any kind of treatment, are not only focused on therapist-client interaction but also on what happens in the group as a whole. The work done within an art therapy group can be largely individual or mostly conjoint, depending on the goals of the group, the nature of the patients, and the bias of the art therapist (Yalom & Leszcz, 2005).

The form taken by the different stages in therapy outlined in Chapter 6 is also slightly different with groups than with individuals, but the overall process is the same. What also occurs, however, is a progressive change in the group itself, which starts out as a series of separate individuals, each linked with the art therapist leader, and evolves in complex ways into a more integrated unit, developing pairings and subgroups within it.

The ways in which groups express resistance and anxiety are especially fascinating, and it helps if the art therapist understands both the developmental and the dynamic aspects of group process. It is more difficult to follow group process, however, when the group itself is not a consistent one, as is often the case in brief hospitalization and is certainly true of an open studio.

Families, of course, are a special kind of group, who have a long history of interaction with one another. They do not disperse when they leave the therapist like the members of an outpatient group but have to go home and deal with whatever came up in the art session. To a lesser extent, this is also true of inpatient groups, who live in close proximity on the unit. This fact of living together places a special strain on inpatient group art therapy as well as on family art therapy, whether you are seeing the entire nuclear family, the couple, the extended family, or a multiple-family group.

It is my own feeling that conducting family art therapy over any substantial period of time, especially if it is the sole form of treatment, is as "hot" a clinical situation as art therapists are likely to encounter. Family art therapy is fascinating and challenging and requires particularly strong clinical skills and some training in family therapy—or, especially if you are just beginning, a co-therapist with experience in family treatment (Goldenberg & Goldenberg, 2007).

Collaboration With Coworkers

There are many ways to collaborate with your colleagues, depending on the situation in each setting. One way is to work parallel to others, meeting regularly with any other clinicians who are also dealing with the same patients. In most inpatient work, the art therapist is part of a multidisciplinary team, all of whom combine their varied skills to help patients individually, in groups, and sometimes with their families.

However, this is not always the case. When I first worked with children in a psychiatric hospital, I attended the morning staff meetings on the day I came to do individual art therapy but did not know or have contact with all of the child psychiatry residents, each of whom was seeing one of the children with schizophrenia on the unit. Although the director had told the residents about my once-a-week presence, some chose to make contact and share, and some did not.

One of the most awkward situations involved a resident who seemed not to know of my existence until the day each of us had to present our work to visiting professor Erik Erikson in front of a large crowd of local mental health specialists at Grand Rounds. Since the child had expressed herself much more articulately in art than she was able to in her verbal therapy, the inevitable comparisons made by Erikson were uncomfortable for me and, I imagine, for the resident as well. After that experience, I resolved to overcome my shyness and to be more assertive, making contact with each resident whose child case I was seeing and offering to share what the youngster had done in art.

Although you would think that I might have learned from that embarrassing incident, I was still rather naïve when I started work at the child guidance center several years later. After observing art therapy groups during a special summer therapeutic day camp program, each of three child psychiatry residents requested adjunctive art therapy for a youngster they were seeing individually.

I then met with each resident to decide together on frequency and format. Each differed slightly according to the resident's perception of the needs of the case, and I thought we were doing a fine job of collaborating. We were, on the surface, but what I was not sufficiently sensitive to was the possible competition and threat for these young psychiatrists—fresh from their general (adult) residency and new to work with children—of someone else seeing his patient and using another modality.

As it turned out, one of the three was secure and was able to talk openly and helpfully about how he felt when either of the two patients we shared—a mother and her child—disclosed something in art therapy not yet expressed in verbal or play therapy. This young doctor was delighted to get a hint of what was forthcoming during our weekly collaborations and dubbed the art "a preview of coming attractions."

The other two responded in different ways to each of the children's greater comfort in and fondness for art therapy. One decided that he should stop seeing the youngster, and that I should become the primary therapist; the other concluded that I should stop seeing the child individually and referred her to an art therapy group I had recently formed. In my own insecurity, I was unable to see beyond my confusion and went along rather meekly with whatever each doctor suggested. But, the lesson was an important one, which I finally grasped, and is relevant for anyone doing adjunctive art therapy in any setting.

Although competition is probably most loaded in the kind of outpatient situation described, it exists whenever art therapy is successful and valued and other approaches are less so. The ability of the other professionals involved to rejoice that something has finally worked seems to be directly proportional to their own feelings of security and competence.

Because of the intrinsic pleasures available in art therapy, especially for children, it is not uncommon that many prefer art to talk therapy.

Also, as noted earlier, the relative visibility of art therapy seems to have made it more easily noticed in the psychiatric hospital where we offered all of the arts therapies, and perhaps it was less threatening in many ways. Whatever the reason, there were more requests for additional art therapy services than in any of the other creative modalities, stimulating some envy and resentment on the part of the dance, music, and drama therapists. As co-directors of the program, my drama therapist colleague and I needed to deal with this unanticipated sibling rivalry among our small expressive therapies family.

Similar but even more insidious feelings of jealousy can easily be aroused in other staff members, who try hard but are often less able to reach patients who, for one reason or another, respond well in art therapy. It is important for art therapists to be alert to the potential of the modality to evoke such envious feelings, so that they can note clues to their emergence and can work to build alliances that will serve to make such situations both less likely and less disruptive.

In schools, there is a similar risk of envy when the art therapist is more popular among the children than the counselor who relies only on words. Although collaborating on an IEP (individualized education program or plan) requires all professionals seeing a child with a disability to meet together, that does not mean that they always have regular contact afterward.

In fact, an art therapist is often somewhat isolated, depending on the administrative setup and the nature of her schedule. Working in more than one school in a district seems to be as common as working on more than one unit in a hospital or working in different physical locations within the same health care system. In such instances, it is vital to find a way to meet and collaborate with others involved in serving the same individuals if at all possible.

Doing Co-therapy

Doing co-therapy is one of the most common forms of collaboration and is probably one of the best ways to broaden and deepen your clinical skills with families and groups. One of the healthiest ways to build alliances with other staff members is to work together in this way, which is also a useful way to learn from someone with more training and experience in either mode. But co-therapy is no bed of roses either. It is complicated, demanding, and can be potentially unpleasant if not carried out carefully.

It is vital, from the first, to understand and respect the style and point of view of the other clinician. One way to begin is to observe each other at work, with similar populations if possible. It is then necessary to plan together for each session and to provide time for mutual discussion between each meeting. Although the pressures of schedule and location make this difficult, it greatly enriches the experience for all.

When I conducted an adolescent expressive therapy group with a drama therapist and a child psychiatrist, for example, the three of us found that we needed at least 2 hours as well to collaborate on the 2-hour weekly sessions. One hour was spent reviewing and discussing what went on, in terms of group process and individual progress, in the presence of a consulting psychiatrist, an expert in group therapy.

The other (separate) hour was spent sharing with each other the thoughts and feelings stimulated in each of us by the youngsters' responses and to each others' handling of situations in the group. Had we not been able to share our discomforts or disagreements, we could probably not have tolerated the intense transferences and countertransferences that developed among us and the members over the 2 years of the existence of the group.

Co-therapy is extremely tricky since no two individuals have identical styles of working with other human beings, and it is difficult to monitor and to manage the inevitable complications, such as competition for the patients' affection. Successful co-therapy requires that the partners be aware of their relative levels of clinical development. If one is significantly more advanced than the other, one becomes the assistant to the other, who functions as the leader, which is useful in training.

However, it is qualitatively different from a co-therapy situation in which the leadership is genuinely shared. When that is the case, great care must be taken to develop an open-and-honest relationship, as well as an understanding of each other's perspectives, before and throughout the time of working together. Most important is the mutual sharing of feelings about one another—perhaps even more critical at certain times than collaborating about the patients—although that is also necessary. If the two therapists do not continually express and work out the tensions and differences that inevitably arise between them, then their work with their clients will—just as inevitably—suffer in some way, not necessarily apparent at first.

Since it is rather unusual that two art therapists at the same level of development choose to work together in co-therapy, the intense competition likely in such a case rarely occurs. Because both are specialists in the visual arts, the disagreements about how to set up, to motivate, to help, and to reflect could be numerous. In my few such experiences, our different notions of what to present and how to relate to the patients created significant tensions for each of us.

More often, the art therapist is the acknowledged art specialist of the team, while the partner is the expert in group, family, or a particular type of treatment (e.g., Gestalt) or another creative therapy (e.g., dance, drama, or music). Having different and clearly defined areas of expertise is a great asset since each then has a defined territory in which their opinions or wishes are given priority.

Nevertheless, there are still inevitable tensions and conflicts when any two people work closely together in the pressure cooker of group expressive arts therapy, and specialization does not remove all problems. It may minimize them, as when an art therapist agrees to take responsibility for presenting the art experiences to the patients, while the other clinician agrees to lead the discussion or another activity. Eventually, as each becomes more familiar and comfortable with the other's modality or area of expertise, each is likely to have more and more opinions about how the other is functioning.

I hope that pointing out the potential pitfalls of parallel or co-therapy will not deter you from trying it. It can be great fun, there is a tremendous amount of learning possible, and—in my experience—it usually increases the potential for growth in clients when done with care. I believe they have more opportunities when they have available two possible transference objects, two modalities, and two trained clinicians to help them with their problems.

For each therapist, it is helpful to be able to discuss clients regularly with another professional who is equally invested in their progress. This makes the work much more tolerable when things become stressful, an inevitable component of successful therapy. It also makes it a much richer experience, from which you can usually learn more than from working alone with the same individual, family, or group.

Knowing Different Therapeutic Modes

As with settings and populations, any art therapist beginning work in a new mode, whether couple or family or some other configuration—like brief psychotherapy—first ought to find out what has been done in that kind of art therapy by others. For no matter how imaginative you may be, it never hurts to become informed about what has worked. Since the literature often deals with theory as well as technique, reports by other art therapists working in the same modes can also help anyone to better understand what is happening.

Making a decision regarding which mode is best when you have a choice is not an easy matter, and it takes many years of clinical experience with each to be able to choose in an informed way. There are certainly assets and limitations to any particular mode of art therapy, and there is no rulebook saying that only one kind may be offered at a time. One of my favorite cases included family art therapy as well as individual treatment for two of the four children (one in art therapy) and eventual couple therapy for the parents.

At the risk of oversimplifying, it would seem that, when a problem has been internalized in the patient (has become part of his basic personality structure), then individual art therapy makes the most sense. Group art therapy makes sense as the only mode of treatment when the people involved cannot, for some reason, handle individual therapy or when their problems are not so much internal as with the external world.

It is naïve, however, to think that just because someone has difficulty relating to peers, putting him into a group for treatment will successfully address that problem. If he suffers from a "delusion of uniqueness," discovering that others have similar troubles may, of course, be helpful. Also, if he is able to relate to people with some awareness of their separateness, a group can certainly be a place for him to learn about the impact of his behavior on others.

Group therapy as adjunctive is, of course, different from group as the primary mode of treatment, in art as in any other form of therapy. The same considerations hold for family art therapy, that the existence of intrafamilial tensions does not necessarily indicate that family therapy is the treatment of choice.

Many factors need to be weighed, including the perceived needs of the patients and their apparent readiness for one or another mode of therapy. Art therapists are rarely in the position of making decisions about the type of treatment offered to someone unless they are in private practice, and it is certainly not always possible to make group art therapy available, even though you might think it would be optimal.

If and when you have such a responsibility, however, you need to understand not only the nature of each mode, but also those client characteristics that would make any one the treatment of choice. When someone is totally unable to use group art therapy, for example, that usually becomes quickly apparent, as in the patient's excessive withdrawal, disruptiveness, or demanding behavior.

Sometimes it is not so much the fault of the mode itself, but rather the size, makeup, or length of the particular group that, if modified, might make it possible for the client to participate constructively. There are many variables to be considered, some of which may sometimes be manipulated as in the following example.

With the children on one inpatient unit, we found that, because of a larger-than-usual number with conduct disorders—due to a research study underway there at the time—the projected group size of six was simply not manageable. Four was a more realistic number, and the art therapy sessions also worked better when shortened in length and increased in frequency.

Finally, it was found that screening patients in individual art interviews prior to placing them in groups made it possible to have more functional group compositions. For those few children who were still unable to share space, materials, or the therapist, individual art therapy was made available. These conclusions were reached after a fair amount of trial and error, as in most clinical decision making in institutional settings.

On some of the adult units in the hospital, we found that making the art therapy groups more homogeneous facilitated the clinician's work, while on others, more heterogeneous groupings seem to enhance what happened. There are, of course, advantages to both, and it is always necessary to balance the gains and losses in each in order to decide what will work best for any setting or population.

The same kind of reasoning holds true for the room in which the art therapy occurs and the length of each session when there is a choice of either. Sometimes a smaller space helps greatly to facilitate interaction, but at other times it can be too close or too intimate for patient comfort. Similarly, a larger space offers more options in closeness or distance, which may enable some people to function better, while others can be overwhelmed, confused, or lost in too vast a space, especially if it is one with a great many stimuli.

What probably matters most in regard to different modes of art therapy is that you become knowledgeable about whichever ones you are called upon to use. Taking a course, doing some reading, getting some consultation or supervision, or even going into that form of treatment yourself are all excellent ways to learn. Working collaboratively, either parallel or together, has many advantages for growing as a clinician and for creating a more secure place for yourself in any system.

Co-therapy, as noted earlier, is probably the most difficult, yet one of the most rewarding, ways to learn and grow. Study groups are also great fun if organized around topics of mutual interest. Developing as an art therapist, in other words, is a lifelong task if you are to achieve true artistry. Regardless of where you are in your professional development, it is always vital to know when you are needing consultation, supervision, or a referral to someone else. This is a simple matter of ethics.

References

Casement, P. (1985). *On learning from the patient.* London: Routledge.

Goldenberg, I., & Goldenberg, H. (2007). *Family therapy: An overview* (7th ed.). Los Angeles: Brooks/Cole.

Lacan, J. (2007). *Ecrits* (B. Fink, Trans.). New York: Norton.

Yalom, I. D., & Leszcz, M. (2005). *The theory and practice of group psychotherapy* (5th ed.). New York: Basic Books.

Recommended Readings

Arrington, D. B. (2001). *Home is where the art is.* Springfield, IL: Thomas.

Kerr, C., Hoshino, J., Sutherland, J., Parashak, S. T., & McCarley, L. L. (2008). *Family art therapy: Foundations of theory and practice.* New York: Routledge.

Kwiatkowska, H. Y. (1978). *Family therapy and evaluation through art.* Springfield, IL: Thomas.

Landgarten, H. B. (1987). *Family art psychotherapy.* New York: Brunner/Mazel.

Liebmann, M. (2005). *Art therapy for groups* (2nd ed.). London: Routledge.

McNeilly, G. (2006). *Group analytic art therapy.* London: Kingsley.

Moon, B. L. (2010). *Art-based group therapy.* Springfield, IL: Thomas.

Proulx, L. (2002). *Strengthening emotional ties through parent-child-dyad art therapy.* London: Kingsley.

Riley, S. (2001). *Group process made visible.* New York: Brunner-Routledge.

Riley, S., & Malchiodi, C. A. (2004). *Integrative approaches to family art therapy* (2nd ed.) Chicago: Magnolia Street.

Skaife, S., & Huet, V. (Eds.). (1998). *Art psychotherapy in groups.* London: Routledge.

Working together on a large surface without talking was helpful for this family. After creating silently on a shared space, there was a vigorous discussion of what had happened.

Students in an art therapy class take turns showing and discussing their individual creations with the group.

PART 5

Related Service

In addition to the basics of art therapy and their application to different people, places, and modes covered in the first four parts of this book, there are other areas that are not essential but are useful to know, especially if you are to fully develop your talents in the service of the profession. For any discipline to continue, some way must be found to impart its essentials to those who wish to learn. Some are trainees, who need assistance to develop their own skills. Specifically, they need to be taught and they need to be supervised, so that knowing both *teaching* and *supervision* is essential for any art therapist who finds herself in the position of training others.

Then there are those who may not wish to become art therapists but who need to understand the field well enough to make appropriate referrals of patients for either assessment or treatment through art. Sometimes, these people work in the same setting, in which case the intervention is usually called *in-service training*. At other times, they work elsewhere, in which case the intervention is more often called *consultation*.

Whatever the nomenclature, the important thing to remember is that these are all an *indirect* use of the art therapist's skills, as opposed to the *direct* use of those skills in work with clients. Both indirect and direct service involve helping relationships, but there are differences between therapy and supervision or therapy and consultation. An art therapist needs to have a clear understanding of what is meant by each of these roles, to know the areas of overlap as well as those of differentiation.

So, after some internal debate, I decided to add several chapters to those about the basics and their application. The chapters in this section—which I considered omitting from the revision but which my consultants felt would be a mistake—are extras for beginners. They are, however, essential for experienced art therapists, who are often involved in indirect service to the profession. The three chapters about such work deal with *teaching, supervision*, and *consultation*.

There is yet another important "extra" that could even be considered "basic" if viewed broadly, but it is usually thought of in a more narrow and specialized fashion: *research*. Although it had been relatively neglected when this book was first written, it is now a requirement in training programs. This is a wonderful development because it is one of the most critical areas for the ultimate acceptance and expansion of art therapy. In the chapter on research, I note some of the issues especially relevant to art therapy research as well as what an art therapist needs to know to be able to understand research findings in related disciplines.

Although refining the artistry of art therapy in our direct work with patients is related to the growth and development of our field, these other areas are also vital to our survival in the world of human services since they often influence those who decide whether to hire or refer people to art therapists. Less political and more enduring, the development of *artistry* in teaching, supervision, consultation, and research in art therapy is necessary in order to better understand and to utilize the powerful creative modality we offer. These "extras," while not essential for each individual practitioner, become increasingly relevant as you assume a more generative role in the future development of the profession.

There is one last "extra" of interest to only a minority of art therapists, but also important for the further growth of the discipline: *theory*. In the section on "The Therapy Part," the importance of knowing and understanding the different theoretical models of personality and psychotherapy in current use was often noted (Corey, 2008). It is fortunate that this is usually part of graduate training (Rubin, 2001).

The development of a valid theory about art therapy is a more demanding task, yet it may be the most important "extra" of all. For if we are unable to account for our effectiveness in a logical and communicable way, we will continue to be viewed as either charming romantics or hopeless airheads, depending on the bias of the perceiver. In the chapter on theory, I shall describe the kind of theorizing that seems appropriate to art therapy and some of what people need to know in order to develop in that direction.

I am not suggesting that most clinicians are interested in becoming theorists any more than I would expect most art therapists to want to conduct research. But I do think that art therapists, once they have learned to do their work artistically, have a responsibility to those they may train, advise, supervise, or inform to be able to understand theory in their own field and in related disciplines, just as they have a responsibility to be able to read and grasp relevant research studies.

Another reason for including this section on "extras" is that, while many art therapists are not formally designated as teachers, supervisors, consultants, researchers, or theorists, *all* art therapists informally assume each of those roles, often without even being aware that they are doing so. If nothing else, this section of the book serves to raise the issues involved in each chapter to a more conscious level, so that individuals can decide whether they wish to pursue further training and greater sophistication in any of these extra but vital dimensions of art therapy.

I have also included an addendum, "Knowing What You *Don't* Know." Perhaps this is the highest level of professional development in art therapy, as elsewhere—a sense not only of wonder but also of openness, a conviction that people and art and therapy are complex, and that simple answers are simply inadequate. Along with humility, a healthy dose of skepticism is useful, although both need to exist in a matrix of overall confidence in yourself and in your discipline. While I sometimes have doubts about me, I never have doubts about the value, the potential, and the power of art therapy.

References

Corey, G. (2008). *Theory and practice of counseling and psychotherapy* (8th ed.). Belmont, CA: Brooks/Cole.

Rubin, J. A. (Ed.). (2001). *Approaches to art therapy: Theory and technique* (2nd ed.). New York: Brunner-Routledge.

Participants in an art therapy workshop warm up by drawing silently with chalk on a large piece of paper.

Art therapy education involves a number of different interventions, including didactic lectures, as in this photo.

CHAPTER 16

Knowing Teaching

Introduction

Although the principles of good pedagogy probably apply to the teaching of any subject matter, it is my impression that art therapists, like most clinician-educators, find themselves offering courses or leading seminars without any background or training in higher education (cf. Milne & Noone, 1996). Sadly, they are often unable to convey what they know about their discipline because they are uninformed about how best to help people to learn. Their approach is usually based on that of teachers they have admired during their own education, and if they are lucky, they have had good models to emulate.

This book is not the place for a detailed treatise on teaching methodology. But, it seems appropriate to briefly alert those art therapists who find themselves instructing others without formal preparation for that role to some of the issues that are especially pertinent to learning in our discipline. Most apply to any teaching situation, whether the students are one-time workshop attendees or 2-year master's degree candidates. As with the difference between short- and long-term therapy, the goals and objectives in diverse situations are likely to be different, but the keys to effective learning remain virtually the same.

Deciding What to Teach

The first issue in any kind of teaching situation is being clear about what you wish to convey. While you might think that is simple, already defined by the title of the course, workshop, or lecture, there are always choices to be made among the many facets of any subject in art therapy. One criterion, of course, is your own sense of what is most important for these people to learn about the topic involved.

To make that decision intelligently, however, you need to find out just what it is the students or audience *already know*—"where they are" in any specific subject matter. You may be able to find out by asking what learning experiences they have already had (e.g., previous required courses), although it is likely, even in a sequentially designed curriculum, that people will be at different levels of awareness, knowledge, and sophistication on any topic.

The decision you then have to make is just where to "pitch" the course, lecture, or workshop, given the fact that there is probably a range of preparedness among those attending. My own preference is to try to communicate to a level around the *middle,* between the most sophisticated and the least informed, and then to provide in some fashion for those at the extremes. This is a challenge, but it is best if your listeners do not feel either that you are "talking down" to them or that you are speaking "over their heads."

This requires a nimble dance on your part as a teacher, but like artistry in doing art therapy, it is also an enjoyable task. One way I have found to guard against being "out of synch" with the learning level of participants is to invite them repeatedly to ask any questions they may have about anything you have said or asked them to do.

In addition to your own ideas about the key learnings in any area and the preparation level of the students, an instructor should also gear what is taught to the particular needs and interests of any specific group of learners. Given the broad range of subject matter within any area in art therapy, another variable governing selection of topics should be the students' greatest concerns.

What this means in practice is that some time at the beginning of any learning experience, short or long term, is well spent in finding out where people are in regard to their areas of special interest. It is analogous to beginning diagnostically when dealing with patients in therapy since what the art therapist has to offer, in either case, can only be received if presented at a level that they can assimilate and that is in accord with their particular interests and motivation for being there.

All of this might seem self-evident, but I have been surprised at the number of times I have assessed learner level and interest and have heard from the students that they were not used to being asked such questions. Of course, the knowledge domains that are part of a prescribed curriculum need to be covered, but there can certainly be variation in how that is done.

Like some clients in art therapy, some students prefer to be spoon-fed, even force-fed, to have the academic "diet" pre-selected for them, and to be told with no ambiguity what to do, what to read, and what to write (or draw). The type of food or "nourishment" offered may well need to be decided by someone who knows more than they do about art therapy nutrition. However, it is important that they have some options as well.

I am reminded of the classic study by a child psychologist in which infants, offered nothing but healthy foods from which to choose, ended up selecting balanced diets, although they did go on periodic food binges in the course of the study (Davis, 1928). Similarly, the academic "diet" made available to weekend workshop or semester course participants needs to be "good" stuff, any and all of which is relevant to the topic and nutritious for the student. But, the sequence in which they partake and the shifts from breadth to depth in approach can, in fact, be determined by the interests of the learners.

The reason for recommending such an approach to teaching, within the structure of any curriculum or objective, is that self-motivated learning always seems to take hold faster and with more lasting effect than that which is dictated primarily or solely by others. Even if the students' freedom is limited to participating in decisions about the sequence of subjects or the relative time spent on different facets of a topic, I am convinced that such involvement pays off handsomely in a high level of interest and the subsequent retention of material.

If, for some reason, flexibility in course subjects or sequence needs to be limited, you can still make it possible for students to choose such things as term paper or project topics according to their own special interests. I am not suggesting that *all* the decisions come from the learners, but that within the structure provided by the teacher's definition of the essential facets of any topic, there should be enough freedom for people to go in directions that are especially fascinating to them as individuals. Motivation, in other words, leads to better learning.

Well, you might say, that is all very fine if you have a whole semester of a 3-credit course within which to shift topics and priorities, but what if you are limited to a 3-hour seminar or a 1-day workshop? Is it not the teacher's responsibility to decide what is most important for people to learn in such a tight time frame? Yes, of course. The instructor has that same responsibility in any time span, and the shorter it is, the less flexibility you will have. But, the importance of trying to reach the level and meet the needs of the learners remains. The two are really not incompatible, and inviting students to collaborate in the learning exercise is always a good idea.

Much of the information gathering about both may have to be done in advance, by inquiring, for example, of the person inviting you for a lecture or workshop about the level of sophistication and particular needs or interests of the group. I usually suggest that the liaison person ask, at a gathering close in time to the one I will be leading—like a scheduled staff meeting or class—just what aspects of art therapy they most want to learn about.

Even in a brief encounter, you can be prepared to go in one direction or another, which can sometimes be assessed at the time. I often decide exactly which exercise I will use or which film segment or image I will show after meeting the participants, even in a short presentation. Needless to say, you have to have options available in art or audiovisual supplies to be able to shift gears on any specific activity at short notice. As if to remind me of unexpected circumstances and the need to assess group sophistication, I had such an experience while I was writing this book.

I had been asked by the Women's Issues Group of the Barrier Island Group for the Arts on Sanibel to present at one of their 2-hour meetings. I had discussed what might be of inter-est with the woman who had invited me as well as with the coordinator and had reviewed it with both of them again a week before the presentation. Based on what each of these women said, I prepared a number of film clips regarding women in art therapy and burned two DVDs, which I brought with me.

However, as it turned out, I had to quickly adapt to the audiovisual equipment—which was not what I had requested—as well as the level of understanding of the group. I had asked for and had been assured that there would be an LCD projector as well as a sound system (either in-room or speakers). I had been asked to bring my laptop and necessary connect-ing cables—all of this in writing. However, after I arrived, the young man who handled the audiovisual material told me that the room the group met in had no sound equipment, neither speakers nor a portable microphone that could augment the sound coming out of the computer speakers. So, I had to abandon my plan to show the video clips I had edited.

This was discouraging to say the least, but it was not the first time I was unexpectedly confronted with audiovisual equipment problems, especially since deciding some years ago that video clips of active work with art are superior to separate still images. Despite having run into film-playing and projection difficulties at New York University, which has a famous film school, I still prefer to use film whenever possible, as in the DVD that accompanies this book. But, since I could not show film in that room except with inadequate sound, I had to change gears on the spot.

Fortunately, having used slide images of artwork for most of my career, I decided to find whatever was on my computer and to shape my remarks according to the questions of the group. I was as lucky in their sophistication as I had been unlucky in the equipment. While exploring their interests, I discovered that most of them were retired mental health professionals, so that allowed me to speak at a more professional level than I had been led to believe would be appropriate. And, it was really lucky that I had—on the hard drive of my little laptop—the contents of a DVD I had recently put together for another book revision (Rubin, 2010).

So I switched gears, and instead of the material I had prepared but could not present, I used images from several sections of the DVD to build a presentation based on the comments and questions that the women were asking. Now, I realize that not everyone carries a laptop to their presentations or has images on their computer. My guess is that most instructors probably prepare a PowerPoint presentation that can be played on a computer already at the facility. My message to art therapists who teach is not about the specifics of my recent experience; rather, it is to be prepared and, above all, to be flexible since you really never know what or who you might find when you go to give a presentation.

Level of sophistication is important, whatever the nature of the group addressed. It is also important, whether the audience is composed of laypersons or professionals from other disciplines, to use language and ideas that make sense and are familiar to the group. I might use the same set of images with parents, teachers, or psychiatrists, but I would say slightly different things about them with each group since I would try to speak in terms both meaningful and comprehensible to the audience.

Similarly, I might ask a group of child care workers or psychologists to engage in the same art activity (like a scribble drawing or a nonverbal dyadic drawing), but the terms in which I would discuss it with each set of learners would probably be slightly different. The rationale given each group for the experience also might differ, depending again on the nature of the members and the context of the exercise. The discussion afterward would, of course, be based on what the participants had to say about the experience, following their lead as you would with a client group.

Deciding How to Teach

In teaching situations, you need to decide not only on the *content* of what you will offer but also on the *form* in which it will be conveyed. For many years, I have been convinced that direct involvement in art activities—along with a chance to look at them reflectively and relate them to whatever is being taught—is the ideal combination. While I am not always successful in making such an experience possible, I usually attempt to do so, even if the involvement is as minimal as doodling with pencil on paper on the arm of a chair or manipulating a piece of plasticine or some chenille stems while sitting in an auditorium seat. I generally present it as "fooling around," which allows people to listen while doing it and not to worry about the final product.

Art therapy, by its very nature, involves both doing and reflecting. It makes sense, then, that any time you want to teach others about it, whether at a deep or a superficial level, they will understand best if they can be directly involved in creating something they can then examine. The emotional impact of discovering something about yourself is of a far different order from the intellectual discovery of the power of art therapy, even through seeing dramatic case studies.

The very best situation for learning about art therapy, then, involves both direct involvement and subsequent reflection—along with a more distant perspective, usually by hearing from the presenter about the topic. To present such information only in words is to lose the most central and valuable element of art therapy: visual imagery.

Although most art therapists do use either original artwork or reproductions in their presentations, I have been surprised to find that this is not always the case. I suspect that if you are really convinced of the necessity to illustrate any descriptions of your work with visual images, you will try to make sure in planning and preparing that proper equipment will be available, even if you have to bring the paintings or the computer yourself.

Another problem many teaching art therapists seem to have is that, even when they have put images together to illustrate a talk, the art products are shown as a group *after* the main (verbal) presentation, with descriptive commentary that is not always clearly related to what was said earlier. It takes time and planning but is infinitely more useful to the audience if the images shown literally *illustrate* the verbal presentation and are viewed at those points in the talk at which they best fit. The simultaneous hearing of description and seeing of illustration facilitates the ability of the audience to fully integrate the message from the art therapist.

A personal anecdote may be relevant here. For 6 years during the late 1970s, I served on the board of an organization founded by Jeanne Kennedy Smith—now known as Very Special Arts and dedicated to bringing the arts to people with disabilities. I had given a fair number of talks for the group, using my favorite method of preparation, which by then was to think of the theme I wanted to present, to select slides to illustrate the ideas, and to speak extemporaneously based on the images, controlling the slide projector myself as I went along. When Mrs. Smith asked me to write speeches for her, just like the ones she had heard me give, I had to explain that they were not written. She had a hard time believing that, and was pretty persistent, so in the end I sent her a paper I had done along with some slides.

Another anecdote is even more amusing. In the early 1970s, I was invited to give a talk in an art therapy lecture series at Hahnemann Medical College, home of the first operational degree program in the field. Although to illustrate my talk I had brought slides in a carousel (holder) as usual, it turned out that the projector was an old one, and the slides needed to be put in one at a time. More upsetting was the fact that I was not going to be able to operate the sequence myself since the talk was in an old-fashioned medical school lecture room, very steep, with me at the bottom and the projectionist at the top.

I gave him the carousel, however, asking him to put the slides in the projector in the order in which they were placed in the tray. The next thing I knew, he had taken the slides out, put them in a pile, and they spilled onto the floor. Since they were not numbered (I had just put them in an order that made sense to me), and the doctors were filling up the seats and we had to begin, I asked the projectionist to just show one at a time—and had no idea what was coming next. So, I had to do quite a verbal tap dance to make sense out of the sequence in my ad-libbed remarks.

Those images included not only artwork that had been done in the group I was describing, but also pictures of the youngsters engaged in creating it. It seems that while many art therapists show art products, relatively few presenters show pictures of people at work. Yet for the naïve listener, what is impossible to imagine is how the room looked, how the participants behaved, and just how those creative products became realities in time and space. Images, videotapes, or films of the art therapy situation in action give concrete form to what might otherwise look quite different in the imagination of those in the audience.

You might object that pictures of clients violate rights of privacy, but in my experience people are agreeable to having their pictures taken, in many different settings, if they are assured that they will be used only for educational purposes. Of course, it is essential for both legal and ethical reasons to obtain written consent from the client or guardian.

Another safeguard that makes sense to me is never to show pictures of people who might be recognizable to groups in the same city.

Since this book was first written, there has been increasing concern with litigation, and of course art therapists need to be sensitive to that and to obtain informed consent from anyone whose image (art or person) is being shown to any group, lay or professional. Ironically, at the same time that institutions and individuals have become more cautious about showing people, the rapid posting and accessibility of still and video images of actual art therapy on the Internet has led to new questions about the ethics involved.

With the speed of changes in communications technology, I do not think the questions stimulated by these developments will be answered in a day, a month, or even a year. The profession of art therapy, which is inherently visual, is now challenged to find ways to tell the world what we can do, at the same time respecting the individuals we serve and their right to privacy if they so desire.

Putting It Into a Broader Context

A final important element in the ideal art therapy learning situation is relating what has been experienced, heard, and seen to a broader picture. The larger scene might be the field in general—locally, statewide, or nationally—at that moment in time. Or, it might be a histori-cal perspective, perhaps about the role of art therapy in the particular area being discussed, whether it is work with families or the prison system.

Just as it is best to include some direct involvement and reflection and to present some vivid clinical material that illustrates what can be done, so it is ideal if whatever has been experienced by the learners can be put into a larger context. This might involve, in addition to lecturing, the assigning of readings or projects, especially in an ongoing teaching situation.

You might argue that the three approaches just advocated as the ideal elements in the *form* of a presentation are relevant for any subject matter and are not unique to art therapy. However, the integration of doing and reflecting and of imagery with words, which I have recommended for teaching, is also the essence of art therapy itself.

The last element, putting the learning into a larger perspective, is also part of good art therapy, in which the client is helped to use the experience in a way that enables him to understand and to enrich his life in general, not just the moments he spends with the art therapist. If teaching, like therapy, is to have any kind of lasting impact, it must be internal-ized and eventually generalized by the learner.

Learning by Doing

This leads to yet another recommendation about the teaching of art therapy, especially to students training for the profession. Any didactic learning should always be complemented by something more direct—first, in the form of observation—onsite or on videotape. But, as soon as possible, the learner needs to do something herself. Anyone who has conducted an art interview with another human being has an understanding that is much fuller than would ever be possible from reading or observing alone. If such "practice" activities can then be examined in some detail, either individually or in a group, the potential for learning is further extended.

Even in an introductory course, students can be required to conduct art sessions with any individuals or families who are willing and can learn a great deal by discussing these in the group. A related approach is to use role-play, which is the most practical for short-term learning situations like workshops, at which participants pretend to be therapists or clients—whether as individuals, groups, or families. In this way, they can at least get a feel for the kinds of tensions and dilemmas involved in art therapy as well as the pleasures and the joys.

Just as people are known to learn more when they are interested in a topic, so they are known to learn more when they are emotionally involved as well as intellectually stimulated. Creating their own art, role-playing with other students, and practicing on willing helpers, are all excellent ways for trainees to be involved in the learning process at a feeling level.

What is critical, however, is that the doing always be integrated with the didactic learning of the moment. Just as images are best shown along with the words of a lecture, so the activity components of the learning process are best if connected by the instructor with the theoretical, technical, and historical information being taught.

Not only is action plus cognition a good formula for learning technique, but it is also the only possible way of making theory come alive. No one has ever seen an *id*, an *ego*, or a *superego*, and no one can specify the color of *transference* or the texture of a *working alliance*. Only when these abstract concepts are made concrete in your direct experience do they start to have meaning that can be comprehended and generalized.

Some creative art therapy educators have had the marvelous idea of asking students to create visual representations of such abstract theoretical concepts using art media; the first I was aware of were Pat Allen and Harriet Wadeson (1982). I am sure the students understood the ideas infinitely better after doing so, just as I am sure that drawing a feeling or a "life line" gives anyone a new perspective on the particular theme, even though the person might have thought he "knew" it already.

Teaching Carefully

I have stressed the importance of gauging the level of sophistication of the audience as well as the areas of greatest interest of the individuals in it. In regard to any learning that involves *doing*, which I have recommended, it is also essential to be extremely cautious and to monitor throughout the activity the group's level of comfort or anxiety about the task and the ensuing discussion.

This is most critical when people are doing their own artwork and looking at it reflectively. You then need to use your own clinical judgment about the appropriateness of the task and how far to go in the discussion regarding potentially touchy areas. It is always safer to err on the side of caution and restraint. One of the most dreadful things that can happen is for an art therapy workshop participant to become disorganized. I believe that it usually results from a failure of judgment on the part of the leader.

A conscientious art therapy instructor needs to be extremely careful to avoid overstimulation. Most important is to assure everyone at every step of the way that if they do not want to talk about something they have made or experienced, they do not have to do so. And if they do not want to do any of the exercises or activities you have suggested, that also is their right. It is vital to protect individuals in any art therapy learning situation from undue exposure and discomfort.

One way to protect people and to ensure that everyone gets a chance to talk as much or as little as they wish about what they have experienced is to suggest that people in a group pair up for the discussion time. One partner first presents what he or she has created to the other member of the pair, who then interviews the individual about it, having been given guidance in advance about asking open-ended questions and accepting "I don't know" as an answer. They then switch roles, so that by the end of the time available, everyone has had a chance to see what it feels like to talk about their own creations as well as to interview another person about their artwork.

After they do so, I invite them to think about what was comfortable and what was uncomfortable and to share as much of that as they wish with their partners. Sometimes I invite anyone who so desires to tell the whole group about their experience. The ensuing discussion can have any of a number of possible foci, depending on the nature of the group and the learning situation.

Just as it is useful to promote direct involvement in any learning situation, so it always helps to convey something that the learners can take with them and use. This is one reason why building a presentation on learner interests makes so much sense since they will not only be more involved but also more likely to use what they have learned in the future. It might help to think of that objective in planning as well. Given choices among interest areas that can be conveyed in a given time, which are they most likely to be able to utilize in their own lives or work in the near future?

Future Learning

Another way of thinking ahead is to see as a relevant goal of any learning situation not only taking in something new and valuable but also discovering what more someone needs to learn about a particular topic and perhaps identifying avenues for further growth. This applies to any learner at any level of professional development.

With some groups, simply getting across the understanding that art therapy is complicated and requires a great deal of skill and supervised learning might be the main objective. Many laypeople and even a fair number of professionals still think that all you need is "a paintbrush and a patient" and you become an art therapist, to quote one of our pioneers (Howard, 1964). In such instances, I work hard to convince the audience of the complexity and sophistication of the work so that they will neither conduct nor sanction irresponsible art therapy with people who are vulnerable.

Of course, there is much more that could be written about the teaching of art therapy, whether you are giving a single talk or designing a 2-year master's degree program. Certainly, the latter involves issues of sequencing in training experiences and selection of subjects. There are specific content areas to be covered and a required number of supervised practicum and internship hours as stated clearly in the Education Standards of the American Art Therapy Association (2007).

However, exactly how these learning experiences are to be delivered, when, and by whom is up to program directors and their faculty. It is my hope that this kind of flexibility will continue so that teachers of art therapy can use their own creative resources in providing training, and so that prospective students can look at different programs and choose those that fit them best. Despite different priorities and beliefs among the training programs, I imagine that all would agree that any organized plan ought to build gradually both knowledge and competencies, always linking the doing with understanding, as in art therapy itself.

Evaluating Teaching

Finally, it is best for any kind of teaching situation that it be evaluated by the learners. It may be difficult or awkward to do this in a short talk or presentation, but it can be useful to the presenter. Inviting some kind of assessment by students is the responsibility of every art therapist involved in any substantial amount of teaching or training. I often suggest that such evaluations be anonymous in order to encourage people to be honest about their criticisms.

I have usually stressed, when presenting evaluation forms or questions, that although I, like anyone, enjoy praise, what I need in order to grow is critical feedback, and that I welcome any suggestions for improvement. Having taught at the college level for over 40 years, I have received many such written evaluations and have learned a good deal from them over that time span. Of course, it can be painful to see in black and white a sharp critique of your teaching. But, just as a good art therapist should be constantly evaluating her work, so should a responsible teacher.

One of the most interesting kinds of evaluation of any type of learning is when you are able to follow up your input at some point later in time, to find out not what people write or say at the end of the workshop or course, but whether and how they are using what they were taught. I have sometimes had that opportunity, and it has been both fascinating and helpful.

I have often felt that those who showed the most growth were individuals who already had the potential, and maybe even the knowledge, but who needed permission to use their own creativity in their work. I do not mean to imply that they would not have developed at all without the learning experience, but I do sometimes wonder whether it is possible to teach people who, for reasons of personality more than intellect, are not able to fully use what you have to offer. This dilemma becomes even more acute in clinical supervision, the subject of the next chapter, in which I have sometimes felt challenged to make gold out of straw or to make a silk purse out of a sow's ear.

References

American Art Therapy Association. (2007). *Masters education standards.* Alexandria, VA: Author. Retrieved February 15, 2010 from http://www.americanarttherapyassociation.org/upload/masterseducationstandards.pdf

Allen, P., & Wadeson, H. (1982). Art making for conceptualization, integration, and self-awareness in art therapy training. In A. E. DiMaria et al. (Eds.), *Art therapy: A bridge between worlds* (pp. 83–83). Falls Church, VA: American Art Therapy Association.

Davis, C. M. (1928). Self-selection of diet by newly-weaned infants. *American Journal of Diseases of Children, 36,* 651–679.

Howard, M. (1964). An art therapist looks at her professional identity. *Bulletin of Art Therapy, 4,* 153–156.

Milne, D., & Noone, S. (1996). *Teaching and training for non-teachers (personal and professional development).* London: Wiley-Blackwell.

Recommended Readings

McNiff, S. (1986). *Educating the creative arts therapist.* Springfield, IL: Thomas.

Moon, B. L. (2003). *Essentials of art therapy training and practice* (2nd ed.). Springfield, IL: Thomas.

Rubin, J. A. (2010). *Introduction to art therapy: Sources & Resources.* New York: Routledge.

In this art therapy course, the students are creating—their instructor observes and interacts with each as she moves around the studio.

A supervisor helps an art therapy intern to reflect on and to learn from her work with patients.

CHAPTER 17

Knowing Supervision

Introduction

Most art therapists who find themselves supervising others have not been trained in supervision per se, any more than the majority of art therapists who find themselves educating others have been trained in teaching. During the years since this book was first published, however, there has been a growing awareness within the profession of the need for both instruction and experience in doing supervision.

As of 2009, the Art Therapy Credentials Board—the group that awards registration (ATR, registered art therapist) and certification (BC, board certified)—offered an additional credential, ATCS (art therapy certified supervisor), available to those who have already attained ATR-BC. The requirements for "regular entry" include a semester course in clinical supervision or 35 continuing education credits as well as a letter of endorsement and documentation of 100 hours of supervisory experience. The requirements for "alternate entry," which reflect the fact that courses in supervision are rarely part of art therapists' formal education, are the documentation of 36 months and 500 hours of experience supervising art therapists.

There are writings by professionals in other mental health disciplines about clinical supervision (Bernard & Goodyear, 2008; Campbell, 2006; Ekstein & Wallerstein, 1972). And, in the years since the first edition of this book, there have been articles, book chapters, and several books on supervision in art therapy itself. This is important because, while many issues in the supervision of art therapists are similar to those in the supervision of other mental health professionals, the presence of art making and the art product greatly affects what happens between supervisor and supervisee.

So far, two books have been published addressing the practice of supervision in art therapy. The first was Malchiodi and Riley's *Supervision and Related Issues* (1996). The second is a publication edited by Schaverien and Case (2007) that provides a much-needed resource for the profession. *Supervision of Art Psychotherapy: A Theoretical and Practical Handbook* includes an excellent review of the literature on supervision in art therapy as well as a series of chapters by British and American art therapists who have had extensive supervisory experience.

My comments in this chapter represent my own point of view based on my experiences during the past 47 years as a supervisee, as a member of several peer supervision groups, and as a supervisor of art therapists at various stages in their training and professional development in diverse settings. Just as I believe that each art therapist needs to find her own voice and style as a clinician, so I believe the same to be true for each art therapy supervisor.

While it is clear that supervising someone's clinical work is quite different from administrative supervision, the same individual often has to play both roles, although it is much simpler to do either without the encumbrance of the other. Since the roles are often combined rather than separated, it is important to keep the two areas distinct in your own mind because administrative supervision usually involves many more clear-cut, either-or issues than does the supervision of clinical work.

On the other hand, it is also true that, if only because of the special needs of the art therapist in terms of materials, space, and other arrangements, it is often necessary to deal with administrative matters in order to help the supervisee to be able to do effective art therapy. Elizabeth Stone, for example, learned from pioneer Vera Zilzer that requesting a "map" of the art therapy room may give the supervisor critical information that might not otherwise be disclosed by the supervisee (personal communication, January 4, 2010).

Simply put, a supervisor's primary job as I see it is to develop the skills of the supervisee. Just as it might be easier to do something *for* or to *tell* a patient than to help him to find the answer for himself, so it is often much simpler to give the answer to a supervisee or even to undertake a difficult task on her behalf than to help her to do it herself. But, as with a patient, it is the growth of the other individual that is the supervisor's goal, and if you are to promote that, you need to help that person to think and do for herself.

Although you might imagine you would naturally promote autonomy, since you would not want any supervisee to be overly dependent, the fact remains that there are some gratifications for a supervisor in being seen as omnipotent, omniscient, or essential to the supervisee, just as there are for a therapist with a needy, insecure patient.

We all have a little bit of that infant grandiosity in us, and we probably enter a helping profession partly to be the heroic rescuer of the weak and helpless. It can be a good feeling to be needed by anyone, whether a supervisee or a patient, and it is therefore vital not to abuse the supervision situation in order to obtain such gratifications at the learner's expense.

Ironically, while there are supervisees who virtually beg for a dependent relationship and are eager to be "fed" and led, there are also supervisees who have considerable difficulty taking in whatever you have to offer. They come for supervision, but seem either not to digest or even to "spit out" whatever is given to them and show little evidence over time of having integrated much in the way of learning. Since there are clearly emotional as well as intellectual issues involved in any kind of supervision, knowledge about development, dynamics, and therapy will stand the supervisor in good stead. What you understand about the transference and the working alliance is especially relevant.

Indeed, there are important analogies in supervision to what goes on between therapist and patient. There is a "real" relationship, and there should also be a "learning alliance," in which both partners work conscientiously toward the goal of growth for one of them. As with patients, from whom you can learn a great deal (Casement, 1985), so the supervisor also benefits from the interaction. I have especially felt that way with bright and creative supervisees, who have often taught me more than I taught them.

There are also transference and countertransference reactions in a supervisory partnership, as in everyday life and in psychotherapy (cf. Robbins, 1988). Because the supervisee is usually dependent on the supervisor for some kind of evaluation, and because the supervisor is generally responsible to others in the institution or training program for the supervisee's performance, there are necessarily strains and tensions in this unique learning situation. It is not therapy, but it is also not teaching—except as it resembles a tutorial—and it seems to work best if it is not strictly didactic.

So, what is it? Supervision in art therapy is a peculiar kind of relationship in which one individual agrees to help another to develop clinical skills, but without leading by the hand, showing how (as in an apprenticeship), or even telling in so many words. Yet, in truth, all these modes of helping do become part of any effective supervision—showing, supporting, and even telling—at times when each seems appropriate. It would be hard to have to choose any of them and not have access to all.

In fact, deciding on the best intervention in supervision is as difficult as the clinical decisions with clients about what to do at any moment in time. As is true during an art therapy session, you still need to decide whether to listen, to interrupt, to tell about, to ask about, and, if intervening, just how to do so. In addition, as with someone in treatment, you need to assess from moment to moment the supervisee's readiness for and openness to any given intervention.

To keep the learning curve and the growth goals clear in your mind with a supervisee, you need to remain constantly aware of the not-so-rational elements in the transaction: the transference reactions of either person in this partnership to the other at any moment in time.

Since the supervisor usually has more distance than the supervisee, it may be a little easier for you to become aware of the supervisee's countertransference responses to patients as well as her transferences to other staff members. These are so powerful, and so easily rationalized, that you need to keep an ever-watchful eye on them. You need to be alert for two reasons: first, so they do not distort your understanding of what the supervisee is actually facing in her work, and, second, so that you can help her to become aware of any overdetermined reactions and perceptions that may be present.

Since such irrational responses are so influential, you might wonder whether doing good supervision is not really the same as conducting effective therapy. While there are some similarities, as noted earlier, the two are also quite distinct. The help you have agreed to give to an art therapy supervisee is in relation to developing her clinical skills and understandings, not improving her mental health.

Although it may be tempting—and I have certainly been there myself—I do not agree with those who feel you can do both simultaneously. This seems a rather grandiose notion, and I have yet to meet the individual who can remain neutral enough to be a good therapist, yet explicit enough to be a good supervisor. The role requirements are simply not compatible in my opinion. An even more serious complication is that it places unfair pressures on the supervisee, who cannot use the supervisor without conflict as either teacher *or* therapist and whose growth in both areas may be gravely compromised.

What a good supervisor *can* and should do, however, is to help the supervisee to pinpoint what may be happening in the way of distorted perceptions, reactions, or behaviors and to suggest or support her in obtaining psychotherapy for herself.

A common and fascinating phenomenon is the replaying in the supervisory situation of what is going on between client and supervisee (Ekstein & Wallerstein, 1972; Stoltenberg & Delworth, 1987). This so-called "parallel process" is, just like transference and countertransference reactions, extremely informative if you are aware that it is likely to occur. Being attuned to this potential "reflecting" interaction can, in fact, help both supervisor and supervisee to better understand what is going on between the supervisee and the client. However, because of the nature of the supervisory relationship, you will need to be tactful about explaining and highlighting it.

It is delicate of course to introduce the notion of "transference" within the supervisory relationship itself, but it is not too difficult to introduce even beginning therapists to the idea that the client is likely to perceive them in ways determined by their past significant relationships. Since transference is also part of everyday life, the concept is easy to convey by asking the supervisee about people she has met toward whom she has felt an instant attraction or repulsion. The notion that a new such person might "remind" her of an important individual in her life is not hard to grasp or to accept.

In any case, the issues noted so far have been rather general ones, having to do with the supervisor-supervisee relationship, its goals and objectives, and its potential complications. More specific issues include the question of the best way of structuring the supervision session itself, as well as the advisability of adjunctive modes of training, such as observing, being observed, or working as a co-therapist with the supervisee.

As with clients, it is important to remember that each supervisee is a unique individual, and that what works best with one may be quite inappropriate for another. Nevertheless, there are some guidelines that are broadly applicable to clinical supervision of either trainees or staff members in art therapy.

As with therapy, it makes sense to begin by assessing "where" the individual is in her clinical skills, which includes not only how she behaves but also how she understands what is going on with her clients and herself. In this regard, it is probably best to begin as in an initial art interview, in an open-ended fashion, to see just how this individual approaches the supervision situation. Does she come in with a list of questions, with a record of a single session, with the artwork done by one or more clients, or does she sit back and wait for the supervisor to structure the time?

Does she seem to want to prove her competence, or does she seem overly self-critical or fearful of criticism? In other words, in addition to finding out where someone is in regard to clinical skills, it is helpful to get a sense of how she regards herself as a therapist. Moreover, the initial unstructured supervisory sessions are most helpful in giving a feel for what and how much the individual wants and expects from the supervisor.

To assess the supervisee's clinical skills more systematically, you might suggest that she list any questions occurring to her during the time between your meetings. Eventually, I have usually requested detailed reports of single sessions, preferring a depth to a breadth approach in learning clinical skills. I always ask that any patient artwork be brought along, and if the original is not available, that a photograph or scan be presented instead. I also request that the supervisee note the date and number in sequence of each item created during a session. If she is not already observing such data, this requirement will alert her to them.

Eventually, when the supervisee seems comfortable, I would probably ask to observe a session—if possible, through a one-way vision window or, if necessary, in the same room— more feasible with groups than individuals. If live observation is not possible or seems too threatening to either the therapist or the clients, I would then ask that the clinician videotape a session, and if that is not possible, to tape the audio portion of an interview. Although direct observation is sometimes not feasible, I find that doing so as early as possible in supervision is extremely helpful since no clinician can report to a supervisor on areas that are *blind spots* and are therefore all the more important for your awareness.

In giving feedback after an observation or report, the supervisor needs to be especially sensitive to the clinician's self-esteem and should try hard to find positive as well as negative things to say. Although it sounds rather simplistic, I always try to begin with positive comments, after which I believe negative ones can be more comfortably heard by anyone, no matter how secure the individual may seem to be.

Conscientious reinforcement of a supervisee's strengths and successes is at least as important in helping her to grow as sharply accurate criticism of her work. The way in which comments or questions are worded, the tone of voice in which they are said, and the expression on the supervisor's face are as powerful in their impact as in your communications during therapy. Ironically, many supervisors seem able to be exquisitely sensitive with clients, yet astonishingly callous with supervisees, as if they are working out some hidden agenda of their own in this particular transaction.

Because of the nature of my own training experiences, as both an art therapist and a psychoanalyst, I have had a great many different supervisors, each with his or her own style and approach. Some have been rather casual and passive, allowing me to structure the session according to my own felt needs; others have been insistent on a particular way of reporting and examining work with patients.

Some have been task oriented, using the time to discuss only clinical work; others have been looser about boundaries and have brought up other areas in which our paths have crossed, usually in ways that seemed relevant to the supervision. As with art therapy, supervision is an activity in which each individual needs to develop her own style of work, a way of relating that is syntonic for her. But, as is also true with art therapy with particular clients, it is important that a supervisor adapt her characteristic style to the specific needs of the individual supervisee.

When I wrote the first edition of this book, I had just become the codirector of a department of creative and expressive arts therapies in a large teaching hospital where I was supervising the art and music therapists as well as the art therapy interns. As a result, I was involved in supervising more staff members and graduate students at the same time than ever before, both individually and in groups. This allowed me to become especially alert to the different "flavor" of each supervisory hour, despite the fact that I tried to be relatively consistent throughout. Since then, I have supervised many more individuals in training and in practice, some as part of my job and some at the request of those who sought supervision to improve their clinical work.

After years of experimentation with a variety of ways of structuring the time, I have come to feel that it is best to give some guidance to those who do not spontaneously utilize the opportunity in thoughtful ways that indicate prior preparation. Some supervisees are able to sort out their priorities well and can usually be trusted to use the supervision session in the fashion they most need at any moment in time.

Others, however, need to be taught how to use supervision most effectively, especially if what was called "supervision" in prior learning situations was primarily administrative or clinically more superficial. Naturally, each supervisor will have her own ideas about what is most important, and it is hoped that they will vary with each supervisee, but the essence of the task is to help the supervisee grow as an art therapist.

When staff members are delivering many hours of direct service and are able to reflect on it with a supervisor for only 1 or 2 hours a week, it hardly made sense to use that precious time for a literal reporting of all that has happened, a communication that could occur more efficiently in the brief written descriptions of each art therapy session that were required for record keeping. Nor did it make much sense to use supervision to talk mainly about what went well, although the supervisee's self-assessment is one of the things you want to help her to develop.

For those who had not spontaneously utilized their supervision time productively, I found it helpful to spend some time pinpointing with them their areas of discomfort or feelings of inadequacy and planning together ways of helping them to grow in those domains. This would include specific ways of preparing for the supervision session, as well as other possibilities for professional development.

Although the primary work of clinical supervision takes place in the supervisory session, for the best training in art therapy the supervisor should be flexible about other kinds of recommended activities or uses of herself. Actions you might recommend to a supervisee include reading specific articles or books on a topic needing to be better understood, as well as observing other therapists at work or doing co-therapy.

One problem with most clinical training programs, including those in art therapy, is that the learners are provided with few live models. They read a great deal about what people *say* they do—which is often different from what they *actually* do—and they hear a lot in classes and case seminars about what others *report* they have done. But, except for required observations or an art therapist with whom a trainee may work as an assistant or co-therapist, they rarely if ever get to observe other art therapists at work.

In the first edition of this book (Rubin, 1984), I wrote: "To date, there are few teaching films and tapes that show art therapists working with patients, and because of the editing (selecting) involved, they inevitably present a distorted picture." Alas, that is still the case. One of my dreams is to get funding to make a series of training tapes for art therapy students via a nonprofit my colleague and I started in 1985.

We created Expressive Media Incorporated (EMI) in 1985 in order to be able to take the teaching films and videotapes we had made when we left full-time work at the psychiatric hospital. I revived it in 2004 in order to be able to distribute two films I finished that year, *Art Therapy Has Many Faces* (Rubin, 2008a) and *Beyond Words* (Rubin, 2008b). In 2008, my drama therapy colleague and I re-edited and updated our early films. We also filmed and added historical introductions as well as added features on each DVD (http://www.expressivemedia.org/films.html).

The DVD that is included with this revision of *The Art of Art Therapy* contains sections that parallel those in this book. They are meant to illustrate the topics discussed in the chapters of "The Art Part," "The Therapy Part," "The Interface," "Applications," and "Indirect Service." As such, they offer a "taste" or a sampling of what goes on in an art therapy session.

I hope that someday it will be possible to make available entire sessions so that students can critique and learn from the work of other art therapists. It is fortunate that it no longer requires a great deal of money and a big budget to videotape an art therapy session or to do minimal editing on the computer. Both are available at reasonable cost and are increasingly being used by a generation that is growing up with YouTube videos, a far different world from the one in which I was trained or the one in which I have supervised most of those I trained or for whom I was responsible.

Meanwhile, until much observation, either live or on videotape, is widely available, it is still no doubt true for many art therapists that your own therapist often becomes a model. Sadly, this person is rarely an art therapist, so that the usefulness of identification here is somewhat limited. Yet, in many domains, such as parenting and teaching, the way in which you behave in a role is based largely on experiences with others who had that relationship to you in the past—your own parents and teachers.

However, for the purpose of exploring and developing your own style as an art therapist, I believe that self-knowledge—through your own therapy, which I strongly recommend—is best supplemented by as many observations of other art therapists at work as is feasible. Needless to say, this can also include observations of the supervisor as well, although in such cases you need to be especially alert to the possible transference meaning of such an event for both parties.

Just as grandiose rescue fantasies are probably ubiquitous, so are exhibitionistic ones part of every artist's unconscious power source. It is inevitable that anyone entering the field of art therapy will have a special interest in the voyeurism that can also be sublimated in this kind of work. So, to "show off" and to "peek" have especially loaded meanings in a tilted relationship like the supervisory one and need to be well understood before the supervisee is invited to observe the supervisor.

The reverse situation, while also loaded, is a little less risky and considerably more defensible. As noted, no one's report of what goes on can fully convey the actuality of an art therapy session; therefore, it is extremely helpful to get a direct look when possible at the supervisee's way of working with clients. Despite prior preparation, the supervisee is likely to be self-conscious, so it is especially important to do your observing in a way that is minimally anxiety provoking.

If no one-way observation room is available, for example, it is important as a supervisor to find out just where in the room and at what level of participation your presence will be least disruptive. Since this may be difficult to establish in advance, you may need to explore through trial and error where it is best to sit and whether your participation will be comfortable or awkward for client or therapist. If it seems that some kind of participation on your part is wanted, then you can also use yourself in a casual and natural way as a model of how to interact with, help, and interview clients.

Since supervision is primarily a learning situation—although the curriculum is more flexible and much more personalized than in most teaching—it makes sense to periodically step back and evaluate with the supervisee where she is and where she wants or needs to go and to think together how best to help her to get there. Sometimes this collaboration is limited by time (a one-semester internship) or some other variable (the client's termination or the end of a placement).

When it occurs, a separation from a supervisor has many of the same elements as a termination in therapy and needs to be handled with care and tact, taking into account all of the feelings involved. When there is no arbitrary time limitation (as in the supervision of regular staff members), it is especially important to regularly reassess goals and ways of reaching them with the supervisee.

In some situations, with both students and staff, there is a great deal to be gained through group kinds of supervisory experiences. They can be structured in many possible ways, limited only by the imagination of the participants. In my opinion, group supervision should never be used *instead of* individual supervision, for which there is no adequate substitute, but it can certainly supplement and complement it in a growth-enhancing way.

For example, in organizing the Creative and Expressive Arts Therapy program in our hospital, we planned for individual supervision for each staff member, the length and frequency to be determined as much as possible by individual needs. We also planned for weekly clinical conferences, in which a group of staff members in related disciplines would take turns presenting case material for several weeks at a time, inviting the others to react and discuss in order to get a broader perspective on treatment.

These group learning sessions were also used to review diagnostic art interviews with both individuals and families, sometimes via videotape, and were occasionally more academic, as in reading an article written or recommended by one of the members and of interest to the group. There is clearly value in sharing ideas within a small group about what a painting or a behavior might mean, or discussing possible implications for understanding or action, which is qualitatively different from considering the same material in a one-to-one supervisory situation. Most obvious is the expansion of each individual's experience through sharing that of others. Equally helpful is the stimulation provided by the healthy competition and cooperative brainstorming within the group.

But what about the supervisor? Is growth to occur only in the supervisee? As with therapy or education, while the primary change is in the one receiving services, it is possible for the caregiver to grow as well, especially if you take the time to think about and reflect on your work. Since there are some things that are unique to supervision, it is especially helpful to read some of the relevant literature in both psychotherapy and art therapy supervision in order to discuss the different theories and techniques of supervision and the pros and cons of each. It is also helpful, if at all possible, to get a critique (or a consultation) of your own work as a supervisor.

One of the most useful learning experiences I ever had was in a course required for my doctoral program—group supervision of supervision—in which we each supervised a master's candidate in counseling psychology and audiotaped our sessions. These tapes were next listened to carefully by another group member, who would then replay the tape with the supervisor—raising questions, offering criticisms, and giving suggestions. This feedback was later discussed in a small group in relation to theories of supervision, a course taken the preceding term.

While acting as an administrator, I tried to meet such needs in twice-weekly collaboration sessions with my colleague who co-directed the Creative and Expressive Arts Therapy program. Each of us consulted with the other regarding any questions or problems we were having in work with our respective supervisees. I imagine that if I had not had easy access to someone on the staff with whom I could be so frank, I would probably have dealt with problems as a supervisor in the same way that I dealt with problems as a therapist—by scheduling a formal consultation with a respected colleague.

It is naïve to think that you can ever reach a point at which your own transference reactions, biases, or blind spots could not potentially interfere with your effectiveness in any clinical or educational role, including supervising. What is most important is being alert to such problems and being comfortable with the idea that, no matter how experienced you are, a more objective person can always help you to do your therapeutic or supervisory job better. The clinicians for whom I have the most respect are also those who are quickest to ask for help when they sense they might need it. This may be true for your work as a supervisor at least as often as it is for your work as a therapist.

Using Artwork to Enhance Supervision

In art therapy, there are some other ways in which we can help ourselves and our supervisees through the use of our modality. As a supervisor, I have often found it helpful to draw a picture of the supervisee or the patient. This is something I have sometimes shared with the therapist, but not always. For the most part, I did it for myself since I found that such an exercise usually helped me to identify more clearly any confused feelings I was having about the clinician or the case.

You can also ask the supervisee to represent the patients or staff members with whom she deals, offering another method for reflection on what is happening in the treatment situation. Any topic that comes up in supervision can be the stimulus for an artwork assignment for the supervisee. Having her do it in her own space on her own time probably reduces the self-consciousness of doing it in your presence.

Yet another approach I had used in a workshop he attended was suggested for supervisory pairs by a psychiatrist colleague of mine involved in training residents. It was to draw on the same sheet of paper without talking, followed by a discussion of what was happening in supervision as reflected in the drawing and the process of making it. Although I worried that such an exercise might be too threatening, it turned out to be extremely helpful to both partners in the collaboration, at least according to the reports from those to whom we suggested it. In a pilot study, we tried it out informally with at least a dozen supervisor-supervisee pairs, most of them psychiatry residents in training working with senior clinicians (cf. Lahad, 2000, for a stimulating discussion of expressive arts methods in supervision of other professionals).

Asking each member of a supervision group to create her image of the client being described has also been remarkably helpful in gaining a fuller understanding of the situation under consideration. If, as can easily happen because of the participants' investment in the process, tensions seem to be disrupting the learning orientation of such a group, representations of the group itself are also a way to begin to look at what is going on within it and to learn about group dynamics as well.

There are many other possible uses of art in supervision, limited only by the imagination of the supervisor, parallel to what is true about the infinite number of potential art activities in the therapeutic situation. As with the latter, it is important to utilize such approaches primarily when the need is strongly felt and the relevance of the activity seems clear. In such cases, art can be as powerful a tool in supervision as it is in both assessment and therapy.

One of the most critical questions to ask a supervisee is how she thinks the client perceives her, positively or negatively, and in what sort of role. It may be possible, depending on her degree of self-awareness, to suggest that her perceptions of the client and of you are also colored by her own internal world. If this idea is really hard for her to accept, and if you are convinced that a supervisee's own unresolved issues (with, e.g., aggression or competition) are interfering with her potential as an art therapist, then I believe it is your responsibility to introduce the idea of personal therapy.

I not only see personal therapy as essential for any art therapist but also feel that it is necessary to do some work on yourself more than once or twice in a lifetime. Of course, if you know it will be threatening to the supervisee, you will want to prepare her for it gently and to introduce the idea with compassion and concern. But it is important to remember that, if psychological problems are interfering with a supervisee's work, the answer is not becoming her therapist/supervisor; rather, it is helping her to decide on and to find a competent clinician for herself.

If you feel you must recommend therapy to a supervisee, I believe this is one instance in which personal disclosure is appropriate, as long as you are comfortable doing it. I did not seek psychotherapy myself until both Margaret Naumburg and Edith Kramer recommended it to me when I first asked for their advice. They disagreed on many things, but they agreed that personal therapy was essential to becoming a good art therapist.

Almost 50 years later, I am glad that I did what they recommended, and I am also happy that the training I eventually chose to pursue in psychoanalysis required that I undergo analysis myself. My husband, who had had a few years of counseling in graduate school, was so impressed with how much I changed that he even decided to enter analysis himself at age 48, which in 1978 was considered rather late to begin such treatment.

The other thing recommended by both Naumburg and Kramer was that I obtain supervision from an experienced clinician. I was exceptionally fortunate that during my early work in art therapy I had close supervision on all of my cases by a number of different psychiatrists, psychologists, and psychoanalysts. In fact, it was because the analysts were my most helpful supervisors that I decided to enter analytic training rather than pursuing a doctoral degree in clinical psychology.

Thanks to a well-timed question by my analyst, however, I was also motivated to obtain a doctorate from a department that turned out to be very fortunate. First, they gave credit for my master's degree in art education and for a number of my psychoanalytic Institute courses. In addition, because it was a competency-based program, I could test out of certain domains and do independent study in others—for example, in analytic psychology with a Jungian and in phenomenology with an expert in that area.

Fortunately, since I could demonstrate that there was a need for additional literature in the field (there were very few art therapy books at the time), I was able to write a book on *Child Art Therapy* (Rubin, 2005) as my dissertation. Something else that turned out to be extremely helpful later in my career was that by completing this particular doctoral degree, I was eligible to sit for the licensing exam in psychology.

As described earlier, one of the required courses and competencies in the doctoral program was Supervision. In addition to reading the literature, attending a seminar, and supervising master's candidates, we were required to tape our supervision sessions, which were then listened to and critiqued—first by another student who gave detailed feedback in an individual session and then by the group and the instructor. In other words, the course not only provided information about and experience in supervision, but also was cleverly designed to provide supervision of supervision itself. It was immensely helpful in learning to be a better supervisor.

I have described aspects of my own training in some detail because I know that it is the basis for what I am recommending in this chapter. While coursework and practice were essential, I am convinced that I became a much better art therapist because of the range and intensity of the supervision I received over the years.

Prior to entering analytic training, for the first 10 years of my work in art therapy—because I was in a department and a clinic where others were being trained and because my primary mentor wanted art therapy to succeed—I had the good fortune to have an unusually large number and variety of clinical supervisors. In fact, there were four psychologists, four psychiatrists, and three psychoanalysts. Most supervised individual work, but several supervised family and group art therapy.

During the analytic training, I was required to have weekly supervision on each of my three adult patients and my three child patients for at least the first year of their analyses and regular supervision thereafter, so I ended up experiencing intensive supervision from six more psychiatrists. By the time I had finished formal training, I had been exposed to many styles and methods of supervision. This, too, was wonderful training since I could select from each supervisor what had been helpful to me.

After finishing analytic training, I became part of several peer supervision groups in art therapy. There was a local group of arts therapists who met monthly. And, there was a national group composed of friends and colleagues, including Laurie Wilson, Gladys Agell, and Millie Chapin. That group met for a number of years—for several days prior to the American Art Therapy Association (AATA) conferences, as well as for a long weekend midway through the year.

These were extremely helpful meetings as members presented case material to each other and tried to understand what was going on and to explore possible next art therapeutic steps. Until I retired from full-time clinical practice, I often consulted with colleagues whose expertise was greater than my own, especially on difficult cases. While working with a young adult with borderline personality disorder, for example, I had weekly phone consultations for many months with an expert in another city.

Even since retirement, I have continued to attend a child analytic therapy study group, in which case presentation is the primary activity and is still extremely stimulating. I have presented a number of videotaped art therapy sessions to this group of experienced clinicians and have found their feedback on the fine points of technique to be extremely thought provoking.

It is no doubt clear by now that I consider learning to be a good therapist a lifelong endeavor and would encourage all art therapists at every stage of development to seek out and benefit from whatever resources are available to you. Not only will it make you a better therapist, but it is also enjoyable.

What is somewhat less enjoyable but an equally major responsibility is to help your supervisees understand the legal, ethical, and moral aspects of the work. In most settings, a supervisor is ethically and legally responsible for the actions of a supervisee in a way that a therapist is not for a patient.

Moreover, while the legal and ethical aspects of doing art therapy are much less fascinating than the clinical issues, and although some of this information is covered in the required coursework of a master's curriculum, a great deal must be highlighted and reinforced in vivo on the job. The notion of liability—of being legally responsible and punishable for doing or not doing something correctly—can be frightening to neophytes but is essential for them to understand well.

Indeed, it is the supervisor's responsibility to teach the new art therapist in the context of actual practice about the meaning and importance of confidentiality, along with the need to breach it if duty requires. Here, I am referring to the legal duty of any mental health professional to *warn* if convinced that the patient represents a threat to self or others, as well as the duty to *report* if child abuse or neglect is suspected. In both situations, the reason is to *protect*, but these actions are not easy to take.

This became painfully apparent to me when I left the protective umbrella of the hospital and clinic for full-time private practice. Even though I had by then been practicing for over 20 years and had a great deal of clinical supervision, the hardest part of being an independent practitioner were the times I had to breach confidentiality to fulfill my legal, ethical, and moral duty as a responsible professional.

While I greatly enjoyed the freedom to help people in the way that seemed best to me without having to get the agreement of an entire treatment team, I remember as if it were yesterday the times I had to call a family member or the police when I was convinced that someone was likely to act on a suicidal impulse. Sometimes the patient was in the same city and sometimes not; the latter was even more difficult, but I am convinced to this day that had I not called the police, several young men and women might not be alive.

I remember the agonizing difficulty of having to talk borderline psychotic adults and the family of a psychotic child into going directly to the emergency room of the psychiatric hospital when I thought they were at risk; in several instances, I ended up accompanying them as well. Making the decision to act to protect someone or someone's family was never easy.

What helped in all of these instances was that there had been sufficient trust established with the client and the family that persuasion, while not at all easy, was at least possible.

Indeed, that is a good note on which to end this chapter because supervision, like therapy, is ultimately a collaborative effort. In both, the establishment of as much trust as possible between the two parties allows for the greatest growth on the part of the client and the supervisee. Both therapy and supervision are relatively intimate collaborations, much more so than teaching or consultation. The latter is also a teaching/learning situation and is the subject of the next chapter.

References

Bernard, J. M., & Goodyear, R. K. (2008). *Fundamentals of clinical supervision* (4th ed.). New York: Allyn & Bacon.

Campbell, J. (2006). *Essentials of clinical supervision.* New York: Wiley.

Casement, P. (1985). *On learning from the patient.* London: Routledge.

Ekstein, R., & Wallerstein, R. S. (1972). *The teaching and learning of psychotherapy* (2nd ed.). New York: International Universities.

Lahad, M. (2000). *Creative supervision: The use of expressive arts methods in supervision and self-supervision.* London: Kingsley.

Malchiodi, C. A., & Riley, S. (1996). *Supervision and related issues.* Chicago: Magnolia Street.

Robbins, A. (1988). *Between therapists.* New York: Human Sciences Press.

Rubin, J. A. (1984). *The art of art therapy.* New York: Brunner/Mazel.

Rubin, J. A. (2005). *Child art therapy* (3rd ed.). New York: Wiley.

Rubin, J. A. (2008a). *Art therapy has many faces* [DVD] (rev. ed.). Pittsburgh, PA: Expressive Media.

Rubin, J. A. (2008b). Beyond words. In *Art therapy with older adults* [DVD] (rev. ed.). Pittsburgh, PA: Expressive Media.

Schaverien, J., & Case, C. (Eds.). (2007). *Supervision of art psychotherapy.* London: Routledge.

Stoltenberg, C. D., & Delworth, U. (1987). *Supervising counselors and therapists: A developmental approach.* San Francisco: Jossey-Bass.

Recommended Reading

Dalley, T., Rifkind, G., & Terry, K. (1993). *Three voices of art therapy: Image, client, therapist.* London: Routledge.

Observing a student who is learning how to do art therapy is an important part of the supervision process.

An art therapist consultant to a museum recommended that visiting schoolchildren dramatize their responses to the artwork, as this boy is doing when he "tells off" the discus thrower.

CHAPTER **18**
Knowing Consultation

Introduction

Consultation, like teaching and supervision, is rarely something for which art therapists have formal educational preparation. Yet, it is not an uncommon role for an art therapist, who is often asked by an institution or an individual to serve as a consultant. Consultation, however, is not the same as therapy, nor is it identical to either education or supervision, although it contains elements of all three. There is a literature on consultation in general, as well as more specialized writing in the area of mental health consultation (Brown, Pryzwansky, & Schulte, 2005; Caplan & Caplan, 1999).

In the latter, a distinction is usually made between program consultation and case consultation. Traditional mental health professionals are more likely to be asked to consult with staff groups or individuals on specific case management questions, a role frequently filled by a consulting psychiatrist or psychologist. Art therapists seem to be asked more often to help with program development, although the work may at times involve guiding others in the understanding or treatment of specific cases.

Having been an art therapist for 48 years, I have had many fascinating and gratifying experiences as a consultant. One factor that probably contributed to the amount and kind of consultation I have done is that for over a decade, my job at the community mental health center where I worked was half in direct service and half in what was termed *community service* or *consultation and education*. Because it was a child guidance center, most of the consultation was to institutions or situations that involved children and families.

Before, during, and since that time, however, I have enjoyed consulting to a wide variety of institutions, people, and projects—including research studies and training programs. These opportunities posed many challenging questions about how best to incorporate, teach, or do research in art therapy. Since retirement from full-time clinical practice, I have had the pleasure of doing programmatic consultation in various parts of the world, where art therapy is just beginning to be known and recognized.

Understanding the Larger Picture

One of the most critical variables in institutional consultation is an understanding of the system itself. Just as you need to understand an individual's dynamics or the interaction patterns of a family, so you need to get as full a picture as possible of the way in which any institutional system functions. This includes a historical as well as a current perspective, which requires looking at the history of the institution, especially the role of art and therapy within it. Assessing a system also includes an understanding of present-day dynamics, which primarily means identifying sources of power, their functioning, and the values expressed in how the organization operates. What is publicly presented as the value structure may or may not reflect the latent values of the system.

You may be feeling by now that these ideas sound fine but would be difficult to implement in real life—especially when an institution is asking you for a specific kind of service, like starting an art therapy program, and is not asking to be assessed or even understood in any larger sense. It is true that the position of a consultant is somewhat more ambiguous in this regard than that of a therapist, teacher, or supervisor. With all of these, while there may be anxiety and resistance to your "diagnostic" curiosity, there will also be some understanding of why you want to know about the past and why you need to understand the larger picture.

The challenge, when invited into any kind of system as a consultant, is to find ways to glean the information required that will be minimally threatening and will make the most sense to those asking for assistance. Actually, if you are convinced of the utility of getting a larger picture in order to help, you will probably be able to find some way to do the kind of observation, record reading, and interviewing necessary for a useful systems analysis.

Assessing What Seems to Be Needed

Just as people often ask for something from therapy that is not what they most need (of which they are not yet aware), so institutions often request something from an art therapy consultant that is somewhat peripheral or at best the tip of the iceberg. However, as with therapy, you always need to begin where the institution *is* and, through the kind of assessment described, gradually define larger needs and potential long-term goals. In the beginning, you will simply want to listen carefully to what it is people think they want of you. You may be able to give them just that or you may, after learning more about the situation, feel that it would be best to offer something a little different from the original request.

Equally important as the gradual building of a mental picture of the inner workings of the system is the slow building of alliances with significant individuals and groups within it. To do so, you will want to behave in a way analogous to that which leads to trusting alliances—with patients, students, and supervisees. You need, first and foremost, to listen empathically, to try to understand just what it is that those you meet with are feeling, thinking, and wishing—especially what it is that they seem to want from you.

Rarely, by the way, do they simply want what they say they want. More often, as in other relationships in which one person asks for and pays another for help, they are wanting many things, some appropriate and some not, with perhaps only some of them in their awareness. However, listening with a clinician's "third ear," you can begin to hear and see what is between the lines, which may never be made explicit but will be a great help in figuring out how best to enable the folks in the institution to achieve what they are after.

Asking to observe and to meet with relevant individuals is usually seen as an indication of your interest and, if requested with confidence, of your expertise in knowing what it is you need to know in order to help. If done tactfully and over time, along with the careful building of alliances and trust, it will help you to have an impact on the institution that will potentially reach much further and deeper than simply fulfilling the initial request.

As I think back over the consulting situations in which I have been involved over the past 48 years, I am astonished at how extensive the ultimate input and impact was in some of them. As with treatment, I probably could not have predicted at the beginning just how art therapy would develop in any of these settings or what else might grow from it. Being open to possibilities, being flexible, and allowing institutional growth to be as organic as individual flowering can help to permit and promote exciting change.

Almost inevitably, the initial request made of any art therapy consultant is fairly narrow and specific. And equally inevitably, as the situation develops over time, other needs become apparent with which you may be able to help. If you have built good relationships with individuals who have some degree of power and influence in the system, and if you are deliberate and selective about your timing, you may be able to stimulate movement in directions that may become apparent to you before they are visible to others. Your next step is to find ways to sensitize others to such needs and then to work within the existing structure of the system to implement change.

One important element in my thinking when I have been a consultant is that of economy and the long-term potential of any investment of my time, which is usually limited as specified in a contractual agreement. Given a choice between influencing many people temporarily and making a structural change in the system that could last beyond my tenure, I have always opted for the latter.

For example, the art program I started in 1967 still exists at the institution for children with disabilities where I was a one-day-a-week consultant. The name of the facility has changed, the individuals I supervised have long since moved on, but the program has stayed and has expanded. So have the bulletin boards and display cases, which required many meetings with anxious administrators before they were permitted. Similarly, the preschool for developmentally disabled children where I spent half a day a week for several years still uses, along with a slightly different approach, the creative play materials that were not available until I worked with the director to introduce them.

Although many faces have changed over the years, there is still an art teacher and a creative arts therapist at the school for blind children, as well as a social worker in both the upper and lower schools—and none of these positions existed prior to their gradual implementation during a decade of gratifying consultation. The attitudes toward children's emotional needs and problems are different now in all of these settings, as they are at a school for the deaf where I also consulted for a year.

I do not mean to imply that I, single-handedly, was responsible for all of these changes. What I do mean to suggest is that, when deciding how best to use my consulting time, I almost always preferred a way that could lead to potentially permanent structural changes in the institution. Of course, most of my consultation time at all of these places was spent meeting with various individuals and groups of staff members around a variety of agreed-on tasks, ranging from individual art therapy supervision to the planning and writing of grant applications for new programs.

Art therapy consultation activities are often concrete and practical, like teaching folks how to order appropriate supplies, helping to plan and organize art rooms, doing in-service training, and conducting demonstration interviews. The last reflects another approach I have found useful in consultation. Although normally consultation—like supervision— should involve helping others to change things rather than doing it for them, the idea of using art therapeutically can be so unfamiliar that I have often chosen to begin by doing some kind of pilot program to find out just what that population was capable of in order to be able to plan for appropriate program development.

Expectations, especially of those who are in some way disabled or impaired, are so often beneath the capacities of the people involved that to accept the consultee's judgment about who can benefit from art therapy is rarely indicated. In almost every instance—from physically handicapped children to cognitively impaired preschoolers to multiply disabled blind children to older adults and many adult psychiatric classifications—the expectations of those requesting a program were far below what the individuals could actually accomplish. Doing pilot work is therefore more than a useful way of becoming familiar with the particular population. It can also be helpful in the modification of attitudes and expectations, especially if staff members are invited to observe such art therapy sessions.

Although I have suggested that art therapists are more often asked to consult on program development than on individual cases, the latter does sometimes occur. As with supervision, it is essential to remember that the goal is to increase the understanding and skill of others in coping with the particular individual.

How you choose to do that, however, can vary considerably. In art therapy, it may well require an actual observation of the person, looking through a series of his drawings, or even having an art interview with him. As the creative and expressive therapy program developed in the psychiatric hospital, the art therapists were often asked to work with individuals who were nonverbal or highly resistant and were then invited to share their findings with other staff members.

Sometimes, they were put into a kind of consulting role and asked to clarify for others just what was "wrong" with this person, whether this patient was ready to be discharged or was suicidal, and so on. Although they were members of the treatment team like other staff, the presence of the art product, which may have been the patient's only clear communication, required that they not only present it but also explain it, thereby putting them into a kind of consulting/teaching role.

Having said that, one of the most hazardous kinds of case consultation for an art therapist lies in the seductive invitation to discourse on someone via their products alone. Often, other staff members, who may or may not be psychologically sophisticated, will bring an art therapist one or more examples of work by an individual, asking for help in understanding its meaning and sometimes requesting assistance in getting the person to produce more.

As with a supervisee, you will need to ask many questions about the context in which the work was produced and whether there were any associative comments or actions that might give valid clues to its meaning. If there are too few such clues, it is best to decline the invitation to "interpret" the art, except when you can be explicit about the purely speculative nature of any comments you might offer. You may not think this sounds so seductive, but it is a big temptation for anyone to be able to decipher what others cannot—to have a key that unlocks a code. And, the more artwork you have seen, the more ideas will be generated as potentially useful hypotheses when you see and hear about people's products.

I am not suggesting that you refuse to share your thoughts, but that if you do so, it is essential and ethical to be clear about the amount of guesswork involved, the lack of validity, and the possibility that what you have to say may not be just slightly—but completely—off base. There is nothing I find quite as upsetting as an art therapist who makes a practice of doing "blind analysis" of people's artwork—an exciting, titillating, but risky exercise. I hope it is less common now than it was in the early days of the field, but I fear the temptations are still there.

What you *can* do, which is helpful to most consultees, is to ask how *they* think people might go about understanding the meaning of any art products. Using the examples they have brought with them, you can do a good deal of teaching—perhaps through role-play—of ways in which they can observe and ask questions that lead to a potentially valid comprehension of symbolic meaning.

Even though we art therapists are probably less likely than other clinicians to project our own ideas onto others' artwork, having been trained not to do so—and hopefully know ourselves fairly well through personal therapy—we are still subject to moments of wishful grandiosity, magic, and voyeuristic powers. And knowing all we have learned about symbolism and development in art expression, we can have good educated hunches about anyone's art product, especially when provided with some information about the artist and the context in which the work was produced.

My plea is simply for caution, modesty, and an unyielding position in relation to this particularly titillating temptation for it does our field much more harm than good in the long run and may even do harm to the individuals involved if hunches are taken as certainties by the person asking the art therapist's opinion.

An experience comes to mind that illustrates some possibilities for a response. I was once invited by a police department to consult on a suspected case of child abuse. I was first presented with some drawings done by the youngster and asked to translate their meaning. I refused to do so, explaining that I did not have such magic powers but offered instead to have an art interview with the child.

The girl revealed, through her drawings, doll play, and talk with me, that her stepfather had indeed abused her sexually, but that she had been fearful of saying this in court since she also loved him and did not want him to have to leave home. The expressive nature of the 1-hour interview probably did help this child to say—first symbolically and then directly—what was on her mind. The drawings by themselves simply reflected her confusion and were not sufficient "evidence" for any courtroom or for me as a clinician. I believe that it would have been unethical to render an opinion based on the pictures alone.

I do not in any way wish to minimize the tremendous value of the art product. Just as it is often true that "a picture is worth a thousand words," the advantage of artwork in convincing others of the worth of such activities is probably not quantifiable. Although a direct personal experience with creative media is even more persuasive, you can only introduce that in the context of consultation when asked to do some in-service training. As indicated in the discussion on teaching in Chapter 16, I usually try to arrange for some direct staff involvement with materials, even if it is minimal.

But if that is not possible, it is also true that art produced by an individual or group, especially if it is done over a period of time and shows some modification visible to the observer, can have a powerful impact on those in decision-making positions. This is especially true if they know the artist, but find that they now "know" or "see" something new as a result of seeing the art itself.

This kind of perceptual drama has occurred so often with individuals of all diagnostic classifications in so many settings that I continue to be deeply impressed with the power of art to evoke and to reveal hidden aspects of human beings—most often strengths and capacities. This seems to be true even when the people are under intensive scrutiny by numerous sophisticated professionals, as in the psychiatric teaching hospital in which I worked for many years.

So, I do not wish to throw out the art/baby with the blind analysis/bathwater. I simply want to remind art therapists that we have access to a powerful educational tool if only we do not abuse it. Some of the abuses of the past have led professionals, as well as patients, to be appropriately skeptical about what anyone can tell about people on the basis of their art.

I remember an uncomfortable experience while serving on the Task Panel on the Arts in Therapy and the Environment (President's Commission on Mental Health, 1978) with Joan Erikson. Although she had started a fine arts program at Austen Riggs, an inpatient treatment center (Erikson, 1976), and was herself a dancer, Erikson had a negative impression of art therapy because of some "wild analysis" of artwork that she had observed. Her reaction was justified since such irresponsible pronouncements by art therapists with insufficient training were fairly common in the late 1970s when we served together on the President's Commission on Mental Health.

It is my hope that we will not contribute to any further confusion, but that in a responsible and restrained consideration of people's art as serious and worthwhile data, we might help to regain some of the lost status of projective approaches in general. To do so, I believe that we must respect the limitations as well as the riches of "reading" people from their products.

A similar kind of restraint is perhaps more necessary when doing consultation than in any other role discussed so far, except for that of therapist. The grandiose rescue fantasies that often interfere with clinical work can also interfere with consultation. While there is a similar risk in both teaching and supervision, the temptation to accept the consultee's wishes for massive or miraculous change is similar to the lure of a patient's dreams of carefree recovery. In both instances, someone has deliberately asked and is paying directly for your help; this is rarely true in teaching and only occasionally in the supervision that is usually required for training and on the job.

Of all the possible roles for an art therapist, consultation is probably the one that is most freely chosen by the person asking for assistance, so that the level of motivation and the desire to use what you have to offer are generally quite high. What is important to remember is that institutional change is no less complex or slow going than individual or family modification. It is also true that, despite a sincere wish to make changes, there is always resistance and anxiety involved.

I am not suggesting that when you are an art therapy consultant you be either unduly pessimistic or particularly suspicious, but that you be realistic in your assessment of the situation and as gradual as possible in developing a plan of how best to help. This is true even if you agree immediately to meet for so many hours a week with one or more staff members for teaching or supervision in art therapy in response to an initial request. Your assessment of the system can and should continue throughout the time you are involved, just as, while doing responsible therapy, you are constantly modifying your assessment of the nature of the person's problems and how best to help him grow.

As is also true when working with a client or a supervisee, as a consultant you will probably know about interventions you wish to make long before you actually make them. As in those other helping relationships, you will be looking for the right moment, when you sense that the person or group is ready to hear what you have to say or to see what you want to help them perceive. So, it is probably necessary in consultation, as in supervision, to use many clinical skills appropriate to therapy, especially in the timing and wording of interventions.

If you are open minded about the direction and possibilities for growth in the institution and those with whom you are interacting, participating in indirect change as a consultant can be highly stimulating and rewarding. Like teaching and supervision, it is probably done best if it is done as artistically as possible.

Yet, it is important, in all of these indirect roles, to remember which role you are playing and to respect the boundaries and implicit or explicit contract of each. Of course, there are times when you might feel and act like a supportive therapist while listening to a consultee or student bemoaning a difficult situation. And of course there are genuine educational components in both consultation and supervision, varying according to the needs and readiness of the learner as well as the nature and extent of the intervention.

But in some ways these are analogous to the therapist/supervisor role issues discussed in Chapter 17. If you feel that a consultee really needs to do in-depth learning in a particular area, you would probably refer her to an article, a book, or a class rather than attempt to incorporate that much teaching into the consultation.

It would seem, therefore, that there is a quantitative as well as a qualitative component influencing any recommendation of something else from somebody else, whether it be in therapy, teaching, supervision, or consultation. There is also a small component of each of these in all of the others, but to let it grow any larger would be to blur boundaries and to do any of these jobs less well than if you were clear about your course and stuck to it.

I am spending a good deal of time and space on the issue of role blurring and possible conflict since I have seen these happen so often with intelligent and well-meaning art therapists. I decided to include these "extras" in this book, in fact, partly because of what seems to be a common confusion about these different roles, each of which has validity and can be a part of the others, but each of which ultimately has to have its own clear definition and boundaries. I hope that what I have written here will help to clarify rather than to further blur this admittedly confusing area.

References

Brown, D., Pryzwansky, W. B., & Schulte, A. C. (2005). *Psychological consultation and collaboration: Introduction to theory and practice* (6th ed.). New York: Allyn & Bacon.

Caplan, G., & Caplan, R. (1999). *Mental health consultation and collaboration.* Long Grove, IL: Waveland Press.

Erikson, J. M. (1976). *Activity, recovery and growth.* New York: Norton.

President's Commission on Mental Health. (1978). *Role of the arts in therapy and environment* (Task panel report). Washington, DC: National Committee, Arts for the Handicapped.

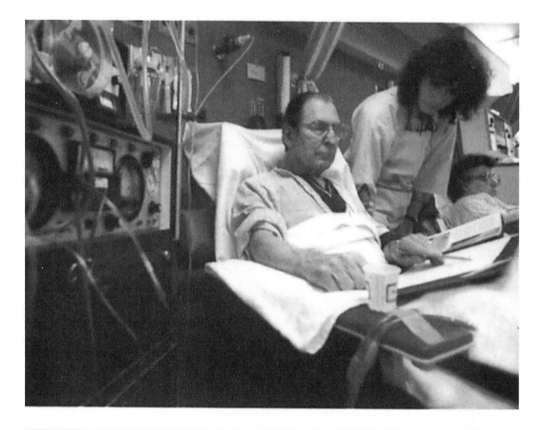

An art therapist consulting to a dialysis unit in a medical hospital did demonstration interviews as part of a pilot program, and art therapy was then made available to these patients.

In an experimental investigation of "tactile aesthetic" perception, a blind "judge" responds to wood scrap constructions made by blind, or partially sighted, children.

CHAPTER 19

Knowing Research

Introduction

Doing research can be exceptionally rewarding, although it has not been particularly appealing to most art therapists. Perhaps this is because there is often less direct interpersonal satisfaction than in doing therapy, teaching, supervising, or consulting. However, it can also be fascinating and fun.

Since my own ideas about research were formed during the early decades of art therapy, my perspective on the topic inevitably reflects the dominance of quantitative methodology in psychology and psychiatry at that time. While I can easily resonate with the postmodern position regarding the ultimate impossibility of differentiating subject and object, what still excites me is the kind of research that asks a question in a clear and systematic fashion and that attempts to answer it equally systematically—and, yes, as objectively as possible. This is the kind of research that art therapists are typically ambivalent about, and that some even find aversive. It represents "science," which until recently made most art therapists uncomfortable and seems to many artists not to be as trustworthy as the creative experience (Kaplan, 2000).

Because of the necessary control of important variables, most "research" as I understand it is rarely as flexible as doing art therapy, let alone teaching, supervising, or consulting. "Art-based research" as described by McNiff (1998) may be the exception, although as exciting as the introspective and self-motivated journeys he describes sound to the artist in me, they also seem to be a very different sort of "hunt" (Kapitan, 2010).

In any case, while there can be a great deal of creative thinking involved in the design of an empirical study or deciding how to sort and understand (analyze) the data, it is often less possible when collecting the information, especially if the procedures have to be standardized in some way. Nevertheless, some sources of satisfaction from doing research are similar to those in other aspects of our work as art therapists.

The primary motivation for doing any kind of voluntary research in art therapy—as elsewhere—is *curiosity*. This is also present when trying to solve the puzzle of how best to help each patient, student, supervisee, or consultee with whom you are working. It also seems to me that the sublimated voyeurism—satisfied in the work of understanding patient art—is an energizing force behind many kinds of studies.

For myself, theorizing (the subject of the next chapter) and doing research are closely related. Both are a way of stepping back and trying to understand the issues in art therapy from a broader, deeper, and more objective perspective. I believe that doing good clinical work is also related, perhaps inextricably so. I cannot imagine "knowing" what to do technically if I were not operating in terms of some theoretical premises about art and therapy. And I cannot imagine ever being able to make significant progress in art therapy theory and technique without at some point validating clinical impressions through well-designed research (cf. Shedler, 2010).

It has become abundantly clear in recent years that art therapy—if it is to achieve its potential to help more people lead more fulfilling lives—needs to prove that it is effective through rigorous outcome studies. In every area of human services, from medicine to education, those who control the funding are now asking for evidence that something works.

The idea that interventions should be "evidence based" is not unreasonable, especially in physical medicine where it first appeared and where randomized clinical trials can result in relatively objective findings. Accomplishing this in mental health is more difficult since so many of the variables are subtle, such as the "fit" between the individual therapist and the particular client. Nevertheless, one extensive study based on reports by a large number of psychotherapy patients concluded that psychotherapy works, that it works best when it goes on for a longer time and when the client has the opportunity to choose the therapist (Seligman, 1995).

For many years—including the conclusion from Seligman's (1995) review of the *Consumer Reports* study—it has been found that no particular theoretical or methodological approach works better than any other. This is sometimes referred to as the "Dodo bird conclusion," from *Alice in Wonderland*, that "everybody has won and all must have prizes." However, recently researchers have had access to the powerful statistical technique of meta-analysis, which allows the findings of disparate studies to be compared. An impressive review stated that, contrary to popular opinion, the effectiveness of psychotherapy is higher than that of medication, and—much to my delight—that the effectiveness of *psychodynamic* psychotherapy is at least as great as that of other approaches (Shedler, 2010).

The complicated issues in outcome research need to be addressed thoughtfully by art therapists. If the personality of the therapist is critical, for example, it is possible to design a study that holds that variable constant. In fact, the research design created many years ago by three of my colleagues at the Pittsburgh Child Guidance Center did just that (Irwin, Levy, & Shapiro, 1972). Their goal was to look at the effectiveness of drama therapy with disturbed youngsters.

So Ellie Irwin, the drama therapist, was the co-therapist in each of three groups to which a group of latency age boys (ages 7–9) were randomly assigned after being carefully matched on a number of measures. All three groups met for 20 weekly sessions. One of the groups had activity therapy, another was a recreation group (the control group), and the experimental group received drama therapy. The change in a number of pre- and posttreatment measures was compared, and it was found that the members of the group that received creative drama improved more than the others at a statistically significant level ($p < .05$). While the specific measures used might be different today, it is helpful to know that even the personality of the therapist can be held constant with experimental and control groups, as in this early investigation.

Empirical research in general and outcome studies in particular are not the most appealing sort of research for most art therapists. There are indeed conceptual and procedural problems with "evidence-based research," as pointed out by British art therapist Andrea

Gilroy (2006). However, while she acknowledged its limitations for interpersonal processes like psychotherapy and art therapy, Gilroy also outlined the steps that art therapists need to take to participate in such studies.

As creative artists, even though we have tried to wear the garments of the psychologist, the sociologist, and the anthropologist, we are naturally drawn to other models of inquiry where the "fit" appears to be better, such as the "art-based research" described by Shaun McNiff (1998). His is one of many publications on research in art therapy since the first edition of this book (Ansdell & Pavlicevic, 2001; Feder & Feder, 1998; Gilroy, 2006; Gilroy & Lee, 1995; Kapitan, 2010; Kaplan, 2000; Karkou & Sanderson, 2006; McNiff, 1998; Payne, 1993; Wadeson, 1992).

This chapter focuses on general considerations regarding art therapy research, based on my own experiences in having conducted and supervised a number of different investigations for 48 years. I actually became involved in studying applied psychological research before becoming an art therapist. During 1959—for a year between teaching art and beginning a family—I worked for an applied behavioral science organization, the American Institutes for Research (AIR). Since you were not allowed to teach in the public schools after the third month of pregnancy in those days, I had looked for a job where I could be employed until our first child was born.

In the late 1950s, the development of behavioral interventions pioneered by Harvard experimental psychologist B. F. Skinner (1961) was being applied to "teaching machines," programmed devices in which the learner was rewarded (reinforced) for the correct answer (cf. Vargas, 2009, for a current overview of the use of behavior analysis to improve teaching). AIR had gotten a contract to develop a teaching machine for "art appreciation," and I had met the principal investigator through a mutual friend. I needed a job that I could work at throughout a pregnancy, and he needed someone who knew something about art. My college major had been art, but at Wellesley in the 1950s that meant art history, and my husband had studied with Skinner, so I was familiar with his work. The combination was right for the AIR project.

My primary assignment in that job was to read and abstract all of the experimental studies I could find on "aesthetic judgment." My secondary assignment at AIR was to read and abstract applied research in "learning theory," an active area of investigation at the time. The idea was to apply what was then understood about learning to the creation of the program for a teaching machine on art appreciation.

In the course of reading and abstracting all of this literature—with the guidance of the psychologist who was my supervisor—I became familiar with the language and methodology of research. I had encountered research tangentially during college when my child psychology professor showed our class some finger paintings that had been collected as part of a study she was doing about child-rearing practices (Alper, Blane, & Adams, 1955). Mrs. Alper, who was usually quite calm, was visibly excited about the findings, which had confirmed her hypothesis. I often wonder how much her palpable enthusiasm about those finger paintings and the associated findings infected me with an interest in research.

I had also bumped into some research in journals during graduate school while exploring the topic of the psychology of children's art for a seminar in child development. It was during those months in the Harvard library stacks that I first read about something called "art therapy" in articles by Margaret Naumburg (1947/1973) as well as "art education therapy" in a book by Viktor Lowenfeld (1957). While most writings on the psychology of children's art were anecdotal accounts of clinical work by various therapists, some of it was experimental—like an early study of line drawings by Ernst Harms, who later cofounded the journal *Art Psychotherapy*.

My education in the area of research has been primarily experiential. In fact, by the time I got to my doctoral program—in which one of the required areas of competency was research and statistics—I was able to test out of any formal study. While there is a great deal to be said for learning by doing, I am pleased that the current standards for master's programs in art therapy require learning about research, and that many programs encourage a research project of some sort as a thesis. Another development that bodes well for the future is the growing number of art therapists who have received doctoral degrees that in many instances required them to conduct some kind of research for their dissertation. As doctoral programs in art therapy itself are being developed, many are run by individuals who have sufficient literacy in both domains to be able to train art therapy students more adequately in this area (cf. Kapitan, 2010).

Meanwhile, although it is important for art therapists to be literate about research, I believe that it is ideal to work with collaborators who are more knowledgeable. Because I spent most of my professional life in multidisciplinary settings, I had the wonderful learning experience of doing a number of studies, most in collaboration with one or more people from other fields who knew more than I about research, experimental design, and statistics. Since these experiences were so helpful to me, I share them in the hope that they will inspire others to undertake similar joint efforts. In addition to telling you something about the research itself, I describe the drama of identifying the questions and ways of answering them. For me, that has always been the most creatively challenging and enjoyable part of the process.

I begin with the first study that, like all research, grew out of a question. It was one that someone posed to me, and when I realized that I did not have an answer, it seemed like a good idea to investigate further. When the chairman of the Child Development Department—who first invited me to work with schizophrenic children in 1963—asked me if you could tell what was wrong with them from their art, I said I really was not sure, in spite of suggestions in the literature that their artwork ought to have certain characteristics that would be clearly diagnostic.

At the time, I was not only working with the children in the hospital unit, but was also doing art with after-school groups at the child study center run by the department—a place that had been founded by Benjamin Spock and Erik Erikson. In an attempt to study the question more rigorously, the psychologist at the study center helped me design a way to collect comparable artistic data from a group of "normal" youngsters matched for mental age and gender. I met with each of the youngsters in the control group in an unstructured art session, offering them the same choice of media and topic available to the schizophrenic children, who were also seen individually.

When I later worked at the Pittsburgh Child Guidance Center, which was part of the Department of Child Psychiatry, the director of research was both a psychiatrist and a psychologist. He helped me to take the next step in answering the question, which was to design the judgment part of the study. This was implemented by having four different groups of judges with different kinds of experience view a random selection of individual products and groups of products.

Their task was to identify each piece of artwork or group of products from a single session as having been done by either a non-schizophrenic or a schizophrenic child (Rubin & Schachter, 1972). Although the judges thought it should be possible to do so, the findings confirmed my clinical impression that, while the children themselves were easy to differentiate, their art was not. Ironically, the few judges who were correct beyond chance expectation were in the group of those who had no experience with children, art, or psychology.

After we completed that study, I had many more ideas for research projects and was thrilled that the director of research was interested in collaborating. So I shared with him the long list of questions I wanted to ask through research. He then asked me one really important question: How valuable or helpful would each of these inquiries be? In other words, given limited time and resources, you first need to prioritize your questions. You then need to find out where your interests coincide with that of possible collaborators. So, we sorted through the topics and focused on what also interested him and the rest of his staff.

Because many clinicians were using family drawings and inferring a good deal from elements like the sequence of figures drawn, figure placement, and their relative size, we collected data for a study that attempted to look at what you could validly infer from family drawings. After considerable discussion, we requested family drawings from a group of parents and children and also asked them to fill out questionnaires about family relationships—who they felt closest to, who they would go to when distressed or happy, who seemed most important in the family, and so on.

The collection of the drawings and the creation of the questionnaires were both designed in collaboration with my colleagues in the research department of the clinic. I was then able to obtain a grant from a faculty support fund in the School of Health-Related Professions, where I was teaching art therapy courses. This grant paid for a sophisticated statistical data analysis program recommended by an external consultant, but as it turned out, it did not provide sufficient support for us to finish the study. It became obvious that we needed to also pay someone with the expertise to analyze the multiple correlations between the scores on the many variables.

This was a painful learning experience in what amounted essentially to poor planning—not anticipating how much funding would be required to sort out the data in order to actually see, understand, and be able to consider the results. For over two decades, I saved the heavy notebooks full of scores and correlations on computer printouts, through a series of office moves. It took me a long time to admit that I was unlikely to be able to finish the study, and I finally discarded a file cabinet full of data, sadder but wiser.

A more modest but more satisfying study was designed and implemented in collaboration with my husband, a speech pathologist who taught courses in linguistics and child language development. This study was a kind of basic research since we did not have a specific hypothesis but were intrigued by the fact that babbling occurs so much earlier than scribbling. Although superficially similar, scribbling happens when children already have a large verbal vocabulary.

We decided to compare the development of art and speech in preschoolers (Rubin & Rubin, 1988), enjoying the creative challenge of designing parallel tasks in language and drawing, as well as ways of analyzing the resulting data. The findings, like the topics investigated, were complex, intriguing, and raised more questions than they answered but were an initial mapping of a previously unexplored territory.

Another qualitative sort of study emerged from questions arising during my work as consultant to a school for blind children, where I had initially done a pilot therapeutic art program. A clinical psychologist friend who had also consulted to that school asked how it was going and what sort of questions were arising. I told him I was intrigued by the fact that the youngsters with no useful vision seemed to have a sense of what felt right when creating something with art materials—a kind of "tactile aesthetic." Since some of the children who were legally blind were actually partially sighted, their responses to what they created were often determined by what they were able to perceive visually, as opposed to the youngsters who were totally blind.

Because the art therapists providing the activities were sighted, I wondered whether we might need to be better attuned to the children's sense of aesthetic rightness or beauty, which might be different for the two groups. My psychologist friend and I met a number of times, trying to figure out a way to investigate this phenomenon. After a good deal of brainstorming, we designed a study in which blind, partially sighted, and sighted judges (with and without blindfolds) responded in various ways to wood scrap sculptures produced by all three groups. There, too, the findings were intriguing and supported the hypothesis that children would prefer work done by someone with their own degree of useful vision—in other words, that they had different aesthetic preferences (Rubin, 1976).

As you can see, most of the research in which I became involved grew out of questions that arose in the course of doing art therapy. In the following instance, the data were collected almost accidentally, but in a way that made them comparable. First, my drama therapy colleague and I decided to work together with a group using both modalities. To select from among all the boys who had been referred, we met with each one for same-day individual art and drama interviews.

After we found that working together in art and drama with a group of latency age boys was fascinating (Irwin, Rubin, & Shapiro, 1981), we decided to see how such a multimodal approach would work with adolescents. Again, we saw each of the boys and girls who had been referred for same-day art and drama interviews in order to select those who would be good candidates for the group.

Having conducted same-day art and drama interviews with both the latency and adolescent youngsters, we realized that we could learn something by comparing the products—the art that had been made and the puppet stories that had been told. As with the art-speech study, we were not sure what we would find but were curious.

We decided to examine the products of the two interviews on dimensions of form and content that would be common to both modalities. Identifying the categories and figuring out ways to rate them was itself a pleasurable creative thinking task. There were a number of intriguing findings, such as the fact that drama tended to elicit more aggressive themes, whereas art tended to elicit more themes of nurturance (Rubin & Irwin, 1976).

There are many issues in art therapy that cry out for well-designed and carefully implemented research. In the area of outcome studies, more investigations involving art therapy are now being conducted using extrinsic measures. While writing this chapter, I heard about one based on the work of Linda Levine Madori (2007), whose educational background is in both art therapy and recreation therapy.

Her method, "therapeutic thematic arts programming" (TTAP) is being used with patients with Alzheimer's disease, and its effects will be assessed using standardized measures like the MMSE (Mini-Mental State Examination), the clock drawing, the Geriatric Depression Scale, and the MDS (Minimum Data Set) to look at appetite, falls, and aggressive behavior (L. Levine Madori, personal communication, January 28, 2010). In a similar fashion, psychiatrist/psychologist Gene Cohen's (2006; Cohen et al., 2006) studies of the effects of creative activities on the health of older people used clear and objective measures of health and well-being, such as the number of doctor visits or the amount of medication used.

Outcome studies are critical in finding out whether and how art therapy is effective. They can in fact be fairly simple, as in the following example: Many years ago, wondering how effective a pilot art program could be with multiply disabled blind children, I designed a somewhat crude outcome study with the woman who had invited me to consult and whose training was in special education (Rubin & Klineman, 1974). I had asked to see each child in a pre-program assessment interview for a number of reasons: in order to decide how to group them and to see how they responded to a set of auditory, olfactory, and tactile stimuli as well as the invitation to use art materials. Parenthetically, it was also a way of orienting the staff and students who were to be helpers in the program to a new way of working in art with these children.

Observers used a 24-item rating scale, rating each child on a variety of behavioral dimensions. At the end of the 7-week after-school program, I met again with each youngster for an individual art evaluation, and these too were rated. The rating scale, designed by myself and a graduate student, was behavioral, and there were changes in a number of areas, some at statistically significant levels (e.g., in independence).

If you want more information about any of the studies noted without having to track down the original journal articles, they are described in greater detail in Chapter 21 of the third edition of *Child Art Therapy* (Rubin, 2005).

Needed Research

Even though there has certainly been more research in art therapy since the first edition of this book, there are still many areas of possible inquiry in addition to outcome studies that would be extremely helpful to the work of the art therapist. Indeed, one thing that art therapy needs more than anything else is a "mapping" of many territories that we now move in without sure guidelines, where we could travel so much better if we but knew the terrain—we could navigate where now we stumble.

For example, there is a need to study in detail the development of art expression in areas other than drawing, as well as its development in non-representational as well as representational modes. Some excellent beginnings have been made by psychologist Claire Golomb (1974) and the studies in the development of symbolization done by Project Zero at Harvard (http://pzweb.harvard.edu/Research/Earlysym.htm), but we still know little about the evolution of normal artistic development in anything other than graphic expression, although some progress has been made (Matthews, 2003).

There have been some attempts to look at artistic development cross culturally (Kellogg, 1969), and now that our ability to communicate with one another globally has expanded so dramatically, it should be possible to see whether our old assumptions about the universality of graphic development are still valid. A study done with children in Chicago and in Japan suggested that there were in fact cultural differences (Toku, 2000), a variable also acknowledged by Golomb (2002). One art therapist has been collecting an archive of "normal" and "typical" drawings from children between 6 and 11 years old from many cultures, to look at this same issue (Alter-Muri, 2002).

There is also a need to define norms for adult artwork in order to be able to make meaningful comparisons and inferences from patient products. A useful beginning has been made with a set of scores for impairment, organicity, distortion, and simplification in adult drawings of the human figure, still the most extensively studied topic at any age level (Mitchell, Trent, & McArthur, 1993).

The area of mental imagery has been mapped so far primarily by cognitive psychologists, with hardly any utilization of expressive visual modes in its study or definition. Similarly, the question of which parts of the brain mediate thought in images as well as in other systems is being investigated by neuroscientists, who may test responses to visual stimuli but are not yet able to measure brain activity during the creative process of making visual art (cf. Solso, 2001). With the growth of art therapy in medical settings, perhaps these kinds of studies will soon become possible. I could go on and on with the kinds of descriptive research that need to be done in order for our work to be based more on fact and less on conjecture (cf. Hass-Cohen & Carr, 2008).

There are also many studies crying for implementation in regard to the influence of the medium or modality—paint versus clay or art versus drama—on the form and content of what someone creates, as well as on self-concept or the ability to gain insight. Sequences of tasks, degree of specificity, nature of therapist involvement—all of these issues of methodology continue to be discussed and occasionally debated, but usually in terms of opinion alone, with hardly any attempt to investigate them systematically.

Even in the area of diagnosis and assessment through art products, there has been a mere trickle of investigations, with the possible exception of those in relation to the Diagnostic Drawing Series (cf. Cohen & Mills, 2010). And when it comes to most issues of technique, such as how much to help educationally and how much to discuss analytically, hot air predominates over hard findings (including most of this book).

Are such studies limited only by the lack of individuals trained in both art therapy and research methodology or the difficulty of finding collaborators and resources? I truly do not know the answer. I just know that it would be helpful to have some objective investigations of such questions. Whatever the cause, and in spite of the growth of interest in research within our profession since the first edition of this book, it still seems to me that much of the research in art therapy has been of mediocre quality, inadequate in both quantity and scope.

Having been so critical, I now want to offer some ideas that I hope will be constructive. One is an approach to learning about (and hopefully liking) research that I have used at the undergraduate level with those training to be art teachers and with graduate students in art therapy. It is a teaching/learning model in which doing always occurs along with didactic instruction. To study research methodology or statistics without applying them at the same time is much too intellectual and difficult for inexperienced researchers to integrate—especially most art therapists, who tend to be uncomfortable with mathematics and abstract conceptualizations.

In fact, the only method I have found that enables people to grasp the thinking behind empirical research is to actually design and conduct a study in art therapy. It need not be complicated; in fact, it can be rather simple. But, going through the process of selecting, defining, and refining the question or hypothesis; living through, with guidance and associated reading/observing, the process of deciding on participants, methodology, and so on; actually gathering the data, experiencing the complexity of controlling variables; and finally, dealing with what has been collected in a logically meaningful way—that seems to be a really viable way for students to learn about research.

You may be wondering how many years or lifetimes this program would require since it might sound a bit too ambitious. Actually, depending on the amount of learning time available, it can be more or less elaborate and more or less formal. It can be as limited as a single assignment for a semester course, or it can be as extensive as a master's thesis or doctoral dissertation. The extent would be a function of the learner's goals and the requirements or expectations of those doing the teaching. If more art therapists had even a mini-experience of this nature, I believe that their attitude toward empirical research would be very different.

In addition to direct experience with conceptualizing and doing research, art therapists would also do well to think of it in less esoteric terms. Research, after all, is simply the systematic asking of questions in a way that enables those that are posed to be answered. Identifying the questions you have and deciding if they are worth the time and effort of serious study is only the first step. Deciding exactly how best to answer them is the creative and challenging part of doing research, as exciting as the development of relevant tasks or activities in doing or teaching art therapy.

For example, you might decide, as I did some years ago, to study intra-individual variability within people's art products. This issue arose after noticing a repeated phenomenon. In this case, it was the fact that people are often highly variable, yet so much of the diagnostic use of art seems not to take this variability into account. What was unknown, however, was what relationship such variability might have to either chronological age or gender.

It was finally decided, after considerable brainstorming with a multidisciplinary research study group, to undertake a normative study and to use a series of human figure drawings as the task (four drawings within 8 days). A minimum of 20 subjects at each age level, half male and half female, all drawn from non-patient school populations, was also recommended by the group. The reason for the numbers was statistical; the reason for the choice of task was that it was so frequently used to evaluate both intellectual level (Harris, 1963) and personality (Machover, 1949), and that there were reliable scoring methods that could be used to compare at least one kind of variability—the differences among the scores for the four drawings from each individual.

Prior to doing the actual study, I wrote to those who were the recognized experts at the time in the use of human figure drawings—Rhoda Kellogg (1969), Elizabeth Koppitz (1968), and Dale Harris (1963)—to ask if any comparable research already existed and for any advice they might have. This was a purely practical move since it would have made little sense to spend the time, energy, and money needed if a similar investigation had already been done. As it happened, there was no such study known to any of our expert consultants, each of whom was enthusiastic about the proposed research and encouraged us to pursue it.

After gathering the drawings (collected in a standardized fashion by classroom teachers) and having them scored by trained judges, it was then necessary to decide how to deal with the numerical data that emerged. We considered treating the four scores obtained for each child by one statistical technique (a repeated measures analysis of variance), but eventually decided on another (the standard deviation among the four scores) as an even more appropriate measure of *score variability*, certainly more refined than the range of lowest to highest score, also considered.

We were then faced with yet another creative challenge: how to measure the variability among drawings that was visually evident but not necessarily related to the score—which reflects primarily the number of details. After experimentation with several sets of measures, we finally developed a 4-point scale of *visual variability*, which allowed judges to give each set of four drawings a single global rating. The same scale also proved to be useful for rating *content variability* as well (man, woman, boy, girl), another way in which the four drawings by each individual were potentially different from one another (Rubin, Schachter, & Ragins, 1983).

This rather detailed description of some of the issues faced in the initiation and implementation of this research project will hopefully not deter the interested art therapist but will rather whet your appetite for the imaginative challenges involved in the systematic asking and answering of questions through research. The findings, in addition, were fascinating since the modification of variability over the age span was not a simple gradual decline, as we had anticipated, but rather an up-and-down phenomenon with peaks and valleys at different chronological ages.

It is, of course, common for research in art therapy to focus on the art product, whether you are measuring or scoring some aspect of it, judging its normality or pathology, or evaluating it in some other way. Unfortunately, while the products of art therapy are eminently concrete and permanent, reliable or valid ways of scoring them are not. For example, while the area of self-esteem is one that we hope will improve as a result of art therapy, the few scales that have been developed for scoring drawings on that dimension are limited to figure drawings in pencil, seem quite unrelated to other indices, and have proved insensitive in the few studies in which I have used them.

The problem here is similar in my opinion to one that also exists in the area of theory—that those who have developed most existing scales for rating drawings or paintings are not artists or art therapists but are more likely to be clinical psychologists with an experimental bent. Perhaps quantification is not the way to get at the qualities meaningful to art therapists in patient art. I am not suggesting that I have an answer; however, if art therapists with an understanding of validity and reliability were to concentrate on such problems, more valid and reliable methods of objectively describing artwork might be developed. If nothing else, it seems important to move once and for all beyond the realm of the pencil drawing of a human figure into the world of color, shape, nuance, and form that is art.

Although there has been some encouraging work in this very direction by art therapists themselves in the years since the initial publication of this book, art therapist Donna Betts's analysis for her 2005 dissertation concluded that "art therapists are still in a nascent stage of understanding assessments and rating instruments, that flaws in the art therapy assessment and rating instrument literature research are numerous, and that much work has yet to be done" (p. 77; cf. also Betts, 2010).

Nevertheless, two standardized art therapy assessments that are widely used also include a rating manual or guide. One is the DDS (Diagnostic Drawing Series) developed by Barry Cohen (1986/1994) with an archive and research studies organized by Anne Mills (Cohen & Mills, 2010). The other is the PPAT, a Person Picking an Apple From a Tree, which was developed by Linda Gantt. These drawings are scored using the illustrated Formal Elements Art Therapy Scale (FEATS; Gantt & Tabone, 1998). Both the DDS Rating Manual and the FEATS include *content* elements as well. And, in both instances, the art therapist researchers have invited colleagues to participate in the collection and analysis of data, as has Rawley Silver, who has developed rating scales for her drawing tests over a long career in the field, spanning more than 30 years (Silver, 2002, 2005, 2007, 2010).

Measuring the Creative Process

Similar problems attend any attempt to measure or describe the creative process. Here, too, we may have gotten caught in the empiricist's numerical web, refusing to recognize the phenomenologically subjective nature of the creative experience. This is recognized in the publications by McNiff (1998) and Kapitan (2010), and it is fortunate that qualitative art-based research can accommodate such aspects better than empirically based studies.

It is indeed possible to develop observation guides and even reliable rating scales of behavior during the art process. As an example of an objective index, the number of times a child asked for help from the art therapist in pre- versus post-program interviews was used in one study and was something that changed to a statistically significant extent following the art program (Rubin & Klineman, 1974). What could not be measured, however, was the look in the child's eyes, the pleading in his voice, or the degree of anxiety felt by the observer listening to the request, all of which were also important aspects of independence/dependence, the variable being measured.

Inferential indices such as the intensity of a person's involvement in the creative task are what we need to find ways of describing—qualitatively if possible, quantitatively if feasible. How often someone steps away from the easel and reconsiders his painting may be as valid a measure of his "observing ego" as his ability to discuss the painting later. Understanding and evaluating the art process are complex challenges that need to be tackled with a more phenomenological methodology, as was suggested many years ago by experienced art education researcher Kenneth Beittel (1973).

But, the hardest thing to measure, and the one most needed if art therapy as a discipline is to fulfill its potential, is the effectiveness of art therapy. Whether the indices are intrinsic (like paintings from the first and last session) or extrinsic (like scores on a written test of self-esteem or the frequency of readmissions to the hospital), it is always difficult to isolate influences in this, as in other, outcome research. Nevertheless, it is in this area that I believe we should concentrate our efforts in order to document the changes that all art therapists feel sure take place but cannot easily communicate without unbiased "evidence."

Art therapist David Gussak collaborated on an article with two other allied health professionals that provided a useful set of "perspectives on clinical outcomes assessment" (Pfeifle, Gussak, & Keegan, 1999). In addition to some single-case studies, there have been several studies by the art therapist-psychiatrist team of Linda Gantt and Lou Tinnin of the success of their protocol for the intensive treatment of posttraumatic stress disorder (PTSD), which includes art therapy (Gantt & Tinnin, 2007). They have continued to update the data from their clinical research (http://www.traumatherapy.us/research.htm).

A second area we need to study in order to improve the work of art therapists is the effectiveness of different methodologies, such as more versus less structure in tasks or the optimal amount of therapist-initiated intervention. Each kind of issue also needs to be addressed with different populations. While it is indeed difficult to conceptualize, let alone control, all of the relevant variables involved in answering such questions, we will be on much sounder ground and will gain significant respect if we attempt to look more objectively at ourselves, at what we do and how we do it.

It is my hope that the efforts that have been made since the first edition of this book was published will help future art therapists to be less uncomfortable with the idea of research. If so, they will be able to initiate as well as respond to interest on the part of others. Collaborating with other mental health professionals on questions of common interest is surely much more than a way for an individual art therapist to grow in understanding research. It is also a way to build bridges, based primarily on a shared intellectual excitement.

If we can view ourselves as capable of learning how to do meaningful research and can be viewed by others as potentially valuable collaborators, our stature will grow, and we will begin to make contributions in yet other realms of mental health, beyond bringing the arts to those who are troubled. For, as noted earlier, there is a great deal to be understood about the mind and its functions through a more detailed, in-depth understanding of how it works when making art.

In addition to the challenge and importance of conducting well-designed research in and about art therapy, it is important for any art therapist in a position of responsibility to be able to understand and evaluate relevant research in related fields. Without some comprehension of what is involved in experimental design or in the handling of data, it is really impossible to make sense of reports of research by others. This is significant for several reasons. First, there is much that is of value to us and related to our work in studies from allied disciplines, but we need to be able to evaluate its quality and comprehend its implications in order to make use of it.

In an issue of *Studies in Art Education* that was published while I was writing the first edition of this book, for example, there was a report of an investigation of "the effects of students' sense of agency or self-determination as a motivational force in art learning" (King, 1983). All of the outcome measures, including both achievement and attitude, favored the student choice condition. What this means is that, at least for the subjects in this study (208 sixth graders involved in different art-learning situations for 3 months), the condition in which they could select their own activities resulted in greater progress in art achievement, in self-concept, and in attitudes toward art.

The relevance of this study for methodology in art therapy is clear. What makes it so important is that it was also carefully designed, so that the independent variable of choice was isolated and controlled much more precisely than is usually the case, making the findings all the more significant. In the same issue, a review of the literature on "cognitive style" and its implications for research in art production (and art criticism) also had relevance for our field (Lovano-Kerr, 1983).

However, despite the fact that there are hopeful signs now on the horizon, things have really not changed as much as I would wish. On November 12, 2009, art therapist Cathy Malchiodi wrote what I consider to be an accurate assessment of where we are today in a piece for her Internet blog on the healing arts for *Psychology Today*. Her piece was a response to an anonymous correspondent who asserted that "Art therapy is a fake!" It was also a wake-up call to American art therapists to "put aside all the excuses and distractions once and for all and make research the prime directive in the profession so we can understand—and preserve—this field." Some excerpts follow:

> Evidence to justify the efficacy of art therapy is seriously deficient. … Leaders in the field of art therapy talk and talk and talk every year about the need for more large-scale outcome studies on posttraumatic stress disorder, autism, Alzheimer's disease, and the currently popular disorder du jour. Academics continue to churn out more chapters and articles on why art therapy research is needed [I plead guilty on this one] while very few outcome studies are undertaken, never mind verified by conventional peer review or published anywhere but in art therapy journals.
>
> As is also the case for other forms of expressive therapy, research into the effectiveness of art therapy has not been conducted with sufficient detail or quality to support claims of its clinical effectiveness. (http://en.wikipedia.org/w/index.php?title=Art_therapy&oldid)

Malchiodi (2009) went on to point out that, despite arguments by some that creative activity cannot be evaluated by the usual scientific measures, this has not been true for music therapy, which "has used accepted instruments to successfully evaluate the effect of music on physiology, behavior, and memory."

Hopefully, we will not be so insular that we have to reinvent the wheel too many times, and we will be able to harness our strengths to those of others for all of that needed and exciting research in the future. Hopefully, too, many of us can learn to enjoy doing such work so that there will be more and better studies designed by those who really understand the discipline. As noted earlier, since art therapists competent in research methodology are likely to remain a rare breed, a reasonable solution is to collaborate with colleagues who possess the needed expertise. Doing collaborative work in research has many of the same pros and cons, stresses and pleasures, as doing co-therapy. However, if the work is carefully planned, the advantages far outweigh the possible hazards.

In the United Kingdom, a collaborative structure for research has been developed, thanks to the efforts of pioneer art therapist Diane Waller. In September 2009, the International Centre for Research in Arts Therapies (ICRA) was founded in the Department of Psychological Medicine at Imperial College in London. Its goal is to "coordinate multidisciplinary research in the arts and arts therapies, psychotherapy, and mental health. … The Centre (ICRA) aims to act as a facilitator for improving the evidence base in arts therapies in particular. Its location within a Division of Neuroscience and Mental Health will be of particular value to new proposed research that will examine the effects of arts therapies for people with Alzheimer's Disease, Parkinson's Disease and other neurological disorders as well as for conditions that impact on mental health and well-being" (preliminary announcement, International Centre for Research in Arts Therapies. Art, Dance and Music Therapy).

This development makes me more optimistic than ever about the potential for constructive change and growth in the systematic asking of questions and trying to find answers in art therapy via what is known as "research."

References

Alper, T., Blane, H. & Adams, B. (1955). Reactions of middle and lower class children to finger paints as a function of class differences in child-training practices. *Journal of Abnormal and Social Psychology, 51*, 439–448.

Alter-Muri, S. (2002). Viktor Lowenfeld revisited: A review of Lowenfeld's preschematic, schematic and gang age stages. *American Journal of Art Therapy, 40*, 170–192.

Ansdell, G., & Pavlicevic, M. (2001). *Beginning research in the arts therapies.* London: Kingsley.

Beittel, K. E. (1973). *Alternatives for art education research.* Dubuque, IA: Brown.

Betts, D. J. (2005). *A systematic analysis of art therapy assessment and rating instrument literature.* Unpublished doctoral dissertation, Florida State University.

Betts, D. J. (2010). Positive art therapy assessment. In A. Gilroy, R. Tipple, & C. Brown (Eds.), *Assessment in art therapy.* London: Routledge.

Cohen, B. M. (Ed.). (1986/1994). *The Diagnostic Drawing Series Rating Guide.* Available from the editor at P.O. Box 9853, Alexandria, VA, USA 22304.

Cohen, B. M., & Mills, A. (2010). *2010 Report on the DDS.* Alexandria, VA: DDS Project.

Cohen, G. D. (2006). Research on creativity and aging: The positive impact of the arts on health and illness. *Generations, 30*(1), 7–15.

Cohen, G. D., Perlstein, S., Chapline, J., Kelly, J., Firth, K. M., & Simmens, S. (2006). The impact of professionally conducted cultural programs on the physical health, mental health, and social functioning of older adults. *The Gerontologist, 46*, 726–734,

Feder, B., & Feder, E. (1998). *The art and science of evaluation in the arts therapies.* Springfield, IL: Thomas.

Gantt, L., & Tabone, C. (1998). *The formal elements art therapy scale: The rating manual.* Morgantown, WV: Gargoyle Press.

Gantt, L., & Tinnin, L. (2007). Intensive trauma therapy of PTSD and dissociation. *The Arts in Psychotherapy, 34*, 69–80.

Gilroy, A. (2006). *Art therapy, research and evidence based practice.* London: Routledge.

Gilroy, A., & Lee, C. (1995). *Art and music: Therapy and research.* London: Routledge.

Golomb, C. (1974). *Young children's sculpture and drawing.* Cambridge, MA: Harvard University Press.

Golomb, C. (2002). *Child art in context.* Washington, DC: American Psychological Association.

Harris, D. B. (1963). *Children's drawings as measures of intellectual maturity.* New York: Harcourt, Brace, & World.

Hass-Cohen, N., & Carr, R. (Eds.). (2008). *Art therapy and clinical neuroscience.* London: Jessica Kingsley.

Irwin, E., Levy, P., & Shapiro, M. (1972). Assessment of creative drama program in a child guidance setting. *Group Psychotherapy and Psychodrama, 25*(3), 105–116.

Irwin, E., Rubin, J. A., & Shapiro, M. I. (1981). Art and drama: Partners in therapy. In G. Schattner & R. Courtney (Eds.), *Drama in therapy* (Vol. 1). New York: Drama Book Specialists.

Kapitan, L. (2010). *An introduction to art therapy research.* New York: Routledge.

Kaplan, F. (2000*). Art, science, and art therapy.* London: Kingsley.

Karkou, V., & Sanderson, P. (2006). *Arts therapies: A research-based map of the field.* London: Churchill Livingstone.

Kellogg, R. (1969). *Analyzing children's art.* Palo Alto, CA: National Press Books.

King, A. (1983). Agency, achievement, and self-concept of young adolescent art students. *Studies in Art Education, 24*, 187–194.

Koppitz, E. M. (1968). *Psychological evaluation of children's human figure drawings*. New York: Grune & Stratton, 1968.

Levine Madori, L. (2007). Use of the therapeutic thematic arts programming TTAP Method, for enhanced cognitive and psychosocial functioning in a geriatric population. *American Journal of Recreation Therapy, 8*, 25–31.

Lovano-Kerr, J. (1983). Cognitive style revisited: Implications for research in art production and art criticism. *Studies in Art Education, 24*, 195–205.

Lowenfeld, V. (1957). *Creative and mental growth* (3rd ed.). New York: Macmillan.

Machover, K. (1949). *Personality projection in the drawing of the human figure*. Springfield, IL: Thomas.

Malchiodi, C. (2009). @im_inebriated to @arttherapynews: Art Therapy Is a Fake! (http://www.psychologytoday.com/blog/the-healing-arts/200911/iminebriated-arttherapynews-art-therapy-is-fake)

Matthews, J. (2003). *Drawing and painting: Children and visual representation* (2nd ed.). London: Chapman.

McNiff, S. (1998). *Art-based research*. London: Kingsley.

Mitchell, J., Trent, R., & McArthur, M. A. (1993). *Human figure drawing test (HFDT)*. Los Angeles: Western Psychological Services.

Naumburg, M. (1947). *Studies of the free art expression of behavior problem children and adolescents as a means of diagnosis and therapy* (Nervous and Mental Disease Monograph, No. 71). (Reprinted as *An introduction to art therapy*. New York: Teachers College Press, 1973.)

Payne, H. (1993). *Handbook of inquiry in the arts therapies*. London: Kingsley.

Pfeifle, W. G., Gussak, D. E., & Keegan, C. A. (1999). Perspectives on clinical outcomes assessment: A view for allied health professions. *Journal of Allied Health, 28*, 240–246.

Rubin, J. A. (1976). The exploration of "tactile aesthetic." *The New Outlook for the Blind, 70*, 369–375.

Rubin, J. A. (2005). *Child art therapy* (3rd ed.). New York: Wiley.

Rubin, J. A., & Klineman, J. (1974). They opened our eyes. *Education of the Visually Handicapped, 6*, 106–113.

Rubin, J. A., & Rubin, H. (1988). Art and speech in preschoolers: A developmental study. *American Journal of Art Therapy*.

Rubin, J. A., & Schachter, J. (1972). Judgments of psychopathology from art productions of children. *Confinia Psychiatrica, 15*, 237–252.

Rubin, J. A., Schachter, J., & Ragins, N. (1983). Intra-individual variability in human figure drawings. *American Journal of Orthopsychiatry, 53*, 654–667.

Seligman, M. E. (1995). The effectiveness of psychotherapy: The *Consumer Reports* study. *American Psychologist, 50*, 965–974.

Shedler, J. (2010). The efficacy of psychodynamic psychotherapy. *American Psychologist, 65*(2), 98–109.

Silver, R. A. (2002*). Three art assessments*. New York: Brunner-Routledge.

Silver, R. A. (2005). *Aggression and depression assessed through art*. New York: Routledge.

Silver, R. A. (2007). *The Silver drawing test and draw a story: Assessing depression, aggression, and cognitive skills*. New York: Routledge.

Silver, R. A. (2010). *Identifying risks for aggression and depression through metaphors*. New York: Purple Finch Press.

Skinner, B. F. (1961). *Teaching Machines*. New York: Freeman.

Solso, R. L. (2001). Brain activities in a skilled versus a novice artist: An fMRI study. *Leonardo, 34*(1), 33–34.

Tinnin, L., Bills, L., & Gantt, L. (2002). Short-term treatment of simple and complex PTSD. In M. Williams & J. Sommer (Eds.), *Simple and complex post-traumatic stress disorder: Strategies for comprehensive treatment in clinical practice* (pp. 99–118). New York: Haworth Press.

Toku, M. (2000). Cross-cultural analysis of artistic development: Drawing by Japanese and U.S. children. *Visual Arts Research, 23*, No. 1, Issue 53. Retrieved from http://www.csuchico.edu/~mtoku/vc/Articles/toku/Toku_Cross-cultural_VAR01.htm

Vargas, J. S. (2009). *Behavior analysis for effective teaching*. New York: Routledge.

Wadeson, H. W. (Ed.). (1992). *A guide to conducting art therapy research*. Mundelein, IL: American Art Therapy Association.

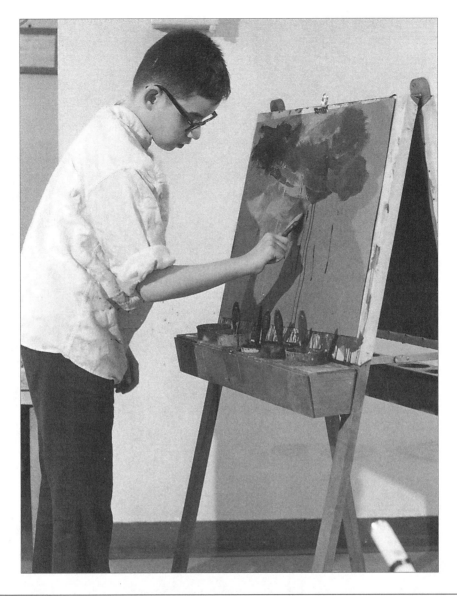

This boy is painting during a post-program interview done after 7 weeks of group art therapy. Observers rated 24 behaviors using a 5-item scale during both pre- and post-program interviews. There were statistically significant gains in some areas, such as independence.

Any viable theory of art therapy has to be able to account for this rare example of self-therapy through art. A rural laborer told me how much it had helped him to carve this larger-than-life-size trunk following the untimely death of his young wife.

CHAPTER 20

Knowing Theory

The Mixed Blessings of Borrowed Theory

Having made a strong pitch for collaboration with those from other disciplines in developing sound research in art therapy, I now make what will probably appear to be a 180-degree turn and argue for greater independence in our thinking in the area of theory. It is understandable that a number of art therapists had to obtain advanced training in some other discipline, largely because such training was not available in our own.

While it is exciting to enrich our field with the well-digested perspectives of others, it is also somewhat depressing. What I find really sad is that we so often seem to borrow theories to explain what happens when people create, just as we attach to ourselves the identities of others when we obtain doctorates in other disciplines. This may sound odd coming from me since I find psychoanalytic theories about development and about intrapsychic as well as interpersonal functioning so useful. The weaker area in psychoanalysis, as in most such general theories—with individual exceptions—is how they understand the creative process itself.

This is not really surprising since those who have theorized about the creative process and its relationship to psychological functioning and mental health have rarely been artists, although they may have done creative thinking in other realms. Psychologists like Rudolf Arnheim (1967), Abraham Maslow (1968), Rollo May (1975), Mark Turner (2006), Mark Runco (2007), or Mihaly Csikszentmihalyi (2008) have added considerably to our understanding of the creative process. Psychiatrists like Sigmund Freud (1900), Silvano Arieti (1976), and Pinchas Noy (1999) have done much to further our understanding of what motivates creative behavior and how it works. And we have learned a great deal from the formulations of psychoanalyst/art historian Ernst Kris (1952) and philosopher of art Susanne Langer (1953). The work of psychoanalyst D. W. Winnicott (1971a, 1971b), who used drawing himself and was a highly creative therapist and thinker, is most apt for us.

While it is important to be literate and knowledgeable about existing theories regarding the creative process, it is also vital to remember that they tend to be intellectualized, based as they are on observation, interview, or speculation about the direct experiences of others. Although there have been some artists who have written thoughtfully about their work, most have not been trained in either psychology or psychopathology (Kandinsky,

1912/2009). Their notions, therefore, while often pregnant with intuitive truths, are as one sided as those of non-artist psychologists and psychoanalysts.

Our "pioneers," incidentally, are not by any means the first people who worked with patients using art. But they *are* the people who wrote thoughtfully about their work. Moreover, they wrote not only descriptively but also analytically, always trying to understand *why* what they were doing was having the effects they observed. In other words, they developed theories about the use of art in therapy, in which they tried to synthesize their knowledge of both art and psychology. The writings of Naumburg (1966), Kramer (1958, 2000), and Ulman (1961, 1971) are distinguished by this attempt not only to describe but also to understand. They have given us excellent models.

In art therapy itself, we have a discipline that combines a sophisticated understanding of the art process with an equally sophisticated understanding of psychology and psychotherapy. Thus, it makes sense that theories about the therapeutic aspects of art can best be developed by those who understand both art and therapy. Some art therapists have followed our pioneer theorists in the years since the first edition of this book was published.

In 1987, I invited a number of colleagues to write chapters for a book, *Approaches to Art Therapy: Theory and Technique,* and when I revised it in 2001, I invited others to contribute as well. All of the authors were selected because they had done a fine job of taking existing theories of personality and psychotherapy and applying them to art therapy in an imaginative way. In my opinion, this was a necessary first step. I believe, however, that what is needed now is the development of meaningful theoretical constructs from within the matrix of art therapy itself.

But, art is art and people are people, you might say, so it makes sense that we have much to learn and to legitimately borrow from those who have studied either creativity or human beings in some depth. While I do not for a moment deny the relevance of theories from other disciplines and their application to our own, I feel some uneasiness about the possibility that we may have been forcing art therapy into theoretical molds that do not quite "fit." What distinguishes the contributors to *Approaches to Art Therapy* (Rubin, 1987, 2001) is that they each found creative ways to extract what made sense from their particular theoretical orientation and equally imaginative ways to apply it to art therapy.

Although this may sound inconsistent with my plea not to reinvent the wheel or to isolate ourselves in our research endeavors, I believe that theory is qualitatively different. Of course, in order to be able to converse and to communicate with students and other professionals, it is necessary to know and understand the similarities and differences between things like Gestalt psychology and Gestalt therapy or classical psychoanalytic drive theory and recent developments in object relations. It is my belief that the chapter authors in *Approaches* (Rubin, 1987, 2001) did a good job of explaining such ideas while showing how they have applied them to art therapy.

Being familiar with different theories of how and why people function in general, and particularly in art, cannot but deepen our understanding of the phenomena with which we deal. It is especially useful, if possible, to read the original—not just someone else's translation of meaning—to fully grasp something like Freud's theory of dream formation and its technical implications (e.g., Altman, 1975; Freud, 1900). But that should be only the beginning.

Thinking Theoretically

The goal is to study and *think about* what goes on in art therapy as we do, advise, and supervise such work, as well as to try to explain the effects of a full art experience in ways that truly fit the facts of actual practice. Now you may object that, insofar as technique is derived from theory, the way in which different individuals practice art therapy will vary according to their underlying models of mental and creative functioning. That is probably true, but it is also likely that in most cases the art therapist herself has never really thought consciously, or at least clearly, about the constructs that inevitably lie behind her work. I am simply suggesting that more art therapists try to do just that.

I am also suggesting that, if we are to enable people to truly understand the theories of others or, if possible, to develop their own, they will need some help and some practice with guidance in order to feel comfortable in this realm. In this respect, theoretical thinking is similar to research, something often seen by most art therapists as alien, esoteric, and much too difficult. While it is even more abstract than empirical research studies, such thinking is not beyond the grasp of the average practitioner.

Unfortunately, our educational system, with its neglect of philosophy, has done little to train or encourage this capacity, but it is as latent in most people as the ability to work creatively with art media. One way to encourage its development would be to initiate projects in training and supervision similar to those suggested for the promotion of research abilities.

This means asking art therapists at all stages of development to sit back and think about how they conceptualize the creative functioning of an individual or group at any moment in time and then to think reflectively about their own behavior and what they expect will come from it, that is, their underlying theoretical constructs about the mechanisms involved in promoting change and growth. Alternating such reflective exercises (in writing as well as orally) with those in which art experience is looked at in terms of one or another existing theory will certainly help art therapists to become more comfortable with such thinking. Theory is only meaningful and worthwhile if it helps to explain the phenomena with which it deals in a way that enables us to do our work better.

To learn or to develop theories about art therapy without actually applying them to real treatment situations is to grasp neither their meaning nor their significance. Theory and technique should go hand in hand—the one based on and growing out of the other, each constantly modifying the other over time. A theory is a hypothesis about connections and causality. In that sense, testing theories in practice is a kind of "research." Learning from what you observe involves accepting or rejecting theories, whether they originated with someone else or are your own ideas.

Writing this reminded me of my early skepticism about the Freudian notion of "penis envy" and the importance of that body part for both boys and girls. It was the "laboratory" of what happened in our household that taught me I was wrong and the theory was right. Briefly, our third child was a boy, and one day I happened on his two older sisters, who did not realize that I had come into the bathroom. There they were, each having drawn and cut out a penis that she had then taped onto her crotch.

Putting that discovery together with the more frequent creations by boys of towers and girls of enclosures, I had to reconsider my discomfort with that part of Freud's theory of psychosexual development. Feminists may be offended, but the truth is that—as Fred Rogers wrote in a song—"some are fancy on the outside, some are fancy on the inside," and it is true. So, children do have to deal with that anatomical difference, and after overcoming my resistance to its ubiquity, I realized that for boys it created a sense of vulnerability, while for girls it evoked envy.

Similarly, one of my patients was a very bright clinical psychologist who wanted to understand why the paintings that she did at home and brought in to me had been so therapeutic for her, even though she insisted that we not analyze them, so we did not. On her own, she found the writings of Susanne Langer and had an "aha!" recognition that what Langer had written about art felt like what she had discovered for herself. She rejected the writings of Edith Kramer and Margaret Naumburg because they did not fit her experience. That is how I think theory works. It explains something.

Although this may sound too intellectual for most art therapists, it may be as important to the continued development of our field as defining the basics. Thinking theoretically is a kind of creative problem solving that is more abstract than art. But art itself is an abstraction of reality, whether representational or non-figurative in its manifest form. Theories are usually expressed in words, although that does not mean that they must be or that they are always best conceptualized in that modality. In fact, I have often thought that certain theoretical ideas would be better represented in images.

It is significant that several major theoretical constructs in the natural sciences were stimulated by intuitive apprehensions of visual imagery—the visual thinking about which Arnheim (1969) wrote so persuasively and that lay behind Kekulé's discovery of the benzene ring or Einstein's theory of relativity. It is quite probable that the intentional use of visual imagery, both two and three dimensional, would extend our power to theorize, to conceptualize, and to hypothesize the invisible forces with which we deal and that we hope to influence.

One of my frequent thoughts as I went through classical psychoanalytic training was that I could imagine the id, ego, and superego much more easily as sounds, shapes, textures, or movements than as abstract concepts or agencies of the mind. Or when thinking of conflict theory, of the dynamics of impulse, prohibition, and compromise involved in defense mechanisms and symptom formation, I often found myself imagining something three dimensional and in motion. They could best be represented, I reasoned, in an animated film, which would capture more fully than any words or linear diagrams the actuality of internalized conflict and the psyche's dynamic attempts at resolution. I still think so, although I do not have the technical expertise to actualize the idea.

In an informal study, I explored with various individuals the creation of one image after another in various media in order to get an idea of what the mind would do with "free association" in art imagery (rather than in words). I deliberately consulted with a non-psychoanalyst—a psychiatrist and psychologist who has had a lifelong interest in art and therapy, Dr. Irene Jakab—who helped me to conceptualize how to explore this idea, which I did with an artist friend in a class at the Psychoanalytic Center (Rubin, 1982). Although visual thinking in art is a territory barely defined and hardly charted, it is one that is full of implications for thinking in general, including theoretical kinds about the work we do.

I do not yet have a formed theory to propose in 2010, any more than I did in 1984. But I still hope that all art therapists will work toward such a goal and will do so as much as possible within the context of our work itself and what it involves. I do not wish to suggest that we throw out all those other theories as useless, but that we be careful not to see in them what we want and need to see in a way that distorts either their original meaning or our own experience with art in assessment and therapy.

Does the Shoe Fit?

This danger is especially acute with those constructs that best seem to "fit" our field, like Langer's notion of art as forms of human feeling (1953); psychoanalysts' ideas about symbolization (Jones, 1916/1948; Petocz, 1999) or sublimation (Hartmann, 1955; Loewald, 1988);

Maslow's concept of "peak experience" (1968), Arieti's concept of the "tertiary process" (1976); and so on. These notions are indeed relevant and related but not quite as syntonic as we might wish. Langer, for example, seemed to be using "feeling" in a much broader way than it is usually understood or meant by art therapists, who would not find some of her associated ideas so congenial.

Sublimation, still a hotly debated concept in psychoanalysis, seems a rather limited and perhaps overly sociological way of referring to what is involved in creating art. While the containment of drive energies in an aesthetic form is indeed pleasing and does relieve tension for the moment, it rarely seems to achieve any kind of lasting problem resolution for the individual.

Perhaps more important, while it seems to be a component of many a creative process, it is not always definably present or ever the totality of the event. In other words, without nitpicking, we seem to have grabbed hold of partially digested and appealing ideas in our eager efforts to make sense of what we do. This may have been a necessary first step and has certainly enabled us to communicate meaningfully with those from other disciplines. But, the time has come to take yet another step, this time toward a theory of art therapy itself that grows out of its own essence, nature, and being.

In the years since the publication of the first edition of this book, some art therapists have ventured to think theoretically. I am referring to the formulations of Arthur Robbins (1987, 1989), Pat Allen (1995), Aina Nucho (2003), and Shaun McNiff (1989, 1994, 2004) as well as the contributions of Mimi Farrelly-Hansen (2001), Paolo Knill (2005), and their collaborators.

A Tentative Theoretical Beginning

Having been so critical of others, I now feel obliged to expose some of my own partly formed notions, which may someday lead to a useful theory of art therapy. I hope that in so doing I will encourage others to share their thoughts as well, so that we can engage in the kind of collaborative theory building that people have done for so long in philosophy, psychology, and other scholarly domains. I start with the art part, as in the organization of this book, for I believe, despite my fondness for reflection and awareness, that art is and must be at the core of art therapy.

First, some thoughts about the creative process itself, the central event in art therapy no matter which end of the art therapy continuum you occupy. The art process has its own internal rhythm and essence, which involve a human being not only in mastery of media, but also in a kind of temporary fusion with the work itself. Art making also involves a person in an externalization of the self in concrete form, a new way of saying "me" or "I" and, perhaps even more important, a new way of saying "I *do*" or "I *can* do."

In a fashion that reminds me of looking in a mirror, a creation in any medium becomes a new kind of self-reflection for the artist. In this way, it provides human beings at all developmental levels with an important experience of self and nonself, yet the nonself has paradoxically been created by the self. In this sense, I am talking about something related to Winnicott's (1953) notion of the "transitional object," but not quite the *same*. That, by the way, is one of the many constructs I believe we have wisely apprehended as relevant but may have swallowed whole too quickly, without selecting the parts that we really can incorporate as art therapists.

In this peculiar experiential duality, the art process provides an individual with temporary fusion (partial or total) and loss of boundaries, along with an experience of heightened separateness from another object, which is yet, paradoxically, *of* and *from* the self. Such experiences, perhaps unique to the visual arts, are extremely important in the internal construction of what some have called a "self-representation." This is not a clearly defined or always stable visual image, any more than the body image is literally a mental picture. But, there is a set of feelings about the self in regard to the environment, human and nonhuman, that are intimately related to the experience of creating in art.

The art object can, of course, also be related to as if it were totally nonself. It can be attacked, admired, and dealt with in any way needed by the individual at that moment in time to maintain his psychic equilibrium. No such freedom is present when dealing with other concrete objects or with other human beings. Indeed, the absolute and complete freedom the creator enjoys in relation to his or her art is probably unique in human experience. If this seems extensive in regard to a finished product (which can ultimately be preserved or destroyed by the artist), just think how infinite it is when dealing with media in their unstructured form.

Despite the fact that each medium has its own built-in limitations and constraints, it is possible within these boundaries for the artist to do anything he can imagine and accomplish. The value of such an experience of near-total freedom in a world that cannot permit or tolerate it in other realms is something of which most practicing artists are well aware. It is also of significant value in art therapy. Needless to say, the patient's freedom is limited by the extent to which the art therapist tells him what to do with the medium; however, it is also true that his ability to use it creatively may be enhanced by the lending of idea or ego by the clinician.

Most people who have psychological problems do not feel free to use their resources in the way that they could or should. If they are not overly constricted, they may be unable to control or channel their energies in a way that is constructive. In either case, art provides a place where both not only *can* happen but also *must* inevitably happen if art is to occur.

That is, a creative situation in art therapy provides for an experience of freedom—within a safe and securely bounded framework—that can be liberating to the human spirit in a way that may never be measurable. Yet creating in art, because it requires discipline, control, decision making, and forming, also provides people with an experience of channeling energies in a constructive and potentially coherent fashion.

The creative art experience also draws on all parts of the mind. Whatever we call the part that creates our dreams or our waking fantasies, we know that in sleep and in periods of altered consciousness our images are more frequent and our thoughts more playful, less logical. In a complete art experience, the creator is able to get in touch with and draw on this kind of largely visual thinking, sometimes called "primary process." Although this used to be thought of as primitive (developmentally earlier and less sophisticated), recent work in hemispheric specialization and psychoanalysis suggests that this is not an *inferior* mode of thought but simply a *different* mode of thought.

There is even a good deal of evidence for the possibility that such thinking has its own developmental line, that it is not simply something prior to or lesser than secondary process (linear, logical) thought (Noy, 1999). This relatively new way of viewing this kind of holistic, image-rich, fantastic thinking is synchronous with the experience of artists over the ages, as well as with those cultures that for various reasons have valued the mystical and the irrational.

In any case, no one will deny that art, if it is to have energy and derive from the inner world of the creator, must draw on the storehouse of imagery buried deep in that part of the mind not conscious during waking hours. But—and this is also undeniable—for such unconscious or preconscious thinking to become art, it must be given form. A dream may be the stuff that art is made of, but by itself it is no more art than ramblings are poetry.

Any raw material must be shaped, selections made, parts omitted, and other parts added or extended. The creation of art, therefore, also involves the other part of the mind, whatever we call it, which organizes and gives form. Perhaps it is true, as Arieti (1976) suggested, that it is a third part—intermediary between the fantasy of the one and the logic of the other—that creates artistic form, what he called the "tertiary process."

It probably does not matter how many components we theorize exist in the human mind. As with stages of artistic development, it will probably be possible some day to make increasingly finer discriminations. What is important is that there is clearly more than one distinct mode of thought, and that art creation is one of the few human activities available to all age levels in which it seems that virtually all modes must be operative.

And, if they are to be successful as art, these modes must also be integrated or synthesized. This may be the greatest reason of all for the value of art in therapy—that it requires the integration of so many usually separated, isolated parts of the mind and aspects of human experience. I believe this to be true, whether we see art as an integration of inner and outer worlds, of self and nonself, of good and bad, of primary and secondary processes, of matter and mind, or of any other such polarities.

Art in the Presence of Another

I have focused so far on those values in the art experience that seem to be inherently therapeutic and growth-enhancing. But art in therapy is art in the presence of someone else and there, I believe, derives an additional aspect of its healing power. Not only do you create a situation in which others are supported in creative art making, but also you function in a variety of significant ways in relationship to those other human beings.

This peculiar combination of supporter/teacher/helper, reflector/witness/analyzer/healer, and symbolic object of positive/negative transference feelings gives immense power to the art therapist's role. If you were simply an art teacher, you might be moderately helpful, but nowhere near as much as you potentially are in the unique artist/teacher/therapist combination of art therapist.

Indeed, I think Edith Kramer was correct that it is in the very nature of art therapy that you are required to be all three—an artist, a teacher, and a therapist. It is also true that therapist is the primary role, to which the others are subservient. But to experience another human being in this rare combination of roles is probably as unique for most clients as having a genuinely creative encounter with art materials.

In addition to being useful to the person as an object of transference with whom unresolved issues and conflicted longings can be experienced, understood, and worked through, you are simultaneously a collaborator—a guide and helper, not only in the journey through the mind provided in every psychotherapy, but also in the realm of creating art—a new, exciting, potentially frightening and thrilling world. The adventure undergone with an effective art therapist is therefore threefold: *into* the self, but also *out* of the self and, in a concrete way, into the *world*.

Most clients, whether in clinical or community settings, have great difficulty comfortably accepting either themselves or the world. Since art therapy encompasses all aspects of the self—destructive as well as constructive—you can make available a wide range of experiences through which the person can make visible—and can eventually learn to accept—unwanted and rejected aspects of the self.

And because making art involves acting on and sometimes representing the physical world, it requires a real encounter with real things as part of the difficult task of coming to grips with reality. The art therapist helps in the task of translating the client's often-distorted psychic reality into a better approximation of what is "really" out there—what he must eventually accept with comfort if he is to live successfully within it.

We often forget or minimize the importance of integrating physical, concrete, motor-kinesthetic expressions of the self with more verbal, intellectual images of the self. Art therapy necessarily involves the body, more with certain media than others, but it is always present and active in some way. The additional component of visual thinking, plus verbalizing about the experience and the product, may enable an acceptance of the self's experience or perceptions in a much more integrated way than is possible through any single modality like words.

Art activity is at least as much a motor activity as it is a cognitive or affective one. Watching a videotape of an art therapy session *without sound* is one good way of tuning in to this dimension, which often escapes us in our usual focus on the visual/verbal axis. In any case, it may well be that it is this truly multimodal aspect of any art process that makes it so helpful as an integrating experience.

We also cannot overemphasize the usefulness of the art product, which enables a person to sit back and look at what he has made—to reflect on both the process and the external object in a way that is not possible while immersed in the doing of it. We are thereby engaging not only the experiencing, doing, active self, but also the observing, reflective, receptive self in relation to the same art object. These two modes of being are related but not identical to the two modes of thinking noted above. In this regard, as in the utilization of both linear and holistic mentation, art therapy also helps human beings to integrate different aspects of themselves.

To be immersed in creating is different from looking at your creation and allowing yourself to become involved in it as a stimulus for thought. The associations can be either logical or illogical. The state of the viewer is more physically relaxed but more mentally active than that of the creator during the doing part of the process. Both ways of being are essential to healthy living and growing.

To be able to engage fully in an activity, whether it is painting, dancing, playing tennis, or making love, requires that you let go of certain controls or inhibitions and allow the motor-rhythmic parts of yourself to be in charge. To be able to reflect on the outcome of that activity, as when you look at the art product you have created, requires that you adopt a more consciously thoughtful state, one in which the loosening of logical controls can also facilitate a freer associative process.

Eventually, however, after the associations that have hopefully been relatively unfettered by logic, it is necessary in art therapy to adopt yet another state of mind. This is a deliberate and thoughtful one that attempts to find and to express some meaning and order in what has been perceived. This ordering of your thoughts in response to the art product is analogous to the ordering of elements in the creative work itself, yet now both the free play of ideas and the attempt to find form take place entirely in the realm of thoughts expressed in words, quite different from the two similar components in the active, making phase.

While it is possible and sometimes necessary to focus more on one component than the other in doing art therapy, for the fullest use of the modality it is important to try to enable both involved doing and relaxed reflection. Of course, there are clients for whom one or the other may not ever be possible or only to a minimal degree. But we give people the most integrated and integrating experience when we try to provide both for everyone we see.

I expect that others will differ with one or another aspect of this position, but it is hoped, along with the refinement of theory in the field, there will come increasingly sophisticated research studies in which we can test out the validity of the sometimes-incompatible assumptions that we now debate.

Meanwhile, it is good to see the beginning of a blossoming of theory within the field, and I expect that there will be more over time, as others begin to wonder why this magical thing called art therapy seems to work so well. That it *does* is clear. That we need to *demonstrate* it (research) is also clear. That we need to understand the *reasons* (theory) is also clear. With progress in both of these critical areas, the *art* of doing good (effective, evidence-based) *art therapy* will become even more clear over time.

The second edition of this book simply reflects one art therapist's ideas about how to do good art therapy. I hope that it will stimulate the same sort of thinking in others. I have been an art therapist since 1963, a time before there existed a professional organization, a literature, standards of education, practice, ethics, or any of the many advances that have been made in the last half century. It has been a pleasure and a privilege to watch the development of this discipline over this period of time. It has been deeply rewarding work, and it is exciting to see it now spreading around the world. If we can continue to refine our thinking about how to do art therapy in the most careful, concerned, and thoughtful way, I believe the profession will continue to thrive.

References

Allen, P. B. (1995). *Art is a way of knowing.* Boston: Shambhala.

Altman, L. L. (1975). *The dream in psychoanalysis.* (2nd ed.). New York: International Universities Press.

Arieti, S. (1976). *Creativity: The magic synthesis.* New York: Basic Books.

Arnheim, R. (1967). *Toward a psychology of art.* Berkeley: University of California Press.

Arnheim, R. (1969). *Visual thinking.* Berkeley: University of California Press.

Csikszentmihalyi, M. (2008). *Creativity: Flow and the psychology of discovery and invention.* New York: Harper Perennial Modern Classics.

Farrelly-Hansen, M. (Ed.). (2001). *Spirituality and art therapy.* London: Kingsley.

Freud, S. (1900). *The interpretation of dreams* (standard ed., (Vols. 4 and 5). London: Hogarth.

Hartmann, H. (1955). Notes on the theory of sublimation. *Psychoanalytic Study of the Child, 10,* 9–29.

Jones, E. (1948). The theory of symbolism. In *Papers on psycho-analysis* (5th ed., pp. 87–144). Baltimore: Williams & Wilkins. (Original work published 1916)

Kandinsky, W. (2009). *Concerning the spiritual in art.* Las Vegas, NV: IAP. (Original work published 1912)

Knill, P. J., Levine, E. G., & Levine, S. K. (2005). *Principles and practice of expressive arts therapy: Toward a therapeutic aesthetic.* London: Jessica Kingsley.

Kramer, E. (1958). *Art therapy in a children's community.* Springfield, IL: Thomas.

Kramer, E. (2000) *Art as therapy: Collected papers* (L. A. Gerity, Ed.). London: Kingsley.

Kris, E. (1952). *Psychoanalytic explorations in art.* New York: Schocken.

Langer, S. K. (1953). *Feeling and form.* New York: Scribner's.

Loewald, H. W. (1988). *Sublimation: Inquiries into theoretical psychoanalysis.* New Haven, CT: Yale University Press.

Maslow, A. H. (1968). *Toward a psychology of being* (2nd ed.). New York: Van Nostrand.

May, R. (1975). *The courage to create.* New York: Norton.

McNiff, S. (1989). *Depth psychology of art.* Springfield, IL: Thomas.

McNiff, S. (1994). *Art as medicine* Boston: Shambhala.

McNiff, S. (2004). *Art heals.* Boston: Shambhala.

Naumburg, M. (1966). *Dynamically oriented art therapy.* New York: Grune & Stratton.

Noy, P. (1999). *Psychoanalysis of art and creativity.* Tel Aviv, Israel: Modan.

Nucho, A. O. (2003). *Psychocybernetic model of art therapy* (2nd ed.) Springfield, IL: Thomas.

Petocz, A. (1999). *Freud, psychoanalysis and symbolism.* Cambridge, U.K.: Cambridge University Press.

Robbins, A. (1987). *The artist as therapist.* New York: Human Sciences Press.

Robbins, A. (1989). *The psychoaesthetic experience.* New York: Human Sciences Press.

Rubin, J. A. (1982). Art and imagery: Free association with art media. In A. E. Di Maria (Ed.), *Art therapy. A bridge between worlds.* Falls Church, VA: American Art Therapy Association.

Rubin, J. A. (2001). *Approaches to art therapy* (2nd ed.). New York: Brunner-Routledge.

Runco, M. (2007). *Creativity: Theories and themes.* New York: Elsevier.

Turner, M. (Ed.). (2006). *The artful mind: Cognitive science and the riddle of human creativity.* New York: Oxford University Press.

Ulman, E. (1961). Art therapy: Problems of definition. *Bulletin of Art Therapy, 1*(2), 10–20.

Ulman, E. (1971). The power of art in therapy. In I. Jakab (Ed.), *Psychiatry and art* (Vol. 3, pp. 93–102). New York: Karger.

Winnicott, D. W. (1953). Transitional objects and transitional phenomena. *International Journal of Psycho-Analysis, 34,* 89–97.

Winnicott, D. W. (1971a). *Playing and reality.* New York: Basic Books.

Winnicott, D. W. (1971b). *Therapeutic consultations in child psychiatry.* New York: Basic Books.

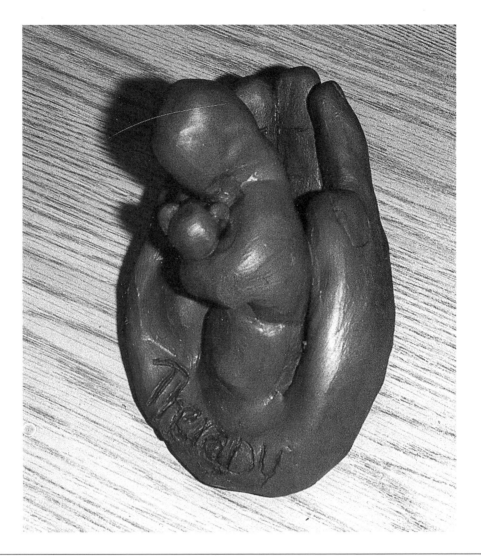

Art therapy takes place in what some have called a "holding environment" and must be true to both art and therapy. This is beautifully represented in a patient's sculpture done on her final day.

Addendum: Knowing What You Don't Know

This book has been all about what you need to know if you are to be an effective art therapist. In addition to the "basics" about art and therapy and the interface in which they combine to become art therapy, I have added some "extras" for those who deliver indirect as well as direct service. I have also noted some considerations regarding different populations, settings, and modes of art therapy of which you need to be aware in order to do any kind of work in the field.

I have done my best to outline the knowledge, experiences, beliefs, and ways of being that seem to be necessary for good work in art therapy, at least as I see it. A final essential, one of which I become more certain each year, is to be aware of what you don't know and to do something about rectifying it, especially when that seems needed in order to do your work properly and well.

An attitude of humility is one that best fits the present development of our field. Art therapy is still young, and we are working in territory that is largely uncharted and not at all well understood. We do not have precise or definite answers about the meanings of art products as much as others would like us to have them. We also do not have clear and certain answers about optimal art activities, much as many wish that we did.

We are, as a discipline, still feeling our way, and we need to acknowledge that fact in our interactions with others, whether patients or professionals. An inappropriate brashness or unwarranted certainty in statements or presentations can do art therapy much more harm than good. We can believe, without ambivalence, in the healing power of art and in the value of the visual image as symbolic speech. However, we do not need in any way to pretend that we have answers that we simply do not have.

What is required, therefore, is modesty, both as individuals and as a group; a never-ending attitude of inquiry, of open-mindedness, of flexibility; an ability to try and to err or to try and to fail. I believe that only such a stance will promote the full development of art therapy, with its thrilling but largely undefined potential for understanding and helping all human beings, especially those in pain.

Appendix A

Books in Art Therapy and Related Areas

Abraham, R. (2004). *When words have lost their meaning.* New York: Praeger.

Achterberg, J. (2002). *Imagery in healing.* Boston: Shambhala.

Adamson, E. A. (1984). *Art as healing.* London: Coventure.

Akeret, R. U. (1973). *Photoanalysis.* New York: Wyden, Inc.

Allan, J. (1988). *Inscapes of the child's world.* Dallas, TX: Spring.

Allan, J., & Bertoia, J. (1992). *Written paths to healing.* Dallas, TX: Spring.

Allen, P. B. (1995). *Art is a way of knowing.* Boston: Shambhala.

Allen, P. B. (2005). *Art is a spiritual path.* Boston: Shambhala.

Alschuler, R., & Hattwick, L. (1947). *Painting and personality* (Vols. 1 and 2). Chicago: University of Chicago Press.

Alschuler, R., & Hattwick, L. (1969). *Painting and personality* (rev. one ed.). Chicago: University of Chicago Press.

American Art Therapy Association. (1975). *Art therapy: Beginnings* [DVD].

American Art Therapy Association: *Proceedings,* 1976–1982: Full papers:

      1976: Creativity and the art therapist's identity (Shoemaker & Gonick-Barris)

      1977: The dynamics of creativity (Mandel, Shoemaker & Hays)

      1978: Art therapy: Expanding horizons (Gantt, Forrest, Silverman, Shoemaker)

      1979: Focus on the future: The next 10 years (Gantt & Evans)

      1980: The fine art of therapy (Gantt & Whitman)

      1981: Art therapy: A bridge between worlds (Di Maria, Kramer, Rosner)

      1982: Art therapy: Still growing (DiMaria, Kramer, Roth)

      1983–2007 Proceedings of annual conferences (1-page abstracts)

American Psychiatric Association. (2000). *Diagnostic and statistical manual of mental disorders* (4th ed., text revision) Washington, DC: Author.

Anderson, F. E. (1992). *Art for all the children* (2nd ed.). Springfield, IL: Thomas.

Anderson, F. E. (1994). *Art-centered education and therapy for children with disabilities.* Springfield, IL: Thomas.

Anderson, W. (Ed.). (1977). *Therapy and the arts.* New York: Harper & Row.

Andreas, C. (2009). *Promote visual perceptual development through therapeutic art.* Saarbrucken, Germany: VDM Verlag.

Andsell, G., & Pavlicevic, M. (2001). *Beginning research in the arts therapies.* London: Kingsley.

Arieti, S. (1976). *Creativity: The magic synthesis.* New York: Basic Books.

Arnheim, R. (1954). *Art and visual perception.* Berkeley: University of California Press.

Arnheim, R. (1967). *Toward a psychology of art.* Berkeley: University of California Press.

Arnheim, R. (1969). *Visual thinking.* Berkeley: University of California Press.

Arnheim, R. (1988). *The power of the center.* Berkeley: University of California Press.

Arrington, D. B. (2001). *Home is where the art is.* Springfield, IL: Thomas.

Arrington, D. B. (Ed.). (2007). *Art, angst, and trauma.* Springfield, IL: Thomas.

Atkins, S. (2002). *Expressive arts therapy.* Boone, NC: Parkway Publishers.

Atkins, S., Williams, L. D., & Suggs, M. S. (2007). *Sourcebook in expressive arts therapy.* Boone, NC: Parkway Publishers.

Ault, R. E. (1986). *Art therapy: The healing vision* [DVD]. Topeka, KS: Marilynn Ault.

Ault, R. E. (1996). *Drawing on the contours of the mind.* Unpublished manuscript.

Bach, S. R. (1990). *Life paints its own span.* Zurich: Daimon.

Barnes, M., & Berke, J. (1971). *Mary Barnes: Two accounts of a journey through madness.* New York: Ballantine Books.

Barnes, M., & Scott, A. (1989). *Something sacred.* London: Free Association Books.

Baynes, H. G. (1961). *Mythology of the soul.* Princeton, NJ: Bollingen.

Beittel, K. E. (1973). *Alternatives for art education research.* Dubuque, IA: Brown.

Bejjani, F. J. (Ed.). (1993). *Current research in arts medicine.* Pennington, NJ: Cappella Books.

Bender, L. (Ed.). (1952). *Child psychiatric techniques.* Springfield, IL: Thomas.

Berensohn, P. (1972). *Finding one's way with clay.* New York: Simon & Schuster.

Bertman, S. L. (Ed.). (1999). *Grief and the healing art.* Amityville, NY: Baywood.

Bertoia, J. (1993*). Drawings from a dying child.* New York: Routledge.

Betensky, M. G. (1973). *Self-discovery through self-expression.* Springfield, IL: Thomas.

Betensky, M. G. (1995). *What do you see?* London: Kingsley.

Betts, D. J. (Ed.). (2003). *Creative arts therapies approaches in adoption and foster care.* Springfield, IL: Thomas.

Bion, W. R. (1961). *Experiences in groups.* London: Tavistock.

Birkhauser, P. (1991). *Light from the darkness* [German and English]. Basel, Switzerland: Author.

Bodtker, J. S. (1990). *Beyond words: Interpretive art therapy.* London: Karnac Books.

Brooke, S. L. (1997). *Art therapy with sexual abuse survivors.* Springfield, IL: Thomas.

Brooke, S. L. (2004). *Tools of the trade: A therapist's guide to art therapy assessments* (2nd ed.). Springfield, IL: Thomas.

Brooke, S. L. (Ed.). (2006). *Creative arts therapies manual.* Springfield, IL: Thomas.

Brooke, S. L. (Ed.). (2007). *The use of the creative therapies with sexual abuse survivors.* Springfield, IL: Thomas.

Brooke, S. L. (Ed.). (2009a). *The use of the creative therapies with autism spectrum disorders.* Springfield, IL: Thomas.

Brooke, S. L. (Ed.). (2009b). *The use of the creative therapies with chemical dependency issues.* Springfield, IL: Thomas.

Brown, W. (1967*). Introduction to psycho-iconography.* New York: Schering.

Buchalter, S. I. (2004). *A practical art therapy.* London: Kingsley.

Buchalter, S. I. (2009). *Art therapy techniques and applications.* London: Kingsley.

Burns, R. C. (1987). *Kinetic house-tree-person drawings.* New York: Brunner/Mazel.

Burns, R. C. (1990). *A guide to family-centered circle drawings.* New York: Brunner/Mazel.

Burns, R. C., & Kaufman, S. H. (1970). *Kinetic family drawings.* New York: Brunner/Mazel.

Bush, J. (1997). *The handbook of school art therapy.* Springfield, IL: Thomas.

Camilleri, V. A. (Ed.). (2007). *Healing the inner city child.* London: Kingsley.

Campbell, J. (1993). *Creative art in groupwork.* Bicester, UK: Winslow.

Campbell, J., Liebmann, M., Brooks, F., Jones, J., & Ward, C. (Eds.). (1999). *Art therapy, race and culture.* London: Kingsley.

Cane, F. (1983). *The artist in each of us.* Chicago: Magnolia Street. (Original work published 1951)

Capacchione, L. (1979). *The creative journal.* Athens, OH: Ohio University Press.

Caprio-Orsini, C. (1996). *A thousand words.* Quebec: Diverse City Press.

Cardinal, R. (1972). *Outsider art.* New York: Praeger.

Carey, L. J. (1999). *Sandplay therapy with children and families.* New York: Aronson.

Carey, L. J. (2005). *Expressive and creative arts methods for trauma survivors.* London: Kingsley.

Carpendale, M. (2009). *Essence and practice in the art therapy studio.* Bloomington, IN: Trafford.

Case, C. (2005). *Imagining animals.* London: Routledge.

Case, C., & Dalley, T. (Eds.). (1990). *Working with children in art therapy.* London: Tavistock.

Case, C., & Dalley T. (2006). *The handbook of art therapy* (2nd ed.). London: Routledge.

Case, C., & Dalley, T. (Eds.). (2008). *Art therapy with children.* London: Routledge.

Cattanach, A. (Ed.). (1999). *Process in the arts therapies.* London: Kingsley.

Chaiklin, S., & Wengrower, H. (2009). *The art and science of dance/movement therapy: Life is dance.* New York: Routledge.

Chickerneo, N. B. (1993). *Portraits of spirituality in recovery.* Springfield, IL: Thomas.

Chilvers, R. (2007). *The hidden world of autism.* London: Kingsley.

Chodorow, J. (Ed.). (1997). *Jung on active imagination.* London: Routledge.

Clements, C. B., & Clements, R. D. (1984). *Art and mainstreaming.* Springfield, IL: Thomas.

Cohen, B. M. (Ed.). (1985). *The Diagnostic Drawing Series handbook.* (Available from Barry M. Cohen, P.O. Box 9853, Alexandria, VA, USA 22304).

Cohen, B. M. (Ed.). (1986/1994). *The Diagnostic Drawing Series rating guide.* (Available from Barry M. Cohen, P.O. Box 9853, Alexandria, VA, USA 22304).

Cohen, B. M., Barnes, M.-M., & Rankin, A. B. (1995). *Managing traumatic stress through art.* Baltimore: Sidran Press.

Cohen, B. M., & Cox, C. T. (1995). *Telling without talking.* New York: Norton.

Cohen, B. M., Giller, E., & W. L. (Eds.) (1991 *Multiple personality disorder from the inside out.* Baltimore: Sidran Press.

Cohen, G. (2001). *The creative age: Awakening human potential in the second half of life.* New York: Harper.

Cohen, G. (2007). *The mature mind: The positive power of the aging brain* (2nd ed.). New York: Basic Books.

Colarusso, C. A. (1992). *Child and adult development.* New York: Plenum Press.

Coleman, V. D., & Farris-Dufrene, P. B.(1996). *Art therapy and psychotherapy.* New York: Taylor & Francis.

Coles, R. (1992). *Their eyes meeting the world* (M. Sartor, Ed.). New York: Houghton Mifflin.

Collot d'Herbois, L. (1993). *Light, darkness and colour in painting-therapy.* Hamburg: Goetheanum Press.

Connell, C. (1998). *Something understood: Art therapy in cancer care.* London: Wrexham.

Cox, C. T., & Heller, P. O. (Eds.). (2006). *Portrait of the artist as poet.* Chicago: Magnolia Street.

Cox, M. V. (1992). *Children's drawings.* London: Penguin Books.

Cox, M. V. (1997). *Drawings of people by the under-5's.* London: Folmer Press.

Craig, C. (2009). *Exploring the self through photography.* London: Kingsley.

Crepeau, E. B., Cohn, E. S., & Schell, B. A. (2008). *Willard and Spackman's occupational therapy* (11th ed.). Philadelphia: Lippincott, Williams & Wilkins.

Crowley, R., & Mills, J. (1989). *Cartoon magic.* New York: Brunner/Mazel.

Dalley, T. (Ed.). (1984). *Art as therapy.* London: Routledge.

Dalley, T., Halliday, D., Case, C., & Schaverien, J. (1987). *Images of art therapy.* London: Routledge.

Dalley, T., Rifkind, G., & Terry, K, (1993). *Three voices of art therapy.* London: Routledge.

Danneker, K (Ed.). (2004). *Internationale perspektiven der kunsttherapie* Graz, Austria: Nausner & Nausner.

Darley, S., & Heath, W. (2008). *The expressive arts activity book.* Springfield, IL: Thomas.

Davis, W. B., Gfeller, K. B., & Thaut, M. H. (2008). *An introduction to music therapy: Theory and practice.* Washington, DC: American Music Therapy Association.

Dax, Eric C. (1953). *Experimental studies in psychiatric art.* London: Faber & Faber.

Dewey, J. (1934). *Art as experience.* New York: Capricorn Books.

Di Leo, J. H. (1970). *Young children and their drawings.* New York: Brunner/Mazel.

Di Leo, J. H. (1974). *Children's drawings as diagnostic aids.* New York: Brunner/Mazel,

Di Leo, J. H. (1977). *Child development.* New York: Brunner/Mazel.

Di Leo, J. H. (1983). *Interpreting children's drawings.* New York: Brunner/Mazel.

Dissanayake, E. (1995). *Homo aestheticus.* Seattle: University of Washington Press.

Dokter, D. (Ed.). (1994). *Arts therapies and clients with eating disorders.* London: Kingsley.

Dokter, D. (Ed.). (1998*). Arts therapists, refugees and migrants.* London: Kingsley.

Drachnik, C. (1995). *Interpreting metaphors in children's drawings.* Burlingame, CA: Abbeygate Press.

Dreifuss-Kattan, E. (1990). *Cancer stories.* Hillsdale, NJ: Analytic Press.

Dreikurs, S. E. (1986). *Cows can be purple.* Chicago: Adler School of Professional Psychology.

Edwards, D. (2004). *Art therapy.* Thousand Oaks, CA: Sage.

Engel, L., & Ferguson, T. (1990). *Imaginary crimes.* Lincoln, NE: Authors Choice Press.

Erikson, E. H. (1950). *Childhood and society.* New York: Norton.

Erikson, E. H. (1977). *Toys and reasons.* New York: Norton.

Erikson, E. H., Erikson, J., & Kivnick, H. (1986). *Vital involvement in old age.* New York: Norton.

Erikson, J. M. (1976). *Activity, recovery and growth.* New York: Norton.

Evans, K., & Dubowski, J. (2001). *Art therapy with children on the autistic spectrum.* London: Kingsley.

Farrelly-Hansen, M. (Ed.). (2001). *Spirituality and art therapy.* London: Kingsley.

Fay, C. G. (1994). *At the threshold* [Videotape]. Dallas, TX: C. G. Jung Center.

Feder, E., & Feder, B. (1981). *The expressive arts therapies.* Englewood Cliffs, NJ: Prentice-Hall.

Feder, B., & Feder, E. (1998). *The art and science of evaluation in the arts therapies.* Springfield, IL: Thomas.

Fein, S. (1976). *Heidi's horse:* Pleasant Hill, CA: Exelrod Press.

Felstiner, M. L. (1997). *To paint her life.* Berkeley: University of California Press.

Fincher, S. F. (1991*). Creating mandalas.* Boston: Shambhala.

Fincher, S. F. (2009). *The mandala workbook.* Boston: Shambhala.

Fleshman, R., & Fryrear, J. L. (1981). *The arts in therapy.* Chicago: Nelson-Hall.

Fordham, M. (1944). *The life of childhood.* London: Kegan Paul.

Frank, L. K. (1948). *Projective methods.* Springfield, IL: Thomas.

Freud, A. (1936). *The ego and the mechanisms of defense. Writings of Anna Freud* (Vol. 2). New York: International Universities Press.

Freud, A. (1965). *Normality and pathology in childhood. Writings of Anna Freud* (Vol. 5). New York: International Universities Press.

Freud, S. (1916–1917). *Introductory lectures on psycho-analysis* (Standard ed., Vol. 12). London: Hogarth Press.

Freud, S. (1923). *The ego and the id* (Standard ed., Vol. 19). London: Hogarth Press, 1964.

Freud, S. (1949). *An outline of psychoanalysis.* New York: Norton. (Original work published 1939)

Frostig, K., & Essex, M. (1998). *Expressive arts therapies in the schools.* Springfield, IL: Thomas.

Fryrear, J. L., & Corbit, I. E. (1992a). *Instant images.* Dubuque, IA: Kendall/ Hunt.

Fryrear, J. L., & Corbit, I. E. (1992b). *Photo art therapy.* Springfield, IL: Thomas.

Fryrear, J. L., & Fleshman, R. (Eds.). (1981). *Videotherapy in mental health.* Springfield, IL: Thomas.

Fugaro, R. A. L. (1985). *A manual of sequential art activities for classified children and adolescent*s. Springfield, IL: Thomas.

Fukurai, S. (1974). *How can I make what I cannot see?* New York: Van Nostrand Reinhold.

Furrer, P. J. (1982). *Art therapy activities and lesson plans for individuals and groups.* Springfield, IL: Thomas.

Furth, G. M. (2002). *The secret world of drawings.* (2nd ed.). Toronto: Inner City Books.

Gantt, L., & Schmal, M. S. (1974). *Art therapy: A bibliography.* Washington, DC: National Institutes of Mental Health.

Gantt, L., & Tabone, C. (1998). *The formal elements art therapy scale: The rating manual.* Morgantown, WV: Gargoyle Press.

Gardner, H. (1980). *Artful scribbles.* New York: Basic Books.

Gardner, H. (1982*). Art, mind and brain.* New York: Basic Books.

Gardner, R. (1971). *Therapeutic communication with children.* New York: Science House.

Gat, G. (2003). *Solution-oriented art therapy with children and adolescents* [VHS]. Los Angeles: Master's Work Video Productions.

Gedo, J. E. (1983). *Portraits of the artist.* New York: Guilford Press.

Gedo, M. M. (Ed.). (1985). *Psychoanalytic perspectives on art* (Vol. 1). Hillsdale, NJ: Analytic Press.

Gedo, M. M. (Ed.). (1987). *Psychoanalytic perspectives on art* (Vol. 2). Hillsdale, NJ: Analytic Press.

Gedo, M. M. (Ed.). (1988). *Psychoanalytic perspectives on art* (Vol. 3). Hillsdale, NJ: Analytic Press.

Gerity, L. (1999). *Creativity and the dissociative patient.* London: Kingsley.

Gil, E. (1991). *The healing power of play.* New York: Guilford Press.

Gil, E. (2006a). *Essentials of play therapy with abused children* [DVD and guide]. New York: Guilford Press.

Gil, E. (2006b). *Play therapy for severe psychological trauma* [DVD and Guide]. New York: Guilford Press.

Gillespie, J. (1994). *The projective use of mother-and-child drawings.* New York: Brunner/Mazel.

Gilroy, A. (2006). *Art therapy research and evidence based practice.* London: Routledge.

Gilroy, A., & Dalley, T. (Eds.). (1989). *Pictures at an exhibition.* London: Routledge.

Gilroy, A., & Lee, C. (Eds.). (1995). *Art and music: Therapy and research.* London: Routledge.

Gilroy, A., & McNeilly, G. (2000). *The changing shape of art therapy.* London: Kingsley.

Gilroy, A., Tipple, R., & Brown, C. (Eds.). (2010). *Assessment in art therapy.* London: Routledge.

Gladding, S. T. (2005). *Counseling as an art* (3rd ed.). Washington, DC: American Counseling Association.

Golomb, C. (1974). *Young children's sculpture and drawing.* Cambridge, MA: Harvard University Press.

Golomb, C. (1992). *The child's creation of a pictorial world.* Berkeley, CA: University of California Press.

Golomb, C. (2002). *Child art in context.* Washington, DC: American Psychological Association.

Gong, S. (2004). *Yi Shu: The art of living with change: Integrating traditional Chinese medicine psychodrama and the creative arts.* St. Louis, MO: Robbins.

Goodenough, F. L. (1926). *Measurement of intelligence by drawings.* New York: Harcourt, Brace World Books.

Goodnow, J. (1977). *Children drawing.* Cambridge, MA: Harvard University Press.

Graham-Pole, J. (2000). *Illness and the art of creative self-expression.* Oakland, CA: New Harbinger.

Graves, S. K. (1994). *Expressions of healing.* Van Nuys, CA: Newcastle.

Green, G. (1969). *The artists of Terezin.* New York: Hawthorn Press.

Greenberg, P. (1987). *Visual arts and older people.* Springfield, IL: Thomas.

Grözinger, W. (1955). *Scribbling, drawing, painting.* New York: Humanities Press.

Gussak, D., & Virshup, E. (Eds.). (1997). *Drawing time: Art therapy in prisons and forensic settings.* Chicago: Magnolia Street.

Hagood, M. M. (2000). *The use of art in counselling child and adult survivors of sexual abuse.* London: Kingsley.

Hall, M. D., & Metcalf, E. W. (Eds.). (1994). *The artist outsider.* Washington, DC: Smithsonian Institution Press.

Hammer, E. F. (Ed.). (1958). *The clinical application of projective drawings.* Springfield, IL: Thomas.

Hammer, E. F. (Ed.). (1997). *Advances in projective drawing interpretation.* Springfield, IL: Thomas.

Hampe, R. (Ed.). (2007). *Crossing boundaries.* Berlin: Frank & Baum.

Hanes, K. M. (1982). *Art therapy and group work: An annotated bibliography.* Westport, CT: Greenwood Press.

Hanes, M. J. (1997). *Roads to the unconscious.* Oklahoma City, OK: Wood 'n' Barnes Press.

Harding, M. E. (1965). *The parental image.* New York: Putnam.

Harris, D. B. (1963). *Children's drawings as measures of intellectual maturity.* New York: Harcourt Brace & World.

Harris, J., & Joseph, C. (1973). *Murals of the mind.* New York: International Universities Press.

Harris, P. (1993). *A child's story.* St. Louis, MO: Cracom.

Hartley, N., & Payne, M. (Eds.). (2008). *Creative arts in palliative care.* London: Kingsley.

Hartley, R., Frank, L., & Goldenson, R. (1952). *Understanding children's play.* New York: Columbia University Press.

Hass-Cohen, N., & Carr, N. (Eds.). (2008). *Art therapy and clinical neuroscience.* London: Kingsley Press.

Hauschka, M. (1985). *Fundamentals of artistic therapy.* London: Rudolf Steiner Press.

Hedges, L. (1983). *Listening perspectives in psychotherapy.* New York: Aronson.

Heegaard, M. E. (1996). *Facilitator guide for drawing out feelings.* Minneapolis, MN: Woodland Press. (and 18 workbooks for children and parents on different topics)

Henley, D. (1992). *Exceptional children, exceptional art.* Worcester, MA: Davis.

Henley, D. (2002). *Clayworks in art therapy.* London: Kingsley.

Herbert, G., Deschner, J. W., & Glazer, R. (2006). *Artists-in-residence.* New York: Creative Center.

Herrera, H. (1983). *Frida: A biography of Frida Kahlo.* New York: Harper & Row.

Hetland, L., Winner, E., Veenema, S., & Sheridan, K. M. (2007). *Studio thinking: The real benefits of visual arts education.* New York: Teachers College Press.

Hill, A. (1945). *Art versus illness: A story of art therapy.* London: Allen & Unwin.

Hill, A. (1951). *Painting out illness.* London: Williams & Northgate.

Hillman, J. (1977). *Re-visioning psychology.* New York: Harper Paperbacks.

Hillman, J. (2004). *Archetypal psychology* (3rd ed.). Dallas, TX: Spring.

Hinz, L. D. (2006). *Drawing from within.* London: Kingsley.

Hinz, L. D. (2009). *Expressive therapies continuum.* New York: Routledge.

Hiscox, A., & Calisch, A. (Eds.). (1997). *Tapestry of cultural issues in art therapy.* London: Kingsley.

Hogan, S. (Ed.). (1997). *Feminist approaches to art therapy.* New York: Routledge.

Hogan, S. (2001). *Healing arts: The history of art therapy.* London: Kingsley.

Hogan, S. (Ed.). (2003). *Gender issues in art therapy.* London: Kingsley.

Hornyak, L. M. & Baker, E. K. (Eds.). (1989). *Experiential therapies for eating disorders.* New York: Guilford Press.

Horovitz, E. G. (1999). *A leap of faith.* Springfield, IL: Thomas.

Horovitz, E. G. (2002). *Spiritual art therapy* (2nd ed.). Springfield, IL: Thomas.

Horovitz, E. G. (2005). *Art therapy as witness.* Springfield, IL: Thomas.

Horovitz, E. G. (Ed.). (2007). *Visually speaking: Art therapy and the deaf.* Springfield, IL: Thomas.

Horowitz, M. J. (1983). *Image formation and psychotherapy.* New York: Aronson.

Hubble, M. A., Duncan, B. L., & Miler, S. D. (1999). *The heart and soul of change: Delivering what works in therapy.* Washington, DC: American Psychological Association.

Innes, A., & Hatfield, K. (2001). *Healing arts therapies and person-centred dementia care.* London: Kingsley.

Irwin, E. C., & Rubin, J. A. (2008). *The green creature within* (2nd ed.) [DVD]. Pittsburgh, PA: Expressive Media.

Jakab, I. (1956). *Pictorial expression in psychiatry: Psychiatric and artistic analysis* (2nd ed. 1998). Budapest, Hungary: Akademiai Kiado.

Jakab, I. (Ed.). (1968). *Psychiatry and art* (Vol. 1). New York: Karger.

Jakab, I. (Ed.). (1970). *Art interpretation and art therapy* (Vol. 2). New York: Karger.

Jakab, I. (Ed.). (1971). *Conscious and unconscious expressive art* (Vol. 3). New York: Karger.

Jakab, I. (Ed.). (1975). *Transcultural aspects of psychiatric art* (Vol. 4). New York: Karger.

Jakab, I. (Ed.). (1981). *The personality of the therapist.* Pittsburgh, PA: American Society of Psychopathology of Expression.

Jakab, I. (Ed.). (1986). *The role of the imagination in the healing process.* Pittsburgh, PA: American Society of Psychopathology of Expression.

Jakab, I. (1990a). *Art media as a vehicle of communication.* Brookline, MA: American Society of Psychopathology of Expression.

Jakab, I. (Ed.). (1990b). *Stress management through art.* Boston: American Society of Psychopathology of Expression.

Jakab, I. (1998). *Pictorial expression in psychiatry: Psychiatric and artistic analysis* (2nd ed.). Budapest, Hungary: Akademiai Kiado.

Jakab, I., & Miller, L. (Eds.). (1978). *Creativity and psychotherapy.* New York: Karger.

Jamison, K. R. (1993). *Touched with fire.* New York: Free Press.

Japan Broadcasting Corporation. (1977). *Unforgettable fire.* New York: Pantheon.

Jeffrey, C. (1995). *That why child.* New York: Free Association Books.

Jennings, S., & Minde, A. (1993). *Art therapy and dramatherapy.* London: Kingsley.

Jewish Museum of Prague. (1993). *I have not seen a butterfly around here.* Prague.

Johnson, D. R. (1999). *Essays on the creative arts therapies.* Springfield, IL: Thomas.

Johnson, D. R., & Emunah, R. (Eds.). (2009). *Current approaches in drama therapy* (2nd ed.). London: Kingsley.

Jones, P. (2005). *The arts therapies: A revolution in healthcare.* London: Routledge.

Jung, C. G. (1964). *Man and his symbols.* New York: Doubleday.

Jung, C. G. (1972). *Mandala symbolism.* Princeton, NJ: Princeton University Press.

Junge, M. B. (1998). *Creative realities.* Lanham, MD: University Press of America.

Junge, M. B. (2008). *Mourning, memory and life itself.* Springfield, IL: Thomas.

Junge, M. B. (2010). *The modern history of art therapy in the United States.* Springfield, IL: Thomas.

Junge, M. B., & Asawa, P. P. (1994). *A history of art therapy in the United States.* Mundelein, IL: American Art Therapy Association.

Junge, M. B., & Wadeson, H. (Eds.). (2007). *Architects of art therapy.* Springfield, IL: Thomas.

Jungels, G. (1982). *To be remembered.* Buffalo, NY: Potentials Development.

Kalff, D. M. (1980). *Sandplay.* Boston: Sigo Press.

Kalmanowitz, D., & Lloyd, B. (Eds.). (2005). *Art therapy and political violence.* London: Routledge.

Kapitan, L. (2003). *Re-enchanting art therapy.* Springfield, IL: Thomas.

Kapitan, L. (2010). *An introduction to art therapy research.* New York: Routledge.

Kaplan, F. (2000). *Art, science, and art therapy.* London: Kingsley.

Kaplan, F. (Ed.). (2007). *Art therapy and social action.* London: Kingsley.

Karkou, V. (Ed.). (2009). *Arts therapies in schools.* London: Kingsley

Karkou, V., & Sanderson, P. (2006). *Arts therapies: A research-based map of the field.* London: Churchill Livingstone.

Katz, F. L., & Katz, E. (1977). *Creative art of the developmentally disabled.* Oakland, CA: Creative Growth.

Katz, F. L., & Katz, E. (1990). *Art and disabilities* (Rev. ed.). Cambridge, MA: Brookline Books.

Kaufman, B., & Wohl, A. (1992). *Casualties of childhood.* New York: Brunner/Mazel.

Kaye, C., & Blee, T. (Eds.). (1996). *The arts in health care.* London: Kingsley.

Kellogg, J. (1980). *MARI card test.* Clearwater, FL: Mandala Research Institute.

Kellogg, J. (2002). *Mandala: Path of beauty* (3rd ed.). Belleaire, FL: Association for Teachers of Mandala Assessment (ATMA).

Kellogg, R. (1959). *What children scribble and why.* Palo Alto, CA: National Press.

Kellogg, R. (1969). *Analyzing children's art.* Palo Alto, CA: National Press Books.

Kerr, C., Hoshino, J., Sutherland, J., Parashak, S. T., & McCarley, L. L. (2008). *Family art therapy.* New York: Routledge.

Keyes, M. F. (1983). *The inward journey* (Rev. ed.). La Salle, IL: Open Court.

Kiell, N. (1965). *Psychiatry and psychology in the visual arts and aesthetics.* Madison, WI: University of Wisconsin Press.

Kinget, G. M. (1952). *The drawing completion test.* New York: Grune and Stratton.

Kirchner, L. (1977). *Dynamic drawing.* Spring Valley, NY: Mercury Press.

Klein, M. (1932). *The psycho-analysis of children.* London: Hogarth.

Klepsch, M., & Logie, L. (1982*). Children draw and tell.* New York: Brunner/Mazel.

Klinger, E. (Ed.). (1980/1982). *Imagery* (Vol. 2). New York: Plenum.

Klorer, P. G. (2000). *Expressive therapy with troubled children.* Northvale, NJ: Aronson.

Kluft, E. (Ed.). (1993). *Expressive and functional therapies in the treatment of multiple personality disorder.* Springfield, IL: Thomas.

Knill, P. J., Barba, H. N., & Fuchs, M. N. (2004). *Minstrels of soul* (2nd ed.). Toronto: E*G*S Press.

Knill, P. J., Levine, E. G., & Levine, S. K. (2005). *Principles and practice of expressive arts therapy: Toward a therapeutic aesthetics.* London: Kingsley.

Koplewicz, H., & Goodman, R. (1999). *Childhood revealed.* New York: Abrams.

Koppitz, E. M. (1968). *Psychological evaluation of children's human figure drawings* New York: Grune & Stratton.

Koppitz, E. M. (1984). *Psychological evaluation of HFD's by middle-school pupils.* New York: Grune & Stratton.

Kovner, A (Ed.). (1968). *Childhood under fire.* Israel: Sifriat Poalim.

Kramer, E. (1958). *Art therapy in a children's community* Springfield, IL: Thomas.

Kramer, E. (1971). *Art as therapy with children*. New York: Schocken Books.

Kramer, E. (1979). *Childhood and art therapy*. New York: Schocken Books.

Kramer, E. (2000). *Art as therapy: Collected papers* (L. A. Gerity, Ed.). London: Kingsley.

Krauss, D. A., & Fryrear, J. L. (1983). *Phototherapy in mental health*. Springfield, IL: Thomas.

Kreitler, H., & Kreitler, S. (1972). *Psychology of the arts*. Durham, NC: Duke University Press.

Kris, E. (1952). *Psychoanalytic explorations in art*. New York: International Universities Press.

Kubie, L. (1958). *Neurotic distortion of the creative process*. New York: Noonday Press.

Kuri, E. (2008). *Helping to make them see*. Saarbrucken, Germany: VDM Verlag.

Kwiatkowska, H. Y. (1978*). Family therapy and evaluation through art*. Springfield, IL: Thomas.

Lacan, J. (2007). *Ecrits* (B. Fink, Trans.). New York: Norton.

Lachman-Chapin, M. (1994). *Reverberations*. Evanston, IL: Evanston.

Lahad, M. (2000). *Creative supervision*. London: Kingsley.

Laing, J., & Carrell, C. (Eds.). (1982). *The special unit, Barlinnie Prison*. Glasgow: Third Eye Center.

Lambert, D. (1995). *The life and art of Elizabeth "Grandma" Layton*. Waco, TX: WRS.

Landgarten, H. B. (1981). *Clinical art therapy*. New York: Brunner/Mazel.

Landgarten, H. B. (1987*). Family art psychotherapy*. New York: Brunner/Mazel.

Landgarten, H. B. (1993). *Magazine photo collage*. New York: Brunner/Mazel.

Landgarten, H. B., & Lubbers, D. (Eds.). (1991). *Adult art psychotherapy*. New York: Brunner/Mazel.

Langer, S. K. (1953). *Feeling and form*. New York: Scribner.

Lantz, B. (1955). *Easel age scale*. Los Angeles: Test Bureau.

Leavy, P. (2008). *Method meets art: Arts-based research*. New York: Guilford Press.

Le Navenec, C.-L., & Bridges, L. (Eds.). (2005). *Creating connections between nursing care and the creative arts therapies*. Springfield, IL: Thomas.

Lesage, A. (2009). *Gates to meaning*. Saarbrucken, Germany: VDM Verlag.

Leuner, H. (1984). *Guided affective imagery*. New York: Thieme Medical.

Levens, M. (1995). *Eating disorders and magical control of the body: Treatment through art therapy*. New York: Routledge.

Levick, M. F. (1983). *They could not talk and so they drew*. Springfield, IL: Thomas.

Levick, M. F. (2001). *The Levick cognitive and emotional art therapy assessment* (LECATA) (2nd ed.). Boca Raton, FL: Author.

Levick, M. F. (2009). *Levick emotional and cognitive art therapy assessment: A normative study*. Bloomington, IN: AuthorHouse.

Levine, E. G. (2003). *Tending the fire* (2nd ed.). Toronto: E*G*S Press.

Levine, S. K. (1992). *Poesis*. Toronto: Palmerston Press.

Levine, S. K. (Ed.). (2002). *Crossing boundaries*. Toronto: E*G*S Press.

Levine, S. K. (2009). *Trauma, tragedy, and therapy*. London: Kingsley.

Levine, S. K., & Levine, E. G. (Eds.). (1999). *Foundations of expressive arts therapy*. London: Kingsley.

Levy, F. J. (Eds.). (1995). *Dance and other expressive art therapies*. New York: Routledge.

Lewis, P. B. (1993). *Creative transformation*. Wilmette, IL: Chiron.

Liebmann, M. (Ed.). (1990). *Art therapy in practice*. London: Kingsley.

Liebmann, M. (Ed.). (1994). *Art therapy with offenders*. London: Kingsley.

Liebmann, M. (Ed.). (1996). *Arts approaches to conflict*. London: Kingsley.

Liebmann, M. (2005). *Art therapy for groups* (2nd ed.). London: Routledge.

Liebmann, M. (Ed.). (2008). *Art therapy and anger*. London: Kingsley.

Liebowitz, M. (1999). *Interpreting projective drawings*. New York: Brunner/Mazel.

Lindsay, Z. (1972). *Art and the handicapped child*. New York: Van Nostrand Reinhold.

Linesch, D. G. (1988). *Adolescent art therapy*. New York: Brunner/Mazel.

Linesch, D. G. (Ed.). (1993). *Art therapy with families in crisis*. New York: Brunner/Mazel.

Linesch, D. G. (2000). *Celebrating family milestones*. Toronto: Firefly Books.

Lisenco, Y. L. (1971). *Art not by eye*. New York: American Foundation for the Blind.

Lowenfeld, M. (1971). *Play in childhood* (2nd ed.). New York: Wiley.

Lowenfeld, M. (1979). *The world technique*. London: Allen & Unwin.

Lowenfeld, V. (1952). *The nature of creative activity* (2nd ed.). London: Routledge & Kegan Paul.

Lowenfeld, V. (1957). *Creative and mental growth* (3rd ed.). New York: Macmillan.

Lowenfeld, V., & Brittain, W. L. (1987). *Creative and mental growth* (8th ed.). Englewood Cliffs, NJ: Prentice-Hall.

Lucas, X. (1980). *Artists in group psychotherapy*. Athens, Greece: Litsas.

Luscher M. (1969). *The Lüscher color test*. New York: Random House.

Lusebrink, V. B. (1990). *Imagery and visual expression in therapy*. New York: Plenum Press.

Luthe, W. (1976). *Creativity mobilization technique*. New York: Grune & Stratton.

Lyddiatt, E. M. (1971). *Spontaneous painting and modeling*. London: Constable.

Lynn, D. (1994). *Myself resolved: An artist's experience with lymphoma*. New York: Author.

MacGregor, J. M. (1989). *The discovery of the art of the insane*. Princeton, NJ: Princeton University Press.

MacGregor, J. M. (1992). *Dwight Mackintosh*. Oakland, CA: Creative Growth.

MacGregor, J. M. (1999). *Metamorphosis*. Oakland, CA: Creative Growth Art Center.

Machover, K. (1949). *Personality projection in the drawing of the human figure*. Springfield, IL: Thomas.

Maclagan, D. (2001). *Psychological aesthetics*. London: Kingsley.

Magniant, R. C. P. (Ed.). (2004). *Art therapy with older adults: A sourcebook*. Springfield, IL: Thomas.

Makarova, E., & Seidman-Miller, R. (1999). *Friedl Dicker-Brandeis, Vienna 1891–Auschwitz 1944*. Los Angeles: Tallfellow Press.

Makin, S. A. (1994*). A consumer's guide to art therapy*. Springfield, IL: Thomas.

Makin, S. R. (1999). *Therapeutic art directives and resources*. London: Kingsley.

Makin, S. R. (2000). *More than just a meal*. London: Kingsley.

Malchiodi, C. A. (1997). *Breaking the silence* (2nd ed.). New York: Brunner-Routledge.

Malchiodi, C. A. (1998). *Understanding children's drawings*. New York: Guilford Press.

Malchiodi, C. A. (Ed.). (1999a). *Medical art therapy with adults*. London: Kingsley.

Malchiodi, C. A. (Ed.). (1999b). *Medical art therapy with children*. London: Kingsley.

Malchiodi, C. A. (2000). *Art therapy and computer technology*. London: Kingsley.

Malchiodi, C. A. (2002). *The soul's palette*. Boston: Shambhala.

Malchiodi, C. A. (2003). (Ed.). *Handbook of art therapy*. New York: Guilford Press.

Malchiodi, C. A. (2004). (Ed.). *Expressive arts therapies*. New York: Guilford Press.

Malchiodi, C. A. (2006). *The art therapy sourcebook* (2nd ed.). New York: McGraw-Hill.

Malchiodi, C. A. (Ed.). (2008). *Creative interventions with traumatized children*. New York: Guilford Press.

Malchiodi, C. A., & Riley, S. (1996). *Supervision and related issues*. Chicago: Magnolia Street.

Martin, N. (2009). *Art as an early intervention tool for children with Autism*. London: Kingsley.

Martinovitch, J. (2009). *Creative expressive activities and Asperger's syndrome*. London: Kingsley.

May, R. (1975). *The courage to create*. New York: Norton.

Mazza, N. (2003). *Poetry therapy: Theory and practice*. New York: Routledge.

McConeghey, H. (2003). *Art and soul*. New York: Continuum.

McElhaney, M. (1969). *Clinical psychological assessment of the human figure drawing*. Springfield, IL: Thomas.

McNeilly, G. (2006). *Group analytic art therapy*. London: Kingsley.

McNiff, S. (1981). *The arts and psychotherapy*. Springfield, IL: Thomas.

McNiff, S. (1986). *Educating the creative arts therapist*. Springfield, IL: Thomas.

McNiff, S. (1988). *Fundamentals of art therapy*. Springfield, IL: Thomas.

McNiff, S. (1989). *Depth psychology of art*. Springfield, IL: Thomas.

McNiff, S. (1994). *Art as medicine* Boston: Shambhala.

McNiff, S. (1995). *Earth angels* Boston: Shambhala.

McNiff, S. (1998a). *Art-based research*. London: Kingsley.

McNiff, S. (1998b). *Trust the process*. Boston: Shambhala.

McNiff, S. (2003). *Creating with others*. Boston: Shambhala.

McNiff, S. (2004). *Art heals*. Boston: Shambhala.

McNiff, S. (2009). *Integrating the arts in therapy*. Springfield, IL: Thomas.

McWilliams, N. (1994). *Psychoanalytic diagnosis*. New York: Guilford Press.

Meares, A. (1957). *Hypnography*. Springfield, IL: Thomas.

Meares, A. (1958). *The door of serenity*. London: Faber & Faber.

Meares, A. (1960). *Shapes of sanity.* Springfield, IL: Thomas.

Meerloo, J. A. M. (1968). *Creativity and eternization.* New York: Humanities Press.

Meijer-Degen, F. (2007). *Coping with loss and trauma through art therapy.* Delft, The Netherlands: Eburon Academic.

Michael, J. A. (Ed.). (1982). *The Lowenfeld lectures.* University Park: Pennsylvania State University Press.

Milbraith, C., & Trautner, H. M. (Eds.). (2008). *Children's understanding and production of pictures:* Cambridge, MA: Hogrefe & Huber.

Milia, D. (2000). *Self-mutilation and art therapy.* London: Kingsley.

Miller, E., & Miller, K. (2008). *The girl who spoke with pictures.* London: Kingsley.

Milner, M. (1957). *On not being able to paint.* New York: International Universities Press.

Milner, M. (1969). *The hands of the living god.* New York: International Universities Press.

Milner, M. (1987). *The suppressed madness of sane men.* London: Tavistock.

Mitchell, R. R., & Friedman, H. S. (1994). *Sandplay.* New York: Routledge.

Mitchell, S. A., & Aron, L. (Eds.). (1999). *Relational psychoanalysis.* New York: Analytic Press.

Moon, B. L. (1996). *Art and soul.* Springfield, IL: Thomas.

Moon, B. L. (1998). *The dynamics of art as therapy with adolescents.* Springfield, IL: Thomas.

Moon, B. L. (2001). *Working with images.* Springfield, IL: Thomas.

Moon, B. L. (2003). *Essentials of art therapy training and practice* (2nd ed.). Springfield, IL: Thomas.

Moon, B. L. (2006). *Ethical issues in art therapy* (2nd ed.). Springfield, IL: Thomas.

Moon, B. L. (2007a). *Introduction to art therapy* (2nd ed.). Springfield, IL: Thomas.

Moon, B. L. (2007b). *The role of metaphor in art therapy.* Springfield, IL: Thomas.

Moon, B. L. (2009). *Existential art therapy* (3rd ed.). Springfield, IL: Thomas.

Moon, B. L. (2010). *Art-based group therapy: Theory and method.* Springfield, IL: Thomas.

Moon, B. L., & Schoenholz, R. (2004). *Word pictures.* Springfield, IL: Thomas.

Moon, C. H. (2002). *Studio art therapy.* London: Kingsley.

Moon, C. H. (Ed.). (2010). *Materials and media in art therapy.* New York: Routledge.

Moore, R. W. (1981). *Art therapy in mental health.* Washington, DC: National Institutes of Mental Health.

Morgenthaler, W. (1921). *Madness and art.* Lincoln: University of Nebraska Press.

Moriya, D. (2000). *Art therapy in schools.* Boca Raton, FL: Author.

Morris, D. (1962). *The biology of art.* New York: Knopf.

Mortensen, K. V. (1991). *Form and content in children's human figure drawings.* New York: New York University Press.

Mueller-White, L. (2002). *Printmaking as therapy.* London: Kingsley.

Murphy, J. (Ed.). (2001). *Art therapy with young survivors of sexual abuse.* Philadelphia: Taylor and Francis.

Naevestad, M. (1979). *The colors of rage and love.* London: Whitefriars Press.

Naumburg, M. (1928). *The child and the world.* New York. Harcourt, Brace, & World.

Naumburg, M. (1947). *Studies of the "free" art expression of behavior problem children and adolescents as a means of diagnosis and therapy* (No. 17). New York: Nervous and Mental Disease Monograph.

Naumburg, M. (1950). *Schizophrenic art.* New York: Grune & Stratton.

Naumburg, M. (1953). *Psychoneurotic art.* New York: Grune & Stratton.

Naumburg, M. (1966). *Dynamically oriented art therapy.* New York: Grune & Stratton.

Naumburg, M. (1973). *An introduction to art therapy: Studies of the "free" art expression of behavior problem children and adolescents as a means of diagnosis and therapy* (2nd ed.). New York: Teachers College Press, 1973.

Neumann, E. (1971). *Art and the creative unconscious.* Princeton, NJ: Princeton University Press.

Nichols, J., & Garrett, A. (1995*). Drawing and coloring for your life.* Overland Park, KS: Gingerbread Castle.

Nicholson, C., Irwin, M., & Dwivedi, K. N. (Eds.). (2010). *Children and adolescents in trauma: Creative therapeutic approaches.* London: Kingsley.

Nicolaides, K. (1941). *The natural way to draw.* New York: Houghton Mifflin.

Nucho, A. O. (1995). *Spontaneous creative imagery.* Springfield, IL: Thomas.

Nucho, A. O. (2003). *Psychocybernetic model of art therapy* (2nd ed.). Springfield, IL: Thomas.

Oaklander, V. (1978*). Windows to our children.* Boulder, CO: Real People Press.

Oster, G. D., & Crone, P. G. (2004). *Using drawings in assessment and therapy* (2nd ed.). New York: Brunner-Routledge.

Oster, G. D., & Montgomery, S. (1996). *Clinical uses of drawings.* Northvale, NJ: Aronson.

Pacey, P. (1972). *Remedial art: A bibliography.* London, UK: St. Albans School of Art.

Palmer, J., & Nash, F. (1991). *The hospital arts handbook.* Durham, NC: Duke University Medical Center.

Panter, B. (Ed.). (2009). *Creativity and madness: Psychological studies of art and artists* (Vol. 2). Burbank, CA: AIMED Press.

Panter, B., Panter, M. L., Virshup, E., & Virshup, B. (Eds.). (1995). *Creativity and madness: Psychological studies of art and artists* (Vol. 1). Burbank, CA: AIMED Press.

Paraskevas, C. B. (1979). *A structural approach to art therapy methods.* Elmsford, NY: Collegium.

Pasto, T. (1964). *The space-frame experience in art.* New York: Barnes.

Payne, H. (Ed.). (1994). *Handbook of inquiry in the arts therapies.* London: Kingsley.

Pearman, H., & Abrams, H. (2007). *Art therapy for children of all ages.* Denver, CO: Outskirts Press.

Pearson, M., & Wilson, H. (2009). *Using expressive arts to work with mind, body and emotions.* London: Kingsley.

Petrie, M. (1946). *Art and regeneration.* London: Elek.

Pickford, R. W. (1967). *Studies in psychiatric art.* Springfield, IL: Thomas.

Plokker, J. H. (1965). *Art from the mentally disturbed.* Boston: Little, Brown.

Pratt, M., & Wood, M. (Eds.). (1998). *Art therapy in palliative care.* London: Routledge.

President's Commission on Mental Health, Task Panel Report. (1978). *Role of the arts in therapy and environment.* Washington, DC: National Committee, Arts for the Handicapped.

Prinzhorn, H. (1922). *Artistry of the mentally ill.* New York: Springer.

Proulx, L. (2002). *Strengthening emotional ties through parent-child-dyad art therapy.* London: Kingsley.

Rambert, M. (1949). *Children in conflict.* New York: International Universities Press.

Ramsay, G., & Sweet, H. (2009). *A creative guide to exploring your life.* London: Kingsley.

Rappaport, L. (2009). *Focusing-oriented art therapy.* London: Kingsley.

Read, H. (1958). *Education through art.* New York: Pantheon Books.

Rees, M. (Ed.). (1998). *Drawing on difference.* New York: Routledge.

Rhyne, J. (1995). *The gestalt art experience* (2nd ed.). Chicago: Magnolia Street.

Riccio, L. L., & Rollins, J. (2001). *ART is the HeART.* Washington, DC: WVSA Arts.

Richards, M. C. (1962). *Centering.* Middletown, CT: Wesleyan University Press.

Richards, M. C. (1966). *The crossing point.* Middletown, CT: Wesleyan University Press.

Ridker, C., & Savage, P. (1996). *Railing against the rush of years.* Pittsburgh: Unfinished Monument Press.

Riley, S. (1999). *Contemporary art therapy with adolescents.* London: Kingsley.

Riley, S. (2001). *Group process made visible.* New York: Brunner-Routledge.

Riley, S., & Malchiodi, C. A. (2004). *Integrative approaches to family art therapy* (2nd ed.). Chicago: Magnolia Street Publishers.

Robbins, A. (1980). *Expressive therapy.* New York: Human Sciences Press.

Robbins, A. (1987). *The artist as therapist.* New York: Human Sciences Press.

Robbins, A. (1988). *Between therapists.* New York: Human Sciences Press.

Robbins, A. (1989). *The psychoaesthetic experience.* New York: Human Sciences Press.

Robbins, A. (1994*). Multimodal approach to creative art therapy.* Bristol, PA: Kingsley.

Robbins, A. (Ed.). (1998). *Therapeutic presence.* London: Kingsley.

Robbins, A. (2001). *Dancing on blood.* Videotape. London: Kingsley.

Robbins, A., & Sibley, L. B. (1976). *Creative Art Therapy.* New York: Brunner/Mazel.

Robertson, S. (1963). *Rosegarden and labyrinth.* London: Routledge & Kegan Paul.

Rogers, E. (Ed.). (2007). *The art of grief: The use of expressive arts in a grief support group (death, dying and bereavement).* New York: Routledge.

Rogers, N. (1993). *The creative connection.* Palo Alto, CA: Science & Behavior Books.

Rollins, J. (2004). *Arts activities for children at bedside.* Washington, DC: WVSA Arts Connection.

Rollins, J., & Mahan, C. (1996). *From artist to artist-in-residence: Preparing artists to work in pediatric healthcare settings.* Washington, DC: Rollins & Associates.

Rosal, M. (1996). *Approaches to art therapy with children.* Burlingame, CA: Abbeygate Press.

Rosen, D. (2002). *Transforming depression* (2nd ed.). New York: Nicolas-Hays.

Rosenthal, R., & Jacobson, L. (1992). *Pygmalion in the classroom.* New York: Irvington.

Ross, C. (1997). *Something to draw on.* London: Kingsley.

Rubin, J. A. (1984). *The art of art therapy.* New York: Brunner/Mazel.

Rubin, J. A. (1998). *Art therapy: An introduction.* New York: Brunner/Mazel.

Rubin, J. A. (Ed.). (2001). *Approaches to art therapy* (2nd ed.). New York: Brunner-Routledge.

Rubin, J. A. (2002). *My mom and dad don't live together anymore.* Washington, DC: Magination Press (American Psychological Association).

Rubin, J. A. (2005a). *Artful therapy.* New York: Wiley.

Rubin, J. A. (2005b). *Child art therapy* (3rd ed.). New York: Wiley.

Rubin, J. A. (2008a). *Art therapy with blind children* [DVD]. Pittsburgh: Expressive Media.

Rubin, J. A. (2008b). *Art therapy has many faces* (Rev. ed.) [DVD]. Pittsburgh: Expressive Media.

Rubin, J. A. (2008c). *Art therapy with older adults* [DVD]. Pittsburgh: Expressive Media.

Rubin, J. A. (2008d). *The arts as therapy with children* [DVD]. Pittsburgh: Expressive Media.

Rubin, J. A. (2009). *Introduction to art therapy: Sources and resources.* New York: Routledge.

Rubin, J. A. (2010a). *Hospital drawing book.* Pittsburgh: Expressive Media.

Rubin, J. A. (2010b). *Me, myself, and I.* Pittsburgh: Expressive Media.

Rubin, J. A. (2010c). *When bad things happen.* Pittsburgh: Expressive Media.

Rugh, M. M., & Ringold, F. (1989). *Making your own mark: A drawing and writing guide for senior citizens.* Tulsa, OK: Council Oak Books.

Safran, D. (2002). *Art therapy and AD/HD.* London: Kingsley.

Salomon, C. (1998). *Life? Or theater?* London: Royal Academy of Arts.

Sandle, D. (Ed.). (1998). *Development and diversity.* New York: Free Association Books.

Sarason, S. B. (1990). *The challenge of art to psychology.* New Haven, CT: Yale University Press.

Schaeffer-Simmern, H. (1961). *The unfolding of artistic activity.* Berkeley: University of California Press.

Schaverien, J. (1992). *The revealing image.* London: Routledge.

Schaverien, J. (1995). *Desire and the female therapist.* London: Routledge.

Schaverien, J., & Case, C. (Eds.). (2007). *Supervision of art psychotherapy.* London: Routledge.

Schaverien, J., & Killick, K. (Eds.). (1997). *Art, psychotherapy and psychosis.* London: Routledge.

Schilder, P. (1950). *The image and appearance of the human body.* New York: Wiley.

Schildkrout, M. S., Shenker, I. R., & Sonnenblick, M. (1972). *Human figure drawings in adolescence.* New York: Brunner/Mazel.

Schnetz, M. (2005). *The healing flow.* London: Kingsley.

Schroder, D. (2005). *Little windows into art therapy.* London: Kingsley.

Searle, Y., & Streng, I. (Eds.). (2001). *Where analysis meets the arts.* London: Karnac.

Sechehaye, M. (1951). *Symbolic realization.* New York: International Universities Press.

Seftel, L. (2006). *Grief unseen.* London: Kingsley.

Seiden, D. (2001). *Mind over matter.* Chicago: Magnolia Street.

Seiden, D. (2007). *Artobiography.* Chicago: Fisheye Graphic Services.

Shaw, R. F. (1938). *Finger painting.* Boston: Little, Brown.

Sherwood, P. (2004). *The healing art of clay therapy.* Melbourne, Australia: ACER Press.

Shorr, J. E. (1995). *Psychotherapy through imagery.* Santa Barbara, CA: Fithian Press.

Shorr, J. E., Sobel, G. E., Robin, P., & Cannella, J. (Eds.). (1980). *Imagery: Its many dimensions and applications* (Vol. 1). New York: Plenum.

Shorr, J. E., Sobel-Whittington, G. E., Robin, P., & Cannella, J. (Eds.). (1983). *Imagery: Theoretical and clinical applications* (Vol. 3). New York: Plenum.

Siegel, D. J. (1999). *The developing mind.* New York: Guilford Press.

Silver, R. A. (1978). *Developing cognitive and creative skills in art.* Baltimore: University Park Press.

Silver, R. A. (2001). *Art as language.* New York: Brunner-Routledge.

Silver, R. A. (2002*). Three art assessments.* New York: Brunner-Routledge.

Silver, R. A. (Ed.). (2005). *Aggression and depression assessed through art.* New York: Routledge.

Silver, R. A. (2007). *The Silver drawing test and draw a story.* New York: Routledge.

Silver, R. A. (2010). *Identifying risks for aggression and depression through metaphors*. New York: Purple Finch Press.

Silverstone, L. (1997). *Art therapy: The person-centred way* (2nd ed.). London: Kingsley.

Silverstone, L. (2009). *Art therapy exercises*. London: Kingsley.

Simmons, L. L. (2006). *Interactive art therapy*. Binghamton, NY: Haworth Press.

Simon, R. (1992*). The symbolism of style*. London: Routledge.

Simon, R. (1997*). Symbolic images in art as therapy*. London: Routledge, 1997.

Simon, R. (2005*). Self-healing through visual and verbal therapy* (S. A. Graham, Ed.). London: Kingsley.

Simonds, S. L. (1994). *Bridging the silence*. New York: Norton.

Singer, F. (1980). *Structuring child behavior through visual art*. Springfield, IL: Thomas.

Skaife, S., & Huet, V. (1998). (Eds.). *Art psychotherapy in groups*. London: Routledge.

Smith, S. L. (1979). *No easy answers*. Cambridge, MA: Winthrop.

Smith, S. L. (2000). *The power of the arts*. Baltimore: Brookes.

Smith, S. L. (2005). *Live it, learn it*. Baltimore: Brookes.

Snow, S., & D'Amico, M. (2009). *Assessment in the creative arts therapies*. Springfield, IL: Thomas.

Solomon, M., & Siegel, D. (Eds.). (2003). *Healing trauma*. New York: Guilford Press.

Spaniol, S. E. (1990). *Organizing exhibitions of art by people with mental illness*. Boston: Center for Psychiatric Rehabilitation, Boston University.

Spencer, L. B. (1997). *Heal abuse and trauma through art*. Springfield, IL: Thomas.

Spiegel, D. (Ed.). (1999). *Efficacy and cost-effectiveness of psychotherapy*. Washington, DC. American Psychiatric Press.

Spring, D. (1993). *Shattered images*. Chicago: Magnolia Street.

Spring, D. (2001). *Image and mirage*. Springfield, IL: Thomas.

Spring, D. (2007). *Art in treatment*. Springfield, IL: Thomas.

Steinhardt, L. (2000). *Foundation and form in Jungian sandplay*. London: Kingsley.

Stepney, S. A. (2009). *Art therapy with students at risk* (2nd ed.). Springfield, IL: Thomas.

Stevens, A. (1986). *Withymead: A Jungian community for the healing arts*. London: Coventure.

Stewart, E. G. (2006). *Kaleidoscope … color and form illuminate darkness*. Chicago: Magnolia Street.

Thevoz, M. (1976). *Art brut*. New York: Skira.

Thomas, G. V., & Silk, M. J. (1990). *An introduction to the psychology of children's drawings*. New York: New York University Press.

Thomson, M. (1989*). On art and therapy*. London: Free Association Books.

Tinnin, L. W., & Gantt, L. (2000). *Trauma Recovery Institute manual and video, "Instinctual trauma response."* Morgantown, WV: Gargoyle Press.

Trechsel, G. A. (Ed.). (1995). *Pictured in my mind: Contemporary American self-taught art*. Birmingham, AL: Birmingham Museum of Art.

Tubbs, C., & Drake, M. (2006). *Crafts and creative media in therapy* (3rd ed.). Thorofare, NJ: Slack.

Twitchell-Allen, D. (1958). *Twitchell-Allen three-dimensional personality test: A 1958 revised guide for administration and recording*. New York: Stoelting.

Ude-Pestel, A. (1977). *Betty*. Palo Alto, CA: Science and Behavior Books.

Uhlin, D. M. (1972). *Art for exceptional children*. Dubuque, IA: Brown.

Uhlin, D. M., & DeChiara, E. (1984). *Art for exceptional children* (3rd ed.). Dubuque, IA: Brown.

Ulman, E., & Dachinger, P. (Eds.). (1975). *Art therapy in theory and practice*. New York: Shocken Books.

Ulman, E., Kramer, E., & Kwiatkowska, H. (1977). *Art therapy in the United States*. Craftsbury Common, VT: Art Therapy.

Ulman, E., & Levy, C. (Eds.). (1981). *Art therapy viewpoints*. New York: Schocken Press.

Van Sommers, P. (1984). *Drawing and cognition*. Cambridge, UK: Cambridge University Press.

Viola, W. (1948). *Child art and Franz Cizek* (2nd ed.). London: University of London Press.

Viorst, J. (1986). *Necessary losses*. New York: Simon & Schuster.

Virshup, E. (1978). *Right brain people in a left brain world*. Los Angeles: Art Therapy West.

Virshup, E. (Ed.). (1993). *California art therapy trends*. Chicago: Magnolia Street.

Volavkova, H. (Ed.). (1962). *I never saw another butterfly*. New York: McGraw-Hill.

Wadeson, H. (1980). *Art psychotherapy*. New York: Wiley.

Wadeson, H. (1987). *The dynamics of art psychotherapy.* New York: Wiley.

Wadeson, H. (2000). *Art therapy practice.* New York: Wiley.

Wadeson, H. (2010). *Art psychotherapy* (2nd ed.). New York: Wiley.

Wadeson, H., Durkin, J., & Perach, D. (Eds.). (1989). *Advances in art therapy.* New York: Wiley.

Wadeson, H. W. (Ed.). (1992). *A guide to conducting art therapy research.* Mundelein, IL: American Art Therapy Association.

Wallace, E. (1990). *A queen's quest.* Santa Fe, NM: Moon Bear.

Waller, D. (1991). *Becoming a profession: The history of art therapy in Britain 1940–1982.* London: Routledge.

Waller, D. (1993). *Group interactive art therapy.* London: Routledge.

Waller, D. (1998). *Towards a European art therapy.* Philadelphia: Open University Press.

Waller, D. (1999). *Treatment of addiction.* London: Routledge.

Waller, D. (Ed.). (2007). *Arts Therapies and progressive illness: Nameless dread.* London: Brunner-Routledge.

Waller, D., & Gilroy, A. (Eds.). (1992). *Art therapy: A handbook.* Bristol, PA: Open University Press.

Waller, D., & Mahony, J. (Eds.). (1999). *Treatment of addiction.* London: Routledge.

Waller, D., & Sibbett, C. (Eds.). (2005). *Art therapy and cancer care: Facing death.* Bristol, PA: Open University Press.

Wallin, D. J. (2007). *Attachment in psychotherapy.* New York: Guilford Press.

Warren, B. (Ed.). (2003). *Using the creative arts in therapy and healthcare* (3rd ed.). New York: Routledge.

Watkins, J. G. (1992). *Hypnoanalytic techniques.* New York: Irvington Press.

Watkins, M. M. (1984). *Waking dreams* (3rd ed.). New York: Gordon & Breach.

Weaver, R. (1973). *The old wise woman.* New York: Putnam's.

Weiser, J. (1993*). Phototherapy techniques.* San Francisco: Jossey-Bass.

Weiss, J. (1984). *Expressive therapy with elders and the disabled.* New York: Haworth.

Wilkinson, V. C., & Heater, S. L. (1979). *Therapeutic media and techniques of application.* New York: Van Nostrand Reinhold.

Williams, G. H., & Wood, M. M. (1977). *Developmental art therapy.* Baltimore: University Park Press.

Wilson, L. (2003). *Alberto Giacometti: Myth, magic and the man.* New Haven, CT: Yale University Press.

Winner, E. (1982). *Invented worlds.* Cambridge, MA: Harvard University Press.

Winnicott, D. W. (1971a). *Playing and reality.* New York: Basic Books.

Winnicott, D. W. (1971b). *Therapeutic consultations in child psychiatry.* New York: Basic Books.

Winnicott, D. W., Winnicott, C., Shepherd, R., & David, M. (Eds.). (1989). *Psycho-analytic explorations.* Cambridge, MA: Harvard University Press.

Wiseman, A. S. (1989). *Nightmare help.* Berkeley, CA: Ten Speed Press.

Wohl, A., & Kaufman, B. (1985). *Silent screams and hidden cries.* New York: Brunner/Mazel.

World Health Organization (WHO). (1992). *International Classification of Diseases, 9th Revision, Clinical Modification* (6th ed.). (Rev. NCHS, National Center for Health Statistics. Geneva, Switzerland: World Health Organization).

Wysuph, C. L. (1970). *Jackson Pollock: Psychoanalytic drawings.* New York: Horizon.

Yalom, I. D., & Leszcz, M. (2005). *The theory and practice of group psychotherapy* (5th ed.). New York: Basic Books.

Yelen, A. R. (Ed.). (1995). *Passionate visions of the American South: Self-taught artists from 1940 to the present* (Rev. ed.). Jackson: University Press of Mississippi.

Zinker, J. (1977). *Creative process in Gestalt therapy.* New York: Brunner/Mazel.

Appendix B

Contents of the DVD

A Note to the Viewer ...

The Art of Art Therapy covers a great deal of ground in a rather broad fashion. The **Figures** that frame each section are also general and, like the examples cited in the text, are meant to illustrate the contents of the book.

The **DVD** is organized exactly like the book, its Scenes corresponding to each of the chapters therein. It is meant to be played on a DVD player, although it can also be played on a computer.

Like the **Figures** in this book, the **DVD** is meant to *illustrate* rather than to *instruct*. None of the video examples is intended to show the *only* or *best* way to think about art, therapy, the interface, or the many possible ways in which art therapy is extended through applications and related services. Instead, like the images in the text, the Scenes on the DVD convey one or more instances of the material in the chapters.

Each Scene consists of a series of clips from a variety of sources related to the topic of the chapter. In some instances, there is narration or voice-over from the original source; in others, there is a musical background. Although it was not possible to provide a continuous narration, and it is certainly not a completed film in the usual sense, I believe that the sequence of moving images on each topic is self-explanatory and should assist the reader.

While the majority of the illustrative clips are from unfinished film and tape materials, some are excerpts from finished works, some of which are still available for purchase. I have therefore included any relevant information, as well as an indication of those individuals and institutions that have generously given permission for their inclusion.

About Confidentiality

Although not all of the people on this DVD are patients, it is important to note that many were, and that they agreed to be photographed or videotaped for the purpose of professional education. Since this book is intended to be used by art therapists and others in the helping professions, I trust that viewers will respect the privacy of everyone who allowed themselves to be filmed and will maintain the same kind of confidentiality normally accorded to any clinical material.

Contents of the DVD

Part I. The Art Part

Chapter 1. Knowing Materials

Unstructured Materials Are Best: *Children and the Arts* by Judith A. Rubin. Available on a DVD with related films: *The Arts as Therapy With Children*, courtesy of Expressive Media: http://www.expressivemedia.org/f4.html

A Reason for Choosing Clay: *At the Threshold* by Carolyn Grant Fay, Jung Center of Houston: https://www.junghouston.org/bookstore/store_item.asp?id=143

Having Choices Helps: Footage courtesy of Ellen Speert, California Center for Creative Renewal: http://www.artretreats.com

Different Materials for One Picture: from *Le Chemin Brut de Lisette et Romain*. Copy of film courtesy of Julia Byers.

Things to Draw With, Things to Paint With, Things to Model With, Things to Construct With: Excerpted from multiple sources. Music: Express Yourself by Charles Wright, with permission from Warner/Chappell.

Chapter 2. Knowing Processes

Different Processes: Montage excerpted from multiple sources.

Observing the Process: Terry Ouderkirk, Kansas State School for the Deaf: *Art Therapy: The Healing Vision* by Robert Ault. Available from Marilynn Ault: *marilynnault@mac.com*.

Observing the Process: Natalie Rogers: *Person-Centered Expressive Arts* Therapy, courtesy of Allyn & Bacon. Available from Psychotherapy.net: http://www.psychotherapy.net/video/Natalie_Rogers_Expressive_Arts_Person_Centered

Chapter 3. Knowing Products

Art Products Are Concrete. They Can Be Taken Home: *A Brush With Life* by Glen Salzman and Martin Duckworth, courtesy of Julia Byers.

They Can Be Brought in to Therapy: *Stevie's Light Bulb* by Ralph D. Rabinovitch, courtesy of Ralph Rabinovitch and the Hawthorn Center.

They Can Be Displayed, They Can Be Left With the Therapist: KDKA-TV.

They Can Be Stored in the Art Studio: *Art and Therapy With Vera Zilzer.* Available from Majie Lavergne: Majie@telus.net.

They Can Be Stored in the Art Studio: *Art Therapy Is … .* Available from Lore Baer: lorebaer@gmail.com.

They Can Be Looked at Any Time: Footage courtesy of Paula Howie, WRAMC.
They Can Be Shown to a Parent: Footage courtesy of CBS News Archives.
Additional footage of demonstration interview, courtesy of WRAMC-TV.
They Can Be Compared: Natalie Rogers: *Person-Centered Expressive Arts Therapy*, courtesy of Allyn & Bacon. Available from Psychotherapy.net: http://www. psychotherapy.net/video/Natalie_Rogers_Expressive_Arts_Person_Centered
They Can Be Re-viewed: Lore Baer: *Art Therapy Is … .* Available from Lore Baer: lorebaer@gmail.com.
Art Is a Valuable Source of Information:
  Alzheimer's Disease: Pictures from Judith Wald.
  Migraine Headache: Pictures from Randy Vick.
Eliana Gil on Artwork and Child Abuse: *Essentials of Play Therapy With Abused Children*, courtesy of Guilford Press.

Part II. The Therapy Part

Chapter 4. Knowing Development

Home movies and a clip from KDKA-TV.
Raw footage from *Creative Healing in Mental Health: Art and Drama in Assessment and Therapy.* Available from http://www.expressivemedia.org.
Most Nonartist Adults Draw Like Children: Courtesy of Irene Rosner-David.

Chapter 5. Knowing Dynamics and Deviations

Carrie's Dynamics Seen in Art Therapy: *Art Therapy: The Healing Vision* by Robert Ault. Available from Marilynn Ault: marilynnault@mac.com.

Chapter 6. Knowing Therapy

Robin's Progress in Art Therapy: Tessa Dalley: *Art Therapy*, courtesy of Diane Waller, John Beacham, and Goldsmiths, University of London.

Chapter 7. Knowing Art Therapy

Robert Ault: Public TV Program: Courtesy of Marilynn Ault.
Myra Levick: 25th Anniversary Interview (1994): Courtesy of the American Art Therapy Association and Doris Arrington.
Arthur Robbins: EMI Interview (2007): Courtesy of Expressive Media.
Robert Ault: TV Interview and 25th Anniversary Interview (1994): Courtesy of Marilynn Ault and the American Art Therapy Association.
Harriet Wadeson: 25th Anniversary Interview (1994): Courtesy of the American Art Therapy Association and Doris Arrington.
Mildred Lachman Chapin: 25th Anniversary Interview (1995): Courtesy of the American Art Therapy Association and Doris Arrington.
Mildred Lachman Chapin: Demonstration Interview: Courtesy of Mildred Lachman Chapin and the Walter Reed Art Therapy Archives.
Laurie Wilson: Photographs courtesy of Laurie Wilson and Alfred Strasser.
Rawley Silver: *Rawley Silver, Art Therapist and Artist* by Christine Turner. Available from Marylhurst University: cturner@marylhurst.edu.
Bobbi Stoll and Gladys Agell Painting and Drawing: Raw footage filmed by Judy Rubin during the first few years of the AATA Quickdraw event.

Part III. The Interface

Chapter 8. Setting the Stage

Teenagers Help to Create Their Space: Courtesy of Kit Jenkins, RAW Art Works.

Vera Zilzer Sets the Stage With Materials: *Art and Therapy With Vera Zilzer.* Available from Majie Lavergne: Majie@telus.net.

Carolyn Grant Fay Sets the Mood: *At the Threshold* by Carolyn Grant Fay, Jung Center of Houston: https://www.junghouston.org/bookstore/store_item.asp?id=143

Natalie Rogers Suggests Relaxation: *Person-Centered Expressive Arts Therapy,* courtesy of Allyn & Bacon. Available from Psychotherapy.net: http://www.psychotherapy.net/video/Natalie_Rogers_Expressive_Arts_Person_Centered.

Selma Ciornai Adds Guided Imagery: Footage courtesy of Selma Ciornai.

Chapter 9. Evoking Expression

Eliana Gil: "Anything You Want": *Essentials of Play Therapy With Abused Children,* courtesy of Guilford Press.

Judith A. Rubin: Choose Materials and Topic: Courtesy of Paula Howie, Walter Reed Art Therapy Archives.

Judith A. Rubin: Family Representations: Courtesy of Expressive Media Archives.

Patti Ravenscroft: Joint Family Picture: Courtesy of Paula Howie, Walter Reed Art Therapy Archives.

Elinor Ulman: Scribble Drawing: Courtesy of George Washington University Art Therapy Program and Elinor Ulman.

Linda Gantt: Clay Scribble: Courtesy of Frank and Linda Gantt.

Patsy Nowell-Hall: Round Robin: *Art Therapy,* courtesy of Diane Waller, John Beacham, and Goldsmiths, University of London.

Chapter 10. Enabling Creation

Edith Kramer: "Art Therapist's 3rd Hand": *Art Therapy: Beginnings,* courtesy of the American Art Therapy Association.

Bruce Moon: Creating Alongside: Courtesy of Bruce Moon.

Millie Chapin: Creating Alongside: Courtesy of Mildred Chapin and the Walter Reed Art Therapy Archives.

Janet Bush: "How Would This End?": Courtesy of Janet Bush.

Violet Oaklander: "Imagine That This Is Sarah": *A Boy and His Anger: A Therapy Session.* Available from: http://www.violetoaklander.com/video.html.

Active Observation-Witnessing: Roger Arguile: *Art Therapy and Children,* courtesy of Diane Waller, John Beacham, and Goldsmiths, University of London.

Active Observation-Witnessing: Cindy Westendorf: Courtesy of CBS News Archives and Amanda's Easel.

Active Observation-Witnessing: Sue Hammons: *Art Therapy,* courtesy of Diane Waller, John Beacham, and Goldsmiths, University of London.

Chapter 11. Facilitating Reflection

Interviewing During the Process: Judith A. Rubin: Home movies and demonstration interview from Walter Reed Hospital, courtesy of EMI Archives.

Interviewing During the Process: Laurie Wilson: Courtesy of Laurie Wilson and the filmmakers:

Interviewing After the Process: Mala Betensky: *Making a Scribble,* courtesy of Aina Nucho, University of Maryland School of Social Work.

Inviting Projected Imagery: Judy Rubin: From *Lisa,* courtesy of EMI Archives.

Moving to the Image: Carolyn Grant Fay: *At the Threshold*, courtesy of Jung Center of Houston: https://www.junghouston.org/bookstore/store_item.asp?id=143

Comparing Drawings: Natalie Rogers: *Person-Centered Expressive Arts Therapy*, courtesy of Allyn & Bacon. Available from Psychotherapy.net: http://www.psychotherapy.net/video/Natalie_Rogers_Expressive_Arts_Person_Centered

Comparing Family Pictures: Patti Ravenscroft and Mari Fleming: Courtesy of Paula Howie and the Walter Reed Art Therapy Archives.

Chapter 12. Working Artistically

Art as Empathic Feedback: Paula Howie: Courtesy of Paula Howie and the Walter Reed Art Therapy Archives.

Art as Reflection and Feedback: Millie Chapin: Courtesy of Mildred Chapin

A Creative Assessment for Couples: Harriet Wadeson: Courtesy of Harriet Wadeson and Claire Whittaker.

Representing Body Memories: Linda Gantt: Courtesy of Linda Gantt.

Part IV. Applications

Chapter 13. Different Populations

Art Therapy for Physical Disabilities: Nina Viscardi Ochoa: *Ventilator Dependent Children at School*, courtesy of Nina Viscardi and Rich Greenberg.

Art Therapy in Rehabilitation: Irene Rosner-David: Interview courtesy of EMI Archives; *Medical Art Therapy,* courtesy of Irene Rosner-David.

Art Therapy for Substance Abuse: Judy Rubin: Courtesy of KDKA-TV.

Art Therapy for Alzheimer's Disease: Shirley Riley: Courtesy of Shirley Riley, Cathy Malchiodi, and Lauren Helfand of OPICA.

Chapter 14. Different Settings

Walter Reed Army Medical Center: Paula Howie and Donna Betts: Courtesy of Paula Howie, Donna Betts, and the Walter Reed Art Therapy Archive.

Bellevue Hospital Creative Arts Therapy: Irene Rosner-David: Interview courtesy of EMI Archives; B-Roll, courtesy Irene Rosner-David.

Elementary School—Crisis Intervention: Sandra Graves-Alcorn: Raw footage courtesy Sandra Graves-Alcorn.

Chapter 15. Different Modes

Individual Therapy—Phototherapy: Ellen Hiltebrand: Footage courtesy of Glaxo-Wellcome and Ellen Hiltebrand.

Individual Art Therapy: Laura Greenstone—Cindy Westendorf: Footage courtesy of CBS News Archives.

Mother-Child Art Therapy: Footage courtesy of CBS News Archives.

Family Art Therapy: Shirley Riley: Footage courtesy of Mary Blaylock.

Family Video Art Therapy: Irene Jakab and Judy Rubin: EMI Archives.

Parent-Child Dyad Art Therapy: Lucille Proulx: Footage courtesy of Lucille Proulx.

Open Studio for Families in Hospital: Donna Betts: Footage courtesy of Paula Howie, Walter Reed Art Therapy Archives.

Group Art Therapy With Puppets: Lani Gerity: Footage courtesy of Lani Gerity.

Group Art Therapy: Introductions: Byron Fry: *Art Therapy: The Healing Vision* by Robert Ault. Available from Marilynn Ault: marilynnault@mac.com.

Part V. Related Service

Chapter 16. Knowing Teaching

Training Group in Art Psychotherapy: Diane Waller: *Art Therapy,* courtesy of Diane Waller, John Beacham, Goldsmiths, University of London.

Art Therapy Class—Sociogram: Charles Anderson: Footage courtesy of Charles Anderson and Emporia State University.

Demonstration Interview Discussion and Viewing Videotape: Edith Kramer: Footage courtesy of Paula Howie and the Walter Reed Art Therapy Archives.

Case Presentation Using Slides: Ellen Speert: Footage courtesy of Ellen Speert, California Center for Creative Renewal: http://www.artretreats.com.

Lecture Institute of the Arts in Healing: Judy Rubin: Courtesy of EMI Archives.

Chapter 17. Knowing Supervision

Art Therapy Supervision Session: Diane Waller: *Art Therapy,* courtesy of Diane Waller, John Beacham, and Goldsmiths, University of London.

Videotapes in Art Therapy Supervision: Robert Grant: Courtesy of EMI Archives.

Group Supervision of Child Care Workers: Judy Rubin: Courtesy of EMI Archives.

Review of Art Therapy Internship: Paula Howie and Donna Betts: Courtesy of Paula Howie, Donna Betts, and the Walter Reed Art Therapy Archives.

Chapter 18. Knowing Consultation

Art Therapist Consults With Other Staff: Roger Arguile: *Art Therapy and Children,* courtesy of Diane Waller, John Beacham, and Goldsmiths, University of London.

Consultation With Child Life Department: Judy Rubin: Footage courtesy of the Child Life Program, Children's Hospital of Pittsburgh and Expressive Media.

Follow-up Sessions at Bedside: Footage courtesy of Expressive Media.

Chapter 19. Knowing Research

Need Research on Art Therapy Efficacy: Judy Rubin: EMI Institute talk.

Effects of Art Activity on the Elderly: Irene Rosner-David: Courtesy of EMI Archives.

Effects of Glass Artmaking on Orphans: James Minson: *Glass Art as Therapy.* Available on *The Arts as Therapy With Children,* EMI: http://www.expressive-media.org/f4.html

Post-Program Self-Assessments: "Art Expressions": Footage courtesy of the Mt. Lebanon Public Schools and Expressive Media.

Stories and Drawings Lower Anxiety: Eleanor C. Irwin: Footage courtesy of the Child Life Program, Children's Hospital of Pittsburgh and Expressive Media.

Centre for Arts Therapy Research, Imperial College London: Dr. Mike Crawford and Dr. Diane Waller: Footage from launch of the center.

Chapter 20. Knowing Theory

Jung's Theory of Active Imagination: Carolyn Grant Fay: *At the Threshold,* courtesy of the Jung Center of Houston: https://www.junghouston.org/bookstore/store_item.asp?id=143

Natalie Rogers Person-Centered Expressive Arts Therapy Theory and Art Interview: *Person-Centered Expressive Arts Therapy,* courtesy of Allyn & Bacon. Available from Psychotherapy.net: http://www.psychotherapy.net/video/Natalie_Rogers_Expressive_Arts_Person_Centered

Phenomenological Art Therapy: Aina Nucho, Mala Betensky: *Louis and the Blue Fish,* courtesy of Aina Nucho, director/producer, University of Maryland at Baltimore, Graduate School of Social Work.

Index

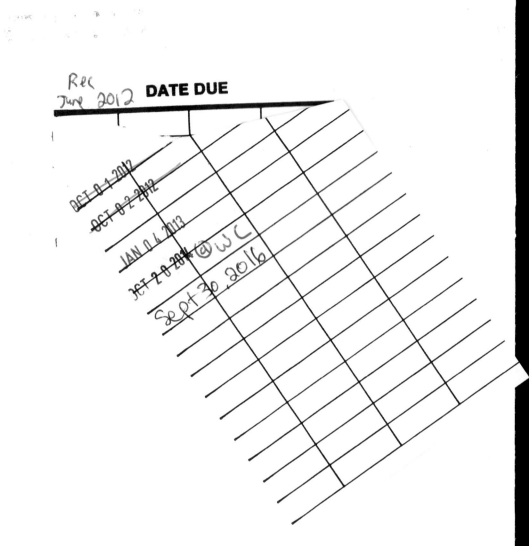

Rec
June 2012

DATE DUE

OCT 0 1 2012

OCT 0 2 2012

JAN 0 6 2013

OCT 2 0 2014 @ WC

Sept 30, 2016